FORCE

——— AND ———

STATECRAFT

Diplomatic Challenges of Our Time

FOURTH EDITION

Paul Gordon Lauren
Gordon A. Craig
Alexander L. George

New York   Oxford
OXFORD UNIVERSITY PRESS
2007

Oxford University Press, Inc., publishes works that further Oxford University's
objective of excellence in research, scholarship, and education.

Oxford New York
Auckland Cape Town Dar es Salaam Hong Kong Karachi
Kuala Lumpur Madrid Melbourne Mexico City Nairobi
New Delhi Shanghai Taipei Toronto

With offices in
Argentina Austria Brazil Chile Czech Republic France Greece
Guatemala Hungary Italy Japan Poland Portugal Singapore
South Korea Switzerland Thailand Turkey Ukraine Vietnam

Copyright © 1983, 1990, 1995, 2007 by Oxford University Press, Inc.

Published by Oxford University Press, Inc.
198 Madison Avenue, New York, New York 10016
http://www.oup.com

Library of Congress Cataloging-in-Publication Data

Lauren, Paul Gordon.
Force and statecraft : diplomatic challenges of our time / Paul Gordon Lauren, Gordon A.
Craig, Alexander L. George. — 4th ed.
p. cm.
Includes bibliographical references and index.
ISBN-13: 978-0-19-516248-6 — ISBN-13: 978-0-19-516249-3 (pbk.)

1. World politics—19th century. 2. World politics—20th century. 3. World
politics—21st century. 4. Diplomacy. I. Craig, Gordon Alexander, 1913- II. George,
Alexander L. III. Title.

D363.L34 2006
909.81—dc22

2005058997

Printing number: 9 8 7 6 5 4 3 2
Printed in the United States of America on acid-free paper

Frontispiece: *Diplomacy* by Maximiano Alves,
Sao Bento Palace, Lisbon, Portugal

to Gordon
teacher, colleague, collaborator, and friend

CONTENTS

PREFACE
—————— TO THE ——————
FOURTH EDITION

This book grew out of the authors' long-standing concern over international peace and security and their conviction that it would be very valuable to examine the kinds of challenges involving force and statecraft that confront policy makers from the combined perspectives of history and strategy. We have had the great pleasure and the privilege of working together as valued colleagues, collaborators, and friends for nearly forty years in this interdisciplinary endeavor. The process began when the three of us first developed a course with these objectives in mind at Stanford University, selecting for focused comparison a variety of historical cases from the past in order to help us understand diplomatic challenges of our own time. The success of that original course and others modeled after it, both in the United States and abroad, the enthusiastic responses of readers to three previous editions of the book, our own continuing collaborative work, and the momentous developments in global politics and war in recent years all encouraged us to write, under the leadership of Paul Lauren, this thoroughly revised and updated edition.

Part One focuses upon the historical context of force and statecraft. Following a completely new Introduction, it ranges from a substantially restructured discussion of the early techniques, instruments, and ideas of diplomacy to the profoundly dangerous changes brought about by contemporary weapons of mass destruction and terrorism. Chapters cover the emergence of the Great Powers, the classical system of diplomacy, the diplomatic revolution, the creation of the United Nations, the rise and fall of the Cold War, globalization and the consequences of the Internet, and events as recent as 9/11, the Bush Doctrine, the "war on terrorism" and the American-led war in Iraq, nuclear proliferation in Iran and North Korea, and the World Summit of global leaders. Significant new material is added to this edition on the critical subject of human rights and its relationship to international peace and security.

Part Two begins with the completely new and pivotal chapter on the subject of "Lessons of History and Knowledge for Statecraft." Each subsequent chapter then proceeds to systematically examine an especially important and challenging subject in diplomacy by means of delineating its theoretical principles and then analyzing three very specific historical cases in equal detail. The first of these always is drawn from the classical system of the nineteenth century, and the other two follow in a progression toward increasingly more recent events in contemporary international affairs. Particular care has been taken in this edition to include a number of new cases that reveal the truly

global dimensions of these diplomatic challenges and thus range from Europe and the United States to the Middle East and Asia.

Part Three opens with an entirely new chapter entitled "Ethics and Other Restraints on Force and Statecraft." This explores practical, structural, and political restraints upon policy makers; the debate over the nature of ethics and international politics; ethical restraints in foreign policy; and the difficult matter of observing ethical restraints, such as those of just war tradition, in warfare itself. A completely rewritten and updated Conclusion brings the major themes of the book together and offers a number of reflections about history, theory, the diplomatic revolution, and challenges ahead.

Every chapter concludes with a section called "Suggestions for Further Exploration." Here readers will find references to citations within the text, bibliographical entries ranging from classical works to the most updated scholarship on the topic at hand, and newly created websites, where appropriate. Each of the analytical chapters now provides suggestions of other historical cases for those who wish to explore specific topics in more detail. In addition, maps and illustrations are included in this edition for the first time.

We will be delighted if this book continues to stimulate serious thought, discussion, and reflection about how force and statecraft are used in the world.

PAUL GORDON LAUREN
GORDON A. CRAIG
ALEXANDER L. GEORGE

— INTRODUCTION —

I t is likely that there is no issue on earth more elemental than that of survival. From the beginning of time to the present, individuals and societies
have struggled with how they and their descendants might find peace and
security in a world where war and violence are always possible or present.
Primitive petroglyph drawings in caves, ancient Hindu texts and Chinese
strategist Sun Tzu's *Art of War*, accounts in the Torah and Qu'ran, and traditional literary epics from highly diverse cultures all record early and frequent
recourse to threats or to the use of armed force when people are unable or
unwilling to resolve their disputes by peaceful means. The famous Greek historian Thucydides, writing in his *History of the Peloponnesian War* 400 years
before the birth of Jesus, tells us how force was threatened by the powerful
Athenians to intimidate the much weaker Melians. Failure to comply with their
demands, they declared, would result in devastation:

> You, by giving in, would save yourselves from disaster . . . [for] your actual
> resources are too scanty to give you a chance of survival against the forces
> that are opposed to you at this moment. You will therefore be showing
> an extraordinary lack of common sense if . . . you still fail to reach a conclu-
> sion wiser than anything you have mentioned so far. . . . Think it over again
> . . . and let this be a point that constantly recurs to your minds—that you
> are discussing the fate of your country, that you have only one country,
> and its future for good or ill depends upon this one single decision which
> you are going to make.

The Athenians brutally summarized their approach with the often-quoted statement that "the strong do what they have the power to do and the weak accept
what they have to accept." Similar expressions have been heard throughout
history, as well as today, from those wanting to take full advantage of their
unrivaled power, weapons of mass destruction, sheer numbers of troops, highly
sophisticated military technology, or willingness to kill innocent civilians in
terrorist acts, all to gain advantage over their adversaries. The persistence of
war and violence in our own time bears all-too-ample and painful evidence
that the dangers continue.

When confronted with this experience, for better or for worse, most leaders
responsible for the survival of their people have concluded that in a world
of ever-possible anarchy where no central governing authority exists, there
are times armed force is an absolute necessity. If peaceful means and rational persuasion do not always succeed in resolving conflicts and competition,
and if adversaries exist who might engage in aggression and only seem to
understand the language of force, they have reasoned, then sheer prudence

requires that force be one of the instruments of statecraft. Even those who have no aggressive designs at all and genuinely desire peace need to acknowledge this, for as the Chinese sage Confucius expressed it centuries ago:

> The superior man, when resting in safety, does not forget that danger may come. When in a state of security, he does not forget the possibility of ruin. When all is orderly, he does not forget that disorder may come. Thus, his person is not endangered; his states and all his clans are preserved.

But herein lies the fundamental dilemma for force and statecraft. Although armed force may be necessary in certain circumstances, it also can be extraordinarily dangerous. It may be used to maintain peace and security, defend vital interests, protect innocents from egregious human rights abuses and atrocities, provide collective security, and enforce international law. At the same time, it can be used for aggression, territorial conquest, genocide, to inflict pain against innocent civilians, subjugation, and intimidation. Armed force is a blunt and dangerous instrument that is not always effective, cannot always be controlled, and sometimes even triggers unwanted wars that might otherwise have been avoided. Indeed, its very existence threatens others, increases the risk of escalation in crises, and carries a seductive appeal to those who believe that military might will enable them to act as they wish and get what they want.

The enormous tension between the necessities and the dangers of armed force thus long has challenged those deeply concerned about survival. Indeed, it has posed one of the most central and difficult questions in the entire theory and the practice of statecraft: If, when, how, and/or under what conditions can force be used legitimately and most effectively as an instrument of diplomatic efforts to achieve peace and security?

Countless numbers of people have struggled with this problem throughout history. They have feared the wanton chaos, destruction, pain, and taking of human lives made possible by the use of armed force, and therefore have searched for ways in which they might prevent or control violent conflict. Some have attempted to do this by relying upon their own resources and efforts alone, while some have sought to work with others in partnership for collective security. Some have placed their hopes on normative values of self-imposed ethical restraints or religious codes teaching compassion and forbidding the resort to war. Others have turned to legal agreements or negotiated treaties to restrict or abolish the use of certain kinds of weapons or to limit the use of military force. Some have relied on particular military doctrines or strategies designed to match the level of violence to political objectives and thus avoid unnecessary destruction or death.

Still others have attempted to combine these various elements and approaches in such a way that they might use force and statecraft together as a means of regulating and controlling the behavior of highly competitive states capable of launching wars and causing great harm to others. They have turned to diplomacy and the creation of viable international systems with an accepted body of normative values and sufficient force in a balance of power

to keep rivalries within certain bounds and to make wars unprofitable or dangerous to aggressors. The Portuguese sculptor, Maximiano Alves, captures some sense of this in his interesting and perceptive allegorical statue entitled "Diplomacy." The figure appears modest, but possesses an obvious depth of dignity and strength. Her facial expression and body posture reveal that she has an understanding of the magnitude of the decisions she sometimes must make; and, because she appears to be pregnant, that her choices will have consequences for the well-being of future generations. Her right arm is uncovered, and in her hand she holds an olive branch of peace poised above documents and books representing the rule of law, treaties, and ethical precepts. At the same time, her left arm is draped with her garment and her hand is clasped around the hilt of a sword to be threatened or used if armed force becomes necessary.

As long historical experience demonstrates, considerable skills are necessary to wisely use the tools in each of these hands. It is not at all easy to use diplomacy to create and maintain viable international systems capable of maintaining peace and security. War and severe competition, for example, were endemic features throughout the seventeenth and eighteenth centuries. Only after the twenty-five years of warfare caused by the French Revolution and the ambitions of Napoleon Bonaparte did the statesmen assembled at the diplomatic Congress of Vienna in 1814–1815 create a system that successfully avoided general war for two generations and then, as modified by Otto von Bismarck, for most of the rest of the century. But that impressive example has not been duplicated by later statesmen. After the First World War, Woodrow Wilson attempted to establish a new system of collective security to replace the one that had finally collapsed so disastrously in 1914, and during the Second World War Franklin D. Roosevelt and others tried to set the stage for a postwar system with the United Nations that would extend into peacetime the cooperative working relations that characterized the wartime alliance of the United States with the Soviet Union, Great Britain, and China. Richard Nixon, Henry Kissinger, and later Mikhail Gorbachev then attempted in their own ways to develop a relationship that would serve as the foundation for an international system that would overcome the intense strains of the Cold War, but these met with only brief successes. In the wake of the 9/11 terrorist attacks and the wars against Afghanistan and Iraq, and with seemingly unrelenting violence in the Middle East, a dominant single superpower, and sharply contested concepts of legitimacy around the world, international stability and order often appear remote at best.

Both the fact that it took until the nineteenth century for the European states to create an effective concert of powers and the failure of recent attempts to achieve the relative success of that earlier experiment can be explained by four challenging requirements of a viable international system. (1) In the first instance, there must be a consensus or genuine agreement among the principal states concerning shared goals and objectives that they are seeking to enhance in creating and maintaining the system. To achieve this, the actors must be able to recognize that they share common interests and well as issues of competition,

and thus are partners as well as rivals within the system. (2) Second, there must be a structure appropriate to the number of states interacting with each other, the geographical boundaries or scope of the system, the relative distribution of power or capabilities among the actors, and the stratification and status hierarchy among them. (3) Third, there must be commonly accepted values and procedures or norms, methods, rules, practices, and institutions for the achievement of the aims and objectives of the system as a whole. These normative values must include shared conceptions about when and how armed force can be legitimately threatened or used. During the long stretch of time that intervened between the breakdown of the authority of the Holy Roman Empire and the religious wars that followed the Reformation, centuries in which Europe was composed of a welter of political units of indeterminate sovereignty and ill-defined borders, not even the most gifted political leaders could be expected to conceive of, let alone develop, anything so ambitious. As will become apparent, it was only in the seventeenth century, when modern states possessed efficient institutions, strong armed forces, and a rational theory of statecraft, that any progress toward effective collaboration became possible. Even then it took a century of intermittent conflict and the threat of domination by a single power before the major states were able to achieve an agreement with respect to basic objectives and the structural and procedural requirements of a viable system.

The eventual collapse of the nineteenth-century system and the twentieth- and twenty-first-century failures to find a practicable substitute for it can be explained by another critical characteristic of an effective international system: (4) it must be able to adapt to new developments and to internal changes within its membership that affect its performance and its ability to maintain itself. The modern period has been one of profound and continuing changes in military technology, transportation and Internet communication, a globalized market economy, the growing influence of nonstate actors, and the evolution of international human rights and international criminal law, to say nothing of those mutations in the internal political structure of states that have resulted from the rise of public opinion, the emergence of a large variety of organized interest groups, and the increasing scope and complexity of governmental organization itself. It has also been an age of intense nationalism, enhanced by the breakup of the old colonial empires and the multiplication of new sovereign states, and of political and religious ideological conflict on a global scale. All of these forces, singly and in combination, have had an impact upon international politics that results in nothing short of a diplomatic revolution. This has made it increasingly difficult to revive and maintain old structures or to devise new ones. Indeed, adaptation to accelerated change has become the major problem of modern statecraft, testing the ingenuity and the fortitude of those charged with responsibility for devising means both of controlling international violence and of maintaining the survival of their own countries.

To develop a greater appreciation for the richness of history, the importance of context and of change and continuity, the requirements for viable

international systems, the range of attempted experiments, and the way that leaders have wrestled with problems of force and statecraft, Part One of this book focuses upon historical context of past and present. We begin with the evolution of diplomacy and emergence of modern states, the conflict in the eighteenth century between their desire for order and their anarchic tendencies, and the laborious and painful birth of the successful nineteenth-century system, its procedures and norms, and the various changes in its structure before its collapse during the First World War. The book moves on to the beginning upheavals of the diplomatic revolution of the twentieth century and the ways in which this crippled subsequent system-building experiments, including those of the 1919 Paris Peace Conference and of the post–1945 Cold War period replete with war and violence in Asia, Africa, the Middle East, the Persian Gulf, and Latin America. We then provide a detailed discussion of the critical period in history that we now face with the search for a new international system in the wake of globalization, the "war on terrorism," weapons of mass destruction, the controversies between the vision of the United Nations and the traditional claims of national sovereignty, expanding definitions of "security" and the growing desire to protect human rights and the creation of the International Criminal Court, the expansion of NATO, the emergence of China, cultural heterogeneity, and the overwhelming power of the United States.

With this historical context established, Part Two seeks to provide an analysis of longstanding and continuing issues that arise with force as an instrument of policy. We make the transition between history and policy by first examining how knowledge can be used for statecraft and how policy makers use or misuse the "lessons" of history. We then employ the methodology of structured, focused comparison and use specific historical cases to explore the value of theory and to carefully and systematically examine the nature of four particularly important and challenging subjects: negotiation, deterrence, coercive diplomacy, and crisis management. Here we make a particular effort to delineate principles and to analyze why certain strategies succeeded and why others failed.

Part Three addresses restraints and reflections on force and statecraft. At a time when increasing numbers of citizens have religious or conscientious concerns about the tendencies, methods, and dangers of contemporary international relations, we believe that it is only appropriate to include a chapter on the difficult and thought-provoking problem of the role of ethics in global politics, especially during times of war. This leads us, finally and naturally, to some concluding reflections about the relationship of the past to the present, theory and practice, and the continuing diplomatic challenges of force and statecraft in our time.

FORCE
AND
STATECRAFT

PART ONE

FROM THE PAST
TO THE PRESENT

— 1 —

The Emergence of Diplomacy
and the Great Powers

The origins of diplomacy go back to the beginnings of recorded history itself. When organized groups of men and women came into contact with others different from themselves, they realized their desperate need to develop techniques that might facilitate interaction beyond the resort to violence and war. Their survival depended upon it. No negotiations could possibly take place over the disposition and use of territory or the conditions that might create a truce, for example, unless messengers from both sides were granted certain privileges and protections. Consequently, various oral traditions and the classic epics of poetry and literature often describe the use of envoys and emissaries to convey messages from one ruler to another. Homer discusses the value of heralds in the *Iliad*, and in the second letter to the church in Corinth, the Apostle Paul describes himself as an ambassador. City-states, empires, dynastic states, and nation-states, among others, each in its own way and often by trial and error over centuries, created various methods and institutions to facilitate relations between themselves and with others. They all contributed various threads to the complex tapestry known as diplomacy, creating what historian M. S. Anderson describes as "the system of regulated and organized contacts between states which Europe had evolved . . . and which, with all its faults, was one of her more important gifts to the world."

The Early Techniques, Instruments,
and Ideas of Diplomacy

A number of the techniques and instruments of diplomacy emerged during the height of Greek civilization when the emergence of several city-states increased the level of competition among them and thereby raised issues of force and statecraft to the fore. As Thucydides reveals so brilliantly in his *Peloponnesian War*, this required that they carefully consider the advantages and disadvantages of remaining isolated or of working in partnership with others. When the representatives of Corcyra approached Athens, he records, they spoke as follows:

3

We used to think that our neutrality was a wise thing, since it prevented us being dragged into danger by other people's policy; now we see it clearly as a lack of foresight and as a source of weakness. . . . We recognize that, if we have nothing but our own resources, it is impossible for us to survive, and we can imagine what lies in store for us if they overpower us. We are therefore forced to ask for assistance, both from you and from everyone else; and it should not be held against us that now we have faced the facts and are reversing our old policy of keeping ourselves to ourselves.

In this environment, Thucydides tells us, there were those who argued that "the strong do what they have the power to do and the weak accept what they have to accept." But there were many others who understood that this approach, as discussed in our introduction, represented no more than a recipe for international anarchy that would produce only more tumult and warfare. They sought instead to develop ways that would reduce the level of friction, facilitate their interaction, and create restraints that might keep their competition within certain bounds.

For this reason, the Greeks began to create some of the diplomatic practices that are still used today. From the sixth century B.C. onward they developed the practice of choosing ambassadors, or those who would represent them, from among the finest orators and most plausible forensic advocates they could find. The task of these representatives was to plead the cause of their city-state before the assemblies of foreign leagues or other city-states, and their speeches were often eloquent. This was extremely important, for as Demosthenes observed: "Ambassadors have no battleships at their disposal, or heavy infantry, or fortresses; their only weapons are words and opportunities." Over time these ambassadors were accorded special privileges and immunity in order that they might be able to fulfill their missions. In addition, the Greeks also established rules of procedure for the exchange of ambassadors, diplomatic conferences, the functions of consuls, the status of neutrality, the ratification of treaties, the right of asylum, extradition, and techniques of arbitration. Thucydides provides an example with the following account:

When the Corcyreans heard of these preparations they sent an embassy to Corinth, accomplished by some envoys from Sparta and Sicyon to support them. There they demanded that Corinth should withdraw her troops and colonists from Epidamnus. . . . They were prepared, however, if Corinth wished to put in a counter claim, to accept arbitration. Cities in the Peloponnese should be chosen by mutual agreement to act as arbitrators, and the colony should go to whichever side the arbitrators awarded it.

These practices helped to establish some of the first rules for the conduct of diplomacy.

The statesmen of Rome, on the other hand, were interested more in empire that in negotiation. They were not interested in bargaining among equals, but rather in holding their vast holdings together through superior organization whenever possible. Toward this end, their contribution to diplomacy was in the area of administrative rules, legal contracts, and the early development

of international law. Their ambassadors were appointed by the Senate and provided with official credentials. They extended the traditions of immunity granted to visiting ambassadors to their staffs as well. They established the profession of trained archivists to be specialists in diplomatic precedents and procedure. In addition, they created normative rules and laws to address declarations of war, the conclusion of peace, and the handling of hostages. In addition, the Romans gave great attention to developing legal concepts like *ius gentium* (the law of nations), *ius naturale* (the law that is common to all mankind), and *pacta sunt servanda*, or the importance of respecting legal obligations and of honoring the sanctity of treaties.

The Byzantine emperors who followed those of Rome increasingly appreciated the necessity of seriously addressing the needs of external relations and statecraft. For this reason, they were the first to organize a special and permanent governmental department to deal with foreign affairs. They made considerable effort to train professional negotiators to serve as their ambassadors, providing them with guidelines about how to behave and with written instructions about their precise missions. In this regard, they were instructed to furnish full reports as to the domestic situations in foreign governments and the relations of those governments to each other. For this purpose, they required more than the qualities of the herald or orator and needed those with trained powers of observation, experience, and sound judgment.

These various techniques, instruments, and ideas were passed on to the Italian city-states of the Renaissance, which made their own contributions and created the origins of modern diplomacy as we know it. They were both interconnected by geography and common interests and divided by intense rivalries. With constant commercial competition and the presence of armed neighbors, all existing in an unstable equilibrium, these states quickly realized that their survival required constant vigilance and acute attention to foreign affairs. To accomplish this, Venetian leaders of the fifteenth century came to understand that they needed to distance themselves from the traditional practice of sending out ambassadors on an ad hoc basis to solve a particular problem or crisis and instead to establish permanent diplomatic missions with a systemized diplomatic service. Venice therefore developed a sophisticated network of representatives who pursued the interests of the republic by providing accurate information, realistic appraisals of opportunities and risks, and skillful negotiations, all with an unusual freedom from sentimentality and illusion.

This practice of systematic diplomacy was quickly adopted by other states on the Italian peninsula, such as Florence, Milan, Mantua, and Tuscany, which, because they were situated in a political arena of incessant rivalry and coalition warfare, always recognized their vulnerability to external threats. They too considered diplomacy so essential that they began to establish permanent embassies abroad. Through time, they also began to write early diplomatic manuals describing the characteristics and skills that diplomats should possess and providing clear advice about how diplomats should act. Not surprisingly, this produced differing opinions, as it would in our own time. Some, like Bernard

du Rosier, the provost and later archbishop of Toulouse, wrote a treatise based heavily upon his religious beliefs in which he argued that the business of an ambassador must always be peace, that diplomats must labor for the common good, and that they should never be sent to stir up wars or internal dissensions. Others, like Ermalao Barbaro, argued in sharp contrast that "the first duty of an ambassador is exactly the same as that of any other servant of government: that is, to do, say, advise, and think whatever may best serve the preservation and aggrandizement of his own state." Regardless of the disagreements over what diplomats actually ought to do, all sides understood the importance of accurate information. For this reason, the Italian city-states became the first to preserve their diplomatic archives in systematic form. They realized that in the field of international relations, facts need to be scrutinized closely and dispassionately before any action can be undertaken. This placed a premium upon collecting all relevant information, registering and indexing all transactions, and thereby making it readily accessible to policy makers whenever needed.

The necessity of establishing such techniques and norms of diplomacy became all the more evident by the persistence of unremitting competition and nearly continuous warfare. As Philippe de Commynes, a Flemish solider-diplomat of the fifteenth century, argued, there was nothing at all glorious about war and violence. He feared the consequences of unrestrained rivalries and saw clearly that states were dependent upon each other whether they liked it or not. This line of thinking became more pronounced by the next century with the writings of the Dominican theologian and law professor Francisco de Vitoria, his Jesuit successor Francisco Suarez, and professor of law Alberico Gentilli, all of which stressed the need to establish commonly held, international legal principles and norms for justice of and in war.

All these developments contributed to a larger movement that sought to approach problems of statecraft in a systematic and rational manner. Some observers of the time actually began to construct certain theories about the nature of government and the conduct of statecraft itself, thereby creating the modern discipline of political science. The most noted of these was Niccolò Machiavelli, a man who had been in the diplomatic service for the republic of Florence, but then was forced to watch in horror as French invaders completely defeated and overthrew his ruler. He himself was dismissed from office, imprisoned and tortured, and then condemned to exile. It is in this context that he set about to write the *Discourses, Art of War,* and his most famous, or infamous, treatise in 1513, entitled *The Prince.* The preface of this book began by expressing his desire to learn lessons from history, warning of the dangers of weak government, and arguing that "when princes think more of luxury than of arms, they lose their state." This led him directly into a discussion of the relationship between force and statecraft:

> You must know that there are two methods of fighting, one by law, the other by force; the first method is that of men, the second of beasts; but as the first method is often insufficient, one must have recourse to the second. It is therefore necessary for a prince to know well how to use both the beast and the man.

Machiavelli stressed the importance for leaders "to keep good faith and live with integrity" in their relations with others, but when it came to advancing the interests of the state, he brutally concluded in language that has haunted his work ever since: "the end justifies the means."

Such thinking produced both intense condemnation by many for its dismissal of Christian ethics and glowing praise among others for its advocacy of power politics. For those who sought to amass greater political power, Machiavelli's writings appeared to provide justification for their methods and their objectives. They believed that in the new age that was rising, the small Italian city-states of the past would be irrevocably dwarfed in magnitude and strength by those monarchies capable of forging powerful nation-states. The French political philosopher Jean Bodin encouraged this idea even further by enunciating the principle of sovereignty in his 1576 book *Les Six livres de la république*. The future belonged to states, he asserted, that possessed sovereignty, which he defiantly described as "power absolute and perpetual," "supreme," and "subject to no law." Indeed, claimed Bodin, such sovereign power provided "the distinguishing mark of a state," giving it the sole authority to decide how it would treat its own people, how would behave in the world, and how it would use armed force.

STATES AND *RAISON D'ÉTAT* IN THE SEVENTEENTH CENTURY

When the seventeenth century began, therefore, emerging states in Europe possessed certain customs and practices of diplomacy and began to experience growing assertions about the prerogatives of their sovereignty. But what would eventually be called the Great Powers still did not exist. In 1600, for instance, Russia was a remote and ineffectual land, separated from Europe by the large territory that was called Poland-Lithuania with whose rulers it waged periodic territorial conflicts, as it did with the Ottoman Turks to the south. Prussia did not exist in its later sense but, as the Electorate of Brandenburg, lived a purely German existence, like Bavaria or Württemberg, with no wider European significance. England, a country of considerable commercial strength, was not accorded much geopolitical importance. As a result of internal anarchy and strife, France seemed destined to play a minor role in European politics. The strongest political center in Europe was the old Holy Roman Empire with its capital in Vienna and its alliance with Spain, which still possessed a vast empire and formidable military power.

Why did this situation not persist? To put it another way, why was the European system transformed so radically that the Holy Roman Empire became an insignificant political force and the continent came in the eighteenth century to be dominated by Britain, France, Austria, Prussia, and Russia? The answer, of course, is war. War shaped the formation, the character, and the development of modern states.

From 1618 until 1721, a long series of raging wars changed the rank order of European states by exhausting some and exalting others. Virtually all of the major dynastic rivalries, religious differences, the drawing of borders,

possession of cities and fortresses, trade routes and colonies, and ultimately the destinies of kingdoms and empires were decided by the use of armed force in war. At the beginning of the century, a European battle might involve as few as 25,000 troops on both sides. Within a few decades, France alone created an army of 400,000. As if bent upon supplying evidence for the later nineteenth-century Darwinians, the states that became the Great Powers proved themselves in the grinding struggle of the age to be the fittest, the ones far better organized and more efficient than the feudal or mercantile states that they replaced to meet the demands of protracted competition in warfare. Only they could marshal the resources to destroy another state. Only they could defend themselves from external attack. Only they could convene peace settlements.

The process of transformation began with the Thirty Years' War, which stretched from 1618 to 1648. It is sometimes called the last of the religious wars, a description that is justified by the fact that it was motivated originally by the desire of the Catholic House of Habsburg to restore the Protestant parts of the empire and because, in thirty years of fighting, the religious motive gave way to political considerations and, in the spreading of the conflict from its German center to embrace all of Europe, some governments—notably France—waged war against their coreligionists for material reasons. For the states that initiated this wasting conflict, the war was an unmitigated disaster. The Hapsburgs became so debilitated by it that they lost their former control over the German states and their empire became a mere adjunct of the Austrian crown lands. Austria, moreover, emerged so weakened by the exertions and losses of the war that after 1648 it barely could protect its eastern possessions and watched in horror when in 1683 the Turkish army threatened to capture Vienna itself. At the same time, its strongest ally, Spain, squandered an infantry once judged to be the best in Europe in bloody battles like that at Nördlingen in 1634. Spain's long and irreversible decline began not with the failure of the naval Armada in 1588, but rather with the terrible losses suffered in German territory and the Netherlands during the Thirty Years' War.

In sharp contrast, some states profited from the war. One of these was the Netherlands which, under leaders like Maurice of Nassau and Jan de Witt, won its independence from Spain and became a commercial and financial center of major importance. Sweden, led by the "Lion of the North" Gustavus Adolphus and his use of the combined arms of infantry, cavalry, and artillery, emerged as the strongest power in the Baltic region. And, of particular importance, there was France, which entered the war formally in 1635 and emerged at the end of it as the most powerful state in western Europe.

It is no accident that these particular states were so successful, for they represented excellent examples of the process that historians describe as the emergence of the modern state, the three principal characteristics of which were effective armed forces, an able bureaucracy, and a theory of state that restrained dynastic exuberance and defined political interest in rational, practical terms. Indeed, the seventeenth century saw the emergence of what came to be called *raison d'état* or *ragione di stato*—the idea that the state was more than its ruler and more than the expression of his wishes; that it transcended

crown and land, prince and people; that objectives should never be sought in excess of capabilities; that it had its particular set of interests and a particular set of necessities based upon them; and that the art of government lay in recognizing those interests and necessities and acting in accordance with them, even if this might violate ethical standards based upon religious belief. The effective state, argued its supporters, must have the kinds of servants who would interpret *raison d'état* wisely and be willing to use the kinds of material and physical resources necessary to advance it.

One of the foremost spokesmen for, and practitioners of, this approach was Armand Jean du Plessis, Cardinal Richelieu, who served as the chief minister of France from 1624 to 1642. In this capacity, he relentlessly promulgated and ruthlessly pursued the concept of *raison d'état* for the benefit of his state. With specific reference to diplomacy, he created a centralized Ministry of External Affairs to supervise the rational pursuit of foreign policy. He also wisely stressed the importance of carefully selecting skilled ambassadors, of calculating risks and opportunities, of giving continuous attention to foreign affairs, and of faithfully honoring all treaty commitments. These valuable contributions, however, often were overshadowed by Richelieu's extremes; like others who sometimes fancy themselves as unusually shrewd practitioners of statecraft, he seemed to recognize few limits or restraints. He placed French political goals above everything else, including the religious values that he supposedly represented as an official of the church. Indeed, upon learning of his death, the pope allegedly responded, "If there is a God, the Cardinal de Richelieu will have much to answer for. If not . . . well, he had a successful life." In order to advance what he regarded as the interests of France, for example, he aggressively crushed domestic adversaries, employed a vast network of spies and agents, launched and deliberately prolonged foreign wars, subsidized Protestants to wage war against Catholics, bribed, manipulated, and fomented insurrections. As he stated in his *Political Testament*, "In matters of state it is necessary to profit from everything possible; whatever is useful is never to be despised." The end to be achieved, he declared directly, was simple: "power."

Such a maxim of statecraft hardly went uncontested. In fact, the views and practices of Richelieu often provoked outrage among those who viewed them as deeply offensive to legal and ethical values. One of the most devastating critiques came from the renowned reformist theologian Cornelius Jansenius, who wrote:

> Do they believe that a secular, perishable state should outweigh religion and the Church? . . . Should not the Most Christian King believe that in the guidance and administration of his realm there is nothing that obliges him to extend and protect that of Jesus Christ, his Lord? . . . Would he dare say to God: Let your power and glory and the religion which teaches men to adore You be lost and destroyed, provided my state is protected and free of risks?

The brilliant Dutch jurist and diplomat, Hugo Grotius, similarly argued that if the leaders continued to condition their behavior exclusively on narrow

definitions of *raison d'état* and expediency, they would only perpetuate international violence and anarchy. As he observed the world around him, according to his powerful 1625 book, *On the Law of War and Peace*, he saw

> a license in making war of which even barbarous nations would have been ashamed; recourse was had to arms for slight reasons, or for no reason; and when arms were taken up, all reverence for divine and human law was thrown away; just as if men were henceforth authorized to commit all crimes without restraint.

The only way to break this vicious pattern, Grotius argued, could be found in creating a broader order or system based upon norms that respected the "laws of nations," the "natural rights" of human beings, and specific criteria for a "just war" that placed clear limits upon the use of force in statecraft. Others went even further in protesting prevailing practices, including the Quakers, who issued their famous testimony of pacifism opposing all war as a matter of ethical principle.

Despite these arguments, the exercise of power in the seventeenth century was such that Grotius was imprisoned and the protestors largely silenced, while Richelieu continued to rise in prominence. His success, that of his even more ruthless and less popular successor Cardinal Mazarin, and the capacity of modern states to create and mobilize armed forces, a centralized administration, and statecraft based upon rational calculations of interests were not only demonstrated in the Thirty Years' War but confirmed by the 1648 Peace of Westphalia. This settlement resulted from lengthy negotiations held in the two cities of Osnabrück and Münster and established a landmark in the history of diplomacy. It provided a legal recognition of a new society composed not of feudal, imperial, or ecclesiastical actors, but rather of powerful, juridically independent, and autonomous states. As one noted expert on international law writes:

> The Peace of Westphalia, for better or worse, marks the end of an epoch and the opening of another. It represents the majestic portal which leads from the old into the new world. . . . In the political field it marked man's abandonment of the idea of a hierarchal structure of society and his option for a new system characterized by the coexistence of a multiplicity of states, each sovereign within it territory, equal to one another, and free from any external authority.

The publication of the influential and uncompromising *Leviathan* by English political philosopher Thomas Hobbes only three years later provided even further theoretical justification for the idea that there was no authority above that of the sovereign state. As such, kings and other government leaders increasingly argued that they could act in the name of their state largely as they wished or were able, safe in the knowledge that they were shielded from individual responsibility for their actions, including the abuse of human rights or the conduct of war.

The newfound power of these states, and the prerogative of sovereignty that they so vociferously claimed, could be seen in a number of cases. One of

these was Brandenburg-Prussia under the leadership of Frederick William, the so-called Great Elector, who inherited a loose collection of territories overrun with foreign troops with a population depleted by famine and pestilence. He calculated that a close, reciprocal relationship existed between military and political institutions. If he desired to create a functioning state out of lands surrounded by adversaries, he believed that he could never do so without an efficient bureaucracy and a strong army. The last was the key to the whole. As he wrote in his political testament, "A ruler is treated with no consideration if he does not have troops of his own. It is these, thank God!, that have made me *considerabel* since the time I began to have them." Thus, in the course of his reign from 1640 to 1688, he organized one of the first departments of war to oversee the details of creating a large and efficient military force. It was to administer this army and to collect taxes to pay for it that Frederick William laid the foundations of the soon famous Prussian bureaucracy which, in turn, helped him to further build and centralize state power. All this inspired a young, energetic, and determined czar who would eventually earn the name of Peter the Great to believe that similar efforts on his part could transform his state from its fragmented past into the modern world, thereby making an emerging Russia parallel an emerging Prussia.

No state proved to be better at harnessing resources and accelerating this process of the centralization of power than France. Over time, some of the victors of the Thirty Years' War lost their strength: Sweden threw its gains away under a less rational ruler, and the Netherlands yielded its commercial and naval supremacy to England, which, among other victories, had conquered the Dutch colonial possession of New Netherland in North America and renamed it New York. But this was not the case in France. Indeed, the ascendancy of France under Louis XIV, who ruled his absolutist state from 1643 to 1715, was evident in European politics, culture, architecture, science, art, administration, warfare, and diplomacy. The extraordinary influence of France itself seemed to be embodied in its best resident ambassadors, who linked the capitals and courts of Europe and whose instructions, reports, and skills served as a model of diplomatic practice for years to come. It was at this time, in fact, that the French language became the *lingua franca* of diplomacy itself.

Serious attention to diplomatic method also appeared with the publication in 1681 of a book written by Abram de Wicquefort entitled *L'Ambassadeur et ses fonctions*. Based on his own observations about statecraft, well-seasoned by his checkered career as a diplomat, this work provided both a commentary on the political ethics of the seventeenth century and an incisive analysis of the art and practice of diplomacy. Wicquefort was not abashed by the peccadilloes of his colleagues, which varied from financial peculation and sins of the flesh to crimes of violence. He believed that in a corrupt age, one could not expect that embassies would be oases of virtue. A state could afford to be served by bad men, but not by incompetent ones. Competence began with a clear understanding on the diplomat's part of the nature of his job, which "consisted in maintaining effective communication between the two Princes,

in delivering letters that his master writes to the Prince at whose court he resides, in soliciting answers to them, . . . in protecting his Master's subjects and conserving his interests." In this pursuit, Wicquefort stressed that prudence and moderation were the qualities that should be cultivated most assiduously. The former he equated with caution and reflection, and the latter with the ability to curb one's temper and remain cool and collected in moments of tension. "Those spirits who are compounded of sulphur and saltpeter, whom the slightest spark can set afire, are easily capable of compromising affairs by their excitability, because it is so easy to put them in a rage or drive them to a fury, so that they do not know what they are doing."

The means of diplomacy, however, are not the same as the ends to which they are employed. As the French writer Jean de la Bruyère wrote mockingly, the diplomats of the age "spoke only of peace, alliance, and public tranquility . . . and thought only of their special interest." This became perfectly clear as Louis XIV continued to amass power and wealth and to grow in strength. Through time, the skill, style, and sophistication of his diplomats could not mask the fact that he wanted them used to secure the political ends of greater glory and influence, dreaming that both domestic and foreign affairs might revolve around him as the planets revolve around the sun. He used diplomacy when he could, but when he wanted more he quickly turned to warfare as the means of challenging the territorial settlements of Westphalia. His armies were the most powerful and most feared in Europe. It was no accident that in his luxurious palace of Versailles, built on a scale never seen before, his throne was located adjacent to his *Salon de Guerre*, or war room. He maintained alliances with the Swedes in the north and the Turks in the south to prevent Russian interference while he placed his own candidate on the throne of Poland. He also used his Turkish connection to distract Austria on its eastern frontiers so that he could simultaneously dabble in German politics. Bavaria and the Palatinate were bound to the French court by marriage, and almost all of the other German princes accepted subsidies at one time or another from France. He employed the same methods of infiltration in Italy, Portugal, and Spain, where the young king married a French princess and French ambassadors exerted considerable influence in internal affairs. In addition to all of this, Louis sought to undermine the independence of the Netherlands and bribe Charles II with a pension in order to reduce the possibility of English interference as he did so. When Louis XIV's army invaded the Low Countries, they quickly crushed their opponents. Only flooding caused by the opening of the dikes prevented the French from entering the province of Holland itself.

This growing French dominance became so great in the second half of the seventeenth century, in fact, that it threatened not only other states, but European peace and security as a whole. As such, the overpowering influence and hegemony of France invited resistance on the part of others, and out of that resistance combinations and alliances were bound to take place. This is exactly what happened, and they began to formulate an appreciation for a balance of power. That is, they began to understand that if any state or

combination of states became too powerful, the peace and security of all the others would be seriously threatened. The only way to prevent this and to maintain some kind of balance, they believed, would be to create countervailing power through collective security. In the words of the German historian Leopold von Ranke, "The concept of the European balance of power was developed in order that union of many other states might resist the pretensions of the 'exorbitant' court, as it was called." This is a statement worth noting. A balance of power, of course, had been practiced in Machiavelli's time in the intermittent warfare between the city-states of the Italian peninsula, but now it was being deliberately invoked as a principle and an instrument of statecraft, as a safeguard against domination. As we shall see, this concept evolved further in the eighteenth century, and during the nineteenth century it became one of the basic principles of the diplomatic system itself.

Such thinking played a significant role as the powers attempted to respond to France's continued and dangerous expansion. They worried as Louis XIV sent his troops into Alsace and captured the vital bridgehead city of Strasbourg. Their fears intensified as he then moved into northern Italy. They finally took action when he attempted to seize the city of Cologne and thereby launched what came to be the Nine Years' War that raged from 1688 to 1697. The result was the formation of the first of the great balance-of-power coalitions. This included the land forces of Austria, which a short time before had repulsed the Turks at the gates of Vienna; the Dutch, who were threatened most directly in a territorial sense by the French; and maritime England, which had just overcome the debilitating effects of a civil war and named the gifted William of Orange of Holland to become their new king, William III. The contending forces were so evenly matched that the war dragged on and settled little, but it demonstrated that a coalition could be formed when necessary to counter a serious threat.

War and Competition in the Eighteenth Century

The eighteenth century opened, continued, and closed with warfare. One of the great paradoxes of the age is that the century that produced an articulation of the principles of democracy and human rights from the Enlightenment philosophers, the ethical restraints proposed by Immanuel Kant, the exquisite music of Mozart and Handel, enormous advances in the sciences, and called itself "The Age of Reason," also witnessed an anarchy of all against all, ruthless competition, cynical opportunism, and nearly constant aggression and violence between states. Virtually all of the alliances of the period were calculated to expand capabilities and to aggrandize territory. It was a century in which there were three systemic wars involving all or most of the Great Powers and seven wars involving at least two of them, resulting in battlefield deaths estimated to be seven or eight times greater than those that would occur in the following century.

All this began with the Great Northern War of 1700–1721, fought over supremacy in the Baltic area. Denmark and Saxony launched the war by invading

Sweden but, to their considerable dismay, were routed and driven from the country by armed forces led by the eighteen-year-old and daring ruler, Charles XII. The Danes capitulated at once, and Charles without pause threw his troops against a much larger Russian force advancing on Narva and quickly routed them. But brilliant military victories sometimes create the foundation of greater defeats, for they often lead to an exaggerated sense of strength and ability and a corresponding lack of perspective and restraint. Now overconfident, Charles determined to punish the Saxons and to exert his control over Poland. It proved to be his undoing, for it distracted him from the more serious threat of an emerging Russia under the leadership of Peter the Great. If anyone was forced to acknowledge the constant presence of warfare during this time, it surely was Peter. Indeed, during his entire reign from 1689–1725 he experienced only eighteen months of consecutive peace. Survival required that he institute reforms that would bring Russia into the modern world. He had carefully observed that those states emerging in the West all had done so because of their ability to create a centralized bureaucracy, build a standing army and navy, and practice *raison d'état*. He used this as a model for his own country, and when his armed forces were ready, he sent them into action. Charles responded with an invasion—and this, like other later invasions of Russia, was defeated by winter and famine and ultimately by a monumental military loss at the Battle of Poltava in 1709. The new Russian fleet subsequently defeated the Swedish navy. All this broke the power of Sweden, eventually enabling Peter to gain possessions in the West, build his new capital of St. Petersburg, and establish a foreign ministry and permanent diplomatic service, thereby confirming the dramatic emergence of Russia as a Great Power and shifting the political axis of Europe.

Warfare simultaneously raged in the West with the outbreak of the War of Spanish Succession fought between 1702 and 1714. When the elaborate efforts to find a suitable and mutually acceptable heir to the throne of Spain failed, the rivalries and ambitions of the Bourbon and the Hapsburg dynasties exploded into open warfare. To control as much territory as possible, Louis XIV again sent his troops smashing into the Netherlands. This threatened the others, and, in response, William III formed the Grand Alliance, the largest coalition of forces aligned against a single power that modern Europe had ever seen. The allied objectives were to prevent any unification of the thrones of France and Spain and thereby thwart domination by Louis XIV. In this campaign, the resources of the Netherlands, Austria, and Prussia were all brought to bear, in addition to England's significant contributions of finances, naval forces, and a land army of nearly 70,000 troops. This resulted in the brilliant military partnership of John Churchill, the Duke of Marlborough, from England and Prince Eugene of Savoy from Austria, a team that defeated a supposedly invulnerable French army on several occasions, including the Battle of Blenheim in 1704 and the Battle of Ramillies in 1706.

These and other victories laid the basis for two agreements of 1713 and 1714, collectively known as the Treaty of Utrecht. According to its terms, France was forced to renounce the idea of a union of the French and Spanish

thrones, give up the Spanish Netherlands to Austria, renounce all territorial gains east of the Rhine River, raze the fortifications at Dunkirk, and surrender important territories in North America to Great Britain (as England was known after its union with Scotland in 1707). Britain also acquired the strategically valuable base of Gibraltar from Spain at this time. In addition, the treaty extended recognition to Prussia as a member of the society of states. The broader significance of the Utrecht settlement is that it marked the first European treaty that specifically mentioned a balance of power. In the letters patent that accompanied the treaty between Queen Anne and King Louis XIV, the French ruler noted that the terms expressed the hope of "obtaining a general Peace and securing the Tranquility of *Europe* by a Ballance of Power," and the king of Spain acknowledged the importance of "the Maxim of securing for ever the universal Good and Quiet of Europe, by an equal Weight of Power, so that many being united in one, the Ballance of the Equality desired might not turn to the Advantage of one, and the Danger and Hazard of the Rest."

Some of the most serious and profound thinking about the subject of force and statecraft, as we shall see, usually occurs at the end of a prolonged war or in the wake of a dangerous crisis. These are the times when issues of survival are most acute and when leaders and peoples alike become vitally interested in finding ways of avoiding future wars or crises. The end of the War of Spanish Succession, for example, brought Louis XIV himself to the point of reflection on the exercise of power in the world, and he said to his great grandson and heir with great solemnity: "My child, you will one day be a great king. Do not imitate me in my taste for war. Always relate your actions to God and make your subjects honor Him." The same war also motivated one of Louis XIV's most gifted diplomats, François de Callières, to write his famous *On the Manner of Negotiating with Princes* in 1716. This has been called "a mine of political wisdom" and has been described by no less an authority than diplomat and historian Sir Harold Nicolson as a work that "remains to this day the best manual of diplomatic method ever written." Callières stated his purpose in the introduction:

> To give an idea of the personal qualities and general knowledge necessary in all good negotiators; to indicate to them the paths which they should follow and the rock which they should avoid; and to exhort those who destine themselves to the foreign service of their country, to render themselves capable of discharging worthily that high, important, and difficult office before entering upon it.

Among these various qualities, one needed "an observant mind, a spirit of application which refuses to be distracted by pleasures or frivolous amusements, a sound judgment which takes the measure of things, as they are, and which goes straight to its goal by the shortest and most neutral paths without wandering into useless refinements and subtleties which as a rule only succeed in repelling those with whom one is dealing." Important also were careful discernment, self-control, creativity, a patient temperament, easy and agreeable manners, and a sense of moderation. In this regard, he cautioned

DE LA MANIERE
DE NEGOCIER
AVEC
LES SOUVERAINS.

De l'utilité des Negociations, du
choix des Ambaſſadeurs & des
Envoyez,& des qualitez neceſſai-
res pour réüſſir dans ces employs.

Par Monſieur D E C A L L I E R E S *;
Conſeiller Ordinaire du Roi en ſes Con-
ſeils , Secretaire du Cabinet de Sa Ma-
jeſté , cy-devant Ambaßadeur Extraor-
dinaire & Plenipotentiaire du feu Roy ,
pour les Traitez de Paix conclus à
Riſwick. Et l'un des Quarante de
l'Academie Françoiſe.*

A P A R I S ,
Chez M I C H E L B R U N E T, Grand'-
Salle du Palais , au Mercure Galant.

M. DCC. XVI.
Avec Approbation & Privilege du Roy.

"A Mine of Political Wisdom": François de Callières,
On the Manner of Negotiating with Princes (Library of
Congress)

against large diplomatic conferences and heavy reliance upon lawyers in negotiations, arguing that the legal mind was at once too narrow, too intent upon
hair-splitting, and too contentious to be useful in a field where success, in
the last analysis, was best assured by agreements that provided mutuality of
advantage. Of particular interest, and in sharp contrast to those who callously
argued that an ambassador was no more than "an honest man sent to lie abroad
for the good of his country," Callières warned of those who tried to get what
they wanted by dishonesty. The good diplomat, he wrote,

> will never rely for the success of his mission either on bad faith or on promises
> that he cannot execute. It is a fundamental error, and one widely held, that
> a clever negotiator must be a master of deceit. Deceit is indeed the meas-
> ure of the smallness of mind of him who uses it; it proves that he does not
> possess sufficient intelligence to achieve results by just and reasonable
> means. Honesty is here and everywhere the best policy. . . . Apart from the
> fact that a lie is unworthy of a great Ambassador, it actually does more harm
> than good to negotiation, since though it may confer success today, it
> will create an atmosphere of suspicion which tomorrow will make further
> success impossible. . . . The negotiator therefore must be a man of probity
> and one who loves truth; otherwise he will fail to inspire confidence.

Perhaps the most distinctive feature of Callières's treatise was the passion
with which he wisely argued that a nation's foreign relations should be conducted by professionals trained for the task rather than by politically connected

amateurs. He complained bitterly of the grave damage done to state interests by those novices "appointed so to speak over-night to important embassies in countries of which they know neither the interests, the laws, the customs, the language, nor even the geographical situation." Governments should seriously reflect, he insisted, upon the story of the Duke of Tuscany who, upon complaining to a visitor about the inadequate capacities of a Venetian resident at his court and receiving the answer, "I am not surprised. We have many fools in Venice," retorted with spirit: "We have many fools in Florence, but we take care not to export them." An incompetent envoy could do serious harm to their country's interests, and for that reason the most extreme care should be taken in the selection of one's foreign representatives. They should be carefully educated in the lessons of history and trained in diplomatic skills and techniques, and should know "exactly the state of the military forces both on land and sea" in order to understand force and statecraft. "Diplomacy," he declared,

> is a profession by itself which deserves the same preparation and assiduity of attention that men give to other recognized professions. . . . [T]here are many qualities which may be developed with practice, and the greatest part of the necessary knowledge can only be acquired, by constant application to the subject. In this sense, diplomacy is certainly a profession itself capable of occupying a man's whole career, and those who think to embark upon a diplomatic mission as a pleasant diversion from their common task only prepare disappointment for themselves and disaster for the cause which they serve.

These words represented not only a personal view but an acknowledgment of the requirements of the age. The states that emerged in the course of the seventeenth and eighteenth centuries were those that could modernize their governmental structure, mobilize their economic and other resources in a rational manner, build up effective and disciplined military establishments, and create a professional bureaucracy that administered state business in accordance with the principles of *raison d'état*. An indispensable part of that civil service was the establishment of a foreign office or foreign ministry, led by single individual known as a foreign minister or state secretary for foreign affairs, and a well-trained diplomatic corps, which maintained permanent missions abroad and had the important task of formulating the foreign policy that protected and advanced the state's vital interests and seeing that was carried out.

If any doubts remained about the effectiveness of this process of state-building, they would have been answered by the emergence of Prussia. When soldier-king Frederick William I assumed the throne during the wars against Louis XIV, he was determined to strengthen his state by whatever means necessary. To do this, he completed the centralization and modernization of the bureaucracy started under the Great Elector, elaborated a body of law that clarified rights and responsibilities for all subjects, nationalized the officer corps of the army, improved its dress and weapons, wrote its first handbook of field regulations, and rapidly expanded its numbers. Indeed, during the course of his reign, he increased the size of his military establishment to 83,000 men, which made Prussia's army the fourth largest in Europe, although the state ranked only tenth from the stand-point of territory and thirteenth in population.

This is the Prussian army and state that he bequeathed to his son, Frederick II, who eventually came to be called Frederick the Great. Here was a man who seemed to combine so many of the paradoxes of the age in his own person. He prided himself on being a product of the Enlightenment and Age of Reason, corresponded with French philosophers like Voltaire, whom he invited to his palace at Sans Souci, studied poetry, loved music and became an accomplished flutist and composer, and wrote a long treatise on politics in which he attacked the advice of Machiavelli. At exactly the same time, he single-mindedly pursued what he perceived as Prussia's *raison d'état* and national interest by further developing a centralized bureaucracy, instituting military reforms, and launching wars of aggression. Indeed, in one of his more famous statements, he declared: "Negotiations without arms produce as little impression as musical scores without instruments."

In 1740, Frederick secured the throne. The same year saw the death of the Austrian emperor, Charles VI, who had asked the European powers before he died to subscribe to a document called the Pragmatic Sanction promising that they would observe the integrity of his possessions under the rule of his young and inexperienced daughter, Maria Theresa. Frederick signed this agreement along with most of the other rulers. Nevertheless, neither his signature nor the arguments against unethical behavior that he himself had used in his *Anti-Machiavel* treatise deterred him now from taking advantage of what seemed to him to be an ideal opportunity for aggrandizement. He consequently wrote a memorandum to his ministers that should be quoted in full for the light that it throws on him and eighteenth-century statecraft:

> Silesia is the portion of the Imperial heritage to which we have the strongest claim and which is most suitable to the House of Brandenburg. The superiority of our troops, the promptitude with which we can set them in motion, in a word, a clear advantage we have over our neighbors, gives us in this unexpected emergency an infinite superiority over all other powers in Europe. If we wait till Saxony and Bavaria start hostilities, we could not prevent the aggrandizement of the former which is wholly contrary to our interest. . . . [As for the other powers], England and France are our foes. If France should mettle in the affairs of the empire, England could not allow it, so I can always make a good alliance with one or the other. England could not be jealous of my getting Silesia, which would do her no harm, and she needs allies. Holland will not care, all the more since the loans of the Amsterdam business world secured on Silesia will be guaranteed. If we cannot arrange with England and Holland, we can certainly make a deal with France, who cannot frustrate our designs and will welcome the abasement of the imperial house. Russia alone might give us trouble. If the empress lives . . . we can bribe the leading counselors. If she dies, the Russians will be so occupied that they will have no time for foreign affairs. . . . All this leads to the conclusion that we must occupy Silesia before the winter and then negotiate. When we are in possession we can negotiate with success. We should never get anything by negotiations alone except very onerous conditions in return for a few trifles.

This memorandum requires little comment. Here is a mind that is completely dominated by *raison d'état*, or (in German) *Staatsräson*, and one that admits no legal or ethical bounds to state ambition. With such calculations and without hesitation, he dismissed his treaty obligations and ordered his armies to invade and seize the rich Austrian province of Silesia. This was a patent act of aggression and one that is still remembered as "the rape of Silesia."

In the end, Silesia fell to Frederick and the whole balance of forces in German-speaking lands tilted in Prussia's favor. But this result was gained only as a result of a complex series of interrelated power struggles and two wasting wars in which the original Silesian issue at times seemed to drop completely out of view. In the first of these, the so-called War of Austrian Succession, extending from 1740 to 1748, Prussia was joined by France, Spain, Bavaria, and Saxony (which changed sides in mid-course), who together resembled a pack of wolves stalking its injured and vulnerable prey, all hoping to gain something at Austrian expense. Britain supported Austria, but many of its troops were sent to attack French and Spanish possessions in the New World. The second was the Seven Years' War, which raged from 1756 to 1763. This began with Frederick's surprise attack on Saxony, but the tactical military advantage of a preemptive attack quickly produced the very strategic alliance of Austria, France, and Russia that he had hoped to prevent. Only Britain and Hanover supported Prussia. In both wars the change of allies from one side to the other resulted not from any overriding principle of an international system or order, but rather from a lust for selfish gain, whether in Europe, India, or in North America, where the struggle was known as the French and Indian War. In fact, these eighteenth-century wars for empire further extended European power over much of the rest of the world.

It is difficult to read of these struggles in which the powers changed sides without the guidance of any but the meanest of principles without thinking of the eighteenth century as an age of anarchy and rapine. Promises and treaty commitments seemed to mean little, and enemies and allies changed with little warning. Frederick had confirmed Prussia's status as a Great Power, but he had engaged in duplicitous diplomacy and bled his country white in twenty-three years of almost continuous warfare to do so. Moreover, the rapaciousness of the age evidenced in so many ways became even clearer with the blatant land grabs in 1772, 1793, and 1795, when Austria, Russia, and Prussia ruthlessly carved up Poland and distributed the spoils between them. All this seemed only to confirm la Bruyere's observation of nations thinking of themselves alone and behaving solely in their own interests. The same conclusion was reached by a contemporary statesman who described the conditions as "a continuous quarrel between people without morals, intent on taking and perpetually hungry."

There were, to be sure, those who attempted to resist these practices of the eighteenth century, who spoke out against them, and who, like Immanuel Kant, sought to establish ethical restraints on force and statecraft. Some, like Emmerich de Vattel who wrote *Le Droit des Gens* in 1758, Fortuné Barthélemy de Félice, the author of *Code de l'Humanité* in 1778, and Georg Friedrich von

Martens in his *Précis du Droit des Gens* of 1789, tried to enunciate certain normative rules for diplomacy, drawing attention to areas of common interest. They argued that in terms of power and influence, there were now five Great Powers that stood above the rest: Britain, France, Austria, Prussia, and Russia (although no one could have foreseen that they would dominate European and world politics until 1914). Some publicists began writing about the idea that these states could perhaps begin to evolve a society or a federation capable of working in concert and reaching some level of agreement on rules for the competition between them. They took some hope in the fact that among these five states, more and more discussion centered around the concept of the balance of power. That is, there was a growing consciousness that their mutual survival required that no single state be allowed to dominate the others. Wars could be fought for limited objectives like territorial adjustments, but not for the complete destruction of another power. In addition, any gain effected by military victory by one should be balanced by compensatory gains for the others major actors, as demonstrated in the elaborate territorial arithmetic seen during the partitions of Poland.

The hopeful also drew attention to the fact that although the powers frequently fought against each other, there were clear restraints on the level of violence. It certainly helped, of course, to engage in wars of tactical maneuver on battlefields restricted to what one could see with the naked eye and to fight in neat line formations with weapons of such limited lethality that brightly colored uniforms could be worn. But there was more. Few statesmen were willing to run the risk of challenging the larger equilibrium as established at Utrecht. In addition, the fear of excessive casualties played a restraining role, as did seasonal weather which annually sent troops into winter quarters. Theologians and philosophers developed theories of just war, and various leaders made tentative efforts to ameliorate some of the rigors of war by developing several laws of war that placed restrictions upon the freedom of military commanders in the field concerning the destruction of crops, livestock, or civilian dwellings and the taking of hostages. No authority existed to enforce these rules, and they were often violated, but their very existence gave hope that some level of cooperation could be obtained to spare civilian society from the horrors that accompanied any war. Even the determined practitioner of war Frederick the Great declared that he wanted to fight his wars without the peasant behind his plow or the townsman in his shop even being aware of them.

But the broader ideas of cooperation, common interests, and mutual restraints often remained largely confined to philosophical discourse and visions of what might be rather than actual practice. During the eighteenth century, they rarely influenced the deliberations and actions of governments dominated by greed, envy, and fear, and going about their intrigue and violent ways without bothering themselves with such thoughts. As historian Friedrich Meinecke starkly concluded in his book *Die Idee der Staatsräson*: "Never was the isolation of the power-state carried so far . . . never, either before or since, did universally European ideas and interests form such a small part, as they

did then, in European policy of the first rank." To make the Great Powers pay attention to such matters, something of sufficient magnitude was needed to frighten them into genuine collaborative action, something that would force them to covert the dream of a European concert into a working reality.

That shock finally came in the form of the French Revolution and the wars of the Republic and the Napoleonic Empire. Yet, when the revolution broke out in 1789, so entrenched were the European powers in their customary, competitive ways that they believed France would become so paralyzed and incapable of conducting foreign policy that they could pick up the spoils. The idea that the domestic revolution might actually have threatening, external consequences hardly seems to have occurred to them. This attitude proved almost fatal, for it allowed the revolutionary forces in France to consolidate themselves before going on the offensive and then made the others highly vulnerable to being divided and conquered once those forces were unleashed. Once this occurred, in the notable words of historian R. R. Palmer, "The wars of kings were over; the wars of peoples had begun."

When France launched its first offensive war in 1792, it did so for a variety of reasons, not the least of which was the ploy of distracting attention away from domestic problems by focusing on a foreign adversary. But even this did not unduly alarm the other powers. The Prussians and the Austrians fought back in uncoordinated campaigns and seemed to be more nervous about each other than about their common enemy, France. Indeed, the Prussians sold out their Austrian ally by a secret treaty that promised the French territory if they received other lands as compensation elsewhere. Many similar examples could be given, as each in turn seemed to be eager to strike their own deals, turning to appeasement, neutrality, alliance, or any other arrangement that might offer them temporary advantage. This kind of selfish, shortsighted, and unreliable behavior enabled the French armies, now made so much stronger by the huge numbers and patriotic zeal of the *levée en masse* or general conscription, to conquer the Rhineland and then to penetrate into southern German lands, Switzerland, and Italy. Once Napoleon Bonaparte seized power in 1799, France was either at war or preparing for war for the next sixteen years, and its imperial conquest gained in momentum and success. Napoleon's new strategic approach to warfare and brilliant military victories defeated Austrian, Prussian, and Russian forces one after the other. His diplomacy held the British at bay, established satellite kingdoms, and continually thwarted attempts to build effective coalitions against him. This enabled him by 1810 to extend his empire by direct and indirect means and to become the dominating master of the continent of Europe. "Europe seemed about to be swallowed up by France," observed historian Leopold von Ranke. "The universal monarchy, that had hitherto seemed only a remote danger, was almost realized."

But like other military conquerors, Napoleon suffered from the problem of not knowing when to stop. He fatally overreached himself in 1812 when he decided to invade Russia. The vastness of the land, harsh winter weather, distant lines of communication, and the "scorched earth" policy of the

Russians that sought to deny him any semblance of victory all proved to be too much and shattered the myth of Napoleon's invincibility. It was only in the wake of this that the other powers finally formed a coalition that would bring about his final defeat.

Their successful collaboration produced defeat for French forces during the Battle of Nations at Leipzig in 1813. But their awareness that they had not yet fully escaped danger made them realize the necessity of keeping the coalition together and, at long last, induced them to take the first real step toward converting the aspiration of a concert into action. The agonies of the wars of the eighteenth century and those of Napoleon convinced them that peace and security could not simply be left to the ad hoc residue of the collision of each state narrowly defining and then asserting its own *raison d'état*. It was the disasters that they had experienced that began to make them consider the possibility that their own national self-interest might be well served by considering their collective interests as a whole. Consequently, in the French town of Chaumont, the governments of Austria, Prussia, Russia, and Britain signed a treaty in 1814 in which they agreed not only to continue the war against Napoleon until a definitive victory had been gained, but also—as a conscious design—to continue their alliance well after their victory. As they significantly explained: "The present Treaty of Alliance having for its object the maintenance of the balance of Europe, to secure the repose and independence of the Powers, and to prevent the invasions which for so many years have devastated the world, the High Contracting Parties have agreed among themselves to extend its duration for twenty years from the date of signature." This held the allies together until Napoleon was finally and decisively defeated at the Battle of Waterloo in 1815 and then, remarkably, went on to serve as the basis for the first notable experiment in creating an international system based upon the principles of balance and concert on behalf of peace and security.

SUGGESTIONS FOR FURTHER EXPLORATION

On the origins and development of diplomacy and its methods, see Geoff Berridge et al. (eds.), *Diplomatic Theory from Machiavelli to Kissinger* (London, 2001); Raymond Cohen and Raymond Westbrook (eds.), *Amarna Diplomacy: The Beginnings of International Relations* (London, 2000); Linda Frey and Marsha Frey, *The History of Diplomatic Immunity* (Columbus, OH, 1999); Keith Hamilton and Richard Longhorne, *The Practice of Diplomacy* (London, 1995); M. S. Anderson, *The Rise of Modern Diplomacy* (London, 1993); Torbjörn Knutsen, *A History of International Relations Theory* (Manchester, 1992); Garret Mattingly, *Renaissance Diplomacy* (New York, 1988 ed.); D. E. Queller, *The Office of the Ambassador in the Middle Ages* (Princeton, 1967); the highly readable Harold Nicolson, *Diplomacy* (New York, 1964 ed.); the comparative study of Adda Bozeman, *Politics and Culture in International History* (Princeton, 1960); Heinrich Wildner, *Die Technik der Diplomatie* (Vienna, 1959); Harold Nicolson, *The Evolution of Diplomatic Method* (London, 1954); Leon van der Essen, *La Diplomatie* (Brussels, 1953); and the older, but still instructive, D. P. Heatley, *Diplomacy and the Study of International Relations* (Oxford, 1919). The classics, of course, remain Thucydides, *The Peloponesian War,* and Niccolò Machiavelli, *The Prince,* which appear in many editions.

A wide variety of books deal with force and statecraft during the seventeenth century. Among these are Derek Croxton and Anuschka Tischer, *The Peace of Westphalia* (Westport, CT, 2001); Geoffrey Parker and Simon Adams (eds.), *The Thirty Years' War* (London, 1997 ed.); Henry Kissinger, *Diplomacy* (New York, 1994), with his favorable interpretation of Richelieu; Derek McKay and H. M. Scott, *The Rise of the Great Powers, 1648–1815* (London, 1983); Robert Massie, *Peter the Great* (New York, 1980); William Roosen, *The Age of Louis XIV: The Rise of Modern Diplomacy* (Cambridge, MA, 1976); William Church, *Richelieu and Reason of State* (Princeton, 1972); J.-P. Samoyault, *Les Bureaux du secrétariat d'état des affaires étrangères* (Paris, 1971); Cardinal Richelieu, *The Political Testament of Cardinal Richelieu*, Henry Bertram Hill (trans.) (Madison, WI, 1968); and John B. Wolf, *The Emergence of the Great Powers, 1685–1715* (New York, 1951). There is no modern edition of Abram de Wicquefort's *L'ambassadeur et ses fonctions* (Cologne, 1681), but many editions of Thomas Hobbes, *The Leviathan*, and Hugo Grotius, *On the Law of War and Peace*, are available.

Thoughtful discussions of competitive diplomacy and warfare during the eighteenth century can be found in Armstrong Starkey, *War in the Age of the Enlightenment* (New York, 2003); Geoffrey Parker, *The Military Revolution: Military Innovation and the Rise of the West* (Cambridge, 1996 ed.); M. S. Anderson, *Europe in the Eighteenth Century* (London, 1968); F. H. Hinsley, *Power and the Pursuit of Peace* (London, 1967); Friedrich Meinecke, *Die Idee der Staatsräson* (Munich, 1963 ed.), in translation by Douglas Scott as *Machiavelism: The Doctrine of Raison d'État* (New Haven, CT, 1957); Walter Dorn, *Competition for Empire, 1740–1763* (New York, 1940); and Albert Sorel, *L'Europe et la révolution française*, 8 vols. (Paris, 1885–1904), especially Volume 1; and, for a very different point of view, A. H. L. Heeren, *Handbuch der Geschichte des europäischen Statensystems und seiner Kolonien* (Göttingen, 1811 ed.). On Frederick II, see Frederick the Great, *Frederick the Great on the Art of War*, Jay Luvaas (ed. and trans.) (New York, 1999); Christopher Duffy, *Frederick the Great* (New York, 1988 ed.); Frederick the Great, *The Refutation of Machiavelli's Prince, or Anti-Machiavel*, Paul Sonnino (trans.) (Athens, OH, 1981); and Gordon A. Craig, *The Politics of the Prussian Army* (New York, 1955), especially Chapter I, "The Army and the State." The classic by François de Callières, *De la manière de négocier avec les Souverains* can be found in translation as *On the Manner of Negotiating with Princes*, with many editions. One also should explore his interesting but less well-known *De la science du monde, et des connoissances utiles à la conduite de la vie* (Paris, 1717); and Karl W. Schweizer, *François de Callières* (Lewiston, NY, 1996).

For the revolutionary period, see R. R. Palmer, "Frederick the Great, Guibert, Bülow: From Dynastic to National War," in Peter Paret (ed.), *Makers of Modern Strategy* (Princeton, 1986 ed.); Jonathan Dull, *The French Navy and American Independence: A Study of Arms and Diplomacy, 1774–1787* (Princeton, 1976); R. R. Palmer, *Age of the Democratic Revolution* (Princeton, 1969 ed.); and Felix Gilbert, *To the Farewell Address* (Princeton, 1961). On the Napoleonic era, see Paul Johnson, *Napoleon* (New York, 2002); Robert Asprey, *The Reign of Napoleon Bonaparte* (New York, 2001); Antoine d'Arjuzon, *Castlereagh, ou Le défi à l'"Europe de Napoléon* (Paris, 1995); Henry Kissinger, *A World Restored: Metternich, Castlereagh, and the Problems of Peace, 1812–1822* (New York, 1973 ed.); Enno Kraehe, *Metternich's German Policy*, Vol. I, *The Contest with Napoleon, 1799–1814* (Princeton, 1963); Geoffrey Bruun, *Europe and the French Imperium, 1799–1814* (New York, 1938); and C. K. Webster, *The Foreign Policy of Castlereagh, 1812–1815* (London, 1931).

Broad treatments can be found in Barry Buzan and Richard Little, *International Systems in World History* (Oxford, 2000); Andreas Osiander, *The States System of Europe* (Oxford, 1994); Paul Kennedy, *The Rise and Fall of the Great Powers* (New York, 1987); and Hedley Bull, *The Anarchical Society* (London, 1977).

2

The Classical System
of Diplomacy, 1815–1914

The greatest challenge to statesmen during the nineteenth century was the task of devising a system that would contain international violence and prevent major wars like those they had just experienced. Leaders desperately wanted to avoid a repetition of the disasters caused by the unregulated competition of the eighteenth century and by the more recent upheaval of revolution and Napoleonic domination. They determined that only collective action would guarantee their survival and thus began to speak explicitly of the necessity for a "system" and what was "best for the general interest of Europe *as a whole.*" Three generations of statesmen struggled with this problem, and their efforts found expression in three different approaches to the balance of power, each of which reflected the characteristic tendencies of its time. Yet, despite their differences, they all succeeded in producing what historian Hajo Holborn describes as a

> system whose foundations lasted for a full century. For a hundred years
> there occurred no wars of world-wide scope like those of the twenty-odd
> years after 1792. Europe experienced frightful wars, particularly between
> 1854 and 1878, but none of them was a war in which all the European states
> or even all the great European powers participated. The European wars of
> the nineteenth century produced shifts of power, but they were shifts
> within the European political system and did not upset that system as such.

Their efforts created a period of unprecedented peace, hitherto unknown stability, and a system that, despite its imperfections, is still described as the "classical system" of diplomacy.

Building a System with a Balance of
Power and a Concert

One of the most famous paintings ever made of a diplomatic conference is that of the Congress of Vienna by French portraitist Jean-Baptiste Isabey. Near the center of this large canvas, standing with a proprietary air and a look of satisfaction on his handsome face, is the host of the meeting, the Austrian

foreign minister Prince Clemens von Metternich, while around him are grouped the chief representatives of the other powers: Viscount Robert Castlereagh, the British foreign secretary, with his legs crossed; the king of Prussia, Frederick William III, looking gloomily at the phlegmatic Englishman; the czar of Russia, Alexander I, wearing a uniform with epaulettes so big that one wonders how he will be able to lift himself out of the chair; and the representative of France, Prince Charles Maurice Talleyrand-Périgord, with his forearm on the table, badly powdered wig, pendulous lips, and sardonic eyes. In the background, in bestarred and bemedaled clusters, stand the lesser figures of the congress—resident ambassadors, diplomatic secretaries, military aides, and the like—all bearing on their faces that condescending smirk worn by persons who wish to give the impression that they are privy to mysteries they are pledged not to reveal.

It is well to consider the faces of these statesmen, for they were pathbreakers. There had been other congresses and conferences before, but those meetings had been largely for the purpose of ending hostilities and dividing the spoils of war. The statesmen at Vienna had set themselves another and more important task. Metternich made this clear when he said:

> No great political insight is needed to see that this Congress could not be modeled on any which had taken place. Former assemblies which were called congresses met for the express purpose of settling a quarrel between two or more belligerent powers—the issue being a peace treaty. On this occasion, peace had already been made [he was referring to the First Peace of Paris, which had ended hostilities] and the parties meet as friends who, though differing in their interests, wish to work together towards the conclusion and affirmation of the existing treaty.

What did he mean by "conclusion and affirmation"? He believed that their major task was not to merely end past hostilities, but to actually construct a viable international system of peace and security.

This did not mean that the statesmen gathered at Vienna utterly neglected the kinds of things that usually preoccupy political and military leaders at the end of wars. They made sure that they received compensation in accordance with the degree of their sacrifice and their contribution to the victory and that titles and territories were restored to rulers who had been deprived of them. But they did not allow these matters to obtrude upon their more important task of building a system. In this effort (and in sharp contrast with those who followed them at the Paris Peace Conference of 1919), these skilled negotiators wisely refused to allow themselves to succumb to the temptation for revenge against the recently defeated. Wilhelm von Humboldt, the Prussian ambassador to Vienna, who played a leading role in devising the agenda for the congress, had been in Paris when the Silesian army entered the conquered city and became distressed when the soldiers wanted to blow up all the bridges over the Seine simply because they were named for Napoleonic victories. He and his colleagues knew that this kind of vindictiveness might satisfy temporary emotions, but would harm any chance of consensus, and thereby the long-term maintenance of a system. They understood perfectly well that

they would need France to play its appropriate role as a Great Power in the postwar period, and thus refused to exclude her from the negotiations or to cripple her in any serious way that might sow the seeds of future war. They believed that their own interests were best served by recognizing the legitimate interests of others.

Castlereagh and Metternich served as the two principal architects of this new system. They understood in a most impressive way that any international system requires shared goals and objectives; an appropriate structure; normative values and rules of restraint with procedures, mechanisms, and institutions to make them effective in practice; and the capacity to adapt to new circumstances.

In this regard, both were convinced that one of the keys to the new international settlement must be the principle of the balance of power. They recognized the importance of power rather than ignoring or deploring it, and therefore attempted to address one of the most difficult yet most essential tasks of statecraft: how to put power into the service of peace and security. They believed that those capable of using force needed to be willing and able to maintain an equilibrium and resist any unilateral attempts at domination. The negotiators at Vienna consequently went through enormous efforts to adjust territory, resources, and population as equitably as possible and to distribute capabilities among the Great Powers—balancing off Russian gains in Poland and Finland with Austrian holdings in Italy, Prussian acquisitions in the Rhineland and Saxony with British possessions in the Mediterranean, and constructing buffer zones between them in the Low Countries and in the territories that lay between Prussia and Austria. Such a division of German-speaking lands, for example, as one delegate said later, was designed to serve as a kind of shock absorber and hence had to remain disunited in the interests of peace, preserving the "balance through an inherent force of gravity." These system builders believed that by investing these territorial arrangements with the sanction of legitimacy, they would create a structure that would balance their strengths against each other, deter aggression, and thereby afford the best guarantee for peace and security. They knew that no one would be completely satisfied, but, as Henry Kissinger observes, they wisely understood that this actually would assist in maintaining the system as a whole:

> Paradoxically, the generality of this dissatisfaction is a condition of stability, because were any one power *totally* satisfied, all others would have to be *totally* dissatisfied and a revolutionary situation would ensue. The foundation of a stable order is the *relative* security—and therefore the *relative* insecurity—of its members.

The men who had guided this work were not, however, so naive as to believe that they had created a utopia or insured themselves against future trouble by this elaborate exercise in cartography. They had learned the important lesson from the Utrecht experience that a purely mechanical balance of power could not operate automatically on its own. They had seen many arrangements come and go and were well aware that change would occur and that a new

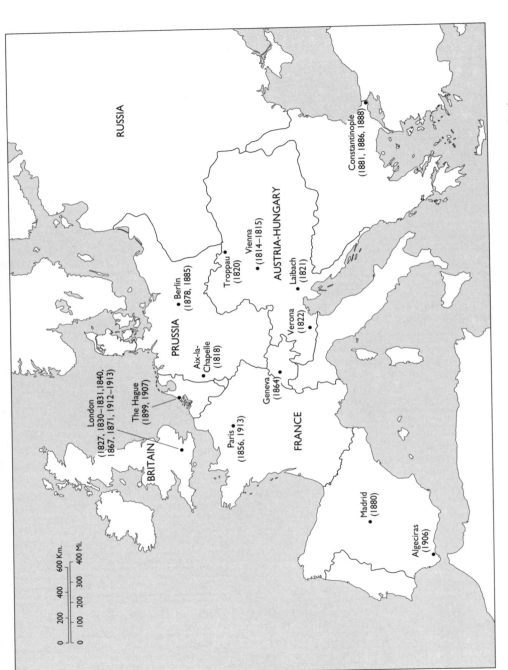

RUSSIA

Constantinople
(1881, 1886, 1888)

Berlin
(1878, 1885)

Troppau
(1820)

Vienna
(1814–1815)

AUSTRIA-HUNGARY

Laibach
(1821)

Verona
(1822)

PRUSSIA

Aix-la-
Chapelle
(1818)

Geneva
(1864)

London
(1827, 1830–1831, 1840,
1867, 1871, 1912–1913)

The Hague
(1899, 1907)

Paris
(1856, 1913)

FRANCE

BRITAIN

Madrid
(1880)

Algeciras
(1906)

0   200   400   600 Km.

0   100   200   300   400 Mi.

A Physical Balance and a Sense of Responsibility: The Classical System's 1815 Settlement and Subsequent Conferences

Frederick or a new Napoleon—or, for that matter, a new revolution—might arise to challenge the status quo. Consequently, they realized the necessity of adding another essential component for peace and security: people with a sense of responsibility to the system as a whole and their determination to maintain and defend it.

To do this, Metternich, Castlereagh, and their colleagues realized that they needed to reach agreement on their common responsibilities to take this new legal order extremely seriously by faithfully observing all treaties and by guaranteeing that no major changes would take place without the general consent of the Great Powers. They consequently decided to build upon their earlier Treaty of Chaumont of 1814, which stressed a commitment to use their forces for collective security, by creating the more permanent Quadruple Alliance of 1815 (soon broadened to include France), stipulating that they would institute an executive body or directorate of their foreign ministers in order that they could hold consultative conferences to address any threats that might emerge "for the purpose of consulting upon their interests, or for the consideration of measures which . . . shall be considered the most salutary for the purpose and prosperity of Nations and the maintenance of the Peace of Europe." In this way, the new system was constructed not only with a kind of constitution but a regulatory mechanism to watch over and protect it. This marked the establishment of what came to be called the Concert of Europe.

Only time and practice, of course, would reveal how this concert would actually work and whether by compromise and consent it could find solutions short of war. The Great Powers would have to decide what was and was not a threat, how their patterns of conflict and cooperation linked them together, or how far they were committed go in taking common action to defend their system. This might not be easy. When Metternich and Czar Alexander became concerned about the threat that liberalism and nationalism posed to the existing thrones of Europe, for example, they tried to turn the Quadruple Alliance into an agency that would automatically intervene in the affairs of any country in which there was a revolution or an agitation against the status quo and suppress by force the revolutionary or democratic movements. The British viewed such attempts as a subversion of the true purpose of the concert, and in a powerful note of 1818, Castlereagh protested that "nothing would be more immoral or more prejudicial to the character of governments generally than the idea that their force was collectively to be prostituted to the support of established power without any consideration of the extent to which it was abused." In a subsequent note of 1820, Castlereagh made it clear that, while Britain could not countenance a policy of joint meddling in the internal affairs of small states, its cooperation could always be counted upon when there was a genuine threat to the peace of Europe and the balance of power. His successors periodically repeated this pledge, as did Lord John Russell in a 1852 House of Commons speech when he declared:

> We are connected . . . with the general system of Europe, and any territorial increase of one Power, any aggrandizement which disturbs the general balance of power in Europe, although it might not immediately lead to war,

could not be a matter of indifference to this country and would, no doubt, be the subject of conference, and might ultimately, if that balance was seriously threatened, lead to war.

These were not only words. The British and the other members of the Concert of Europe were able to work together remarkably well with mutual consultations and collective decisions in every crisis that threatened the peace between 1815 and 1854 by finding solutions that prevented the outbreak of any war between them. This was true in the Belgian crisis of 1830, the Near Eastern crisis of 1838, and the first Schleswig-Holstein crisis of 1850, to mention only some of the more challenging disputes. In all these cases, and in many others, the European concert demonstrated its ability to hold conferences and practice crisis management, as we shall discuss in Chapter 11, and in preserving the balance of power and the system created at the Congress of Vienna when it appeared to be threatened.

There were less dramatic, but nevertheless effective, examples of other forms of cooperation as well. The participants in the Concert of Europe also worked to develop ways of regulating their competition by developing techniques of crisis prevention. That is, in order to help prevent crises and wars from breaking out between them in the first place, they created certain means to coordinate relations, minimize friction, avoid misperceptions and miscalculations, clarify respective interests, establish restraints, and make clear distinctions between legitimate and illegitimate ends and means in the pursuit of policy. Some of these rules of accommodation took the form of binding obligations in explicit treaty form with the force of international law, as when they established the neutrality of Belgium in 1831, in their words, "to prevent events from disturbing the general peace." Others were more implicit in nature, taking the form of tacit understandings, gentlemen's agreements, advanced consultations, or the offering of good offices for mediation, as occurred during the 1826 dispute between Greece and the Ottoman Empire and the 1842 conflict between Britain and France.

This system was not perfect, but there can be little doubt that the balance of power and the Concert of Europe worked particularly well in preventing major wars up to 1854 and in keeping the wars of the 1850s and 1860s within limits and saw to it that they ended with moderate rather than vindictive settlements. It is instructive to ask ourselves why this was so.

One explanation can be found in the fact that statecraft in this period was led by some unusually skilled statesmen and not subject to certain pressures that subsequently caused governments, often reluctantly, to do things that were bound to arouse the suspicion and fear of other powers and to invite violent retaliation. For the most part, and since very few people could vote, leaders of these years did not have to worry about public opinion as they set their course in foreign affairs. There were exceptions to this, of course. Early human rights advocates exerted pressure at the Congress of Vienna to end the international slave trade, and Turkish atrocities against Christians in the Balkans could provoke popular agitation for reprisals. But in general, foreign ministers did not overly concern themselves about what might be in tomorrow's

headlines. Governments were also free from massive pressure from organized economic interests. Industrialization and capitalism had not evolved to the point where business firms were forming lobbies and seeking to influence political decisions, and in this period most businessmen were convinced that the best thing that the government could do for them was to leave them alone. The problem of reconciling desirable foreign policy initiatives with the desiderata of powerful private interests, which in our own time often makes the use of economic sanctions ineffective (as demonstrated in the case of the U.S. grain embargo against the Soviet Union in 1980–1981), did not plague foreign offices.

The maintenance of this system was also enormously enhanced by the limitations upon armed force. In order to avoid the dangerous excesses of the "nation in arms" produced by the French Revolution and used by Napoleon, armies in the first part of the century were deliberately and by mutual agreement scaled back and composed of professionals rather than mass, citizen-conscripted soldiers. There was a virtual absence of any serious arms race, and no military pressure groups issued demands that complicated the policy-making process or disturbed international relations. The technological limits were even more striking. Simple, smooth-bore muskets firing solid lead balls represented the most sophisticated weapons on the battlefield.

This is precisely the context in which one of the most insightful books of the nineteenth century appeared in 1832: Carl von Clausewitz's famous *On War*. Based upon his study of history and his own hard-won experiences in combat, he wrote not only about the essential character of warfare, but about armed force as an instrument of statecraft. In this regard, his most-quoted sentence in the entire book is as simple as it is profound: "war is . . . a continuation of political activity by other means." War, he argued, must never become an end in itself, and priority must always be given to political over military purposes. "The political object is the goal," he wrote, "war is the means of reaching it, and means can never be in isolation from their purpose." When this principle was ignored (as during the First World War when the insubordination of the German military chiefs destroyed the ability of civilian leaders to maintain rational control over the course of operations), the results could be disastrous, but when it was followed, as it was throughout so much of this period, limited ends and limited means significantly reinforced each other and thereby contributed toward maintaining the system as a whole. Clausewitz clearly saw that this would produce a natural resistance in the international community to any aggression, and thus observed:

> If we consider the community of states in Europe today, we . . . find major and minor interests of states and peoples interwoven in the most varied and changeable manner. Each point of intersection binds and serves to balance one set of interests against the other. The broad effect of all these fixed points is obviously to give a certain amount of cohesion to the whole. Any change will necessarily weaken this cohesion to some degree. The sum total of relations between states thus serves to maintain the stability of the whole. . . .

Yet another reason why this system worked so well was the fact that whatever ideological differences existed, they were not sufficient to lead to war. There were moments, to be sure, when serious divisions surfaced. After the revolution of 1830, Europe seemed to be divided between liberal Britain and France and conservative Russia, Prussia, and Austria. The British foreign secretary, Lord Palmerston, acknowledged this fact when he said, "The three and the two think differently and therefore they act differently." But if one examines the record of the years 1830–1854 carefully, it is clear that the powers ignored their ideological differences more than they observed them. The British had no compunction about concluding agreements with the Eastern powers in moments in which they felt the French were threatening their interests; while on the French side, Louis Philippe sought an accommodation with the Eastern powers even at the expense of his entente with Britain. When Metternich became worried about the czar's policy in the Near East, he consulted the British about ways of restraining him; when the czar became annoyed with his Prussian ally's Baltic ambitions, he collaborated with the British to frustrate them.

Finally, whatever differences existed between the powers were largely subordinated to the high degree of consensus and shared values among them. The leaders of virtually all of the Great Powers accepted the balance of power created at Vienna, but they understood that whereas such a balance might inhibit the ability to overthrow the international system, agreement on shared values with their self-imposed restraints inhibits the actual desire to do so. They accepted the legitimacy of the system and were able to establish a high degree of restraint on the part of single powers (Czar Nicholas probably could have exacted a higher price for his aid to the Turks in 1833 but refused to do so because he feared such unilateral action might lead to emulation), a willingness to accept the validity of existing treaties (in no age in modern times was there greater respect paid to the principle *pacta sunt sevanda*), and when single powers seemed on the point of seeking aggrandizement (as was true of France in 1840), a willingness to participate in concerted action to restrain them. This consensus was the essential strength of the international system of the years 1815–1854, represented by Figure 2-2.

The inner squares represent the entente between Britain and France, on the one hand, and the combination of the northern courts, on the other; the arrows

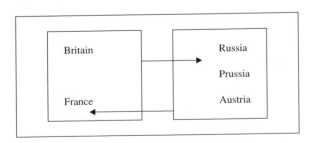

Figure 2-2

signify the interpenetration and collaboration that went on throughout the period; and the outer rectangle represents the consensus that held them all together in an effective concert that preserved the Vienna settlement in its major outlines and maintained an equilibrium of forces in Europe.

CHANGE AND AN EXPERIMENT WITH A DEFENSIVE ALLIANCE SYSTEM

Continuities and changes always co-exist, for the world never stands completely still. Over time, new forces, personalities, ideas, discoveries, and technological developments sooner or later challenge existing arrangements and bring about transformations. In this regard the nineteenth century certainly was no exception, especially with the emergence of the Industrial Revolution and the force of nationalism. After the revolutions of 1848, a new spirit began to emerge in Europe, one that found its strongest expression in the policies of a new generation of young men in a hurry infused with nationalism for their own countries and no longer willing to fully abide by the collaborative principles and practices invented and followed by the statesmen of Vienna. These newcomers included Felix zu Schwarzenberg in Austria, Camillo di Cavour in Piedmont, Otto von Bismarck in Prussia, and Louis Napoleon in France. The vent that opened the way to the fulfillment of the ambitions of these *Realpolitiker* (a term invented in the 1850s by the political activist and writer Ludwig von Rochow to describe those who defined statecraft solely in terms of the calculation and exercise of raw power) was the outbreak of war between Russia and Britain (supported by France and Piedmont) in 1854. The two powers whose collaboration had prevented the revolutions of 1848 from escalating into a major international conflict now slipped into the Crimean War—a senseless struggle that resulted not from any deliberate threat to either power, but rather from imaginary dangers.

By the time the war was over, more soldiers had lost their lives from disease than in military combat and neither side had secured any appreciable gains. This explains in part why the negotiators at the Conference of Paris in 1856 made great strides in addressing certain norms limiting the operation of armed force by formulating rules for naval warfare, protecting the rights of noncombatants, and guaranteeing the rights of neutrals in times of war. But the war and the distrust that it caused also left a situation in which Russia, France, Prussia, and the rising power of Piedmont all wanted some territorial revisions of the balance of power. Britain, wearied by its exertions in the Crimea, emerged in a pronouncedly isolationist mood. After this, the Concert could not always completely manage crises or exert effective restraints, as evidenced by four wars of unification: the Austro-Italian war of 1859, the war between Denmark and the German states in 1864, the Austro-Prussian War of 1866, and the Franco-Prussian War of 1870. These were all limited wars of short duration and not one escalated into a European or system-wide conflict. Nevertheless, they caused the balance of power to be modified by the inclusion of the two new states of Italy and Germany.

Successful statecraft requires the capacity to adjust to changing circumstances. But with these changes after mid-century, the tasks became increasingly more difficult than those that had confronted the statesmen of Vienna. The Industrial Revolution, for example, began to reveal inventions and weapons that would eventually transform battlefields and the costs of war. Psychologically, there was no longer the experience of a commonly shared invasion by an obvious aggressor like Napoleon to remind them of the necessity of working together, and the lessons of history learned by one generation are not always accepted by another. Moreover, there was little relaxation of tension after 1871, as there had been after 1815. The resentments and frustrations left by the wars of unification encouraged a combativeness that was fed by the widespread currency of Darwinism and by the sensationalism of a newspaper press that pandered to a gullible and excitable public and introduced the expression "jingoism." The emotional dimensions of French *revanchisme*, Pan-Slavism, Pan-Germanism, irredentism, and hypersensitive nationalism made this situation even worse. The French, unwilling to forget the annexation of Alsace and Lorraine by Germany, the Austrians, seeking to expand into the Balkans and arousing Russia's anger and distrust, and the Italians, dissatisfied with the extent of their new state and burning to despoil the Austrians of any remaining areas inhabited by Italian minorities, all posed problems for the maintenance of a new balance of power.

The opportunities for friction between the powers also increased due to structural readjustments and political and economic developments. Italian and German unification, for example, managed to significantly reduce the number of buffer zones or shock absorbers created by those assembled earlier at Vienna. The Great Powers now possessed more common borders, and these made them rub up against each other uncomfortably. At the same time, the age of free trade was coming to an end and the age of neomercantilism and imperialism was dawning, so that tariff wars and colonial competition between powers would soon be more likely. Governments interested in following sensible collaborative foreign policies were no longer as free of domestic pressures as Metternich had been. Public opinion still exercised only a sporadic influence on policy determination, but groups with similar economic interests were becoming more organized and beginning to develop techniques for persuading governments to alter policies in their interest. Pressure groups from industry and agriculture, for example, increasingly began to push for tariffs, for colonies, and then for expanded armaments.

All this was a source of concern to the diplomats of Europe, especially to the leading statesman of the period, Otto von Bismarck. His country, Germany, had been the principal beneficiary of the new balance of power that he had done so much to forge, and he was determined to keep the gains secure. Toward this end, he regarded Germany as a sated power and wanted nothing but peace and stability. As he wrote to his ambassador in St. Petersburg, "we do not pursue power-politics, but safety-politics." But history shows few examples of sudden conversions, like the apostle Paul on the road to Damascus, whereby leaders who gained their reputations by launching wars

suddenly became men of peace. Consequently, although Bismarck's objectives had genuinely changed, the other powers did not always trust him, and his subsequent diplomacy continually suffered from the "blood and iron" and *Realpolitik* reputation that he had developed earlier. He quickly learned that it is often much easier to upset a diplomatic system than to maintain it. During the tense crisis of 1875 and the possibility of an Austro-Russian conflict in the Balkans, which would almost certainly involve Germany, it became apparent to Bismarck that wishing for peace was not enough and that he would have to take a more active role. This explains why he worked so hard, as we shall see in Chapter 11, to serve as a crisis manager and act as an "honest broker" in 1878, inviting the contentious powers to the Congress of Berlin and successfully averting a war in the Near East. But at the end of the crisis the Russian government took the line that the settlement was a betrayal of past friendship and began to talk of an alliance with France. It was thus clear to Bismarck that times and conditions had changed and that the traditional friendship among Prussia, Austria, and Russia, forged in the war against Napoleon, could no longer be relied upon. If the existing balance of power, and Germany's place in it, was to be preserved, it would have to be by some new means.

Bismarck reluctantly concluded that the only way of escaping his dilemma would be to maintain a strong army for deterrence and to create defensive alliances that would, at a minimum, relieve Germany of potential isolation and might, if things went well, give him some measure of control over the policies of enough of the other powers to prevent them from embarking upon actions that would threaten the general peace. Later on, he was to define his policy by saying that one must not lose sight of "the importance of being one of three on the European chess-board. That is the invariable objective of all cabinets and of mine above all others. Nobody wishes to be in a minority. All politics reduce themselves to this formula: to try to be one of three as long as the world is governed by an unstable equilibrium of five Great Powers."

This was probably a rationalization after the fact. After the Congress of Berlin, when Germany was in a state of near isolation, Bismarck had more limited objectives. He decided that Germany needed one reliable ally, and he reached out to Austria-Hungary, concluding a treaty that stipulated mutual defense in the event of an attack by Russia and benevolent neutrality if either ally were attacked by a power other than Russia. But this Dual Alliance of 1879 rather unexpectedly brought him the kind of control that was to secure the European balance for the next twelve years. For although the details of the treaty with Austria were secret, the conclusion was not, and it startled the Russians into changing their tune and asking for a renewal of the Three Emperors' League, which Bismarck arranged between Germany, Austria, and Russia in 1881. That success, in turn, brought the Italians to Berlin, asking for protection against French attacks on their interests in North Africa—to which Bismarck agreed on condition that the Italians also make a treaty of accommodation with his partner Austria. This resulted in the Triple Alliance of 1882. Bismarck hoped that all this would greatly reduce the chance of a Russian attack on Germany, block the possibility of a Franco-Russian

alliance, and minimize the possibility of a war between Austria and Russia in the Balkans or a conflict between Austria and Italy. His support of British interests in Egypt completed the isolation of France.

Bismarck's elaborate defensive alliance system thus was dramatically different from the eighteenth-century treaties of aggrandizement as well as from the earlier arrangements of the Vienna system. It tied most—but not all—of the powers in one way or another to Berlin. The Austrians, for instance, were assured of German support in the event that their Balkan interests were subjected to Russian attack, but they were at the same time held on a very short leash by Bismarck's warning that he would not support them if they took the initiative in causing any Austro-Russian war. There were no opposing alliance systems of countervailing power, but Britain was not formally tied by treaty and France remained isolated.

The Bismarckian way of maintaining this equilibrium of forces was a complicated one, and that was its chief weakness. It operated on the basis of insecurity and by means of secrecy, a high degree of disingenuousness, and constant maneuver. Indeed, the German Emperor William I looked at this alliance system and said to Bismarck, "I would not be in your shoes. You seem to me at times to be like a rider who juggles on horseback with five balls, never letting one fall." This became apparent during the tense Bulgarian crisis of 1886–1887, when a renewal of Austro-Russian antagonism in the Balkans dissolved the Three Emperors' League and a simultaneous wave of *revanchisme* in France made a Franco-Russian alliance seem possible. Bismarck was able to contain these dangers and repair his system only by the most questionable means: a deliberately manufactured war-scare designed to intimidate the French and professed support of Russian objectives in the Balkans that was belied by covert connivance with third powers and stock market manipulations that rendered his promises meaningless. Bismarck's performance in this affair has often been described as a tour de force, but the course that he followed was so subterranean and devious that it is difficult to avoid the suspicion that he was beginning to prefer tactical virtuosity to plain dealing. Certainly his methods in the Bulgarian affair saved his alliance system only in a formal sense, while increasing the feeling of the Russians in particular that they had been lied to. As a result, the days of the Bismarckian model of balance of power were numbered. Even if the chancellor had remained in office after 1890, it is difficult to believe that his arrangements could have withstood the strain of his manipulations much longer.

Despite these problems, the fact remains that there were many times in which the Great Powers demonstrated their capacity to act together in concert with flexibility and moderation to reach mutual accommodation in order to maintain the system as a whole. The successes of their numerous diplomatic conferences revealed their sense of responsibility to participate in collective decisions and actions, respect legal treaties, and generally observe restraint in their international actions. They agreed to establish neutral, demilitarized zones in an attempt to prevent crises from occurring between them in the first place, as they did in their 1863 treaty on the Ionian Islands of Greece, pledging to each other that "no armed force, either naval or military, shall

at any time be assembled or stationed upon the territory or in the waters of those islands." The next year they broke dramatic new ground by signing the famous Geneva Convention, the first multilateral treaty in history designed to lay the foundations of humanitarian law and the creation of the International Committee of the Red Cross by protecting the rights of individuals wounded in times of war irrespective of their nationality. The diplomats also successfully worked to localize or contain certain regional and non-European conflicts in order to prevent larger confrontations among themselves, fearing that a minor or peripheral dispute might easily escalate out of control. When an insurrection broke out in Bosnia and Herzegovina in 1875, for example, their negotiations resulted in a collective accord stating:

> The Powers have come to an agreement to make use of all the influence at their disposal in order to localize the conflict, and diminish its dangers and calamities by preventing Serbia and Montenegro from participating in the movement. Their language has been the more effectual from being identic, and has, consequently, testified the firm determination of Europe not to permit the general peace to be imperilled by rash impulses.

They practiced crisis-management techniques sufficient to avert general war, as they demonstrated at the Congress of Berlin in 1878 when defusing danger in the Balkans. Moreover, the diplomats of this period also understood the importance of crisis prevention and worked to draw demarcation lines of interest, set limits, and establish restraints and ground rules for governing their interactions in order to avoid serious misunderstandings and disputes. This was the motivation for the well-known 1884–1885 Conference of Berlin, which, in the words of one authority, "had not been called as the result of a crisis, but rather in an attempt to forestall the possibility of one arising." Such achievements at a time of considerable tension and competition are indicative of what could be done by diplomacy within this classical system.

FURTHER CHANGE AND AN EXPERIMENT WITH BIPOLAR ALIGNMENT

Given the nature of change and the need to adapt to changing circumstances, it is not surprising that with time, other experiments would be tried as well. Thus, the third form assumed by balance of power came in the years from 1907 to 1914, when all of the major European powers (including Britain, which abandoned its "splendid isolation" and its role as "the balance wheel of Europe" upon which it long had prided itself) arranged themselves into a bipolar alignment. It was this particular manifestation of the politics of equilibrium that fastened itself upon the imagination of later generations and, because of its catastrophic end, made balance of power an opprobrious term in the postwar period, particularly in the United States.

It is possible—and not entirely unjustified—to place blame for the emergence of this other experiment, with all of its deplorable consequences, on the nature of German policy after 1890. It was precipitated by the abrupt dismissal of Bismarck from his post and the German government's decision

to eliminate one of the key elements of his alliance system by dismantling the connection with Russia, which they regarded as incompatible with obligations assumed toward Austria in the Dual Alliance of 1879. Whatever the weaknesses of the Bismarckian arrangement, the fact remains that it did not divide Europe into two confrontational camps. Instead, it brought most states into a defensive and interlocking network in which no single power, including Germany, could be assured of support in any unilateral aggressive action. Because the system would come into operation against any effort to upset the system as a whole, as historian Norman Rich observes, it was defensive by nature and thus served as a deterrent to chauvinistic agitators in every country. This critical feature began to change once the German-Russian alliance was severed, for it encouraged the Russians to look elsewhere for friends and left Europe in a much more unstable and fragile condition.

Perhaps things would have evolved differently with more able and restrained leaders, but German foreign policy was now directed by the often impulsive and bombastic Emperor William II, his vain chancellor Bernhard von Bülow, and his assertive chief of the imperial naval office Admiral Alfred von Tirpitz, who together launched a new offensive policy they described as a "new course" of *Weltpolitik* designed to make Germany a global power. They were no longer interested in mere defense, but wanted more. Toward this end, German leaders aggressively sought to acquire imperial possessions and to build a new navy. This immediately brought them into conflict with the spheres of influence of other powers in Africa, the Pacific, and the Middle East in such a way as to seriously annoy the other Great Powers. The Russians, for example, were deeply worried to find the Germans trying to move into the Persian Gulf, and they began to reconsider their options. The British and the French, who were at loggerheads in Africa after 1882 and came uncomfortably close to a war in the Sudan in 1898, discovered that Germany was becoming a potential threat to both of them and began to mend their fences. At the same time, an alliance of domestic conservative political parties and groups that derived their financial support from heavy industry and big agriculture steadily began to push the German government into launching an ambitious naval armaments program in 1898 and 1900 to challenge others on the seas and imposing tariff barriers on trade. This could not help but alienate the other powers, especially the British, French, and Russians, and in the end drive them toward each other. As one insightful British Foreign Office analyst concluded in a famous memorandum: "The union of the greatest military with the greatest naval power in one state would compel the world to combine for the riddance of such an incubus."

It would be a mistake, however, to think of this fateful course as having been caused solely by German clumsiness and impercipience. Even if William II, Bülow, and Tirpitz had been wiser, more responsible, and less provocative, it is difficult to believe that the apprehensiveness of others would have been any different. As historian Paul Kennedy observes, it was the transformation of Germany from a cluster of second-rate states under insignificant princelings to a united empire with a significant population,

impressive industrial resources, and advanced technology that provided the root cause of concern. By the end of the nineteenth century, Germany was not only growing out of its European "skin" but also acquiring the early attributes of a world power. To the British in particular, this change brought about new anxieties and tensions and made it easy for them to slip into the habit of regarding Germany not just as a competitor but as a future foe. Lord Esher was not alone in thinking "there is no doubt that within measurable distance there looms a titanic struggle between Germany and Europe for mastery. The years 1793–1815 will be repeated, only Germany, not France, will be trying for European domination." Such fears increasingly led the British to conclude in the first years of the new century that they could no longer maintain their security by their own resources but must seek to contain the German threat by entering into partnership with Germany's other antagonists.

The resulting experiment in yet another balance of power did not suddenly occur overnight, but took seventeen years to unfold after the first precipitous events of 1890. Diplomats in Paris and St. Petersburg spent the time from 1891 to 1894 transforming an exchange of notes and a military convention into an alliance between republican France and czarist Russia. After considerable negotiation, Britain and France agreed to settle their major differences and signed the Entente Cordiale in 1904, and this was then followed by the Anglo-Russian Agreement of 1907. Together, these various arrangements divided the powers into two groups: the Triple Alliance (Germany, Austria, and Italy) and the Triple Entente (Britain, France, and Russia). This was not as rigid as it might first appear, however, for it is important to remember that when they were signed, both the British-French entente and the Anglo-Russian agreement were bilateral rather than multilateral accords that focused largely on resolving colonial differences rather than establishing military partnerships, and both deliberately avoided using the word "alliance." Similarly, it was clear at even an early stage that regardless of their treaty commitments, Italy would not be a reliable ally to the Germans or Austrians and thus could not be counted in their camp in any meaningful way.

This new iteration of equilibrium possessed both similarities and differences with the other experiments of the nineteenth century. They all involved attempts to balance the power and the interests of the Great Powers of Europe. This latest effort, like the Bismarckian arrangement but unlike the Vienna settlement, relied less and less upon general agreement and more upon formal secret agreements among the selected parties themselves. In addition, this new variant represented a bipolar alignment (like the Cold War that would follow in the next century), and this made it much more unstable and inflexible than the two previous experiments, causing it to last for a much shorter period of time. There was little interpenetration here as there had been after Vienna, and there was no control by a strong alliance leader as there had been at the time of Bismarck. Thus, as this particular experiment began to operate in the years from 1907 to 1914, the predominant characteristics for both parts of the bipolar alignment were constantly accelerating armament programs, war plans and arrangements made by military staffs on their own (sometimes

without any regard for political implications), mutual suspicions, and a growing fear of losing allies to the opposite camp and thus being encircled and destroyed.

Nevertheless, even in the midst of this intense bipolar competition, the Great Powers demonstrated that it was still possible on occasion to manage the relations between themselves through diplomacy. During the Hague Conferences of 1899 and 1907, delegates made pioneering efforts to establish not only the principle of international arbitration but also the practical rules of procedure and a formal institution to settle conflicts, and did so by accepting the restraints of the Convention for the Pacific Settlement of International Disputes and creating the Permanent Court of Arbitration. By means of the Algeciras Conference of 1906, they managed to keep the highly combustible first Moroccan crisis from exploding into war. Similarly, in 1907 and 1908 the powers demonstrated mutual restraint by working to further demilitarize the strategically important Åland Islands astride both the Baltic Sea and the Gulf of Bothnia, recognizing that the possession by any one nation would be regarded as a grave threat by all others. They successfully prohibited weapons and armed force from the islands, as they said at the time, in order "to remove distrust and avoid conflict by means of international agreement rather than have recourse to the sword." The negotiators further pledged that if events threatened international stability in the area, they would "communicate with each other for concerting among themselves" upon ways to take common measures to protect peace and security.

But, as the end approached, it became increasingly difficult to reach these kinds of accommodations and agreements. Recurring crises in the Balkans, Morocco, and other parts of the decaying Ottoman Empire began to take their toll, as governments began to worry how long they could continue to go to the brink and whether or not they might lose allies in the process. It seemed increasingly important to possess allies—and much more dangerous to lose them. Governments seemed to suffer from recurrent nightmares in which they saw themselves abandoned by their friends and encircled by a host of enemies. As a consequence, they sought to strengthen the loyalty of their allies and to avoid even the suggestion of defection. The German government, for example, came to fear isolation and thereby place an excess valuation upon the Austrian alliance. In doing so, they abandoned Bismarck's wise limitation upon his commitment to Austria, namely, that Germany would support it against Russia only if it were attacked by the latter power and not if it took the initiative itself. During one of the Bosnian crises, the German chief of general staff specifically told his opposite number in Vienna that he could rely upon German support, regardless of the origins of the conflict, an assurance that was patently dangerous but seemed necessary in the circumstances. The British and the French began to have similar apprehensions about losing the Russians, and they consequently tended to give them a dangerous degree of freedom and action, instead of warning them that, if they were foolhardy, they would have to stand alone. This not only reduced flexibility and the ability to respond to changed circumstances, but placed the stronger members of the

respective alignments at the mercy of their junior partners. The danger, of course, was that all of the participants of the Triple Entente and Triple Alliance might easily be pulled into a conflict precipitated by their most irresponsible members. Under these circumstances it was difficult to know how much longer the system could last.

CHARACTERISTICS OF THE SYSTEM

Statesmen of the nineteenth century, as we have seen, worked to construct and then maintain a viable diplomatic system for peace and security. Their success left a remarkable record: not one war occurred between the Great Powers for forty years and, after the Crimean War, no general war for another sixty years. To accomplish this, they needed not only to confront their fear of repeating the nearly disastrous mistakes of the past, but to respond to the changes that occurred during their own times. They consequently experimented with three difference experiments or approaches. Although each of these had their differences, they all occurred within the system and shared certain features to a greater or lesser extent that reveal much about the nature of diplomacy and the classical system as a whole.

One of the essential characteristics of this system was its *composition, numbers, and types of actors*. The major participants were the Great Powers of Europe, or what Castlereagh called "the powers of the first order." These included Britain, France, Prussia (then Germany), Austria, Russia, and, to a lesser extent after its unification, Italy. Their relative strength gave them power over much of the rest of the world, and they thus made and enforced the rules of behavior for everyone else. The only other states that showed any serious or sustained interest in international relations at the time also tended to be European. Two others, the United States and Japan, still stood in the wings, waiting but not yet called upon to play their parts. Indeed, when one foreign ministry official once suggested seeking more cordial relations with the United States, Bismarck dismissed the notion with contempt because, as he explained it, Americans "don't matter at all." Such a system, composed only of a very small number of actors that were all nation-states from a single continent, greatly simplified the tasks of statecraft.

The *structure* of this system took the form of a balance among these Great Powers. They believed that a countervailing balance of power, however arranged at any given point of time, was essential for deterring any one state from seeking hegemony against the others. This required that they—as the ones capable of using armed force and thereby doing the most damage to each other and to all other lesser states—each play a role and cooperate as necessary to preserve the balance. Even if one of them was defeated in a war, for example, they needed to be readmitted as a regular member to participate once more in the balancing process. Such structural readjustments worked best when the powers maintained flexibility in making alliances and shifting partners as changing circumstances required, but were at their worst when they tried to isolate one of the members or began to lose their ability to adjust, as

they did in the dangerous years from 1907 to 1914. They also understood that this structure would contribute to the maintenance of the system only if the major actors remained of roughly comparable power *vis-á-vis* one another. Toward this end, they tried to avoid cases of unilateral aggrandizement by a number of means, not the least of which was the application of the principle of compensation: when one of the Great Powers acquired—or wished to acquire—additional territory, population, or resources, it was understood that the other powers had to receive appropriate payoffs in kind, usually at the expense of weaker states in Europe or imperial possessions overseas.

In addition, this structure was designed to support a decentralized, self-regulating system of sovereign nation-states. Power and responsibility remained solely in the hands of the constituent state actors. This obviously marked a significant difference from the structure of other systems, such as Manchu China during roughly the same period, in proposals for world government that have emerged from time to time, or broad-based international organizations. There was, in other words, no single hegemonic power or supranational political authority at the apex of the system to regulate their quarrels, to ensure that international politics did not become anarchic, or to enforce the rules. All these requirements are important for the maintenance of any system, but in this case they were to be achieved by the Great Powers coordinating and regulating their own behavior.

The classical system of diplomacy also possessed the characteristic of *shared goals and objectives*. Statesmen realistically understood that no system can possibly survive unless there is an essential consensus upon fundamental assumptions and aims by all the major participants, especially among those necessary to maintain the system. As mentioned previously, a balance of power inhibits the *capacity* to overthrow a diplomatic system, but agreement on shared values inhibits the *desire* to do so. There could be no major actor so dissatisfied that it questioned the legitimacy of the entire international order and therefore sought to overthrow the system as a whole. The Great Powers agreed upon a common purpose: to insure their own survival by creating a collective security arrangement that would maintain peace and stability. This could not be achieved unless they reached a consensus on basic principles, accepting each others' existence, defining their own interests in terms of the larger good, and agreeing upon their shared responsibility to defend what they created. They therefore had to strike a difficult balance between the desire to pursue purely selfish objectives in rivalry, on the one hand, and the need to maintain the system in partnership, on the other. For this reason, the Great Powers did not perceive each other as implacable enemies engaged in a struggle for elimination, or a "zero-sum" contest in which any gain for one side happened only at the expense of the other. Rather, they viewed each other as limited adversaries in their competition, while at the same time partners within the system. Armed force could be a permissible and legitimate instrument of policy as long as it was employed for limited ends. Any war that seriously threatened the existence of another member, however, and thus jeopardize the entire system had to be prevented.

The statesmen of the period also clearly realized that they needed to develop certain *norms, methods, and rules of accommodation* in order to establish restraints and provide some regulation of their rivalries, to direct change in desired ways, and thereby maintain their system. They were not so naive as to think that the balancing and equilibrium necessary for their system would automatically occur, that they had created a fixed utopia, or that they had protected themselves against future crises simply by redrawing the map or by joining hands at a diplomatic conference. Instead, they recognized that conflict and competition among themselves could not easily be prohibited or eliminated in the real world of international politics. They believed, however, that such competitive behavior need not be totally arbitrary, haphazard, or unrestrained. To deal with this, they reached consensus on a wide variety of normative values, methods, and rules to regulate their competition and keep it within mutually acceptable boundaries, many of which were clearly articulated in the widely used handbook of Carl von Martens entitled *Guide diplomatique*. This required that democracies and absolute monarchies alike accept certain self-imposed restraints and that they honor their commitments and be willing to take collective action to enforce the rules if necessary. Part of this stemmed from pragmatic self-interest with the calculated knowledge that, as they said, "no Power can free itself from treaties without at the same time freeing others." Yet another part was based upon a larger sense of responsibility to the system as a whole. "The Great Powers," observed one leading statesman, "feel they have not only a common interest, but a common duty to attend to." With such attitudes and through such means, they thus hoped that any changes or adjustments that occurred would be *within* the system rather than *of* the system.

The results of their efforts demonstrated an imaginative array of mutual restraints tailored to fit specific problems and took many forms. One of these was the creation of procedures that enabled the Concert of Europe to function in such a way as to promote cooperation and coordination of their foreign policies. They opposed unilateral action and attempted to secure the consent of all for major territorial changes. Methods of crisis management were developed and used, even as late as the time of William II. They developed sophisticated practices and ground rules for crisis prevention, including multilateral consultation and decision making, the creation of buffer states and demilitarized zones, localizing and restricting regional conflicts, delineating areas of special interest, and the pacific settlement of disputes. Moreover, they agreed on the value of the principles of *raison d'état* and national sovereignty, that diplomacy should be a "commerce in mutual benefits," that ideology should not be a determining factor in their foreign policies, that negotiations should be conducted with discretion and in private, that public opinion and pressure groups should play as little a role as possible in their deliberations, and that their attention should be focused not on economic affairs but rather on what they called "high politics," or political and military affairs that involved issues of war and peace.

In this regard, and with specific reference to force and statecraft, those responsible for maintaining this system agreed *that wars, if fought with limited means*

for limited political objectives, could be regarded as legitimate instruments of policy. They did not try to completely eliminate wars or threats of force. Instead, they made a distinction between those that were permissible and those that were not, sometimes drawing upon just war theory. Thus, wars or threats of military action, even with the weapons increasingly made possible by the Industrial Revolution, were permitted as long as they did not threaten the system as a whole or the vital interests of other major powers. In fact, the use of force was regarded as not only legitimate, but even necessary if one state attempted to achieve domination, for this would destroy the balance-of-power itself. With the passage of time and with the bipolar version of the system at the turn of the century, however, the distinction between permissible and impermissible war became increasingly difficult to determine.

Among these various norms, methods, and rules of the classical system of diplomacy was also the agreement to rely heavily upon *professional diplomats.* No system, however cleverly designed, can possibly operate itself. It is completely dependent upon people to make it work. In this regard, statesmen of the time appreciated the wisdom in the advice of de Callières that, given the enormously high stakes of international politics, only the most highly qualified individuals should be employed to conduct the demanding tasks of statecraft. Consequently, they were carefully trained and selected professionals who regarded themselves as members of a like-minded elite and culturally homogeneous corps known specifically as the European *famille diplomatique,* or diplomatic family. These cosmopolitan diplomats moved with ease within the larger system, and many in fact were employed by countries other than their own. They shared common ties of culture and historical tradition, geography, language, religion, class and social status, race, and gender. This made it much easier for them to achieve such a remarkable level of consensus on the nature and purposes of what they called "the art of diplomacy," ethical values, the need to establish certain normative rules and procedures, and a sense of responsibility to make and to enforce collective decisions necessary to protect their system as a whole. Looking back on this system, political scientist Charles Burton Marshall writes that these professionals

> drew on a generally common fund of history. The frame of discourse among them was unified to a degree permitting any government participating significantly in world affairs to be confident of having its utterances understood by others in the sense intended. None was a revolutionary power. Ideologies were 'a minor theme.' . . . The basis of the general order was not at issue. A common notion of legitimacy prevailed.

Finally, these diplomats, like those of any international system, found themselves heavily influenced by *the state of technology.* In terms of transportation and communication, they began the nineteenth century with the same condition as all of their predecessors in human history: no ambassador, no diplomatic instructions, no replies from foreign missions, no military orders, no idea could travel faster than the speed of a horse. The pace was slow, and time, distance, and geography were significant facts of life. In a memorandum

to his secretary of state, President Thomas Jefferson once observed: "We have heard nothing from our ambassador in Spain for two years. If we do not hear from him this year, let us write him a letter." Even in the best of circumstances, it took days for a hand-carried diplomatic dispatch to go from Paris to Vienna, weeks to go from Rome to St. Petersburg, and months to go from Berlin to Tokyo. Despite the obvious limitations, this possessed one great advantage: time to think and time to reflect. By the end of the century, the age of steam had produced railroads on land and steamships on the seas, and electricity had made possible the use of telegraphic communication. This eventually generated what would become a rising tide of information and the growing pressure for critical decisions to be made rapidly, the dangers of which were demonstrated all too well when leaders found themselves suddenly overwhelmed, as we shall see in Chapter 11, during the crisis of 1914 and when Austria first declared war on Serbia—by telegram. But this would not happen until the very end, and statesmen throughout the century enjoyed small foreign ministries with simple organizations and a relaxed atmosphere characterized by the tradition known as *le thé de cinq heures* when officials gathered for tea to socialize. Participants fondly recalled limited working hours and "comparatively idle days," porters meeting horse-drawn carriages, dispatches written by hand, and time to read and reflect. "There were few bathrooms and ice was rare," wrote one diplomat looking back on his own experiences and capturing the mood of the period, "but calm abounded . . . ; there were no telephones, no cars, no deaths on the road or in the air. There were less nerves, less noise; perhaps afer all the world would give that peace which the prayer-book said it couldn't."

Weapons technology always plays a critical role in force and statecraft as well, and the nineteenth century certainly was no exception. The period witnessed the emergence of the Industrial Revolution and with it the change from smooth-bore muskets firing solid balls to rifles projecting expanding bullets, from simple canon to long-range artillery, from soldiers marching on their feet to being transported to battlefields by railroads, and from wooden-hulled sailing ships like the *H.M.S. Victory* to heavily-armored and turbine-driven battleships like the *H.M.S. Dreadnought*. Each of these transformations proved significant, but none produced anything that even came close to a weapon of mass destruction. Indeed, even if the volume and the range of fire increased, most shots still missed. This meant that the limited state of weapons technology reinforced the limited political objectives of warfare and that the cost of diplomatic failure was not catastrophic ruin.

Yet, by the turn of the century, many of these limits and the basic simplicity and homogeneity of the system found themselves being subjected to growing stresses and strains. The Spanish-American War of 1898 and the Russo-Japanese War of 1904–1905 revealed that other actors were anxiously waiting in the wings to play a role in international affairs. The Great Powers of Europe still possessed a rough equilibrium or balance of power, but they increasingly lost sight of their common values and the necessity of self-restraint, as became painfully evident in the summer of 1914, when leaders abandoned

their sense of responsibility to the system and turned instead to war of a very different and devastating nature.

Suggestions for Further Exploration

The classical system of diplomacy long has fascinated students of international relations. See F. R. Bridge and Roger Bullen, *The Great Powers and the European States System, 1815–1914* (New York, 2005 ed.); Ralph Menning, *The Art of the Possible: Documents on Great Power Diplomacy* (New York, 1996); Henry Kissinger, *Diplomacy* (New York, 1994); Norman Rich, *Great Power Diplomacy, 1815–1914* (New York, 1992); Paul Gordon Lauren, "Crisis Prevention in Nineteenth-Century Diplomacy," in Alexander L. George (ed.), *Managing U.S.–Soviet Rivalry* (Boulder, CO, 1983); René Albrecht-Carrié; *A Diplomatic History of Europe Since the Congress of Vienna* (New York, 1973 ed.); Charles Burton Marshall, "The Golden Age in Perspective," *Journal of International Affairs*, 17 (1963): 9–17; Hajo Holborn, *The Political Collapse of Europe* (New York, 1951); and many editions of Carl von Martens, *Guide diplomatique*.

Insightful discussions of system building and the men and motives that guided it include Paul Schroeder, *The Transformation of European Politics* (Oxford, 1994); Alan Sked, *Europe's Balance of Power* (London, 1979); Henry Kissinger, *A World Restored: Metternich, Castlereagh, and the Problems of Peace, 1812–1822* (New York, 1973 ed.); C. K. Webster, *The Foreign Policy of Castlereagh* (London, 1963 ed.); Paul Schroeder, *Metternich's Diplomacy at Its Zenith* (New York, 1962); and Harold Nicolson, *The Congress of Vienna* (London, 1945).

Those interested in the operations of the Concert of Europe should consult Raymond Cohen, "Rules of the Game in International Politics," *International Studies Quarterly* 24 (March 1980): 129–150; Hedley Bull, *The Anarchical Society: A Study in Order in World Politics* (London, 1977); Richard Elrod, "The Concert of Europe," *World Politics* 28 (January 1976): 159–174; Gordon A. Craig and Peter Paret, "The Control of International Violence," *Stanford Journal of International Studies* 7 (1972): 1–21; Carsten Holbraad, *The Concert of Europe* (London, 1970); René Albrecht-Carrié, *The Concert of Europe, 1815–1914* (New York, 1968); and W. N. Medlicott, *Bismarck, Gladstone, and the Concert of Europe* (London, 1956). The balance of power is treated particularly well in F. H. Hinsley, *Power and the Pursuit of Peace* (Cambridge, 1963); Gordon A. Craig, "The Great Powers and the Balance of Power, 1830–1870," in *New Cambridge Modern History* 10 (Cambridge, 1960); and E. V. Gulick, *Europe's Classic Balance of Power* (Ithaca, NY, 1955). The classic treatment of war as an instrument of policy during the period is Carl von Clausewitz, *On War*, especially with the best and most recent translation by Michael Howard and Peter Paret (Princeton, 1976).

The course of international politics and nationalism during and after mid-century can be explored with Winfried Baumgart, *The Peace of Paris 1856: Studies in War, Diplomacy, and Peacemaking* (Santa Barbara, CA, 1981); Paul W. Schroeder, *Austria, Britain, and the Crimean War* (Ithaca, NY, 1972); A. J. P. Taylor, *The Struggle for Mastery in Europe, 1848–1918* (Oxford, 1954); and R. C. Binkley, *Realism and Nationalism, 1852–1870* (New York, 1935). The unification of Italy is treated by D. Mack Smith, *Italy and Its Monarchy* (New Haven, CT, 1989); and Derek Beales, *The Risorgimento and the Unification of Italy* (New York, 1971); while German unification is analyzed by Otto Pflanze, *Bismarck and the Development of Germany*, 3 vols. (Princeton, 1990); Lothar Gall, *Bismarck* (London, 1986); and Fritz Stern, *Gold and Iron* (New York, 1977). Diplomacy during the Bismarckian period is treated in Klaus Hildebrand, *German Foreign Policy from Bismarck to Adenauer* (London, 1989); Stig Förster et al. (eds.), *Bismarck, Europe, and Africa*

(Oxford, 1988); George Kennan, *The Decline of Bismarck's European Order* (Princeton, 1979); William Langer, *European Alliances and Alignments, 1871–1890* (New York, 1964 ed.), and *The Diplomacy of Imperialism, 1980–1902* (New York, 1968 ed.); and B. H. Sumner, *Russia and the Balkans* (Oxford, 1937).

Discussions of the Great Powers on the eve of 1914 can be found in Oron Hale, *The Great Illusion, 1900–1914* (New York, 1971); Barbara Tuchman, *The Proud Tower* (New York, 1966); and Michael Balfour, *The Kaiser and His Times* (London, 1964). More specific topics such as Anglo-German relations and their naval competition are treated in Paul Kennedy, *The Rise of the Anglo-German Antagonism* (London, 1980) and P. Padfield, *The Great Naval Race* (London, 1974); imperialism in Paul Gordon Lauren, *Power and Prejudice* (Boulder, CO, 1996 ed.) and D. K. Fieldhouse, *The Colonial Empires* (New York, 1966); war plans and military interference with policy in Paul Kennedy (ed.), *The War Plans of the Great Powers, 1880–1914* (London, 1979) and Gordon A. Craig, *The Politics of the Prussian Army* (New York, 1955); big business and politics in Eckhart Kehr, *Battleship Building and Party Politics in Germany* (Chicago, 1975); the collapse of the Sick Man of Europe in Marion Kent (ed.), *The Great Powers and the End of the Ottoman Empire* (London, 1984); and the impact of technology on diplomacy in Stephen Kern, *The Culture of Time and Space* (Cambridge, MA, 1986 ed.). On the coming of the war, see James Joll, *The Origins of the First World War* (London, 1992 ed.); Zara Steiner, *Britain and the Origins of the First World War* (London, 1977); and the much-discussed Fritz Fischer, *Germany's Aims in the First World War* (New York, 1967).

3

The Diplomatic Revolution Begins, 1919–1939

In 1814–1815, after almost twenty-five years of intermittent warfare, representatives of the European powers had been able to sit down together —in Metternich's phrase, "as friends,"—and to lay the foundations for a diplomatic system that with readjustments worked remarkably effectively for nearly a century. The First World War that brought this system to a calamitous end lasted only four years, but when it was over and leaders came together in another great peacemaking conference in Paris, their achievement fell far short of that of their predecessors at Vienna. No viable system ever emerged from their labors, and although they tried at times to pretend that it had, the fact that an even greater world war than that of 1914–1918 broke out within twenty years provided dramatic proof of their failure. Part of the explanation for this can be found in the unprecedented destruction and dislocations of the war, and part rests with the personal shortcomings of the statesmen themselves. But the larger, underlying reason for why they failed to build a viable international system can be found in the beginning of a revolution, the features of which slowly emerged over a period of several years but then virtually erupted in fury before their very eyes. This was the diplomatic revolution characterized by the expansion in the numbers and types of actors within the international system, the geographical scope of that system, powerful domestic political forces pressing to ignore the advice of professional diplomats and instead elevate the role of public opinion and promote economic interests, new technology in communications and transportation as well as weapons, and the deliberate rejection by many national leaders of traditional norms of diplomacy and self-imposed restraints on force and statecraft. These forces collectively created pressures that in the end overwhelmed them all.

ATTEMPTS AT PEACEMAKING AND SYSTEM BUILDING

Peacemaking, even in the best of circumstances, presents formidable challenges. But when the First World War ended, the problems appeared particularly difficult as Europe and the world staggered in disbelief over the carnage and

disruption that confronted them. The century's new science and technology in the hands of mass, citizen-conscripted armed forces infused with intense nationalism had unleashed destruction that revolutionized modern warfare and seriously challenged the traditional assumptions of using armed force as a legitimate instrument of policy. The combination of patterns of machine gun fire, barbed wire entanglements, artillery capable of firing exploding shells to targets several miles away, poison gas, land mines, torpedoes, submarines and battleships mobilized on a massive scale, aircraft for combat on the ground and in the sky, and armored tanks laid waste entire provinces, obliterated the traditional distinction between civilian and combatant, and killed an estimated 10 million people.

But there was more. The war destroyed four empires and made it possible for new states to be created from their ashes. It precipitated democratic and Communist revolutions and loosened the ties of colonial empires overseas. The war brought about direct American intervention into European affairs, thereby setting the stage for the beginning of a redistribution of world power. In leaving little distinction between "victor" and "vanquished," the conflict further signaled the collapse of many of the restraints and limited features of classical warfare and diplomacy. Moreover, the internal and external dimensions of the First World War profoundly damaged the earlier cultural and psychological homogeneity and general consensus on ethical values of European civilization itself. Death and exhaustion left, in the mournful words of German writer Erich Maria Remarque, "Fields of craters within and without." "The old Europe that we had known in 1914," wrote one French diplomat, "ceased to exist."

Structurally, for example, there was not much left of some of the known entities the past. Of the five Great Powers that had dominated the old system, more than half—the German Empire, the Russian Empire, and the Austro-Hungarian Empire—had succumbed to revolution and been diminished. The Ottoman Empire no longer existed. How was one to work into any new system such untried elements as the Bolshevik state of Russia and the German and Austria republics, to say nothing of completely new nation-states like Finland, Estonia, Latvia, Lithuania, Czechoslovakia, Hungary, Yugoslavia, and a revived Poland? In addition, countries and former colonial possessions like Canada, Australia, New Zealand, South Africa, the United States, and Japan that had played only minor or sporadic roles in international relations prior to the war now emerged with policies and objectives of their own. How much of a role they would now play, and how to fit them into political calculations or a diplomatic system, were extremely difficult for the peacemakers to determine.

The tasks of peacemaking were further complicated by political passions and pressures that had been unknown in 1814. There was no question now of former friends and foes sitting down together as partners to lay the foundations of peace for the society of states as they had at Vienna, and this meant that the final settlement would not constitute a consensual agreement among all those who had fought the war. The war of 1914–1918 far exceeded the

conflicts of the nineteenth century in duration and ferocity, and in other senses it was revolutionary: it largely divorced military strategy from foreign policy, was fought not as a limited but as a "total" war that involved the whole of the resources at the command of the participants, and broke down the traditional division between the military and civilian parts of society. Indeed, the suffering of the civilian populations was greater than it had been since the horrors of the Thirty Years' War. That war, as we have seen, started as a religious conflict and ended as a political one. One could say of the First World War that it marked a reversal of that process, beginning as a political conflict and ending as a religious one, in which each side began to view the other not as an opponent who must be defeated, but as a kind of anti-Christ who must be extirpated. This transition resulted not only from the extent of suffering and sacrifice, but also from the deliberate manipulation of nationalistic passions and wartime propaganda. As one of the leading propagandists, George Creel, later observed:

> It was in this recognition of Public Opinion as a major force that the Great War differed most essentially from all previous conflicts. The trial of strength was not only between massed bodies of armed men, but between opposed ideals . . . [and] raised issues that had to be fought out in the hearts and minds of people as well as on the actual firing line.

Once passions were aroused, it was difficult to turn them off. Consequently, when the war ended, there was little patience for the traditional practices of diplomacy or a broad sense of proportion on behalf of the system as a whole, little sympathy for letting the defeated enemy express their views during the deliberations, and little sentiment for reconciliation or compromise with the beaten foe. Instead of working in partnership to build a consensus on system-wide principles, leaders focused on rivalry and allowed themselves to succumb to the emotional impulse to rush to judgment and seek revenge.

These domestic forces often were all too well reflected in those political leaders determined to represent their countries themselves at the Paris Peace Conference in 1919, even though they often had little knowledge of international history or understanding of just how complicated a task it would be to make peace in the aftermath of such a devastating war. The mercurial British Prime Minister David Lloyd George had actively campaigned on a slogan not for a new legal order based upon consensus, but rather a settlement based upon revenge against the Germans. "We will squeeze the orange," he asserted, "until the pips squeak." Referring to the art of diplomacy, he expressed contempt for the professionals, saying that "diplomats were invented simply to waste time" and declaring simply: "I want no diplomats." Similarly, President Woodrow Wilson of the United States (described by one career diplomat as "The Dread Amateur") asserted that there was "disgust with the old order of things" and argued that the world needed a "new diplomacy" different in its origins, objectives, and methods of the past. They and their fellow politicians Georges Clemenceau of France and Vittorio Orlando

of Italy put these sentiments into practice at the peace conference when they often rejected the advice offered by their staff experts and relied more upon popular passions or personal intuition to solve intricate international problems. As Winston Churchill so pointedly described it:

> The peoples, transported by their sufferings and by the mass teachings with which they had been inspired, stood around in scores of millions to demand that retribution should be exacted to the full. Woe betide the leaders now perched on their dizzy pinnacles of triumph if they cast away at the conference table what the soldiers had won on the hundred blood-soaked battlefields. . . . The multitudes remained plunged in ignorance of the simplest facts, and their leaders, seeking their votes, did not dare to undeceive them.

One of the results of all this could be seen in the decline of a common set of ethics and normative values in statecraft. When the diplomatic corps of the classical system was filled with professionals who retained their posts for long periods and knew one another well, an incentive existed for them to see themselves as a part of a larger international society, to share a basic code of ethics, and to take personal moral responsibility for their actions. After 1918, when politicians who came in and out of office and whose sense of loyalty focused only on their own national public increasingly insisted upon conducting their own diplomacy, however, this kind of incentive began to disappear, and international relations suffered as a result.

Such a result quickly became evident when these leaders failed to reach a consensus on values or a conceptual basis for a new international order. The negotiators in Vienna a century earlier had shared a common understanding of history and agreed upon the principle of the balance of power to build their system. Some Europeans, particularly the French, still wanted to think in those terms and frequently pressed for treaties of guarantee to enforce the settlement. But this idea was directly challenged by Wilson, who, like many Americans before him, believed that balance-of-power politics was a contrivance of European states that had always been prone to absolutism, militarism, and antidemocratic behavior. He had made his determination to eliminate the old system abundantly clear when he declared:

> There must not be a balance of power but a community of power . . . I am therefore proposing that all nations henceforth avoid entangling alliances that draw them into competitions of power, catch them in a net of intrigue and selfish rivalry, and disturb their own affairs with influences intruded from without. . . . When all unite to act in the same sense and with the same purpose, all will act in the common interest and are free to live their own lives under a common protection.

Wilson wanted to replace the modalities of the old European order with a new League of Nations, a permanent institution composed of free nations that would discuss matters of interest to the international community, adjust their relations with each other, revise the peace treaties when inequities became apparent, and regulate their disputes. The establishment of this body was the

president's principal objective during the Paris negotiations, but the potential advantages that he claimed for it proved to be less than attractive to the other representatives. Premier Clemenceau remained an intransigent supporter of the balance of power as the most effective regulator of relationships between nations, and he refused to abandon this opinion because of sermons by a man whom he regarded as an idealistic schoolmaster from a country with no experience in world affairs. Others were inclined to agree. They wanted to avoid any self-imposed restraints and instead to punish the enemy, to be compensated for their sacrifices, and to construct a new system based on security guarantees.

Peacemaking and system building at Paris became, therefore, the scene of a protracted conflict between Wilson and his former associates. In the end, he gained his major objective, the League of Nations, but only at the expense of many compromises that vitiated his own declared principles. This was particularly evident when one compared the final results with his earlier and highly publicized declarations about a "war to end all wars," a "war to make the world safe for democracy," "peace without victory," "justice," and the "equality of rights." Indeed, the discrepancies between what he had promised and what the Treaty of Versailles delivered were so palpable that Wilson's critics lashed out at him. His role in defeating a provision on human rights and racial equality, for example, prompted the Japanese to publicly accuse Wilson of being nothing more than a hypocrite.

Domestic opponents within the United States were even harsher and mounted a powerful offensive against the whole settlement itself. During debate in the Senate, for example, the League was attacked as an instrument of irresponsible commitments and a dangerous international organization that would threaten national sovereignty, jeopardize the Constitution, interfere in domestic affairs, and "entangle the American nation in a European-Asiatic balance of power." Senator James Reed of Missouri, deeply concerned about race, even declared: "Think of submitting questions involving the very life of the United States to a tribunal on which a nigger from Liberia, a nigger from Honduras, a nigger from India . . . each have votes equal to that of the great United States." Thinking like this fanned the flames of already existing bitter partisanship between Democrats and Republicans, personal feuds, and the refusal of both Wilson and his "irreconcilable" opponents to compromise, and, in the end, the Senate rejected the treaties and forbade American membership in the League entirely.

This was a fatal blow to Wilson's dream, for international systems cannot be built or maintained unless there is genuine collaboration among the major actors to agree on basic principles, including those of self-restraints, and to actively participate in defending them. Thus, from the very beginning the League suffered from what political scientist Inis Claude called "the problem of the empty chair." The Americans refused to join from the outset. Moreover, two other important powers stood outside its membership for most of the period; Germany did not join until 1926 and then withdrew in 1933 along with Japan, while the Soviet Union did not become a member until 1934

and was then expelled five years later. To make matters worse, the only major nations left participating in the League, namely Britain and France, could never agree on its purposes and methods, particularly when force and statecraft were involved. These two governments continually disagreed and actually worked at cross purposes concerning the League's authority to apply sanctions in moments of aggression. The French tried periodically to put teeth into the organization by having its members sign guarantees to act automatically when peace was threatened. This was the whole purpose of the Draft Treaty of Mutual Assistance of 1923 and the Geneva Protocol of 1924, intended to bind League members to take action against states that refused to arbitrate disputes or were designated as aggressors by the League Council. But the British consistently defeated these attempts, taking the line that the League would not survive if too great a strain were placed upon it and that it would be advisable to regard it not as a body that took punitive action against wrongdoers, but simply as a place for debate. The League was forced to confront the fact that its member states were unwilling to take collective security seriously, and this did not bode well for the future.

The pattern of refusing to confront issues of force and statecraft collectively also took place elsewhere. At the Washington Naval Conference of 1921–1922, for example, leaders signed the Five Power Treaty on capital warships, but fundamentally revealed a stark unwillingness to engage in a meaningful restraints or limitations upon their weapons. At exactly the same time, the Four Power Treaty on Asia and the Pacific demonstrated a similar unwillingness to enforce its terms. As Senator Henry Cabot Lodge, who previously had orchestrated opposition to both the Treaty of Versailles and the League of Nations, announced with pride: "There is no provision for the use of force to carry out any of the terms of the agreement, and no military or naval sanction lurks anywhere in the background or under cover of these plain and simple clauses."

In exasperation, the French attempted to build up their own security system by concluding separate alliances with Belgium, Poland, and the so-called Little Entente of Yugoslavia, Romania, and Czechoslovakia. But these arrangements of deterrence, as we shall explore in more detail in Chapter 9, looked far better on paper than they did in practice. The small states had many disputes among themselves and could never contribute significant military force against powerful neighbors like the Germans or the Soviets; France's resources were not sufficient to support their allies unless the British were prepared to give some assistance, and the British were not ready to do any such thing. In fact, in 1925 when the British government signed the Locarno Pact guaranteeing the common boundary between Germany on the one hand and France and Belgium on the other, it wanted to make it "perfectly clear" that it was unprepared to enter into any similar engagements with respect to Eastern Europe. When the historical advisor to the Foreign Office, Sir James Hedlam-Morley, struck a dissenting note by warning that the European balance of power which it protected by supporting the weaker side against the stronger had always been central to Britain's foreign policy, his advice was dismissed. Weakened by this British attitude and by the high cost of military assistance

to its eastern members, the French system appeared in shambles after the conclusion of the Nazi-Polish Pact in 1934. France cast even further doubt upon its own system when it tried to complete the Maginot Line, a gigantic defensive rampart along its frontier from the Switzerland to Belgium, indicating that it would stay inert on the inside of its own borders and thereby abandon others to their fate. These developments could not possibly restrain the designs of any aggressors.

Those statesmen attempting peacemaking and system building also struggled with yet another feature of the diplomatic revolution: the rapid expansion in the number of actors in the international system. Before 1914 there were only about a dozen nations in the whole world that took a continuous interest and share in global affairs, and these were largely European. The Paris Peace Conference provided the first clear demonstration of how radically that condition was about to change, and from that time onward the number of states determined to play independent roles upon the world stage would increase dramatically. As one observer noted, "THIRTY-TWO NATIONS, PEOPLES, AND RACES. . . . Not simply England, Italy, and the Great Powers are there, but all the little nations. . . . Not only groups, but races have come—Jews, Indians, Arabs, and all-Asia." Another participant at the conference described it as: "Chinamen, Japanese, Koreans, Hindus, Kirghizes, Lesghiens, Circassians, Mingrelians, Buryats, Malays, and Negroes and Negroids from Africa and America were among the tribes and tongues forgathered in Paris to watch the rebuilding of the political world system and to see where they 'came in.'" This was something unknown in the annals of diplomacy.

One of the results of this development was the realization that it was much more difficult to create a working system of an international community than it had been when the participating states had been fewer in number. The original membership of the League of Nations, for example, numbered forty-two, including Australia, Canada, China, Haiti, India, Japan, the Latin American states, Liberia, New Zealand, Persia, Siam, and South Africa, among others, who joined with the victorious European powers and successor states. Others, in the name of national self-determination, eventually joined as well. But there was something more than just numbers. This expansion of actors also brought with it a breakdown in what had once been the internal homogeneity of the small, Euro-centric system of classical diplomacy. An important reason for the relative effectiveness of the nineteenth-century system was that is members were bound together by a common historical tradition and language, by shared cultural and religious values, and by ties of race, class, and gender, all of which greatly facilitated communication and cooperation. This did not survive in the aftermath of the First World War, and the adjustments that the new heterogeneity necessitated were sometimes painful. The British found it difficult, for example, to watch the League of Nations pay as much attention to the speeches of Eduard Benes of Czechoslovakia, Nicolae Titulescu of Romania, or Haile Selassie of Ethiopia as it did to their own representatives. They showed disrespect for the small powers, and it was said of Foreign Secretary Austen Chamberlain that when he spoke in the

Assembly, he sometimes seemed to be saying, "We are perfect. We are British. And yet you, you dagoes, dare to come here and criticize US!" With attitudes such as these, it would be most difficult to build an inclusive and effective international system.

Further complications arose as a result of technology that began to transform the pace of diplomacy. The staggering power and speed of invention and practical application affected diplomats as directly as it did millions of other people. Foreign ministries found themselves replacing their horse-drawn carriages with automobiles, their candles and gas lamps with electric lights, their elegant curving staircases with elevators, and their clerks skilled with pen and ink with typists who could do the work faster. Moreover, the growing use of electronic communication and aircraft all revealed further nullifications of former practical limits heretofore imposed by distance, geographical barriers, national boundaries, and—perhaps most critically—time. The speed of these new forms of international communication and transportation reduced the length of time to contemplate, analyze reports, choose between alternative courses of action, assume responsibilities, and issue instructions without the relaxed luxury to think and to reach careful judgment enjoyed just a few years before.

Public Opinion and Foreign Policy

One of the most salient features of the interwar period was the heightened influence that public opinion exercised upon foreign policy. There were a few, like former U.S. Secretary of State Elihu Root, who worked to develop an informed public and, in a famous essay published in the newly created journal *Foreign Affairs,* stressed the necessity of serious education to help citizens learn lessons from history and "acquire a knowledge of the fundamental and essential facts and principles upon which the relations of nations depend." But these were exceptions, for the new emphasis focused more on emotion than facts for people set adrift by war and revolution. Particularly in the democratic countries, this manifested itself in excessive preoccupation with the mood of the electorate and a consequent tendency of governments to follow rather than lead opinion. It also changed the conduct and forms of diplomacy in ways that were not always conducive to maintaining the system.

Here again it was the experience of the First World War that shattered traditional practices. The years and sacrifices required by "total" war and the deliberate use of nationalistic propaganda to win "the hearts and minds" of people at home and abroad brought rising and irresistible pressure from politicians, business interests, journalists, and vocal members of the public at large insistent upon having a voice in determining what the policy of their country should be. They deplored what they called the "secret diplomacy" of the past and announced their determination to end, in the words of the *Berliner Tageblatt,* "an aristocratic collegium unapproachable to the ordinary mortal, like the table of the Holy Grail." Critics argued that they had remained silent and subservient long enough and thus began to insert themselves into

diplomacy, create permanent legislative committees to deal with foreign affairs, and demand that they be kept informed and consulted. Consequently, the professionals in foreign ministries who once had so assiduously refrained from providing any information about their activities to "the masses" were now increasingly forced not only to respond to these public demands, but to attempt to actually shape opinion as well. They found themselves required to spend ever larger amounts of time and effort giving legislative or congressional briefings, guiding junketing politicians, hiring press attachés, recruiting publicists, holding press conferences, making public appearances and answering questions, publishing collections of heretofore classified diplomatic documents in order to win popular support, and attempting to build domestic political coalitions in order to conduct policy. Professional diplomats warned ominously that all this would replace the traditional norms of restraint and practices of discretion with cheap public displays and what they described as "the inflammation of national passions."

Yet, this increasingly would become a feature in the conduct of diplomacy, and any politician who seemed to disregard it ran the risk of being swept away by public indignation. Aristide Briand of France was forced from office in 1922 by a pervasive, and wholly irrational, rumor that his policy at the Geneva reparations conference had been dictated by the British. Lloyd George himself fell from office in the same year when his handling of a crisis in the Middle East led to a public outcry that he was trying to drag the country into another war.

The retribution that public feeling could wreak upon political leaders seeking to deal with complicated international problems was, therefore, real and intimidating. Indeed, the interwar years are full of examples of how great their timidity could become. Thus, when Winston Churchill accused Prime Minister Stanley Baldwin in a 1936 House of Commons speech of irresponsibility for having failed, in view of the manifest dangers in the international situation, to take advantage of the election campaign of the previous year to call for a heightened armament effort, Baldwin answered with a startling ingenuousness. "Suppose I had gone to the country," he replied, "and said that Germany was rearming and we must rearm, does anyone think that this pacific democracy would have rallied to that cry at that moment? I cannot think of anything that would have made the loss of the election from my point of view more certain."

The history of U.S. foreign relations during these years provides other cases of disinclination to challenge public opinion. During the Disarmament Conference of 1932, President Herbert Hoover might have persuaded the French government to modify its opposition to reduce armaments if he had been willing to modify or abandon war debts owed to the United States, but he refused to do so because he believed that such an offer would be unacceptable to American opinion. Like Baldwin, he was afraid of losing an election. Similarly, when President Franklin Roosevelt declared in 1937 that the epidemic of lawlessness that was spreading in the world could only be checked by a quarantine imposed by the peace-loving states, the public response in

his own country was so immediate, massive, and negative that the White House felt compelled to disavow the true intent of the speech and retreat into an inactivity that lasted until the very eve of a new war.

In addition to its tendency to lame the resolution of governments, the power of public opinion had a significant effect upon the conduct of diplomacy itself. For one thing, it ended the virtual monopoly of the professionals. Popular opinion held the view that the professional diplomats and their way of doing business had been largely responsible for causing the war of 1914 and that the sooner their control was broken the better. So strong was this feeling that political leaders sought to reduce the role of the professionals, by which they generally meant that they should take over the functions of the diplomats themselves. This explains why Lloyd George so frequently bypassed the Foreign Office and to a large extent ignored his ambassadors, traveling around with his own staff and conducting negotiations with foreign officials on complicated matters that he did not fully understand. The meager and sometimes disconcerting results of this practice did not discourage others from imitating it. Instead of letting chiefs of mission abroad do what they were trained to do, political leaders, ministers, and special missions of prominent politicians or private citizens often took to doing their business for them. In this regard they were assisted by the new technological inventions of the telephone (that enemy of reflection, which became increasingly accepted as a means of communication) and the airplane to travel abroad and conduct negotiations themselves. A French commission later investigated the deficiencies of this kind of conduct of diplomacy and wrote that

> after the conclusion of the treaties of 1919, ministers had the habit of multiplying their contacts with their colleagues in other countries. The abuse of direct conversations opens the door to numerous dangers. Engagements are entered into too easily. They are often improvised. It is better to define the course of a negotiation by a note which has matured in the silence of the ministry than by chance exchanges that are likely to be imprecise.

Nor was imprecision the only danger inherent in this kind of diplomacy. When politicians engaged in the process of negotiation, they often were apt to feel that their personal reputations were at stake and that a successful result was imperative. This, in turn, could lead to ringing declarations plainly designed to convince a credulous public that great objectives had been achieved—which later, however, proved to be unsubstantiated.

Along with the transformations in the personnel charged with conducting important foreign affairs went a change in format. During the war, Wilson had called for "open covenants openly arrived at," and it soon became an article of public faith that "open diplomacy" was the only acceptable procedure. The result was a rapid growth of diplomacy by conference, which took the form of either large meetings in which many states participated in discussions of subjects of general interest or what came to be called summit meetings, like the Locarno Conference of 1925, in which heads of state or foreign ministers met to deal with particular crises or opportunities. These tended to

gratify the desire for openness and spectacle, but all too often met under the pressure of public impatience and without preliminary talks adequate to lay a basis for fruitful negotiation. They often, indeed, seemed planned more for their public effect than for the substantive issues at stake, as evidenced by the numbers of journalists, photographers, press conferences, inspired leaks, and other inventions of modern public relations. They generally began with public statements by the heads of delegations in which they made their objectives clear in advance. This unfortunately fixed their positions so that they had little room for subsequent maneuver and concession in that any alteration of position might strike their public as a humiliating retreat. In these circumstances not much could be expected, except for a final communiqué that sought to record a success where none existed.

As for summit meetings, the eminent expert on diplomatic practice, Sir Harold Nicolson, pointed out that the political leaders who participated were particularly busy and preoccupied men. "The time at the disposal of these visitors," he noted, "is not always sufficient to allow for patience and calm deliberation. The honors which are paid to a minister in a foreign capital may tire his physique, excite his vanity, or bewilder his judgment." This could be seen with striking clarity with the ill-fated Munich Conference of September 1938 in which the participants were anxious to go home with anything that might be called a success. British Prime Minister Neville Chamberlain desperately wanted to come back with something, so he persuaded Adolf Hitler to sign a loosely stated "Anglo-German Declaration" of future cooperation. When Chamberlain flew home to joyous crowds, he smiled and proudly waved the piece of paper in his hand as proof that he had secured "peace in our time." The public desperately wanted to believe in its credibility. They thus were completely shocked when in March 1939 Hitler invaded Czechoslovakia, demonstrating that the agreement meant nothing at all.

A final result of the heightened importance of public sentiment was a new emphasis on what might be called diplomacy by public declaration. This was the technique of using a public address to send a message not to another government, but rather to the population of another country in the hope of influencing it to bring pressure upon its own government. The master of this was Hitler. Whenever he did something particularly outrageous, he would make a major address in which he appealed to wishful thinking and the uneasy conscience in the West. He then would explain that, far from being provocative or aggressive, what he had just done was simply a means of redressing legitimate grievances, opening up new opportunities for a better world, or removing the last obstacle to peace. These speeches were remarkably effective, principally because his listeners did not want war and they felt more than they thought. This made them more vulnerable and susceptible to manipulation. As such, they could be encouraged to believe in a policy of seeking peace through the increasingly dangerous policy of giving dictators what they wanted, eschewing collective security, and dissuading their own governments from taking effective action that might have discouraged the aggressors from launching a war.

ECONOMICS AND FOREIGN POLICY

The nature of the diplomatic system in the years from 1919 to 1939 also was profoundly influenced by economic issues and by the insensitivity of the various powers to their long-term international consequences and their potential for political damage. Part of the problem, of course, flowed from the consequences of the First World War itself: 10 million killed in combat, 7 million permanently disabled, and the unprecedented destruction of homes and farms, livestock and forests, communication and transportation networks, and industrial plants and shops, all of which had to be rebuilt or replaced. Added to this were the financial problems that resulted from the fact that most of the belligerents had relied upon borrowing rather than taxation to meet the costs of the war, and now were confronted with staggering debts and the threat of mounting inflation. In addition, the victors often demonstrated remarkable ignorance about the simplest of economic facts, and the tactics that they employed were so unrealistic and counter-productive that they fatally weakened the possibility of maintaining a diplomatic system.

Given the losses of the war and the monumental reconstruction that lay ahead, it is not surprising that economic competition among nations would become intensified. It became commonplace to hear bitter rivals speak of each other and their postwar struggle in terms of "business enemies," "financial weapons," "commercial battles," "captured markets," and "economic warfare." Various pressure groups representing chambers of commerce, exporters, businesses, and investors consequently placed considerable domestic pressure upon their foreign ministries to make greater efforts to fuse economics with foreign policy. Toward this end, professional diplomats found themselves increasingly being forced to abandon the traditional administrative distinction between "political" and "commercial" affairs, gather business intelligence and trade statistics, hire commercial attachés, and include businessmen, bankers, and industrialists as active participants in diplomatic negotiations. This was clearly demonstrated in Germany when Walter Rathenau, a part owner or director of eighty-six domestic and twenty-one international enterprises, was named as foreign minister in 1922, symbolizing the role that large-scale business would play in international politics.

But the passion to punish sometimes overrode wise financial decisions, as evident by the issue of reparations at the peace conference. As one economic expert wrote at the time, "Some of the delegates wanted to destroy Germany, some wanted to collect reparations, and some wanted to do both." In the end, they chose to ignore the historical lessons of the generally counterproductive nature of reparations and decided to exact from Germany a punitive amount twice as large as the original estimate, even though Germany's capacity to make such payments had been significantly diminished as a result of losing the war. These terms helped to destroy the new system rather than to build it. It was thus no wonder that the democratic experiment of the Weimar Republic was characterized from the beginning by a deep popular resentment against the West. To make matters worse, the completely different approaches to

collective security taken by the British and French governments became manifest over the reparations question as well. Lloyd George became convinced that only a scaling down of the burden imposed upon Germany would allow the postwar system to operate, a position that the French, under the leadership of the tough and rigid Raymond Poincaré, adamantly opposed. This irreconcilable difference between the two major powers most responsible for maintaining the peace settlement found fateful expression in January 1923 when a German default led, despite British protests, to a French and Belgian military occupation of the Ruhr mining area. The Germans responded with a policy of passive resistance, the costs of which could only be met by printing new money in such large amounts that the country was soon involved in runaway inflation. This impoverished the middle class and strengthened the growing number of rapid nationalist, antirepublican, and discontented political movements, not the least of which was a group known as the Nazis. Whatever advantage the French gained from their invasion was short-lived, for the termination of reparation payments resulted in the collapse of the franc, and the country was saved from bankruptcy only by loans from J. P. Morgan in New York and Lazard Brothers in London.

The growing role of private bankers in place of professional diplomats could also be seen in the various efforts made to devise new and reduced reparations payments and to extend loans to Germany. All this came to an abrupt end, however, with the Wall Street crash of 1929 and the resulting world depression. This, in turn, led to strong isolationist and trade protectionist tendencies in the United States, Britain, and France. In Germany it destroyed the democratic Weimar Republic and brought Adolf Hitler to power. None of these developments could be a source of satisfaction for those who desired peace and collective security.

The possibility of combining economic diplomacy with issues of force and statecraft was seriously considered at the Geneva Disarmament Conference of 1932. The British believed that everything possible should be done to help Germany restore its full sovereignty in foreign affairs, including a revision of restrictions on armed forces in the Treaty of Versailles. The French adamantly opposed this proposal unless accompanied by other security guarantees. This argument and its impact upon the whole subject of peace brought the United States temporarily back to European councils, with President Herbert Hoover arguing that a reduction of armaments would be the best way of promoting recovery from the world depression. Some of his advisors actively encouraged him to use the war debts owed to the United States by France as economic leverage to coerce the French into changing their position. But Hoover did not want to jeopardize his electoral chances with the public by any suggestion of debt reduction, even as a means of pressure to promote disarmament. This, when combined with the reluctance of the participants to accept any meaningful limitations upon their armed forces, caused the conference to collapse and the fateful consequences that would follow.

Under Hitler's direction, the integration of economic diplomacy with political objectives became much closer and more successful. When he launched

the Four Year Plan in 1936, he made it clear that those charged with making economic decisions needed to know that their sole duty was to create the basis for "the struggle for self-realization" that would enable Germany to assert itself in the world. Hitler called for a *Wehrwirtschaft*, or war economy, with an economic mobilization comparable to his military mobilization. "The German economy," he said, "must be capable of supporting war in four years." The key to his success in this effort was the economic strategy, which targeted exchanges of weapons made in Germany for foodstuffs and raw materials from Eastern Europe.

Hitler's open admission that his economic policy was predicated upon war and his rapid success in penetrating Eastern Europe alarmed the foreign policy establishments of Britain and France. Voices were raised to argue that acquiescence in Germany's hegemony over Europe would violate their national interests. Proposals that economic countermeasures be employed, however, encountered strong opposition by the general public, private individuals, and bankers, who argued that cooperation with Germany, rather than opposition, was the best way to secure peace. This became such a force that one diplomat complained: "In spite of all our efforts, Mr. Montagu Norman [the governor of the Bank of England] continues to carry out his own foreign policy, certainly without consulting the Foreign Office and without, I suspect, taking even the Treasury very much into consideration." Such divisions of purpose and policy made an effective answer to Hitler's economic diplomacy impossible.

TOTALITARIAN AND DEMOCRATIC DIPLOMACY AND THE CONTRAST OF NORMS

In September 1938, when Neville Chamberlain went to Godesberg, carrying his allies' approval of the terms for a settlement of the Czechoslovakian crisis on which he and Hitler had agreed two weeks earlier, he was disagreeably surprised to find that his host had changed his mind and had rewritten the agreement, introducing severely harsher conditions. When Chamberlain was handed a paper embodying these changes, he is reported to have said angrily, "This is an ultimatum, not a negotiation!" Pointing to the title page, Hitler replied mildly, "It says memorandum." This incident illustrates how faulty real communication was apt to be between the totalitarian and democratic states in the interwar period. Indeed, these diplomatic conversations took place between rivals rather than partners, and negotiations often resembled what the French call a *dialogue des sourds*, or a conversation between deaf people. The victories of Bolshevism in Russia in 1917, Fascism in Italy in 1922, and National Socialism in Germany in 1933, when combined with the general marginalization of professional diplomats, created three major states determined to actually overthrow the peace settlement and helped to bring about a new ideological age and with one of the most fateful features of the entire diplomatic revolution: the deliberate rejection of heretofore commonly accepted norms of behavior and the resulting collapse of a consensus on values.

The basic reason for this condition was a serious lack of consensus on basic principles and a profound difference in values and aspirations. Great Britain, France, and the United States had developed in the liberal-democratic tradition, and their approach to international relations after 1919 was strongly influenced by their faith in the primacy of reason and the repugnance for war. Western leaders viewed the conduct of diplomacy a rational pursuit among responsible powers that operated according to reasonable and generally accepted rules of law and procedure, self-imposed restraints, and the peaceful settlement of disputes. They believed that in an age that followed the most terrible war in history, any person competent enough to rise to the leadership of a great nation would be intelligent enough to see that war was not to anyone's advantage. In sharp contrast, from the beginning of their existence, the totalitarian states deliberately rejected these values and assumptions and, like playing chess by moving bishops as if they were rooks, operated according to rules that they made up on their own.

It was clear from the very beginning that the Soviet Union had a fundamentally different approach to diplomacy from that of the West. The new Communist leaders had no hesitation about declaring an unremitting ideological war with capitalism, rejecting self-imposed restraints, and overthrowing the established international order. They did this not only by repudiating the debts owed by the czarist government to its Western allies and by confiscating all foreign properties in Russia without compensation to the owners, but also by officially announcing their intent to foment worldwide revolution. V. I. Lenin set about, as he had promised earlier, "to prepare and conduct revolutionary war" and "to at once systematically start to incite rebellion." As a part of this strategy, he sought to reject all the forms of traditional diplomacy, which he regarded as no more than tools in the hands of landlords and capitalists. Thus, when Leon Trotsky became the first commissar for foreign affairs, he announced that he would "issue a few revolutionary declarations to the peoples and then close up the joint [the Foreign Office]." Based upon their belief that they could never co-exist with capitalist states, the Soviets created the Comintern—that "general staff of the world revolution of the proletariat" with the mission of coordinating the activities of Communist parties abroad and encouraging subversion and the use of force against non-Communist governments. Such actions generated great suspicion on the part of others, as indicated in 1920 by U.S. Secretary of State Bainbridge Colby when he wrote:

> It is not possible . . . to recognize the present rulers of Russia as a government with which the relations common to friendly governments can be maintained. This conviction . . . rests upon . . . facts . . . which none dispute [and which] have convinced the Government of the United States, against its will, that the existing regime in Russia is based upon the negation of every principle of honor and good faith and every usage and convention underlying the whole structure of international law, the negation, in short, of every principle upon which it is possible to base harmonious and trustful relations, whether of nations or individuals. . . . There cannot be any

Europe and the Middle East Transformed by War and Revolution: The Settlement of 1919

common ground upon which [the United States] can stand with a Power whose conceptions of international relations are so entirely alien to its own, so utterly repugnant to its moral sense.... We cannot recognize, hold official relations with, or give friendly reception to, the agents of government which is determined and bound to conspire against our institutions.

Soviet ideological beliefs and suspicions were only exacerbated by Western actions. Political leaders forced the Soviet Union into diplomatic isolation by refusing to recognize the new government and deliberately excluding it from all peacemaking and system-building efforts of the Paris Peace Conference. In addition, they used the Treaty of Versailles to take vast swaths of territory

from what had been Russia and gave them to the new successor states, creating what they called a *cordon sanitaire*, or sanitary barrier, to protect against the spread of the "disease" of Communism. The clear purpose of this, according to British General Sir Henry Wilson, was "to create a ring of States all around Bolshevik Russia, the object being to prevent Bolshevism from spreading; to deprive it of supplies and power of expansion, and to reduce it to absolute exhaustion." From the Soviet perspective, this was made even worse when the West launched a military intervention against them, employing force in an attempt to overthrow their new regime.

This strong divergence of values and norms and its effect on any attempts to use diplomacy to build and maintain a viable diplomatic system was seen in subsequent Soviet behavior. Lenin boldly announced that the diplomatic corps had been purged of every "single influential person" from the old regime and reconstituted with ideological loyalists charged with creating "a reliable Communist apparatus" for foreign affairs. It was not unusual, therefore, to find Soviet negotiators like G. V. Chicherin, Maxim Litvinov, and V. M. Molotov, bound by rigid directives that allowed little flexibility, engaging in what has been called "diplomatic guerrilla warfare." Here, they would automatically reject all initial proposals from others, persist in an uncompromising advocacy of Communist ideology, use negotiations not to reach settlements but to block or delay them, and refuse to use diplomacy as a means of reaching real understanding or agreement. Sometimes they entered into discussions largely for the purpose of propaganda or rhetorical fireworks, as they did on the eve of the Anglo-Soviet Trade Agreement of 1921 when they announced: "We are convinced that the foreign capitalists, who will be obliged to work on terms we offer them, will dig their own graves." On other occasions they engaged in negotiations primarily to ingratiate the Soviet Union with third parties, as they did during the Genoa Conference of 1922 and the Disarmament Conference of 1932.

These methods reinforced the conviction that it was difficult under any conditions to carry on political discussions with the Soviet Union and impossible to rely on any agreements made. The belief proved to be a heavy handicap to any revision of view in the years when the Soviets, seriously alarmed by the threat of Hitler's Germany, began to seek agreements with the West that might strengthen their position and the system of collective security. This shift in Soviet diplomacy was marked by placing the Comintern under restraint, gaining diplomatic recognition by the United States in 1933, securing admission to the League of Nations in 1934, and negotiating the Franco-Soviet Pact in 1935. But Western suspicion of Soviet motives remained unabated. Even as the war approached and attempts were made to secure an Anglo-French-Soviet alliance, British Prime Minister Neville Chamberlain remained unmoved and said, "I must confess to the most profound distrust of Russia."

The suspicions of diplomacy during these interwar years was further complicated by the coming to power of Benito Mussolini and the creation of his Fascist government in Italy. His previous experience in journalism left him

with a tendency to be preoccupied with newspaper opinion, with style rather than substance, and with a hankering after sensational strokes and dramatic coups that would look good in headlines. This is why he was forever expressing his contempt for traditional diplomacy, conventional practices, professional diplomats, collaborative negotiations, and restraints on the use of force. Instead, he wanted to talk about what he called the *tono fascista*, or the "Fascist style" of diplomacy that demonstrated a proud and militant bearing, constant posturing and bombast, and a strong orientation toward ideological purity. Its practical effect, made even worse when he appointed his inexperienced son-in-law Galeazzo Ciano as foreign minister, was to make Italian ambassadors conduct themselves not as partners of a common diplomatic community, but rather as if they were in "an enemy camp." When one senior diplomat received the order to represent Italy in France, for example, he naturally requested instructions. "What ought I try to accomplish in Paris?," he asked. "Nothing," replied Ciano. "It will be difficult," the ambassador responded, "but I will do my best." Such an approach often led to a considerable amount of slipshodness in detail, as in the drafting of the Pact of Steel with Germany in May 1939, which imposed rigid conditions upon Italy without stipulating the necessity of consultations or providing any details whatsoever.

In sharp contrast to Mussolini, Adolf Hitler had given much consideration to what could and could not be accomplished by diplomacy and quickly proved himself to be the most skillful of all the totalitarian leaders. His own personal experience in the First World War had demonstrated the importance of public opinion and the power of the state to manipulate it. "It was shown only during the war," he wrote in his autobiography *Mein Kampf* well before he even came to power in 1933, "to what enormously important results a suitably applied propaganda may lead." It could be used to stir aggressive nationalism that stressed patriotic unity, inflame hatred against enemies, portray international cooperation with others as betrayal, or justify war. Here he also articulated his dreams of creating a *Machtstaat*, or power state, to employ force and of tearing up the *Diktat*, or dictated settlement of the Versailles Treaty, in order to fully rearm Germany without restrictions. With such armed force he wanted to secure *Lebensraum*, or living space, at the expense of others and even identified who his potential international targets would be. Importantly for our consideration, he never regarded diplomacy as a means of resolving conflict or preserving peace, but rather as an instrument of preparing for expansion and war. As he wrote himself, "An alliance whose aim does not embrace a plan for war is senseless and worthless. Alliances are concluded only for struggle." It is not surprising, therefore, that Hitler had a deep distrust of professional diplomats, referred to the German Foreign Ministry as "the Idiot House" staffed by incompetent and ideologically questionable bureaucrats, and actually removed his ambassadors from foreign posts when he thought that they might be interested in seeking accommodation or peace when he desired war.

Given these explicit statements and actions, how is one to explain why the West approached the Soviet Union with such immediate and unmistakable

hostility and yet reacted to the other totalitarian states with such blindness? The governments in London and Paris seemed for a long time willing to excuse Hitler's and Mussolini's breaches of treaty law without acknowledging the dangerous threat posed to peace and their own national security. The explanation is to be found in a combination of an intense hatred of Communism and a greater tolerance for other ideologies, ignorance, wishful thinking, and the stubbornness with which the policy of appeasement was pursued. But the fallacies of this policy would have become apparent before 1939, even to its authors, if it had not been for the skills of Hitler, who proved to be particularly adroit in playing to the prejudices of the West, in exploiting their wishful thinking about diplomacy, and thereby in postponing the time when the scales finally fell from their eyes.

Appeasement was the invention of Neville Chamberlain, a politician who had made his way to becoming prime minister by distinguished service in domestic politics, but who knew little of international relations or force and statecraft. Indeed, he had once been interrupted while airing his views on diplomacy by his own brother Austen, one of the authors of the Locarno treaties, who accurately said, "Neville, you must remember you don't know anything about foreign affairs." This proved in the end to be tragically true, but it never seemed to bother him. He argued that the best way to maintain peace and security was to give Hitler and Mussolini what they wanted, in the hopes that once their wants were satisfied, they would play by the rules and become participating partners in the diplomatic system. Like so many other political leaders at the time, he was headstrong in his own opinions, resented the professional diplomats, sought to bypass the Foreign Office as much as possible, dismiss the criticisms of those with considerable international experience such as Foreign Secretary Anthony Eden or Winston Churchill, and surround himself instead with those whose views agreed with his own.

In the end, Chamberlain's critics proved to be absolutely right, and appeasement helped to bring on the very war that the prime minister sought to avoid. This was not, however, solely a result of his own gullibility. Hitler's gifts of persuasion were considerable, and Chamberlain was not the only statesman who was deluded by his ability to mask his true intentions until he felt strong enough to strike. Hitler showed both skill and inventiveness in using the resources and techniques of diplomacy to advance his purposes, to exploit psychological weaknesses, and to deliberately play on the wishful thinking of what others wanted to see and hear.

This can be seen as Hitler carefully went through four distinct phases on this road to war. The first of these, which followed immediately upon his accession to power, may be called the diplomacy of concealment or obfuscation. It was designed to convince other powers that Hitler's regime would bring with it no fundamental changes in German foreign policy. Toward this end, he did not change the personnel in the Foreign Office or the embassies, made every possible attempt to explain to other governments and peoples that whatever unpleasant things were going on inside Germany had no foreign political connotations, and played down whatever earlier statements appeared in

Mein Kampf. Hitler's public statements at this stage were pacific, disarming, and even ingratiating. All of this was designed to divert attention from his real intentions, blunt criticism, and prevent external interference while Germany was still vulnerable.

In the second phase, which began at the end of 1933 and extended through the next year, Hitler's diplomacy was intended to remove the fetters of previous obligations and to protect the country from the possible consequences of doing so. This began with Germany's secret rearmament and departure from the disarmament conference and the League of Nations, an action which Hitler carefully prepared by playing upon the bad conscience of the West with regard to Germany's remaining disabilities under the Versailles Treaty and the resentment that existed in some countries over France's reluctance to make concessions. He used with effect tactics that were to be employed again, constantly raising the level of his demands so that a settlement became impossible, and then withdrawing from the conference and the League on the grounds that the German people would no longer tolerate an imposed inequality. Hitler also devoted considerable effort to avoid any attempt to punish him for his actions. This took the form of a flurry of public and private assurances that Germany was willing to make new engagements and enter into new pacts with any power, including a pact of friendship with Poland in 1934. His smooth promises had such a ring of sincerity that they lulled Western statesmen into a dangerously false sense of security.

The third phase, which extended from 1935 through 1937, was characterized by a diplomacy of testing resolve, designed to discover how much resistance could be expected once Hitler decided to unmask his plans for expansion to the East. It began with the first of his "Saturday Surprises," when (after government officials and military personnel in other countries had already left for the weekend) he announced in March 1935 that Germany had decided to create a new Air Force and that it would no longer be bound by the arms restrictions of the Versailles Treaty. In a revealing example of just how skillful he could be in disarming potential antagonists, Hitler explained his decision as reasonable and a matter of honor, saying that Germany simply wanted to be free to have an Air Force like any other self-respecting state. Even the usually skeptical British ambassador in Berlin, Sir Eric Phipps, was won over, and actually advised his government that Hitler had changed from his "old, somewhat gangster-like days at Munich" and that he could now be trusted: "His signature, once given, will bind his people as no other could." When this deception proved to be successful, Hitler then boldly decided to invade and remilitarize the Rhineland, the last remaining protection for France against an immediate German attack. Only words (rather than actions) of protest occurred in response to this direct challenge to security, and no one marched—except for the Germans. As Hitler later admitted, "If the French had marched into the Rhineland we would have had to withdraw with our tails between our legs, for the military resources at our disposal would have been wholly inadequate for even a moderate resistance." He had tested

the resolve of others to uphold the international order and found that they had none.

The fourth phase was the period of aggression, heralded by Hitler's secret meeting with his military and diplomatic advisers in November 1937, the reorganization of the army, and appointment of the ideologically pure but completely inexperienced businessman, Joachim von Ribbentrop, as foreign minister. In March 1938 he sent his troops into Austria, violating yet another provision of the Versailles Treaty, completely swallowing a sovereign state and member of the League of Nations, and thereby expanding the territory of his new Reich. Then, and with the actual approval of those practicing appeasement at the Munich Conference of September 1938, who assisted in the dismantling of their own system by giving him everything he wanted, an emboldened Hitler took control of the Sudetenland, declaring solemnly that it was his "last demand." Less than six months later he moved his military forces into Prague, seized control of the remainder of Czechoslovakia, and prepared for war against Poland. Last-minute attempts by the British and the French to stop Hitler by attempting to practice a strategy of deterrence could not help but fail; as we shall see in Chapter 9, success often depends upon credibility, and this had long since disappeared. Hitler had no reason to believe that they had either the will or the ability to enforce their threats. Indeed, he described them with one word: "worms."

Hitler's most stunning diplomatic stroke came in August 1939, when he suddenly signed the Nazi-Soviet Non-Aggression Pact with blinding speed literally under the noses of the French and British. This treaty between the two powerful countries who had been deliberately excluded from peacemaking and system building in 1919 and who desired to overthrow the international system itself called for a division of spoils in Eastern Europe and relieved Hitler of any immediate military threat of a two-front war. With this in his pocket, he had no further use for diplomacy and could turn instead to his poised and waiting troops, heavy artillery, armored tanks, Stuka dive bombers, and other new weapons made possible by the most recent technology. In marked contrast to his opposite numbers in London and Paris, he had never regarded it as a means of preserving peace but as an instrument for preparing for the war that he had always wanted. "After all," he said once the war had begun, "I did not raise the army in order *not* to use it." The statement underlines the fact that all of his diplomatic intercourse with the Western governments, upon which they had placed such high hopes, had been nothing but a deliberately contrived *dialogue des sourds*, in which the words he used had secret meanings that the other side would not or could not hear.

SUGGESTIONS FOR FURTHER EXPLORATION

The diplomatic revolution theme is developed in Paul Gordon Lauren, "The Diplomatic Revolution of Our Time," in David Wetzel and Theodore Hamerow (eds.),

International Politics and German History (Westport, CT, 1997); Paul Gordon Lauren, *Diplomats and Bureaucrats* (Stanford, CA, 1976); and the original articulation in Gordon A. Craig, "The Revolution in War and Diplomacy," in *War, Politics, and Diplomacy* (New York, 1966).

The Paris Peace Conference is treated in many books, including Margaret Olwen Macmillan, *Paris 1919: Six Months That Changed the World* (New York, 2002); Manfred Boemke et al. (eds.) *The Treaty of Versailles: A Reassessment After 75 Years* (Cambridge, 1998); Alan Sharp, *The Versailles Settlement: Peacemaking in Paris, 1919* (New York, 1991); Arno Mayer, *Politics and Diplomacy of Peacemaking* (New York, 1967); and Harold Nicolson's personal memoir, *Peacemaking 1919* (New York, 1939 ed.). The literature on Wilson is vast, but good places to start are Lloyd Ambrosius, *Wilsonianism: Woodrow Wilson and His Legacy in American Foreign Relations* (New York, 2002); the chapter entitled "The New Face of Diplomacy," in Henry Kissinger, *Diplomacy* (New York, 1994); Arno Mayer, *Political Origins of the New Diplomacy* (New York, 1970 ed.); Gordon A. Craig, "The United States and the European Balance," *Foreign Affairs* 55 (1976): 189–198; Arthur Link, *Wilson the Diplomatist* (Chicago, 1965); and Alexander L. George and Juliette L. George, *Woodrow Wilson and Colonel House: A Personality Study* (New York, 1964).

For valuable explorations of the diplomacy of the interwar period as a whole, see Zara Steiner, *The Lights That Failed: European International History, 1919–1939* (Oxford, 2005); G. Ross, *The Great Powers and the Decline of the European States System* (London, 1983); Sally Marks, *The Illusion of Peace* (London, 1976); R. J. Sontag, *A Broken World, 1919– 1939* (New York, 1971); Arnold Wolfers, *Britain and France Between the Wars: Conflicting Strategies of Peace* (New York, 1966 ed.); and the classic, Gordon A. Craig and Felix Gilbert (eds.), *The Diplomats, 1919–1939* (Princeton, 1953). Issues of collective security and the League of Nations are discussed in Jonathan Haslam, *The Soviet Union and the Struggle for Collective Security in Europe, 1933–1939* (New York, 1984); John Jacobson, *Locarno Diplomacy* (Princeton, 1972); and F. P. Walters, *A History of the League of Nations* (London, 1952).

Public opinion and foreign policy are treated in John Milton Cooper, *Breaking the Heart of the World* (New York, 2001); Richard Cockett, *Twilight of Truth: Chamberlain, Appeasement and the Manipulation of the Press* (New York, 1989); Ralph Levering, *The Impact of Public Opinion on American Foreign Policy* (New York, 1978); Sir Harold Nicolson, *Diplomacy* (London, 1963 ed.); Winston Churchill, *The Gathering Storm* (Boston, 1948); E. H. Carr, *Propaganda in International Politics* (New York, 1939); Elihu Root, "A Requisite for the Success of Popular Diplomacy," *Foreign Affairs*, 1 (1922): 3–10. Those readers interested in economics and foreign policy should consult Paul Kennedy, *The Rise and Fall of the Great Powers* (New York, 1987); Marc Trachenberg, *Reparations in World Politics* (New York, 1980); David E. Kaiser, *Economic Diplomacy and the Origins of the Second World War* (Princeton, 1980); Charles Maier, *Recasting Bourgeois Europe* (Princeton, 1975); Charles Kindleberger, *Power and Money: The Economics of International Politics and the Politics of International Economics* (New York, 1970); and the provocative John Maynard Keyes, *The Economic Consequences of the Peace* (London, 1920).

The foreign policies of the totalitarian states and the policy of appeasement has long fascinated students of international relations, and much has been written about them. For studies of Hitler's policies, see Gerhard L. Weinberg's two-volume, *The Foreign Policy of Hitler's Germany* (Chicago, 1970 and 1980); Chapter 19 of Gordon A. Craig, *Germany* (New York, 1978); Klaus Hildebrand, *The Foreign Policy of the Third Reich* (Berkeley, CA, 1974); Norman Rich, *Hitler's War Aims* (New York, 1973); Alan Bullock, *Hitler: A Study in Tyranny* (New York, 1962 ed.); Hitler's own revealing autobiography *Mein Kampf*; and, due to the capture of German documents after the Second World War, there is

a most unusual multivolume collection published by the U.S. Department of State entitled *Documents on German Foreign Policy, 1918–1945*. For Soviet diplomacy, interesting insights can be gained from Robert Service, *Lenin* (Cambridge, MA, 2002); Alan Bullock, *Hitler and Stalin: Parallel Lives* (New York, 1991); Anthony Read and David Fisher, *The Deadly Embrace* (New York, 1988); Andre Gromyko and B. N. Ponomarev (eds.), *Soviet Foreign Policy, 1917–1945* (Moscow, 1981); Teddy Uldricks, *Diplomacy and Ideology: The Origins of Soviet Foreign Relations* (Beverly Hills, CA, 1979); and Adam Ulam, *Expansion and Coexistence* (New York, 1974 ed.). Studies of appeasement include Frank McDonough, *Hitler, Chamberlain, and Appeasement* (Cambridge, 2002); Richard Davis, *Anglo-French Relations Before the Second World War: Appeasement and Crisis* (New York, 2001); Keith Robbins, *Appeasement* (London, 1997); D. C. Watt, *How War Came* (London, 1989); Larry Fuchser, *Neville Chamberlain and Appeasement* (New York, 1982); Telford Taylor, *Munich: The Price of Tragedy* (New York, 1979); and Martin Gilbert, *The Roots of Appeasement* (London, 1966).

— 4 —

A Postwar System of Security: Great-Power Directorate or United Nations?

The war that began when Hitler's columns sliced into Poland in September 1939 lasted for almost six years and, long before it was over, proved to be more truly global than its predecessor, more total in its demands on resources and in its impact upon all classes of society, much more sophisticated in its weaponry, and infinitely more destructive in its results. It is estimated that perhaps 50 million people met their deaths during this conflict and that, for the first time, more civilians lost their lives than combatants. As if that were not enough, the war ended with the revelation of the existence of a new category of terrible weapons of mass destruction that promised to multiply these dreadful statistics beyond the limits of human comprehension if statecraft could not control the use of force on a major scale in the future. Allied leaders thus realized that if they failed to establish a viable postwar security system at the end of this most devastating war in human history and at a time of an unabated diplomatic revolution, they would face the prospect of a repetition of the cataclysm—or something even worse.

PLANS FOR A POSTWAR SYSTEM OF SECURITY

Thoughtful statesmen often attempt to learn lessons from history that might guide them in their formulation and implementation of policy, as we shall see in more detail in Chapter 7. In this regard, all those leaders of what British prime minister Winston Churchill called the "Grand Alliance" of the Second World War wanted to succeed where their predecessors after the First World War had failed. They desperately desired to avoid any repetition of those mistakes that had led to the Great Depression, the collapse of the League of Nations, the emergence of aggressive totalitarian regimes, the rejection of existing treaties and international law, genocide in the Holocaust, and a catastrophic global war.

One of the mistakes made by the victors in 1918, as they saw it, was to enter into an armistice with the German government without decisively defeating its armed forces and occupying the country. This led to subsequent

claims by rabid nationalists that Germany had not really been defeated but that the army had been "stabbed in the back" by traitors. Resolved not to make this mistake again, the victors of 1945 agreed this time to convincingly defeat, disarm, and occupy Germany, Italy, and Japan. Other important lessons were drawn from the previous failure to develop economic policies and cooperation that would avoid future depressions and thereby encourage more lasting peace. Plans therefore called for the removal or reduction of trade barriers, the creation of a new monetary system to stabilize currencies and facilitate the flow of capital, and the institution of policies that would expedite healthy economic development and postwar reconstruction. They also came to believe, importantly, that the recent past had taught them that gross violations of human rights constituted serious threats to the peace. Nations like Nazi Germany that violated the rights of their own people became dangerous to the countries around them. They thus began to insist that the world needed to acknowledge that a profound relationship existed between *individual* security, *national* security, and *international* security.

Still another lesson had a particular poignancy for the United States: that one of the most serious mistakes in bungling the peace after the First World War had to do with the fact that it had gone its own way and remained largely unwilling to participate as partners with other nations in the international system. America not only had deliberately refused to join the League of Nations, but even had tried in the early years to thwart some of its efforts. In addition, the United States pursued a policy of isolationism, often popular at home for reasons of domestic politics with its emotional appeal against "foreigners" and "entangling alliances," but fatal for diplomacy and collective security. This contributed significantly to the perception among the aggressors that they had little to fear, and thus led to the onset of the Second World War. With this acutely in his mind, President Franklin Roosevelt (the first president to leave the country in wartime and the first to travel by airplane) determined that this time it was essential for both national self-interest and for the world to not follow the same path, but instead to cooperate with other peace-seeking countries in developing and maintaining a postwar security system.

Such a system, in Roosevelt's view, needed to be based on the realities of power. It could not possibly work unless the states that possessed preponderant force agreed to cooperate in creating and in preserving the peace. He knew that only the fear of a common enemy had brought them together as successful coalition partners in war. Once victory removed that threat, serious differences could easily emerge. The defeat of Nazi Germany, to illustrate, would create a power vacuum in Europe with serious implications for the vital interests of both the Western powers and the Soviet Union. If no international system was created in sufficient time to provide a framework within which they could cooperate, dangerous consequences would result.

How might one accomplish this task? One possibility would be to simply allow unbridled competition among the major powers like in the eighteenth century to generate countervailing forces to keep each other at bay. But this arrangement had failed in the past to bring about peace or deter Napoleon

from trying to achieve hegemony, and was likely to fail again. Britain would be too weak by itself to provide a military counterweight to Russian domination on the European continent, and any long-term American commitment appeared at the time to be highly uncertain. Another possibility would be to try to reduce the potential for conflict by giving each of the major powers generous spheres of influence in areas of special interest to them. Such an approach was initially favored by Churchill and Stalin, who privately reached an agreement for dividing up the Balkans between them. But in the end Roosevelt refused to agree to this scheme. He believed that it would be unstable, would not eliminate competition among the major powers for very long, and would create two armed camps that might well lead to another war. In addition, he doubted that public opinion would support postwar plans for a crass spheres-of-influence agreement that directly contradicted the principles of human rights and self-determination that had been written so prominently and publicly into the Atlantic Charter and Declaration of the United Nations as the peace aims for which they were fighting.

The only alternative, Roosevelt concluded from his reading of lessons of the past and his own personal attendance at the Paris Peace Conference in 1919, was a continuing coalition of the victors to maintain the peace settlement modeled on the concert system established by the Congress of Vienna after the defeat of Napoleon. He called it the "Grand Design." He knew that one of the most serious problems after the First World War was that the final treaties had been decided not by all of the Great Powers—but by only some of them. This not only led to a settlement that lacked widespread consensus and legitimacy, but to resentment and a desire on the part of those who had been excluded to overturn the result. Consequently, Roosevelt envisioned a new, postwar security system in which all of those possessing the greatest power—the United States, Britain, the Soviet Union, and, he hoped, eventually China—would form a consortium. These nations, forming a kind of executive committee, would be known as the "Four Policemen." They would possess exclusive authority to decide on the use of military force, but would consult with each other as a means of collective rather than unilateral decision making. Together they would use force and statecraft to meet whatever threats might arise.

Like the other plans for a postwar system of security, this "Grand Design" suffered from problems. In the first instance, it did not take into account the interests of the many other nations in the world who had actively participated and sacrificed in the war. Military victory had been secured by the combined forces and sacrifices of forty-six different nations, and each believed that it most assuredly had earned a voice in the peace settlement. Not one of these wished to be excluded from participation in whatever new security system might be created or to have the sovereign equality of states be jeopardized or preempted by only four nations acting arrogantly and exclusively by themselves. Proposals like this, observed one diplomat from another country that had contributed much to the war effort, amounted to no more "than an undertaking by the Great Powers to meet from time to time to discuss the

situation as it appeared, and to decide what might best be done, and in taking this course they expected the assistance and collaboration of the smaller powers." Such an approach, if left unmodified, he and many others argued, would negate the very principle of democracy for which the war had been fought and would thereby fail to keep the peace. Still another problem with Roosevelt's initial plan emerged with public opinion at home and abroad, which strongly supported multilateral diplomacy, collective security, and internationalist foreign policies. Since so many sacrifices had been required of civilians during the war, and since domestic political support would be critical for sustaining any postwar security policy, this opinion had to be taken very seriously. As one foreign minister declared: "As we have had a people's war, so shall we now have a people's peace."

For the critics of all the other postwar security system plans, the best solution appeared to be the creation of and greater reliance upon a new and broader international security organization stronger and more effective than the League of Nations, as already promised by the Moscow Declaration of October 1943. After so much wartime suffering and widespread public endorsement for this proposal, Roosevelt eventually reached the same conclusion himself. He came to believe that the best way for the United States to pursue its own interests and secure its own defense would be to work collectively with others countries and, when necessary, accept certain self-imposed restraints and sacrifice its own freedom of action for the common good. Once this vision became clear in his mind, he worked tirelessly to build even further support for a new organization at home and abroad. With history very much on his mind, he wanted to avoid Woodrow Wilson's mistake of failing to secure support in the Senate, and thus went before a joint session of Congress. Here he declared with as much energy and his weakened body could muster: "This time, as we fight together to get the war over quickly, we work together to keep it from happening again." Roosevelt said that the time had arrived

> to spell the end of the system of unilateral action, the exclusive alliances, the spheres of influence, the balances of power, and all the other expedients that have been tried for centuries—and have always failed. We propose to substitute for all these a universal organization in which all peace-loving nations will finally have a chance to join.

This new organization was the United Nations, which would come to be described as "the most ambitious order-building experiment in history."

Force and Statecraft as Envisioned by the United Nations Charter

The delegates of the victorious coalition of the Second World War who met in San Francisco in 1945 to negotiate the details of the United Nations were not wild-eyed idealists. They had just barely survived a catastrophe of "total" war lasting six years and genocide replete with some of the worst cases of

man's inhumanity to man ever known. Hard-earned experience had taught them that their victory against the aggressors had not come from words or moral suasion, but by the application of superior power made possible by the combined armed forces and resources of many different nations. Thus, they understood far better than most the dilemmas presented by both the necessity and the dangers of force in the world. They realized that they had a common interest in keeping the peace and were realistic in their calculation that it could be secured in the future only if they continued their cooperation through collective action. Given this experience, they knew that the threat or the use of force would be very much a part of the statecraft of the new United Nations, as it had been a part of all systems of security in the past. The question for them was not how to eliminate force, but rather how to use diplomacy to guide and control it. They drew upon lessons they had learned from recent history and described their purpose simply enough in the very first sentence of the United Nations Charter: "to save succeeding generations of the scourge of war, which twice in our lifetime has brought untold sorrow to mankind." Toward this end, they importantly pledged as members in partnership to "refrain in their international relations from the threat or use of force against the territorial integrity or political independence of any state" and "to unite our strength to maintain international peace and security, and to ensure by the acceptance of principles and the institution of methods, that armed force shall not be used, save in the common interest."

Agreement upon this critical phrase of "the common interest," what it meant, who would define it, and how it would be defended, it was envisioned, would be determined among the members of the United Nations by diplomatic negotiation (a subject we shall explore at length in Chapter 8). According to the Charter, general principles of cooperation in this international system, including those dealing with human rights "for all without distinction as to race, sex, language, or religion," would be discussed in the General Assembly, where every country was represented equally and where recommendations could be made. Actual authority for action on specific problems and crises, however—especially those involving force and statecraft— would reside in the much smaller Security Council, on which the five most powerful nations at the time (the United States, Britain, France, the Soviet Union, and China) held permanent membership and the power to veto any action they did not like. The preferred means of resolving conflict, of course, would be diplomacy, or what Chapter VI of the Charter called "Pacific Settlement of Disputes." Should these efforts fail, however, Chapter VII on "Action with Respect to Threats to the Peace, Breaches of the Peace, and Acts of Aggression" specifically addressed armed force.

Those who founded the United Nations realized that any viable international system required consensus upon a number of basic principles and normative rules that restrained their competition. As the new American President Harry Truman, who had worked diligently to overcome innumerable obstacles in order to keep Roosevelt's vision alive, quite realistically declared at the San Francisco Conference, "We all have to recognize, no matter how

great our strength, that we must deny ourselves the license to do always as we please." This principle applies to all matters of international relations, but particularly to those dealing with force and statecraft. More specifically, the framers of the Charter understood that no system could survive for very long if they could not reach a consensus upon shared norms or if actors unilaterally decided on their own when they were justified in threatening or using armed force against others.

They spent considerable time, therefore, wrestling with the question of exactly what would constitute a legitimate use of armed force as an instrument of policy. After intense and extensive negotiation, they agreed that only two kinds of cases would qualify:

1. *Self-defense* in the event of an actual armed attack. According to the text,

> Nothing in the present Charter shall impair the inherent right of individual or collective self-defense if an armed attack occurs against a Member of the United Nations, until the Security Council has taken measures necessary to maintain international peace and security. Measures taken by Members in the exercise of this right of self-defense shall be immediately reported to the Security Council and shall not in any way affect the authority and the responsibility of the Security Council under the present Charter to take at any time such action as it deems necessary in order to maintain or restore international peace and security.

2. *International enforcement action.* The Security Council alone was empowered to act as the legitimate authority to "determine the existence of any threat to the peace, breach of the peace, or act of aggression and [to] make recommendations, or decide what measures shall be taken . . . to maintain or restore international peace and security."

Should measures short of the threat or use of armed force prove to be inadequate, according to the Charter, the Security Council "may take such action by air, sea, or land forces as may be necessary," including measures of coercive diplomacy with force and statecraft used in demonstrations, blockades, or other operations. As partners in this endeavor, all members obligated themselves to contribute armed forces, assistance, and facilities when called upon to provide the collective air, sea, or land forces as might be necessary to carry out "the measures decided upon by the Security Council." The Charter called for this body to be assisted by a Military Staff Committee composed of the chiefs of staff of its permanent members that would help to develop plans for "the establishment of a system for the regulation of armaments" as well as for "the application of armed force." Over time these plans came to include various arms control agreements and arms embargoes as well as shows of force for deterrence or coercive diplomacy, peacekeeping forces, humanitarian intervention, and even war itself. In addition, the Charter allowed for the possibility of regional security arrangements.

These provisions on force and statecraft marked a strong and explicit endorsement of shared responsibility for collective security. That is, they proclaimed that any aggression or threat to peace and security would be met by

the concerted efforts of the members of the Security Council and the collective military contributions of the members of the United Nations acting in the name of the international community as a whole.

The Charter thus went considerably further than any previous treaty in history and gave every impression that the United Nations had the very real possibility of satisfying the requirements of a viable security system. There seemed to be an agreement among the member states on the basic aims and objectives for creating and maintaining the system as a whole. The purposes of the organization were stated boldly: to take effective collective measures to maintain international peace and security, to develop universal principles of international law and friendly relations among states, and to promote and encourage respect for human rights and fundamental freedoms. In addition, there appeared to be a structure appropriate to the number of states interacting with each other with a hierarchy among them and a recognition that new states likely would be added through time. The design deliberately created a global organization rather than one of merely European membership, and a clear distinction was made between all nations in the General Assembly and the most powerful on the Security Council. It also recognized, however reluctantly, the necessity of the Great Powers cooperating within, and to a certain extent, dominating the organization. Consequently, it seemed as though the founders of the United Nations had reached a consensus on values and procedures that would help them maintain the system as a whole, including the legitimacy of using force when necessary. It is not at all surprising, therefore, that when the Charter was signed in June 1945 many commentators hailed it as "an epoch-making document" marking "one of the great moments in history."

Not everyone, of course, reacted so positively. Some critics complained bitterly that the United Nations Charter did too little. In their minds it did not fully define what was meant by expressions like "the common interest" or "self-defense." It promoted the principle of international human rights in Article 1, yet supported the Westphalian principle of sovereign nation-states and asserted in Article 2 that the organization could not interfere with matters essentially within the domestic jurisdiction of states. Moreover, according to some commentators, the Charter made little effort to eliminate armed force, created an organization completely dependent upon whatever power its members—jealous of their own national sovereignty—were willing to give it, and granted far too much authority and privilege to the five countries that controlled the Security Council. *Time* magazine, for example, compared the idealistic promises made during the war with the end result and concluded in disappointment that the final agreement represented no more than "a charter for a world of power." Others complained that the Charter did too much. This applied particularly to those who valued the interests of their own nation much more than the needs of the international system. They feared that involving others in collective decision making would jeopardize their sovereignty and thereby restrict their freedom of action to pursue their own national interests as they saw fit.

A number of seasoned diplomats and observers viewed the United Nations Charter neither as a magnificent achievement that would suddenly create heaven on earth nor as a tragedy that would destroy the cherished nation-state. Instead, they saw it in the historical context of the time and considered diplomacy to be the art of the possible, balanced somewhere between the cynics and the perfectionists, and knew that no nation or group could obtain everything that they wanted over the course of a mere two months of negotiations. They believed that those who assembled at San Francisco had accomplished about as much as, if not more, than could realistically be expected given the traditional practices, the circumstances of the war, the magnitude of the tasks, the differences between the Great Powers and the medium and small nations, the divergent opinions of the states and non-governmental organizations (NGOs), and the often exaggerated hopes for the future. They likely would have agreed with the later conclusion of political scientist John Stoessinger, who writes:

> In not attempting the impossible, the founders of the United Nations were realists. But in seeking to go to the very limits of the possible, they were also visionaries. And necessarily so, for the idea of the United Nations had to take into account the full import of the cruel paradox that, in the nuclear age, the national sovereignty of nations would have to be controlled by an international order, but that this international order would have to be created and even controlled by sovereign nations. The plan therefore had to combine the dictates of national power with those of international order.

It is precisely this paradox and the need to combine both the specific interests of sovereign nation states with the broader interests of the international order that presents the central dilemma of any system. Collective security cannot work without the support of the most powerful, and collective security cannot work unless the most powerful can also be restrained.

Statesmen present at the creation of the United Nations had no idea about the magnitude of the challenges and diplomatic problems that lay ahead. As they attempted to learn lessons of history, however, they did know that any system required that its members be willing to make sacrifices for the common good and able to adapt to new developments in order to survive. With this in mind, Truman announced: "This Charter, like our Constitution, will be expanded and improved as time goes on. No one claims that it is now a final or a perfect instrument. It has not been poured into a fixed mold. Changing world conditions will require readjustments."

CHANGING WORLD CONDITIONS AND READJUSTMENTS

The smiles and cooperation that characterized the drafting and approval of the Charter did not last long, and changing conditions occurred much sooner than expected. Within only months, for example, the world watched with deep concern as the United States, Britain, and the Soviet Union failed to reach agreement at the Potsdam Conference on several fundamental features of the postwar settlement, as the Soviets moved troops further into positions in Eastern

Europe and entered the war in Asia, and as the Americans dropped the atomic bombs on Hiroshima and Nagasaki. With the end of the war and the elimination of the common threat that had held them together, the coalition partners of the "Grand Alliance" rapidly fell victim to their own rival national passions, histories, interests, and perspectives. Two days after the beginning of the very first session of the United Nations, the presence of Soviet troops in Iran was brought before the Security Council, quickly followed by a countermove by the Soviet Union complaining about British forces in Greece and India and the refusal of Europeans to end their domination over colonial empires. Shortly thereafter, Winston Churchill delivered his famous "Iron Curtain" speech condemning Soviet behavior in forcibly imposing Communist regimes and securing their grip upon Eastern Europe. One diplomat painfully observed that "the clouds were gathering fast," and these gave every indication that the world (as we shall see in more detail in the next chapter) was rapidly moving from one war into another, known as the Cold War.

Given these ominous treads, global opinion strongly supported the belief that the United Nations remained the best hope for peace and security in a world rapidly becoming dangerous again. Even as late as 1948 national public opinion polls revealed a clear majority within the United States enthusiastically supporting the organization and its mission. Some of this popular enthusiasm for the new organization was doubtless selfish and based on the hope that it would reduce American responsibilities in foreign affairs. Perhaps much more of it was the result of unreasonable expectations by those who wanted to believe that the new organization would be able to act on the international level in much the same way as a government acts on the national level. This was a profound misunderstanding, for as Brian Urquhart, a long-time civil servant posted to the United Nations, writes, "The UN is nothing like a government. It has no sovereignty or power of sovereign decision-making. It is an association of independent, sovereign states which depends for its effectiveness on the capacity of its members to agree and cooperate." At times, this capacity to place the needs of the international system as a whole above those of the nation-state appeared quite limited.

This was certainly true in the case of the most powerful of its members. The dream of maintaining Great Power cooperation and consensus on principles that had formed the basis of Roosevelt's initial "Four Policemen" idea, for example, never materialized. Instead, national interests prevailed and a pattern quickly emerged that one scholar has described as "the moral infection of Great Power disagreement." Britain and France resisted any attempts to dismantle their colonial empires, China experienced revolution and the coming to power of Mao Zedong and his Communist Party, and the Soviet Union and the United States seriously escalated their Cold War conflict. Domestic opinion, which had so strongly supported the United Nations, began to erode. In the United States, for example, public opinion was outraged when other members of the General Assembly did not agree with American positions or dared to criticize racial segregation or lynching. Congress frequently complained about the undue influence of "foreigners" and "the colored peoples

of the world" within the United Nations or the organization's failure to prevent crises that Congress itself had not foreseen. The Red-baiting hysteria surrounding the McCarthy investigations provided a steady stream of highly public accusations that United Nations staff members and certain delegates were "manifesting fellow-traveler tendencies," tainted with a "scarlet hue," and "crypto-Communists."

In addition, there was a tendency on the part of many governments to belittle the achievements of the United Nations while blaming their own foreign policy failures upon it, to insist that it stay out of their own particular areas of interest, or even attempt to emasculate it. President Truman's self-styled realist secretary of state, Dean Acheson, contemptuously referred to those who supported the United Nations as the "True Believers" with "universal Plumb plans," criticized the Charter as "impracticable," complained that the Secretariat was no more than "a crowded center of conflicting races and nationalities," and revealed his attitudes about gender roles by asking V. L. Pandit of India, who became the first female president of the United Nations General Assembly: "Why do pretty women want to be like men?" During the critical crisis caused by Great Britain's admission that it could no longer support the governments of Greece and Turkey against external threats, Acheson bypassed the United Nations completely and eliminated all but the barest reference to it in the Truman Doctrine. A similar disregard, bordering upon contempt, came in 1948 when the organization was desperately seeking a plan for partitioning Palestine that might avert a war between the Arabs and Jewish settlers, whose numbers were being rapidly augmented by refugees from Europe. This time the United States negated the negotiations and precipitated hostilities in the area by abruptly recognizing an independent state of Israel without even informing its own delegation to the United Nations of its intentions. Others tried to deliberately subvert agreement, as the British demonstrated during one series of diplomatic negotiations when they sent ciphered instructions to their representative to kill a particular proposal, but "not give the impression that we are being obstructive. We suggest our right course is to play for time, leaving it as far as possible to other delegations to bring out the difficulties." On other occasions the permanent members of the Security Council cast vetoes if they wished to stop an action they regarded as contrary to their national interests.

When the Great Powers agreed with the Secretary-General of the United Nations, they lavished him with praise, but when they disagreed, they poured out their contempt and criticism. When the first Secretary-General, Trygve Lie of Norway, condemned the North Korean attack on South Korea in 1950, for example, the United States praised him for his courage, "unusual skill," "good judgment," and "understanding mind." When he publicly supported membership in the United Nations for the new Communist-led People's Republic of China, however, the Americans condemned him as no more than "a stooge of the Reds." The British and the French sharply criticized his brilliant successor, Dag Hammarskjöld from Sweden, for trying to "interfere" during their military action against Egypt in Suez Crisis of 1956, but then

eagerly welcomed his offer to provide a face-saving way out of their mistake with some semblance of dignity. When Hammarskjöld worked to facilitate the massive process of decolonization or tackled the problem of apartheid in South Africa, the Soviet Union praised him for his courage and wisdom. But when he worked to build an independent nation in the Congo against Soviet interests, they not only criticized him for being a "tool of the colonialists and capitalists" but actually went so far as to demand that the position of Secretary-General be abolished and replaced with a three-man directorate, or *troika*, representing the three major power blocs, Hammarskjöld correctly viewed this vehement attack as a challenge not just to him, but to the principles of the Charter and the larger international security system and its future. He therefore announced that he would leave whenever the majority of members wanted him to leave, but that he would not be intimidated by Great Power pressure designed to emasculate the organization. "It is not the Soviet Union or, indeed, any other big powers who need the United Nations for their protection," he said, "it is all the others." In the end he declared: "I shall remain at my post." When he finished, the General Assembly rose to a standing ovation with emotional approval and applause.

One of the reasons for this widespread global support, of course, resulted from the fact that the United Nations demonstrated remarkable success in adapting to new circumstances by facilitating one of the most momentous developments of the twentieth century: the collapse of colonial empires, the emergence of newly independent nations and peoples, and the subsequent geographical expansion of the international system itself. A dramatic indication of what was coming could be seen in the San Francisco Conference itself, held not in Europe but in the United States and not on the shores of the Atlantic but rather on the Pacific. When the delegates created the United Nations in 1945 only fifty-one states were admitted to membership. Among these, only three came from Africa, and among the mere three from Asia, only China was independent of colonial rule. The great majority of member states therefore represented the countries of Europe, the Americas, and the white Commonwealth countries. Many assumed that this political dominance by the Western world would continue in the future as it had for centuries in the past. They were wrong, for in the simple words of one observer, "time had run out." Within a single decade, and in the name of national self-determination, twenty-five new states had joined the United Nations. By the end of 1965, forty-one more had been added, swelling the membership to 117. This development marked one of the greatest political changes in international history, shifting power from whites to nonwhites and liberating more than 1 billion people from Western colonial rule in Asia and Africa.

It also dramatically changed the composition and the agenda of the United Nations. The increased membership meant that the West lost its majority in the United Nations. As a consequence, America, Britain, and France became less and less able to control the direction and outcome of negotiations, and thus even less inclined than they had been in the past to view the organization as a major factor in their foreign policies. Perhaps more importantly, it

greatly accelerated that dimension of the diplomatic revolution whereby the cultural homogeneity that had characterized diplomacy for so long increasingly gave way to heterogeneity. The shared similarity among diplomats of the European-dominated past was steadily being replaced with great differences of race, language, religious values, socio-economic status, stages of development, and gender, among other factors. This development demonstrated the remarkable ability of the organization to realize its goal of becoming truly international in scope as well as adjusting to the growing number of states interacting with each other within the system as a whole. The United Nations became the one place in the world where all blocs and ideologies could genuinely be represented. Nevertheless, such diversity brought about new and different assumptions about the nature of international society. These states were not as interested in the political and military questions that absorbed the attention of the superpowers and their allies of the Cold War, not as eager to maintain a static system frozen at the time of the 1945 victory, not as willing to continue letting the Great Powers alone determine the agenda of the United Nations, and more aware that genuine peace and security have many aspects. Consequently, their attention focused on self-determination and decolonization, "people-to people" diplomacy, relief operations, the plight of refugees, social and economic development, education, medical care, the environment, cultural activities, the rule of law, and other global problems like human rights.

Indeed, this expansion of the number of actors and the new majority of small- to medium-sized states provided one of several important features of the diplomatic revolution that increasingly helped to place the whole subject of human rights high on the international agenda. There were others as well. When the technological invention of television was brought into the public deliberations of the United Nations, for example, it forced representatives to explain abusive actions and policies of their governments under journalistic scrutiny and before the eyes of the world as never before in history. This growing openness or transparency of diplomacy in this international forum, in turn, encouraged segments of public opinion to organize pressure groups of very vocal human rights NGOs who passionately believed that respect for individual dignity was closely related not only to freedom and justice but to peace and security. It is for this reason that they often were willing to challenge traditional concepts of the prerogatives of national sovereignty and the relationship between states and their citizens or subjects by stressing the connection between individual, national, and international security and by developing standards and mechanisms that might bring life and substance to the vision proclaimed in the landmark Universal Declaration of Human Rights. Innovative treaties, treaty-monitoring bodies, and special procedures dealing with genocide, racial discrimination and apartheid, civil and political rights, economic and social rights, torture, and women and children, for example, all sought to provide protection to those who suffered and to transform victims of abuse from being mere objects of international pity into actual subjects of international law.

The United Nations also became the one permanent piece of diplomatic machinery that could be put to work at a moment's notice for crisis management (a topic to be discussed in Chapter 11). It served as the one body in which both traditional and democratic, bilateral and parliamentary forms of diplomacy could be brought to bear upon critical problems and crises in order to avert great danger. The United Nations had great importance as a place in which informal contacts could be made, and hints and signals passed outside of official diplomatic channels, thereby sometimes saving the major powers from the possible consequences of their own mistakes. American ambassador Philip Jessup and Soviet ambassador Jacob Malik discovered the great advantages of this during their private conversations in 1949 that prepared the way for the termination of the crisis precipitated by the Soviet blockade of Berlin. The British and the French received the same benefits during the Suez Crisis of 1956. Two years later, after an antigovernment coup in Iraq, the landing of U.S. Marines on the shores of Lebanon (meant to avert a threat that never materialized and, in retrospect, never seems to have been very likely) might have invited a Soviet response had Hammarskjöld not devised a face-saving formula by which the United States withdrew its troops. Any doubts about this potential for crisis management by the United Nations should have been put to rest after the Cuban Missile Crisis of 1962, when the world stood on the brink of possible nuclear annihilation. In this situation, Secretary-General U Thant of Burma initiated direct communication with the Americans, Soviets, and Cubans, offering his good offices, serving as a go-between, suggesting a way to avert catastrophic war, providing an impartial point of reference to which each side could respond without giving the appearance of weakness or surrender, and creating an international observation and supervision mechanism to ensure that the terms of settlement would be acceptable to the antagonists. In the end, courage and wisdom on the part of many individuals made it possible to manage and defuse the crisis, but those who knew the inside details gave Thant and the United Nations considerable credit. A highly unusual and joint official letter sent shortly thereafter stated clearly: "On behalf of the Governments of the United States of America and the Soviet Union we desire to express to you our appreciation for your efforts in assisting our Governments to avert the serious threat to the peace which recently arose."

Tense and dangerous crises, of course, always provide reminders to any international security system not only of the need to try to avert and, if that fails, to manage them, but also of the fact that it may be necessary at times to use force in statecraft in response to threats to peace. As already discussed, this had been envisioned by the Charter itself. In working through changing world conditions and in making adjustments to new circumstances, therefore, the United Nations began to develop policies to do precisely this. Explicit provisions in the text for the possibility of force against aggressors or threats to the peace always provided some measure of deterrence. But if this failed, much more was needed. In an effort to practice coercive diplomacy, for example, the Security Council invoked its authority under Chapter VII in 1966

and imposed the first-ever mandatory sanctions against the white minority regime of Rhodesia, and did so until power was transferred to a black majority and the country was renamed Zimbabwe. Similarly, the United Nations rebuked the white minority government of South Africa on many occasions for its racial policies and control over Namibia, calling for a mandatory arms embargo imposed by the Security Council in 1977. This was lifted only when Namibia gained its independence and when the government repealed its apartheid laws.

Members of the United Nations also dealt directly with matters of force and statecraft by creatively developing both the concept and the practice of international peacekeeping forces, or what was described as "using soldiers as the servants of peace rather than as the instruments of war." They sent military forces into troubled areas to monitor cease-fires, create buffer zones, and keep warring parties apart. These forces were authorized by the Security Council and operated in the collective name of the United Nations, being deployed in, among other places, the Suez Canal and Sinai Peninsula (1956–1967), the Congo (1960–1964), Cyprus (1964 to the present), the border between India and Pakistan (1965–1966), the Golan Heights after the Arab-Israeli War of 1973, Lebanon (1978 to the present), and beginning in 1987 to Afghanistan, Pakistan, Iran, and Iraq. By 1988, nearly 500,000 United Nations personnel from fifty-eight nations had been involved in peacekeeping operations. Viewing all this activity, often in nearly impossible circumstances, one feels compelled to ask where the world would have been during these years without the United Nations.

The most serious use of force and statecraft by the United Nations involved those actual enforcement actions taken under Chapter VII of the Charter—that is, the use of armed forces to enforce the decisions of the Security Council dealing with acts of aggression. This involved collective military intervention on behalf of states that had been attacked. The first of these occurred when the Soviet-equipped armies of North Korea launched a massive and well-coordinated surprise attack against South Korea in June 1950, thus beginning the Korean War and marking, in the words of one observer, "one of the great watersheds in the history of the organization." Since the Security Council found itself foolishly being boycotted by the Soviets at the time, it was able to avoid any veto of opposition and thereby invoke its power to employ as-yet-untested machinery for collective security and approve support for military intervention to defend the south. This effort received even further endorsement when the General Assembly passed its "Uniting for Peace Resolution" indicating strong support from the international community for this United Nations–sponsored use of armed force. Although the coalition of nations who contributed personnel numbered nineteen, the majority came from South Korea and the United States under the command of American General Douglas MacArthur. In the end, but only after the involvement of the Chinese and a considerable loss of human lives, the North Korean invaders were repulsed and the Korean peninsula largely restored to its prewar status quo.

It was the Security Council, in what has been called one of the most important decisions in the history of the organization, that also authorized the use of collective force when Saddam Hussein of Iraq suddenly and brutally invaded neighboring Kuwait in 1990. President George Bush the elder, who had previously served as a U.S. ambassador to the United Nations and therefore understood the importance of diplomacy and collective decision making in serious international problems, worked diligently with other leaders like Mikhail Gorbachev of the Soviet Union to create agreement on mobilizing a coalition to force Saddam out of Kuwait. Efforts were first made to use coercive diplomacy (a strategy to be discussed in Chapter 10) to persuade the aggressor to yield to the demands of the international community. When this failed, the Security Council acted with unusual speed and decisiveness in authorizing the actual use of military force to expel Iraqi troops from the territories they had occupied and "to restore international peace and security to the area." A coalition of thirty-two different nations led by the United States thus launched a massive land, air, and sea assault called Operation Desert Storm in January 1991 and in less than seventy-two hours successfully routed the Iraqi forces and restored independence to Kuwait. As one contributor in *Foreign Affairs* wrote, "the concept of collective security as envisioned in the UN Charter worked" and "the United Nations reclaimed a major role in international relations." In the United States this was popularly hailed as an American victory because the bulk of the air and ground operations were launched by American troops. But it became clear enough that the United States could not have borne the political, military, and financial requirements of the operation alone, and it was realized afterward that in serious matters of force and statecraft unilateral action often can create far more serious problems than it ever attempts to solve.

In retrospect, much of the criticism suffered by the United Nations as an international security system seems mean-spirited and ill-informed. Its successes in preventive diplomacy, peacemaking and peacekeeping, setting normative standards, promoting and protecting human rights, mediation in conflict resolution, crisis management, adaptability to an expanding and heterogeneous world, and the solid record of accomplishment made by its subsidiary bodies specializing in humanitarian aid and relief are undeniable. In addition, its support for the principle of the inviolability of borders, under which borders cannot be changed unilaterally or by military means, was seen clearly in the collective use of armed force in both Korean and Persian Gulf wars. These achievements become even more impressive when seen in light of the sheer complexity of problems in the world, Great Power vetoes, the failure of members to honor their pledges under the Charter, and the fact that the organization can never do any more than its sovereign member states allow it to do. Nevertheless, throughout much of its history there ran a current of carping and criticism from those with exaggerated expectations, governments that in moments of frustration blamed the organization for problems in which they had themselves been impercipient before the event and unwilling to act after it, or adamant opponents such as those in the United

States who viewed the United Nations was an alien and dangerous presence. From his years as Secretary-General, Dag Hammarskjöld tried to provide some perspective on all of this by employing nautical imagery:

> On the seas we sail, we have to face all the storms and stresses created by the ideological, economic, and social conditions of our world. Aboard this new *Santa Maria* we have to meet the impatience of those sailors who expect land on the horizon tomorrow, also the cynicism or sense of futility of those who would give up and leave us drifting impotently. On the shores we have all those who are against the whole expedition, who seem to take a special delight in blaming the storms on the ship instead of the weather.

Despite these kinds of problems, however, support for the United Nations as an indispensable organization in times of mounting international complexity remained strong throughout most of the world. Indeed, 1988 saw such a string of impressive United Nations successes that the often critical *New York Times* declared it "The Year of the UN." In April, after seven years of peace talks led by a United Nations mediator, the Soviet Union agreed to withdraw its forces from Afghanistan. In August, on the basis of a Security Council plan, Iran and Iraq agreed to a cease-fire in a bloody and wasting conflict that had lasted for ten years. In the same month, Secretary-General Javier Pérez de Cuéllar of Peru secured the agreement of Greece and Turkey to hold new talks on the problem of uniting Cyprus, which had poisoned relations between the two NATO allies for more than twenty years. He also began talks in August that promised to end the war between Morocco and the Algerian-backed Polisario guerillas for control of the western Sahara. In September the 10,000-member United Nations peacekeeping forces received the Nobel Peace Prize for their significant—and sometimes vital—contributions to international peace and security. In December, United Nations forces began to monitor the withdrawal of Cuban forces from Angola in accordance with the terms of an agreement between the Angolan, South African, and Cuban governments, mediated by the United States. During the same month, Yasser Arafat's declaration before a meeting of the General Assembly in Geneva that his Palestine Liberation Organization (PLO) would recognize the binding nature of pertinent United Nations resolutions and the right of the state of Israel to exist created the necessary conditions for American Secretary of State George Shultz's decision to establish formal contact with the PLO in the hope of alleviating the Palestine problem. Finally and significantly, and in sharp contrast to several decades of his country's determined efforts to limit the power of the organization and its secretary-general, Mikhail Gorbachev made a breathtaking announcement before the General Assembly that he intended to reduce the number of Soviet troops and called for a greatly enhanced role for the United Nations in global affairs.

There also was something more. Despite its restraints and imperfections, and all of the political problems and magnitude of the challenges and criticisms that confronted it, the United Nations managed to keep its ambitious order-building experiment alive. It continued to hold out the vision created in the wake of a catastrophic war of a larger international community of men

and women united by a common desire for a security system with peace and justice rather than a world constantly divided by human frailties and the anarchy of parochial national interests. Those who supported it knew that sometimes they would succeed and sometimes they would fail, but that, through time, they hoped that their efforts would matter.

As a result of these considerable achievements and a realization that the struggle might be worth the effort, the United Nations began to attract considerably more attention than it had at other times. In fact, a number of states appeared to have discovered new virtues in the organization they had often neglected and abused. This, in turn, led many thoughtful observers and participants to devote considerable attention to how it might best respond to the needs of the future. "After forty-five uncertain, and sometime bleak, years, the prospects for international cooperation are brighter than at any time since the Second World War," concluded a 1990 study entitled *A World in Need of Leadership: Tomorrow's United Nations*. Others expressed similar enthusiasm for an increasingly dynamic and invigorated role for the United Nations. In a special issue called "Beyond the Year 2000: What to Expect in the New Millennium," *Time* predicted that in the future "cooperation with the UN will be the norm" and that "the world will have to utilize the powers of the UN" to solve its global problems.

Whether these predictions would be realized or not would depend—as always—upon whether the Great Powers would let it happen. Historically, any viable order of international peace and security had been dependent upon a very high level of consensus upon interests, principles, values, and restraints among those with the greatest power. In this regard, the United Nations was no different. It depended completely upon the support that the major powers gave over the years. Only the future, of course, would tell whether this could occur. The years ahead would be dramatic and would entail major upheavals in the international system and the diplomatic revolution with profound implications for force and statecraft. These would involve the collapse of the Soviet Union, the emergence of the United States as the world's only superpower, new crises in Europe and Asia, the escalation of violence in the Middle East, violence within states and genocide in the former Yugoslavia and Africa, "failed" states and "rogue" regimes, the proliferation of weapons of mass destruction, and the attacks of September 11, 2001 and the rise of global terrorism. Further turmoil arose when the George W. Bush administration decided to replace the Charter's clear prohibition against the threat or use of force against the territorial integrity or political independence of any state with the announcement that the United States would take preventive action, including forcible "regime change," by launching a war against Iraq in 2003. But these developments lay in the future and remained as yet unknown. Until then, as we shall see in the next chapter, the ability of the United Nations to function as its founders intended depended heavily upon what happened in the struggle known as the Cold War.

SUGGESTIONS FOR FURTHER EXPLORATION

The history of plans for a postwar security system and the creation of the United Nations can be found in Stephen C. Schlesinger, *Act of Creation: The Founding of the United Nations* (Boulder, CO, 2004); Townsend Hoopes and Douglas Brinkley, *FDR and the Creation of the U.N.* (New Haven, 1997); Alexander L. George, "Domestic Constraints on Regime Change in U.S. Foreign Policy: The Need for Policy Legitimacy," in *Change in the International System*, O. R. Holsti, R. M. Siverson, and A. L. George (eds.) (Boulder, CO, 1980); Robert A. Divine, *Second Chance: The Triumph of Internationalism in America During World War II* (New York, 1967); Ruth Russell, *A History of the United Nations Charter* (Washington, DC, 1958); United Nations Information Organization, *Documents of the United Nations Conference on International Organization, San Francisco, 1945* (London and New York, 1946–1955); and Forrest Davis, "Roosevelt's World Blueprint," *Saturday Evening Post*, April 10, 1943.

Discussions and analyses of the United Nations as a whole can be found in Thomas Weiss, David Forsythe, and Roger Coate, *The United Nations and Changing World Politics* (Boulder, CO, 2004); Lawrence Ziring et al., *The United Nations: International Organization and World Politics* (Belmont, CA, 1999 ed.); Stanley Meisler, *The United Nations: The First Fifty Years* (New York, 1997); Paul Gordon Lauren, "The Diplomats and Diplomacy of the United Nations," in Gordon A. Craig and Francis Lowenheim (eds.), *The Diplomats, 1939–1979* (Princeton, 1994); Brian Urquhart, *Ralph Bunche* (Boston, 1993), and his excellent autobiographical account based upon a long career within the organization, *A Life in Peace and War* (New York, 1987); John Stoessinger, *The Might of Nations: World Politics in Our Time* (New York, 1979); the pioneering Inis Claude, Jr., *Swords Into Plowshares* (New York, 1971 ed.); and Thomas Hovet, Jr., "United Nations Diplomacy," *Journal of International Affairs*, 17 (1963). On the relationship between human rights and peace and security, see Paul Gordon Lauren, *The Evolution of International Human Rights: Visions Seen* (Philadelphia, 2003 ed.).

For specific treatment of force and statecraft in the United Nations, see Donald Daniel and Bradd Hayes (eds.), *Beyond Traditional Peacekeeping* (New York, 1995); Paul Diehl, *International Peacekeeping* (Baltimore, 1995 ed.); Michael Howard, "The Historical Development of the UN's Role in International Security," in Adam Roberts and Benedict Kingsbury (eds.), *United Nations, Divided World* (Oxford, 1993 ed.); United Nations, *The Blue Helmets* (New York, 1990 ed.); the pioneering Michael Harbottle, *The Impartial Soldier* (London, 1970); and Gabriella Rosner, *The United Nations Emergency Force* (New York, 1963). On the legal aspects, see Mary Ellen O'Connell, *International Law and the Use of Force* (New York, 2005).

Additional information about this period and these issues can also be found on the Internet, including the home page for the United Nations at www.un.org; the Security Council at www.un.org/Docs/sc; a discussion of the larger system at www.unsystem.org; the UN High Commissioner for Human Rights at www.unhchr.ch; and the UN Department of Peacekeeping Operations at www.un.org/Depts/dpko. See also the reports of organizations with long-standing interests in the United Nations including the United Nations Association of the USA at www.unausa.org, and the Stanley Foundation at www.stanleyfoundation.org.

— 5 —

The Cold War

The Cold War became one of the longest and most costly international conflicts in human history. It was fought first and foremost between the United States and the Soviet Union—along with their respective allies and the Chinese—who employed as many tools and methods as possible to gain advantage, including economic aid, propaganda campaigns designed to influence public opinion and create hatreds, espionage, covert action and political assassinations, military assistance, the construction and maintenance of rival alliances, guerrilla and counterinsurgency warfare, proxy wars, and a massive and terrifying arms race with weapons capable of obliterating opponents. The Cold War was wider in scope than any of the world wars, for it was not only fought on every continent but, considering the space race, *over* each one as well. It also was one of the costliest of all of the world's conflicts. It is estimated that the United States alone, for example, spent more than $13,000,000,000,000 on this struggle. As the authors of *A Hard and Bitter Peace: A Global History of the Cold War* describe it, "For decades the Cold War dominated international relations, profoundly influenced the global economy, and to some extent affected the life of almost everyone on the planet." The magnitude and totality of this struggle could not help but create profound consequences for the diplomatic revolution, domestic politics and institutions, foreign and national security policy, any attempts to create a viable international system, and, most certainly, force and statecraft.

THE ORIGINS AND ESCALATION OF THE COLD WAR

In one sense, the Cold War began with the Bolshevik Revolution in 1917 when Lenin announced that there always would be unremitting hostility between the capitalistic West and the communistic Soviet Union. But the immediate origins of what came to be called the Cold War emerged at the end of the Second World War once military victory eliminated the threat of a common enemy. The hopes that the coalition that had cooperated to win the war would continue to cooperate to win the peace were dashed. The United States, Great

Britain, and France took strong exception to Stalin's attempts to create pro-Soviet regimes in Eastern Europe, particularly in Poland, and vehemently protested his refusal to coordinate policies in the postwar occupation zones of Germany. The Soviets, for their part, expressed their anger when the British and the French sought to move back into their colonial possessions and when the United States announced that it would brook no opposition to its sole occupation of defeated Japan. They also grew deeply suspicious about the American monopoly of a weapon that would become one of the defining characteristics of the Cold War with a profound impact upon subsequent force and statecraft: the atomic bomb.

Weapons in the past had always been characterized by their limited capacity to destroy. The state of technological advance imposed severe limits on their lethality, and large masses of people could never be killed at an instant. It is for this reason that Clausewitz could write with confidence about the historical experience of war genuinely being a continuation of policy by other means. Yet, this feature of all previous weapons changed with America's successful 1945 test in the desert at Alamogordo, New Mexico. As he personally witnessed the first-ever explosion, General Thomas Farrell was nearly overwhelmed when he realized that a critical threshold had just been crossed. He wrote in his official report:

> The effects could well be called unprecedented, magnificent, beautiful, stupendous, and terrifying. No man-made phenomenon of such tremendous power had ever occurred before. . . . Thirty seconds after the explosion came first, the air blast pressing hard against people and things, to be followed almost immediately by the strong, sustained, awesome roar which warned of doomsday and made us feel that we puny things were blasphemous to dare tamper with the forces heretofore reserved to The Almighty.

Serious complications followed almost immediately. In 1946 Winston Churchill visited Fulton, Missouri, and delivered his famous "Iron Curtain" speech, accusing the Soviets of brutally imposing pro-Communist regimes across Eastern Europe, warning that there might be no limits to their expansive and proselytizing tendencies, and declaring: "I am convinced that there is nothing they admire so much as strength, and there is nothing for which they have less respect than weakness." Stalin angrily shot back in response that this was nothing less than a declaration of war against the Soviet Union.

Further confrontations appeared in rapid succession. One exploded in Iran as the British and Americans struggled with the Soviets over access to vital Middle East oil concessions and Stalin supported an ill-fated revolt in Azerbaijan. Another erupted in Turkey as the former allies of the "Grand Alliance" now contested who would control the strategic Bosporus and Dardanelles straits that guarded naval access between the Mediterranean and the Black Sea. Yet another broke out in Greece when the British-supported government suddenly found itself teetering on the very verge of collapse in a civil war against Communist insurgents. Then, in 1947, the United States dramatically enunciated the Truman Doctrine, arguing that in the emerging

"Fate of Nemesis": The Atomic Age Begins (Getty Images)

global ideological struggle it would provide assistance to all countries willing to resist Communism. "At the present moment in world history," Truman declared, "nearly every nation must choose between alternative ways of life"—either democracy characterized by free institutions or totalitarianism based upon terror and political oppression. The Soviets responded by describing this speech as "venomous slander," "aggressive," "hostile and bellicose," and specifically designed "to interfere in the affairs of other countries on the side of reaction and counter-revolution." They, in turn, imposed tighter controls over Eastern European countries occupied by their troops, ruthlessly eliminated political opponents and replaced them with more reliable Moscow-controlled Communists, and in 1948 seriously escalated the Cold War by dismantling the democratic government of Czechoslovakia and installing a puppet government of their own while cutting off all Western access into West Berlin by instituting the Berlin Blockade.

This vicious cycle of action and reaction continued with other events and crises in the relations between the West and the Soviet Union. Each side believed that it was behaving in a justifiably defensive manner in response to obstructionist and threatening behavior on the part of the other. The more sympath-

etic images that Soviet and Western leaders held of each other at the end of the Second World War were now transformed and darkened; each side perceived the other as having hostile intentions. This is not to say that the Cold War was caused merely by mutual distrust and misperception—its origins lie deeper than that, as already indicated, in the real and important conflicts of interest that existed between the two sides—but there is no doubt that they were seriously exacerbated by the psychological dynamics of conflict escalation. False perception and psychological phenomena of this kind are, unfortunately, familiar in international relations, as they are in everyday life. Oliver Wendell Holmes once remarked that in any argument between two persons, six persons are involved: the two as they actually are, the two as they see themselves, and the two as they see each other. No wonder, Holmes exclaimed, that the two talk past each other and become angry! In international affairs, the same sort of psychological multiplication process is apt to take place, with much the same effects.

When government leaders deliberately seek to manipulate negative images of their adversaries in order to generate—and then exploit—fear, this problem becomes even worse. In this regard, the Cold War enormously accelerated that feature of the diplomatic revolution whereby domestic political pressures and public opinion came to exert great influence upon international relations. Secretary of State Dean Acheson, for example, freely admitted in his memoirs that he consciously denigrated Soviet intentions and portrayed Russia as aggressive as a means to gain approval for President Truman's policies. Others of both political parties followed suit, finding hysteria, Red-baiting, and exaggeration of Communist threats useful political expedients. Republican Senator Joseph McCarthy became so successful, in fact, that the term "McCarthyism" was coined to describe these activities. He and his rabid followers gained sufficient political power to actually purge the professional diplomats known as the "China Hands" from the Department of State by accusing them of being "sympathizers," "fellow-travelers," or "card-carrying" members of the Communist Party. The price for doing so, of course, was a further diminution of the professionals and the elimination of America's expert eyes and ears in Asia for many years to come.

Communists, for their own part, also discovered that fear of an enemy can be a very useful tool. Soviet leaders thus depicted the United States as leading the "monopoly bourgeoisie of capitalism," "fascist sympathizers," and "reactionary elements of world imperialism" bent on subversion, military adventurism, aggression, and global domination. When Mao Zedong and his Chinese Communist Party came to power in Beijing in 1949 and created the People's Republic of China as a result of their victory over the American-supported Chiang Kai-shek, they wasted no time in portraying the United States as a

> paradise of gangsters, swindlers, rascals, special agents, fascist germs, speculators, debauchers and all the dregs of society. This is the world's manufactory and source of all such crimes as reaction, darkness, cruelty, decadence, corruption, debauchery, oppression. . . . Everyone who does not want the people of his beloved fatherland contaminated by these criminal phenomena is charged with the responsibility of arising to condemn her, curse her, hate her, and despise her.

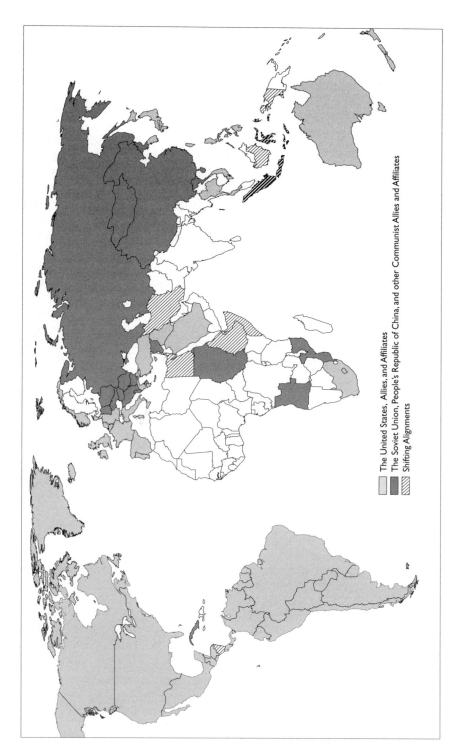

Divisions of the Global Cold War: Formal Alliances and Informal Alignments

The United States, Allies, and Affiliates

The Soviet Union, People's Republic of China, and other Communist Allies and Affiliates

Shifting Alignments

Such a volatile combination of dramatically differing perceptions and seriously conflicting national interests escalated the Cold War to dangerous proportions. In a few years, both the United States and the Soviet Union gained such strength that they came to be known not just as Great Powers, but as superpowers. Each moved quickly to organize and then dominate their respective alliance systems. Under the policy known as Containment, for example, the United States sought to stop the spread of Communism first by intertwining economic development with security guarantees and then creating the North Atlantic Treaty Organization (NATO) in 1949 with Canada and Western Europeans, adding Greece and Turkey shortly thereafter. This was followed by bilateral military agreements with the Philippines and Japan in Asia, ANZUS with Australia and New Zealand in the Pacific, the Southeast Asian Treaty Organization (SEATO), and the Central Treaty Organization (CENTO) in the Middle East. In a particularly important move, the United States strongly pushed to have West Germany, which had been an arch enemy defeated only ten years before, added to NATO in 1955. The Soviets condemned this development as an "imperialistic program of oppression and aggression" and a "revival of German militarism," accused the Americans of seeking "world supremacy," and immediately responded by creating the Warsaw Treaty Organization with its puppet states in Eastern Europe, which it claimed was "a purely defensive organization directed towards safeguarding the peace and security of the peoples of Europe and the rest of the world."

Whether an alliance is offensive or defensive is often in the eyes of the beholder, however, and deterrence to prevent a war by one side easily may be perceived as aggression by the other. Whatever the intentions of the Americans and the Soviets at the time, the fact remains that their policies created a powerful, bipolar structuring of the world during the Cold War. There were not enough major powers of relatively equal strength to make possible the reemergence of a genuine multipolar balance-of-power system. Each superpower sought to dominate its weaker allies and to keep their hegemonic alliances under tight control. There was very little flexibility in making alliances or, for most weaker states, in switching them. Both the United States and the Soviet Union viewed any possible loss of an ally, even a small one, with great apprehension for fear of its effects on the rest of their alliances and thus the perceived credibility of their military threat.

These threats, like those of all military alliances in the historical past, relied heavily on trained troops armed with weapons. But during the diplomatic revolution and the Cold War there was something new, and weapons came to be distinguished as either "conventional" or nuclear. The human capacity to destroy had never known such unlimited possibilities, and this suddenly caused serious practical and ethical problems for those charged with formulating and implementing foreign policy involving force and statecraft. In a thought-provoking 1957 book entitled *Nuclear Weapons and Foreign Policy*, scholar Henry Kissinger observed:

> In Greek mythology, Nemesis, the goddess of fate, sometimes punished man by fulfilling his wishes too completely. It has remained for the nuclear age to experience the full irony of this penalty. Throughout history, humanity

has suffered from a shortage of power and has concentrated all its efforts on developing new sources and special applications of it. It would have seemed unbelievable even fifty years ago that there could ever be an excess of power. . . . Yet this is precisely the challenge of the nuclear age. Ever since the end of the Second World War brought us not the peace we sought so earnestly, but an uneasy armistice, we have responded by what can best be described as a flight into technology: by devising ever more fearful weapons [of mass destruction].

In this new environment, the Americans and the Soviets competed in the most serious, expensive, and potentially deadly arms race in human history. The Soviet Union broke the monopoly of the United States by exploding its first atomic weapon in 1949. In response, Truman's newly created National Security Council issued a policy statement in 1950 known as NSC-68, later described as "one of the key historical documents of the Cold War." It predicted a future of indefinite tension and monolithic Communist aggression on a global scale and saw the contest ahead as primarily military in nature. It therefore called for more force: a tripling of America's defense budget, a massive increase in conventional weapons, and the building of a nuclear arsenal. The United States thus successfully exploded the first hydrogen or thermonuclear bomb in 1952, and the Soviets responded in kind three years later. The race was on, and both sides rushed to build not only their nuclear arsenals but ever more sophisticated means of delivering these weapons to their adversaries. After the first successful launch of the Sputnik satellite by the Soviet Union in 1957, the race entered space. Both developed intercontinental ballistic missiles (ICBMs) with a range of over 3000 miles and thus capable of an attack from one continent to another. With weapons such as these capable of destroying an enemy without ever having to launch an armed invasion as in the past and doctrines like "Massive Retaliation" threatening annihilation against any attack, it is not surprising that both sides began to speak of all-or-nothing Mutual Assured Destruction, or MAD.

The Cold War also escalated the use of intelligence activities for national security. Statecraft throughout time sought to obtain valuable foreknowledge that might help to avoid surprise attacks or threats. Government leaders historically and typically used a variety of means, including spies, to collect and analyze information and to protect their own intelligence sources and methods. During the Cold War, however, these traditional practices were augmented by the increased use of covert action, or secret activities designed to influence the course of events in another country such as destabilization campaigns or political assassination by the superpowers to advance their interests. The Soviets developed their massive apparatus of the Committee for State Security (KGB) to coordinate these activities, drawing upon a long national experience with the czar's secret police. The United States, which had always resisted establishing a permanent intelligence organization, now created the Central Intelligence Agency (CIA). The tenor of the time is well reflected in an infamous memorandum from a top-secret government report recommending that American intelligence operations jettison accepted normative standards and ethical restraints and instead become

more effective, more unique, and if necessary, more ruthless than that employed by the enemy. No one should be permitted to stand in the way of the prompt, efficient, and secure accomplishment of this mission. . . . It is now clear that we are facing an implacable enemy whose avowed objective is world domination by whatever means and whatever cost. There are no rules in such a game. Hitherto acceptable norms of human conduct do not apply. If the U.S. is to survive, long-standing American concepts of "fair play" must be reconsidered. . . . We must learn to subvert, sabotage, and destroy our enemies by more clever, more sophisticated, and more effective methods than those used against us.

Seeking Restraints Through Deterrence, Diplomacy, and *Détente*

Such unremitting hostility, unrestrained competition, and recommendations to become "more ruthless" and observe "no rules" created diplomatic problems of the first magnitude. Without some form of restraint, as we shall see in Chapter 12, international competition becomes unbridled; now, in the Cold War, the superpowers appeared to be heading toward destruction. Every major crisis, whether in Berlin during 1948, 1958–1959, and 1961, in Cuba during 1962, or in any other location around the world, always was coupled with the fear that *any* shooting war between American and Soviet forces, no matter at how modest a level initially, could escalate completely out of control. It therefore gradually became evident to the United States and the Soviet Union that, despite their intense rivalry, they in fact shared one essential goal: the prevention of a Third World War and what would very likely bring about their mutual annihilation.

The practical task thus was how to compete and use force and statecraft in the Cold War while at the same time avoiding thermonuclear war. This presented both superpowers with a serious dilemma and the necessity of choosing between preferred objectives and risks. Policy makers in the United States, for example, constantly had to confront a built-in conflict during every major international crisis: how to contain the international Communism, or to roll it back if possible, and simultaneously to avoid a catastrophic war. Democratic and Republican administrations alike attempted to cope with this dilemma by considering whether in a given situation the *balance of power* between the Soviet bloc and the free world alliance was at stake. If a Communist success in a certain area might critically weaken them or their allies, and the balance of power was thereby threatened, American policy makers demonstrated a willingness to do what they could to prevent that particular outcome, even though to do so meant accepting some danger of war, as in Korea. If, however, a Soviet success would not seriously undermine the ability of the Western alliance to contain the future spread of Communism, then they generally were inclined not to overreact in ways that would risk armed confrontation. This explains why President Dwight Eisenhower, despite all of his talk about the "liberation" of Eastern Europe, greatly feared the possibility of provoking the Soviets into a war and thus refused to intervene when the Hungarians called for help during their revolution in 1956.

In some ways this use of balance-of-power criterion in making critical foreign policy decisions during the Cold War was similar to its employment by the Great Powers in the classical European system. But it is important to recognize that a "balance of terror" is not the same as a multipolar, system-wide balance of power, especially when the major actors lacked a consensus on basic values. The major difference, however, was the fear not of limited conventional war, as in the past, but of a thermonuclear holocaust. The sheer destructiveness of modern weapons thus provided a powerful deterrent by discouraging both superpowers from resorting to war as a way of preventing an undesired change in the existing balance of power if to do so would result in a direct military clash between the United States and the Soviet Union.

The strategy of deterrence, which we will explore in detail in Chapter 9, at times played an invaluable role in restraining the Americans and the Soviets in their rivalry. But this occurred only in the most dangerous of circumstances and certainly did not cover all the other aspects of Cold War competition or of American-Soviet relations. Critics complained that the strategy of Containment, despite its steadfastness, was nevertheless static, purely reactive, and, of particular importance, provided no place for diplomatic initiative. They argued that it often failed to utilize the techniques, institutions, and practices of diplomacy developed over many centuries to help resolve conflict and to facilitate relations among states.

Fearing the consequences of such neglect as well as the lost opportunities for negotiation that would result, some policy makers sought to use what they had learned about diplomacy in the past or to develop some other new method of seeking restraint, regulating rivalry, and promoting some level of cooperation. These included experimentation with crisis prevention, crisis management, and accommodation, or, as we shall see in Chapter 8, negotiation to arrive at agreements to settle or moderate certain conflicts. On some occasions agreements were reached on arms control, as with the decision in 1958 to temporarily suspend nuclear testing. Sometimes these negotiations were conducted within the context of the United Nations when it suited the interests of the superpowers. But most of the time they were not, for neither the Americans nor the Soviets were prepared to consistently honor their obligations under the Charter. Efforts to find restraints thus were episodic and inconsistent and often remained less than effective as long as the two superpowers persisted in placing a higher priority on winning the Cold War.

The dangers of rejecting diplomacy became painfully evident. In 1958 major confrontations occurred over the Taiwan Straits and over Berlin. Two years later the Soviet Union announced that it had shot down an American U-2 spy plane deep inside its own territory, and armed struggle broke out in the Congo and in Laos. After his earlier bombastic threat to the West that "we will bury you," Soviet leader Nikita Khrushchev declared in 1961 that the Soviet Union would actively support "wars of national liberation" in the developing world and then forced another crisis over Berlin, issuing menacing threats and employing what came to be called "atomic blackmail" that resulted in U.S. soldiers being sent down the Autobahn in armored vehicles,

the building of the hideous Berlin Wall, and fear of nuclear war so intense that thousands of Americans began building fallout shelters in their backyards. The same year witnessed the United States launch the ill-fated Bay of Pigs invasion of Cuba in an attempt to overthrow its Communist leader Fidel Castro and the decision of President John F. Kennedy to increase production of nuclear weapons and the missiles to deliver them, double the number of ships in the navy, enlarge the army, build up the number of tactical air squadrons, create special counterinsurgency forces to fight Communist guerrillas, and expand covert actions in order to provide what he described as a "flexible response" to as many contingencies as possible. It is thus not surprising that the experienced U.S. ambassador in Moscow, Llwellyn Thompson, worried aloud: "All of us are going to be dead!"

The potential for catastrophe was revealed with vivid and frightening clarity by the most acute confrontation of the entire Cold War: the Cuban Missile Crisis. In the late summer and early autumn of 1962, and despite his promises to the contrary, Khrushchev secretly deployed a number of medium- and intermediate-range ballistic missiles to Cuba capable of obliterating most cities in the United States. When this was discovered by U-2 reconnaissance aircraft, it brought the superpowers—and the world with them—to the brink of thermonuclear war. Rejecting the recommendation from his military advisors on the Joint Chiefs of Staff to use force immediately by launching an air strike against the missile sites, but nevertheless threatening to do so if necessary, Kennedy undertook a naval blockade of Cuba instead. American and Soviet forces were placed on full alert, Strategic Air Command planes went airborne, and Kennedy announced ominously from the White House he would "regard any nuclear missile launched from Cuba against any nation in the Western Hemisphere as an attack by the Soviet Union on the United States, requiring a full retaliatory response upon the Soviet Union." This brought the antagonists, in the words of one leading participant, "eyeball to eyeball," and the world held its breath. In the end (as we shall analyze in more detail in Chapters 10 and 11), the combination of crisis management by both Washington and Moscow, successful diplomacy at the United Nations, and Kennedy's use of the strategy of coercive diplomacy proved effective. The crisis ceased with a quid pro quo in which Khrushchev agreed to remove the missiles in return for a conditional pledge by Kennedy not to invade Cuba in the future as well as a secret agreement to remove U.S. Jupiter missiles from Turkey.

Once it became more fully understood just how close the world had come to a nuclear holocaust, the impact of the Cuban Missile Crisis became even more profound. Indeed, this crisis marked one of the major turning points of recent history. It had a dramatic, catalytic effect by facilitating a transition from the era of the acute Cold War to a more serious search for a less dangerous and more viable international system, thereby demonstrating that international crisis sometimes can have positive results in improving relations between previously antagonistic states. This interesting feature is conveyed by the Chinese character for "crisis," which has two meanings. The first is the same

as the standard meaning of the word in English, that is, a threat or danger. The second connotation, however, is something quite different—not "threat" but rather "opportunity." This insightful double meaning suggests that a crisis can loosen things up, lead policy makers to question and to revise if not totally discard some of the old beliefs and policies that led to the confrontation in the first place, and perhaps make them more willing to strike out in new directions.

The Cuban Missile Crisis produced precisely this kind of effect. It moved American and Soviet allies to explore ways that they might begin to somehow disengage from the military blocs controlled by their respective superpowers. It also stimulated those new states emerging from the process of decolonization and the bitter legacy of racial discrimination to avoid being drawn too closely into the wakes of either the United States or the Soviet Union by focusing on what they called the Third World and "nonalignment." In the same way, the Cuban Missile Crisis produced a dramatic shift in the thinking of both Khrushchev and Kennedy. Samuel Johnson once remarked to Boswell that nothing concentrates the mind so well as the prospect of being hanged in a fortnight. It is not an exaggeration to say that the terrifying horror of the missile crisis provided a form of shock therapy for both leaders. It brought to a head long-standing dissatisfactions and fears of the Cold War on both sides and strengthened their determination to move away from its worst aspects and seek better alternatives. Almost immediately, for example, the two superpowers reached what they called the Hot-Line Agreement calling for a cable link between Washington, D.C., and Moscow in order to provide direct, secure, and rapid communication to assist in crisis management during any future confrontation. Shortly thereafter they negotiated the Limited Test Ban Treaty prohibiting nuclear tests from being conducted in the atmosphere and marking the first major arms control agreement during the Cold War. Potentially more significant was the fact that the American image of the Soviet opponent and attitudes toward diplomacy appeared to undergo significant modification. Kennedy and other American leaders began to view the Soviet Union as a *limited adversary* rather than as a total enemy and began to see the virtues in diplomatic negotiation. This change was conveyed by Kennedy in a moving speech at American University in which he spoke of peace "as the necessary rational end of rational men" and called upon his fellow citizens to reexamine their dogmatic views on the Cold War if they wanted to save humanity from annihilation. He called for a renewal of traditional diplomacy and warned his listeners not to take "a distorted and desperate view of the other side, not to see conflict as inevitable," and not to regard "accommodation as impossible and communication as nothing more than an exchange of threats." In sharp contrast with previous presidential statements (and in some that would follow), he went on to say about the Soviet Union that "no government or social system is so evil that its people must be considered as lacking in virtue."

Heartening as this sounded, the fact remains that people learn different lessons from history and from their own experiences, leaders change, and

entrenched habits and patterns of thought are hard to break. The assassination of John Kennedy in 1963 and the removal of Khrushchev from office the next year robbed the world of the two leaders who had been most transformed by the dangers of confrontation. After the initial terror of the Cuban Missile Crisis had passed, many American policy makers and members of the public alike began to believe that the "success" in Cuba had been the result not of careful diplomacy, but rather of being tough and firmly resolved to threaten and use force if necessary. Moreover, they found themselves continuing to be dominated by the tendency to overlook distinctions and see problems in universal terms. It was the persistent and indiscriminate assumption that all Communist regimes were identical, linked, and deadly, for example, that fostered the so-called "domino theory" (arguing that if one country fell to Communism, others automatically would do the same) and drew the United States into the long agony of the Vietnam War. This involvement, made against military advice and without any careful assessment of costs and possible outcomes, was escalated dramatically by President Lyndon Johnson who ordered the bombing of North Vietnam for the first time in 1965. Ultimately, the United States would send more than half a million troops to the conflict. At the same time, Khrushchev's successor, Leonid Brezhnev, committed the Soviet Union to supporting America's adversaries in Vietnam, escalated the arms race by more that tripling the number of strategic Soviet ICBMs, invaded Czechoslovakia in 1968, and announced with the Brezhnev Doctrine that he would intervene militarily in other countries as well if Soviet and/or Communist interests were threatened further.

Trouble brewed in Asia as well. At home, the People's Republic of China under Mao persecuted opponents and then descended into the chaos of the Cultural Revolution which consumed perhaps a half million Chinese lives. Its ideological fervor also permeated foreign affairs. The government charged the Soviets of losing their revolutionary zeal and becoming "soft" on capitalism, stationed troops on the border that they shared with the Soviet Union, and contributed to the division known as the Sino-Soviet split that greatly altered the relationship between the world's two largest Communist powers. It also directed its wrath against the United States, accusing America of imperialism and racism, supporting the hated rival regime in Taiwan, killing its soldiers earlier during the Korean War and its allies in Vietnam, arming its neighbors like Japan and the Philippines, excluding it from assuming its rightful membership in the United Nations, and denying it diplomatic recognition.

The renewed international dangers as well as the severe domestic costs resulting from these problems and others involving various allies and client states forced leaders to look again at the value of diplomacy. To describe their efforts, they came to use the French word *détente*, taken from traditional diplomacy and meaning a relaxation of tension between adversaries by means of a conscious policy of engagement, cooperation, and accommodation. Each, for their own reasons, had strong self-interests in creating some restraints for the Cold War competition that threatened to engulf them. For this reason, the Americans and the Soviets began by negotiating an arms control agreement

known as the Nuclear Non-Proliferation Treaty (NPT) in 1968. The following year West German Chancellor Willy Brandt initiated a policy he called *Ostpolitik,* or Eastern Policy, designed to improve relations with the governments of the Soviet bloc in Eastern Europe, including Communist East Germany, and reach an agreement on the divided city of Berlin. The Chinese had their own fears as well, not the least of which were Soviet threats and military confrontation on the Sino-Soviet border, and therefore began to consider better relations with the United States as a means of providing a counterweight to the Soviet Union. For their part, the Soviets feared the deployment of new U.S. multiple warhead missiles (MIRVs) aimed at them, continued unrest among their satellite states, and what they regarded as the unpredictable Chinese, and thus sought to find a means of relaxing a number of Cold War tensions.

These interests coincided with those of the United States, which found itself trying desperately to extricate itself from the Vietnam War that was consuming lives, creating tensions with allies, wrecking havoc with other diplomatic efforts, escalating budget deficits in order to finance the war, and (especially after the American invasion of Cambodia in 1970) increasing domestic opposition and dividing the country more than at any time since the Civil War. At the same time, it was constantly engaged in antagonism with the Chinese Communists and confrontation with the Soviets pursuing an unrestrained arms race with strategic weapons and developing an anti–ballistic missile (ABM) system to defend itself against the U.S. arsenal. This helps to explain why Richard Nixon, despite his reputation as a militant anti-Communist and ardent Cold Warrior of the past, declared in his inaugural address that America was prepared to enter a new "era of negotiation" with its major adversaries. But he and his new national security advisor, Henry Kissinger, wanted *détente* not just to mean a relaxation of tension to advance American interests in foreign policy but hopefully to reach accommodation with former antagonists in order to eventually create a strategic balance of power. Their own political experience and understanding of history convinced them that all nations, including their own, based their policies on what they perceived as their national interests and that this factor should be used to create some arrangement of accommodation to maintain peace and security.

To begin this process of creating restraints by using mutual interests, Nixon and Kissinger began negotiating constructive relationships with their major rivals, trying to ignore ideological differences and issues of human rights, and using a combination of threats as "sticks" and inducements as "carrots" in a triangular configuration of power for leverage. They began with China, for as Nixon had written in an article in *Foreign Affairs,* "any American policy must come urgently to grips with the reality of China. There is no place on this small planet for a billion of its potentially most able people to live in angry isolation." As a result of lengthy negotiations, the Chinese agreed to reduce their level of support for America's adversaries in the Vietnam War and to settle the issue of Taiwan by peaceful means, while the United States promised to gradually reduce its troops in Asia and to reverse their long-standing

opposition to Beijing's admission into the United Nations, and both agreed to establish offices for permanent diplomatic representation in Washington, D.C., and Beijing. Nixon, who personally traveled to China in 1972 to meet Mao Zedong and solidify these agreements, described his trip as "a week that changed the world."

The most critical element of *détente*, of course, involved the two major superpowers of the Cold War, and many agreements ranging from trade and technical exchanges to strategic weapons were signed in a very short period of time. In 1971, for example, the United States and the Soviet Union signed an accord on Berlin, a treaty prohibiting the emplacement of nuclear weapons on seabeds or ocean floors, and agreed to participate in a wide-ranging security conference on Europe and a separate discussion on mutual and balanced reduction of forces. The next year Nixon and Brezhnev signed two arms control agreements based upon their negotiations known as the Strategic Arms Limitation Talks (SALT) placing limits on their offensive and defensive strategic missiles. "Never before," announced Kissinger, "have the world's two most powerful nations . . . placed their central armaments under formally agreed limitation and restraint." They also signed an accord called "Basic Principles of Relations" to define new norms and rules of cooperation and competition, pledging to prevent the development of situations that might dangerously exacerbate their relations, to do their utmost to avoid military confrontations, and to "exercise mutual restraint in their relations and be prepared to negotiate and settle differences by peaceful means." At the 1973 summit in Washington, D.C., the two leaders further signed the "Agreement on the Prevention of Nuclear War," promising to consult and "to refrain from the threat or use of force" against either "the other party" or "the allies of the other party" in situations that might raise the threat of nuclear holocaust.

PERSISTENT PROBLEMS AND THE FINAL DEMISE OF THE COLD WAR

Given all these agreements, it was not at all difficult to imagine the world moving away from the intense rivalry of the Cold War. The efforts to create new restraints and to regulate conflict appeared to have a reasonable chance of success. But, as we have seen from historical experience, such efforts ultimately succeed only if the participants actually honor their commitments regarding the common aims and objectives they are seeking to advance and to follow the norms and procedures on which they have agreed. And this is done only if the participants regard it to be in their interest and can gain sufficient support to do so. *Détente* suffered from both of these problems and, by so doing, revealed much to us about the nature of efforts to create and maintain viable international systems for peace and security.

The expectation that the superpowers would act with greater restraint in their foreign policies, for example, was not always realized in practice. In fact, at times it seemed to be completely ignored. Both superpowers persistently refused to give up the economic, diplomatic, and military advantages that came

from being the world's two largest weapons manufacturers and exporters of arms sales to other nations and rebel factions. Each continued to support their respective client states in the Middle East, with the United States announcing that it was supplying an additional forty-eight modern Phantom jets to Israel and the Soviet Union responding with increased military supplies to Egypt and Syria, which they promptly used to launch an attack in October 1973. The resulting Arab-Israeli War, as we shall see in Chapter 11, immediately escalated into superpower confrontation and demonstrated that both sides were willing to ignore their mutual pledges by trying to intimidate each other, with the Soviets threatening to intervene with troops and placing their Air Force and Strategic Rocket Forces on full alert and the Americans moving to DEFCON III (the maximum defense condition state of readiness short of war) to simultaneously deter and coerce. Moreover, when the citizens of Chile democratically elected a Marxist leader, Kissinger responded that "I don't see why we need to stand by and watch a country go Communist due to the irresponsibility of its own people," and Nixon approved a covert operation to overthrow the government. This resulted in a military coup d'état that brought to power the repressive dictatorship of General Augusto Pinochet. The agreements similarly did little to restrain the Soviets and their support for what they called "progressive" and "liberation" movements in the Third World. All this raised serious doubts about whether the superpowers of the Cold War would place any restraints upon themselves or not, let alone think about the possibility of a larger international system as a whole.

Détente was also plagued by its failure to gather widespread legitimacy and support. Many countries, including a number of allies, complained that whatever understandings or accommodations had been made, there could be no such thing as a truly international "system" as long as the United Nations was ignored and they, as legitimate nation-states, were deliberately excluded from negotiations conducted in secret and from a triangular structure confined exclusively to the Americans, Soviets, and Chinese. This problem was compounded even further by the difficulty of gaining domestic endorsement. As we have seen, Franklin Roosevelt seriously worried about the need to secure public support as he made plans for his postwar security system. Kissinger himself had written about the importance of this same matter earlier in his incisive historical analysis of the foreign policies of Castlereagh and Metternich during the nineteenth century. "The acid test of a policy," he wrote, "is its ability to obtain domestic support. This has two aspects: the problem of legitimizing a policy within the government apparatus . . . ; and that of harmonizing it with the national experience." Ironically, Kissinger's own *détente* policy was to encounter, and then fail to pass, that same test.

Domestic support was difficult to secure, in part, because the pursuit of *détente* required a more sophisticated mental and emotional analysis than that of Cold War rivalry. Previous American leaders had developed and successfully exploited fear, hysteria, and a simplistic image: Communists were bad and anti-Communists were good, and that is all that one needed to know about international relations. The policy of *détente*, however, imposed the more

complicated intellectual task of viewing the Soviets and the Chinese as limited adversaries, neither completely friend nor foe, but something in between, depending upon circumstances. The nature of that something in the context of force and statecraft was not easy for many people to understand. Members of Congress and the public often were unable or unwilling to grasp the subtleties of a strategy that combined both sticks of punishment and carrots of incentive. Whenever the administration engaged in efforts and conciliation and the bestowal of benefits, critical hawks on the right complained that it simply rewarded Communist "adventurism" around the world and thus was nothing less than "appeasement." On the other hand, whenever the administration engaged in threats or punishments, critical doves on the left complained that America risked the outbreak of nuclear war or the descent down a slippery slope into another Vietnam disaster. Added to this was a growing distrust of government leaders after the Watergate scandal and revelations of shocking CIA activities conducted in the name of national security sufficient to cause Congress to pass the 1973 War Powers Act seeking to restrain a president's ability to commit armed forces abroad. Many Americans grew weary of such disputes and duplicity, of diplomacy that required subtlety and nuanced approaches, and of the distrust and acrobatics that accompanied balance-of-power maneuvers, and thus withheld their support.

Given all of these factors, it is not at all surprising that the process of *détente* came to resemble a roller coaster. As both Gerald Ford and then Jimmy Carter came to realize once they became president, especially at a time when opinion ran strongly about "no more Vietnams," the pursuit of consistent and effective foreign policy in the absence of support is difficult if not impossible. There were times when the superpowers found ways to successfully collaborate on areas of mutual concern and let pragmatism transcend ideological rivalry, as with the SALT II accords seeking to reduce a further escalation of the arms race. There were times when others would largely take the initiative in using diplomatic negotiation to reach accommodation and relax tension. This occurred, as we shall see in Chapter 8, when thirty-five nations negotiated the historic 1975 Helsinki Final Act at the Conference on Security and Cooperation in Europe (CSCE), making a direct connection between the human rights of individual security and national and international security, and pledging the signatories to "refrain in their mutual relations, as well as in international relations in general, from the threat or the use of force against the territorial integrity or political independence of any state, or in any other manner inconsistent with the purposes of the United Nations." But there were other times when the antagonism grew worse, as when the Soviets escalated their military buildup, intervened to support their side in the civil war in Angola and then enlisted Castro's Cuba to contribute additional weapons and eventually 11,000 combat troops to the struggle, or publicly rejoiced when American hostages were seized during the Iranian Revolution.

But the real *coup de grâce* was delivered when in December 1979 the Soviet Union forcefully invaded neighboring Afghanistan. This invasion rocked American leaders to the core and led immediately to a renewal of the Cold

War. A shaken and beleaguered Carter, who came into office with the intention of developing a more constructive foreign policy that stressed human rights, disarmament as compared to arms control, and working with the Soviets to create greater global stability, now responded by condemning the invasion as "the greatest threat to world peace since the Second World War." He then cut off sales of technology and grain to Moscow, withdrew SALT II from consideration by the Senate, substantially increased American military spending, accelerated the development of a Rapid Deployment Force to project military power abroad, and signed Presidential Directive 59 shifting U.S. strategic emphasis from merely deterring nuclear war to planning to actually fight and win it. *Détente* was dead.

If any doubts still existed about the renewal of confrontational attitudes in the Cold War, they ended when Ronald Reagan became president in 1981. In his very first press conference he depicted Soviet leaders like Brezhnev as dangerous and dishonorable individuals who were bent on world domination and who would "reserve unto themselves the right to commit any crime, to lie, to cheat" in order to achieve their goals. Later, in the most widely quoted speech of his presidency, he referred to the Soviet Union as "the focus of evil in the modern world" with all "the aggressive impulses of an evil empire." With this as the premise, he challenged the Soviets to "tear down that [Berlin] wall" and called upon Americans to realize their historical destiny by becoming fully engaged in the worldwide contest with Communism—"the struggle between right and wrong and good and evil."

It was in this spirit that the Reagan administration launched its counteroffensive. The first priority was to challenge the Soviet Union by a massive increase in conventional and nuclear weapons. This began with expenditures that funded the largest peacetime buildup in American history at a level doubling the national debt. Billions of dollars were spent on developing and deploying the B-1 bomber, "Stealth" aircraft capable of minimizing radar detection, Trident II submarines with their sub-launched ballistic missiles, air- and ground-launched cruise missiles, Pershing II intermediate-range missiles, the neutron bomb, and the powerful and highly accurate MX missile carrying ten independently targetable nuclear warheads. Reagan also resumed production of poison gas for chemical warfare and called for the development of a space-based defense system that mated laser weapons and other high-energy projection technology with computers in order to destroy Soviet missiles before they reached their targets. He described it as the Strategic Defense Initiative (SDI), while his critics dubbed it "Star Wars." From recently declassified documents and the memoirs of former Soviet leaders, we now know that they thought that the United States was preparing to launch a preemptive strike against the Soviet Union and believed SDI to be simply one step toward such an attack.

The second priority was to counteract any Communist attempts to spread its influence in the Third World. Even though the administration officials were seriously divided over exactly how force should be used in statecraft, as evident in the highly public disagreements between Secretary of Defense

Caspar Weinberger and the Joint Chiefs of Staff, on the one hand, and Secretary of State George Shultz, on the other, the United States intervened in the civil war in El Salvador, mined harbors in Nicaragua, invaded Grenada, and sent Marines to Lebanon. Various forms of support were given to authoritarian anti-Communist regimes, whatever their lack of democracy, rule of law, or record on human rights, such as those in Chile, El Salvador, Guatemala, Haiti, Pakistan, the Philippines, and South Africa, among others. Arms and money were covertly sent to militant Islamic rebels in Soviet-occupied Afghanistan (including one by the name of Osama bin Laden); anti-Communist forces in Angola, Cambodia, and Ethiopia; and the Contras against the Communist-backed Sandinistas in Nicaragua. The obsession to promote this fight was such that agents were not overly scrupulous in their efforts and specific laws passed by Congress to restrain or even prohibit certain actions were broken. The campaign against the Sandinistas, for example, was financed in part by laundered money gained from secret arms contracts with the same Iranian revolutionaries who had captured American diplomats, thereby creating the Iran-Contra scandal. But critics of individual aspects of Reagan's foreign policy were outnumbered by the majority of voters, who were inspired and heartened by the fact that America seemed strong again and movement had been restored to foreign policy after a decade of setbacks and disappointments.

Popularity at home, however, does not necessarily translate into popularity abroad, and Reagan's rhetoric and policies alarmed many other nations. Even close allies in Europe regretted the passing of *détente*, listened in horror as the Americans and Soviets openly spoke about force and "counterforce" strikes, and feared the coming of a new ice age. This was particularly true of Germany, where the Social Democratic party repudiated its own chancellor, Helmut Schmidt, because he supported the deployment of intermediate-range Pershing II and cruise missiles if the Soviets did not agree to remove their large number of mobile, land-based SS-20 missiles. A large and well-coordinated peace movement opposed this deployment and urged withdrawal from NATO if it took place. The Soviets took advantage of this situation to rain threats down upon the new West German government of Helmut Kohl, warning of a sharp deterioration of relations between Moscow and Bonn and the end of the arms control negotiations in Geneva. In the end, the deployment took place and successfully forced the Soviets to change their strategy, but it came at a heavy price and revealed deep concerns within allied countries about the direction of superpower confrontation.

This episode served as a good reminder that diplomacy, by its very nature, involves the interaction among different states, and, within these at a time of the diplomatic revolution, each is heavily influenced by domestic politics. In this regard, a monumental change occurred in 1985 when Mikhail Gorbachev became the new leader of the Soviet Union. More energetic, more thoughtful, and less reverential of the ideological stereotypes of the past than his predecessors, Gorbachev nevertheless faced not only an openly hostile administration in the United States, an exhausting war in Afghanistan, unrest in Eastern Europe, and tension with China abroad, but a country in serious

crisis at home. The long-term, debilitating effects of military and territorial overextension, arms race competition, bureaucratic stultification and mismanagement of a planned economy, absence of accountability, and a system that resisted independent initiative all had driven the Soviet Union into a political and economic state of near collapse.

Gorbachev attempted to salvage this situation by launching a dual policy of what he called *perestroika* (restructuring) and *glasnost* (openness) at home and "new political thinking" abroad. In sharp contrast to his predecessors, he announced before a meeting of his assembled diplomats that the most serious problem facing Soviet foreign policy was no longer the contest with capitalism, but the danger of the arms race that threatened the world with mutual destruction. To deal with this, Gorbachev called for a "fresh start," announced within his first month of assuming office that he would freeze the deployment of Soviet intermediate-range missiles in Europe, and began to cultivate a more personal relationship with Reagan, who, through time and in turn, appeared to be willing to modify some of his earlier positions. The two leaders met at a series of summit meetings in Geneva, Reykjavik, Washington, D.C., and Moscow, one of which yielded the remarkable 1987 Intermediate-Range Nuclear Forces (INF) Treaty that actually eliminated an entire category of weapons. He then undertook a series of surprise, unilateral actions over the objections of many of his own military and intelligence advisors. These included completely removing Soviet troops from Afghanistan, reducing the military budget by 14%, cutting weapons expenditures by 20%, and withdrawing 200,000 troops from Asia. Then, in his famous 1988 speech before the United Nations, Gorbachev announced that his government would work in cooperation with the international community, would reduce Soviet troop strength by 500,000, and would support freedom of choice for all nations, including those in Eastern Europe—"without exception."

Such a dramatic statement signaled that the Soviet Union would no longer use armed force to protect its empire and prop up its puppet regimes. Once this was realized, every one of the Communist governments behind the Iron Curtain—Poland, Hungary, Czechoslovakia, Bulgaria, East Germany, and Romania—either changed its political orientation or was overthrown by popular uprisings within the single year of 1989. Free elections were held and joyous crowds danced on the ruins of the despised Berlin Wall. "Rarely in history," wrote one journalist, "has such a sweeping reorientation of political, economic, and military power taken place so swiftly without military conquest or bloodshed." *Time* magazine reflected on these tumultuous events and in January 1990 concluded:

> With remarkable imagination and daring, he has embarked on a course, perhaps now irreversible, that is reshaping the world. . . . He has been breaking up an old bloc . . . , altering the relationship of the Soviet empire with the rest of the world and changing the nature of the empire itself. He has made possible the end of the Cold War and diminished the danger that a hot war will ever break out between the superpowers. Because he is the

force behind the most momentous events of the 1980s and because what he has already done will almost certainly shape the future, Mikhail Gorbachev is *Time*'s Man of the Decade.

Little could *Time* or even Gorbachev himself imagine what lay immediately ahead, for these events unleashed forces that appeared impervious to control. Although often praised abroad, Gorbachev's reforms and new policies generated great discontent, resistance, and even sabotage at home, especially among hard-line Communists, nationalists, and others committed to pursuing Cold War rivalries. The purchasing power of the ruble plummeted and the economy bordered on complete collapse. East Germany ceased to exist by being peacefully absorbed into a new reunited Germany and brought into NATO. Lithuania, Estonia, and Latvia all declared their independence and broke away from centralized Soviet control.

In November 1990 the leaders of thirty-four member states of CSCE, including the Soviet Union, signed the Charter of Paris reaffirming their belief in the intimate connection between human rights and security and pledging themselves to "a new era of democracy, peace, and unity." By July 1991 the Warsaw Treaty Organization formally dissolved. Plotters then attempted a bizarre and ineffective *coup* in August 1991, holding Gorbachev himself under a humiliating house arrest. In the midst of all these upheavals, Boris Yeltsin, the outspoken and reformist president of Russia, asserted that the Russian Republic also would become independent and that the Communist Party no longer held a monopoly of power. Finally, in December 1991, he and the leaders of most of the other republics announced that the seventy-four-year experiment was finished and that the Soviet Union had ceased to exist.

Why this geopolitical earthquake occurred became a matter of great controversy and surely will remain so. Just as there are intense arguments over the origins of the Cold War, so there are over its demise. Some, including many Americans, give the credit to Ronald Reagan, who steadfastly determined to drive the Soviet Union into a massive and expensive arms race that they could not possibly win, challenging them from a position of strength at every turn, denying them technical and economic assistance, and thereby driving them to collapse. Others claim that Reagan's military buildup actually prolonged the Cold War, and instead praise Mikhail Gorbachev for his bold initiatives and willingness to take unilateral and unreciprocated action to reduce the level of tension between the superpowers, describing him as "the architect of a world transformation." Some credit a whole series of American presidents, Democratic and Republican alike, who together persisted in a strategy of containing the Soviet Union until it finally fell apart. Others explain these events as the logical result of the inherent weakness and impoverishment of the Soviet system and the failure of the ideology and the practice of Communism itself, with its centrally controlled economy and one-party state rather than any pressure imposed on the Soviet Union by the United States, and argue that no one could indefinitely ignore market forces or an essentially repressive regime and somehow "reform the unreformable." Still others credit the ultimate power

of the vision of liberal democracy and human rights for being able to inspire those who were oppressed with a dream of eventual freedom.

Whatever the reason or combination of reasons, the fact remained that the contest that had defined international relations and created so much struggle for decades now came to an end. Thus, in 1992 Mikhail Gorbachev stood at exactly the same spot where Winston Churchill years before had delivered his "Iron Curtain" speech, and told his audience what so many had waited so long to hear: "The Cold War is over—and a new era has begun."

SUGGESTIONS FOR FURTHER EXPLORATION

For good treatments of the Cold War as a whole, see Ronald Powaski, *The Cold War: The United States and the Soviet Union, 1917–1991* (New York, 1998); John Lewis Gaddis, *We Now Know* (New York, 1998) and *The Long Peace* (New York, 1987); Walter LaFeber, *America, Russia, and the Cold War* (New York, 1997 ed.); and Edward Judge and John Langdon, *A Hard and Bitter Peace: A Global History of the Cold War* (Upper Saddle River, NJ, 1996). Discussions about the statecraft of particular leaders can be found in Gordon A. Craig and Francis L. Lowenheim (eds), *The Diplomats, 1939–1979* (Princeton, 1994). New articles of analysis and interpretation constantly appear in the recently established *Journal of Cold War Studies*.

A good sense of the controversy surrounding the origins of the Cold War can be gained by comparing the "orthodox" interpretation of Herbert Feis, *From Trust to Terror* (New York, 1970) with "revisionist" authors like Gar Alperowitz et al., *The Decision to Use the Atomic Bomb* (New York, 1996); Michael Parenti, *The Sword and the Dollar* (New York, 1988); and William A. Williams, *The Tragedy of American Diplomacy* (New York, 1988 ed.); and "neo-revisionist" interpretations of Thomas Paterson, *On Every Front* (New York, 1996 ed.); and Melvyn Leffler, *A Preponderance of Power* (Stanford, CA, 1993 ed.).

Any student of diplomacy needs to appreciate that international relations involve the interaction among different states rather than simply the unilateral policies of a single country. As a consequence, it is extremely important to examine the documents and perspectives of other nations. A good place to begin for the Cold War are official histories from the Soviet Union, and these can be found in B. Ponomarev, Andre Gromyko, and V. Khvostov (eds.), *History of Soviet Foreign Policy, 1945–1970* (Moscow, 1974); and Andre Gromyko and B. Ponomarev, *Soviet Foreign Policy, 1917–1980*, 2 vols. (Moscow, 1981). Contemporary issues of *Current Digest of the Soviet Press* also provide official statements about foreign policy. For the Chinese perspective, see Chen Jian, *Mao's China and the Cold War* (Chapel Hill, NC, 2001).

There are also specific topics that warrant special attention. The role of psychological images and perceptions is treated in John Stoessinger, *Nations at Dawn: China, Russia, and America* (New York, 1994 ed.); and Alexander L. George, "The Transition in U.S.-Soviet Relations," *Political Psychology*, 12 (1991); and McCarthyism is explored in Paul Gordon Lauren (ed.), *The China Hands Legacy* (Boulder, CO, 1987). Containment is discussed in George F. Kennan and John Luckas, *George F. Kennan and the Origins of Containment* (Columbia, MO, 1997); Deborah Larson, *Origins of Containment: A Psychological Explanation* (Princeton, 1985); and John Lewis Gaddis, *Strategies of Containment* (New York, 1982). The arms race is analyzed in Ronald Powaski, *March to Armageddon* (New York, 1993); Robert Jervis, *The Meaning of the Nuclear Revolution* (Ithaca, 1990); and Henry Kissinger, *Nuclear Weapons and Foreign Policy* (New York, 1957).

Deterrence strategy in American Cold War policy is examined in detail in Alexander L. George and Richard Smoke, *Deterrence in American Foreign Policy: Theory and Practice* (New York: 1974). Intelligence and covert action are treated in Loch Johnson, *America's Secret Power* (New York, 1991); Christopher Andrew and Oleg Gordievsky, *KGB: The Inside Story* (New York, 1990); and Paul Gordon Lauren, "Ethics and Intelligence," in Alfred Maurer et al. (eds.), *Intelligence: Policy and Process* (Boulder, CO, 1985). The subject of race is discussed in Mary Dudziak, *Cold War Civil Rights* (Princeton, 2000); and Paul Gordon Lauren, *Power and Prejudice: The Politics and Diplomacy of Racial Discrimination* (Boulder, CO, 1996 ed.). *Détente* is explored by Alexander L. George et al. (eds.), *U.S.-Soviet Security Cooperation* (New York, 1996 ed.); Alexander L. George (ed.), *Managing U.S.-Soviet Rivalry* (Boulder, CO, 1983); Henry Kissinger's autobiographical *Years of Upheaval* (Boston, 1982) and *White House Years* (Boston, 1979); and Dan Caldwell, *American-Soviet Relations* (Westport, CT, 1981).

The debate over the demise of the Cold War can be seen by comparing Richard Herrmann and Richard Ned Lebow (eds.), *Ending the Cold War* (New York, 2004); Peter Schweizer, *Reagan's War: The Epic Story of His Forty Year Struggle and Final Triumph Over Communism* (New York, 2002); Don Oberdorfer, *From the Cold War to a New Era* (Baltimore, 1998 ed.); Archie Brown, *The Gorbachev Factor* (New York, 1997); Richard Ned Lebow and Janice Gross Stein, *We All Lost the Cold War* (Princeton, 1995); and Francis Fukuyama, *The End of History and the Last Man* (New York, 1993).

In recent years there has been considerable effort to use the Internet as a means of making important new findings about the Cold War readily available in electronic format. These include declassified documents, material obtained under the Freedom of Information Act, and previously inaccessible archival sources once hidden behind the Iron Curtain. Some of the most valuable Web sites are those of the Cold War International History Project at www.cwihp.org; the Parallel History Project on NATO and the Warsaw Pact at www.isn.ethz.ch/php; U.S. Department of State, Foreign Relations Series, at www.state.gov/www/about_state/history; Center for Defense Information at www.cdi.org; Center for the Study of Intelligence at www.cia.gov/csi; and the National Security Archive at www.gwu.edu/~nsarchive.

6

The Evolving International System

The end of the Cold War and of the Soviet empire created a widespread mood of euphoria. The prospect that the struggle that had dominated global politics for decades was over seemed to open up a vast new horizon of possibilities. Some observers sighed in quiet and grateful relief that the world had managed to escape nuclear annihilation. Others reacted with a strident sense of triumphalism, believing that their own superiority had brought about victory. Despite their considerable differences of opinion, however, it appeared as though all sides had one thing in common: the opportunity to think about a new future. For the first time in decades, serious consideration could be given to what the world might be like without the dangerous and costly confrontation between the superpowers. Many hoped that they would now see a "peace dividend," an end to the arms race and "balance of terror" of MAD, the elimination of rival alliance systems and covert action, the rule of law, enhanced human rights, and the opportunity for the United Nations to finally realize the role originally designed for it and thereby bring about greater international peace and security. U.S. Secretary of State James Baker gave expression to this mood when he proclaimed: "We live in one of the rare transforming moments in history, with the Cold War over and an era full of promise just ahead." In this setting it was not at all uncommon to hear much discussion about a "New World Order" emerging in a rapidly evolving international system.

"A World in a Rapid State of Transition"

As we have seen from the very beginning, change constantly occurs, and any international system must be able to adapt to geopolitical shifts and to internal changes within its member states that affect its performance and ability to maintain itself. The question of how best to accomplish this in the context of the post-Cold War world was not as easy to resolve as many had hoped and led to sharp and intense debates that continue to this day over the desirability of a broad-based United Nations system of collective security, a

unipolar system dominated by a single superpower, or a multipolar system of several major actors.

Regardless of the various points of departure and differing political perspectives on force and statecraft, however, there was common recognition of the necessity of adapting to a vastly changing world. In his reports entitled *An Agenda for Peace* and *An Agenda for Peace: One Year Later*, for example, United Nations Secretary-General Boutros Boutros-Ghali posed the issue directly: "How the international community can best equip itself to respond to a world in a rapid state of transition." He opposed putting faith in the leadership or direction of any single country, however great or powerful, and advocated instead a reliance upon collective preventive diplomacy, peacemaking, peacekeeping, and peacebuilding. As he observed:

> History is accelerating. The pace is alarming. The direction is not entirely known. At this time of stress, the hard fact is that no power or combination of powers is prepared to take on its shoulders the responsibility for collective security worldwide.

Henry Kissinger sharply contested this conclusion and argued instead that the emerging international system would be better served by embracing *raison d'état*, a balance of power, and strong American leadership. But he also acknowledged in his book *Diplomacy* that the difficulty confronting world leaders in the wake of the Cold War was to bring order to this emerging system with which none of them had much experience:

> Never before has a new world order had to be assembled from so many different perceptions, or on so global a scale. Nor has any previous order had to combine the attributes of the historic balance-of-power systems with global democratic opinion and the exploding technology of the contemporary period.

The challenges that both Boutros-Ghali and Kissinger anticipated were seen soon enough.

One of these was the sheer expansion of the international community itself. In 1990 Namibia and Liechtenstein became members of the United Nations. The following year witnessed the admission of North and South Korea, Estonia, Latvia, Lithuania, Micronesia, and the Marshall Islands. A remarkable twenty new states became members over the next two years, including former Soviet republics like Armenia, Georgia, and Kazakhstan. Today, membership is virtually universal. A walk along First Avenue in New York City in front of the United Nations headquarters reveals a display of the national flags of 191 members. This phenomenal number represents well more than a tripling of independent nation-states just since the end of the Second World War, each with its own history, perceptions, interests, and values. All of these, especially when combined with the burgeoning number of nonstate actors in global politics, as we shall discuss shortly, marked a dramatic escalation of the diplomatic revolution in the number of participants, expanding geographical scope, and resulting complexity within the evolving international system.

Other challenges emerged in this transformation as well, including political instability and the outbreak of violence and wars. Indeed, even as early as mid-July 1990, when the revolutions in Hungary, Poland, Germany, and Czechoslovakia consolidated themselves and the Soviet Union began to betray signs of dissolution, observers in the Middle East noted an ominous massing of Iraqi forces along the border of Kuwait. For some time it had been obvious that the Iraqi dictator Saddam Hussein's ambitions had not been diminished by his long and wasting conflict waged against Iran and fought with American-supplied weapons and financial support. His brutality against political opponents at home, the use of biological and chemical weapons against rebellious Kurdish subjects, and pressure against Kuwait for concessions on disputed oil reserves provided evidence enough. Nevertheless, the United States tended to play down Saddam's excesses, wanting to believe that he was a pragmatist who, if handled in the right way, would see that there was a natural congruence between his own and American interests. Both the Reagan and first Bush administrations turned a deaf ear to domestic and international arguments that pressure should be exerted against the Iraqi regime. This proved to be a serious mistake, for Saddam seems to have concluded that he could pursue his ambitions without meaningful consequences. With no fear to hold him in check, he invaded Kuwait in July 1990.

From that moment on there was no further hesitation on the part of President Bush. He threw himself energetically and skillfully into mobilizing world opinion against Saddam and seeking authorization from the United Nations for action. The already-high geopolitical stakes were made even more acute by the threat posed to vital oil reserves, the possibility of further attacks against Saudi Arabia or Israel, and the unequivocal nature of Iraq's blatant breach of international law. In early August, the UN Security Council denounced Iraq's aggression and, in a series of resolutions and in the name of the international community, voted to employ coercive diplomacy by imposing progressively stiffer sanctions. When this proved to be insufficient, it authorized the actual use of armed force, if necessary, to expel Iraqi forces from Kuwait and to restore peace to the area. With this widespread international backing, President Bush skillfully built up a multilateral military coalition ("Desert Shield") to deter further Iraqi aggression and, after delicate negotiations with a fearful and hesitant Saudi government, dispatched a large ground force, backed by naval units, to Saudi Arabia. As Saddam stubbornly refused to disgorge his spoils, the troop buildup increased and was transformed from more than a defensive shield into "Desert Storm," a military strategy to force him out of Kuwait if necessary. When he disregarded an ultimatum of coercive diplomacy for withdrawal, American and allied war planes began in January 1991 to bomb command-and-control centers in Baghdad and Iraqi military positions in Kuwait. This was followed by a massive ground offensive, which lasted less than 100 hours and captured well over 10,000 Iraqi prisoners in the first day's fighting. At the end of the Gulf War, the president proudly announced that Americans had finally "kicked the Vietnam syndrome once and for all." The limited objective of liberating Kuwait was met, but Saddam remained.

Other challenges of warfare and the use of force continued, seemingly one right after the other. Saddam Hussein's unrelenting persecution of the Kurds later in 1991 resulted in armed forces being sent into northern Iraq to protect them. During the same year, another U.S. client state of the former Cold War, Somalia, erupted into civil war and anarchy. This, in turn, led to American and United Nations troops being sent into the country in the name of humanitarian intervention. At exactly the same time, the centrifugal forces in Yugoslavia began to career out of control. Slovenia and Croatia declared their independence from the Serbian-dominated government in Belgrade, and violence broke out in Bosnia in which Bosnian Serb nationalists, with the support of Serbian president Slobodan Milosevic, attempted to create an ethnically pure region by means of a ghastly process of intimidation, rape, fighting, and mass murder known as "ethnic cleansing." Member states of the United Nations decided to respond by combining diplomacy with the sending of peacekeeping forces and imposing an arms embargo. Although this may have had some advantages in theory, in practice it seriously disadvantaged Bosnian government troops against the already well-equipped Serbs. This became particularly evident in 1994 with a horrifying mortar attack against civilians in a Sarajevo marketplace and especially in 1995 with the shocking massacre of 7000 men and boys at the so-called "safe area" of Srebrenica, an event described as "the worst human rights disaster in Europe since the Holocaust." When the United Nations found itself blocked from taking collective action as a result of threatened vetoes from Russia and China, the British and French urged NATO to deploy its Rapid Reaction Force (RRF) and President Bill Clinton authorized U.S. troops to launch Operation Deliberate Force in the Balkans. In 1994 civil war also broke out in Rwanda between Hutus and Tutsis. All this seemed to belie the dreams of those who had hoped for a post–Cold War "New World Order."

Dramatic transformations revealed themselves in other ways as well, particularly in the area of technology. With specific reference to the use of force, there emerged what some came to call the revolution in military affairs (RMA) that now combined with the diplomatic revolution, especially with the application of advanced sensing and information-reporting computer technologies and precision-guided munitions (PGMs). The Persian Gulf War, for example, utilized cruise missiles with guidance systems capable of comparing landmarks with prerecorded maps to guide them to their targets, jet fighters with radar-evading Stealth technology based upon new aerodynamic shapes and composite materials, electronic jamming equipment, night vision devices, and so-called "smart bombs" guided by lasers, infrared signals, or television cameras. Advanced research continued apace for developing and refining weapons of mass destruction with highly sophisticated delivery systems capable of sending nuclear, chemical, or biological agents toward targets thousands of miles away. At the same time, scientists worked to develop electromagnetic pulse (EMP) weapons and new space and counter-space technologies using particle beams and kinetic energy to project military potential beyond earth's atmosphere. This enabled strategists to go beyond the previous arenas of land, sea, and air warfare into what they called the

new "fourth medium": space. Diplomats and military planners of previous generations, schooled on ideas of limitations from Clausewitz, could not have even imagined such sophisticated developments and their implications for what is today known as C^{4}ISR: command, control, communications, computers, intelligence, surveillance, and reconnaissance.

These technological transformations also greatly influence the collection, analysis, and transmission of information. A visit to the communications center of any major foreign ministry today reveals the effects of the "digital revolution" produced by the microchip and its staggering array of complex devices to encrypt and decrypt classified messages, create and store elaborate data bases on foreign governments and nonstate actors in international affairs, compress and retrieve vast amounts of information, rapidly conduct highly complex mathematical computations, convert photons into electrons and then process these into images, and provide automatic links with Web sites that span the globe. Those charged with the conduct of diplomacy in the contemporary world can use computers, facsimile machines, fiber optics, and various wireless devices instantaneously to send and receive satellite transmissions and maintain constant and secure mobile communications with others virtually anywhere on the planet. It is possible for a secretary of state to transmit instructions and reports, communicate with the president, or even to receive maps and runway patterns of new locations necessitated by unscheduled stops or changing itineraries all while in midair, and to do so with amazing speed. Technical intelligence systems also have created an "information revolution" that makes it possible for diplomats to receive extraordinary intelligence about others in world affairs. The current capacity to collect data and near real-time information through technical means of electronic intercepts, embedded relay chips in telecommunications equipment, hydrophones on the ocean floors, and space-borne assets like spy satellites, and then provide analysis through sophisticated processing and imagery (such as integrating overhead photographic imagery with terrain elevation data to produce a three-dimensional depiction of territory), simply staggers the imagination. As one writer describes the capabilities:

> Cameras carried in satellites [can] photograph missile bases, airfields, submarine pens, harbors, and other defense installations from a hundred miles or more in space with such clarity that they [can] pinpoint a single man walking alone on a vast desert. Sensors in the satellites [are] not blinded by the dark; radar eyes and heat-sensing infrared sensors penetrate clouds and dark skies and [make] photos almost as sharp as those made during a clear day by normal cameras. . . . [E]ach satellite carries a battery of antennae capable of sucking foreign microwave signals from out of space like a vacuum cleaner picking up specks of dust from a carpet.

This vast amount of information and the ease of transmitting much of it also contributes further to that other feature of the diplomatic revolution discussed previously: namely, the accelerating rise of public opinion and "public diplomacy." Indeed, one insider estimates that the staff of the U.S. Secretary of State spends 80–90% of its time thinking about the media and

how policies will "play" with the public. This is further confirmed by the exist-ence and the size of the office of the Under Secretary of State for Public Diplomacy and Public Affairs and by the fact that American Foreign Service Officers now can select a career track designated as "Public Diplomacy Officers." According to their official job description, they are responsible for managing cultural and exchange programs, as well as being assigned to "explain and defend the substance of American foreign policy to ensure that U.S. positions are well understood and that misrepresentations are cor-rected." In this regard, technology increasingly makes it infinitely easier to influence stories in the press, images broadcast over television, and infor-mation made available on the Internet. The foreign ministries of every major nation-state in the world today, in addition to the United Nations, re-gional organizations, and NGOs, maintain active Web sites full of reports, explanations, briefings, news releases, video clips, and digital images designed to provide information and influence public opinion. One recent government commission consequently concludes that "public diplomacy is a strategic com-ponent of foreign policy" and, as such, must be regarded as "indispensable" to contemporary statecraft.

These transformations in public diplomacy are matched, if not exceeded, by those in economics and commerce, and thereby continued yet another feature of the diplomatic revolution. Business firms, bankers and financiers, manufacturers, shipping companies, chambers of commerce, private investors, and many analysts argue with increasing effectiveness that survival depends not upon military success but rather upon the ability of states to compete in the international economic sphere and thereby provide for the well-being of their people. Diplomats, they urge, therefore need to be more aggressive in pro-moting trade and finance in the global marketplace. At the same time, writes one author,

> Governments increasingly recognized that the distribution of goods and cap-ital abroad might be utilized as an instrument of diplomacy. Investment could buy friendships or build and solidify alliances, while monies withheld or economic reprisals could coerce opponents into making certain diplomatic concessions. Financial penetration could facilitate political hegemony in developing countries. Commercial advantages offered to foreign suppliers of strategic raw materials could strengthen security. Moreover, profits from overseas markets could contribute to national wealth and perhaps increase international prestige.

The combination of these private and public interests results in foreign min-istries around the world taking more determined action than ever before to protect and promote trade and investment by recruiting economic special-ists, creating career tracks for "Economic Officers," employing commercial attachés, compiling vital import and export statistics for their nationals, reporting on foreign market conditions and tariff policies, utilizing success-ful business men and women as trade negotiators, and upgrading the qual-ity and professionalism in the consular services. Over time these activities have expanded even further to include close cooperation between business

and diplomacy in areas of investment, trade, technical assistance, foreign aid, and reconstruction projects following in the wake of wars. Said one high-ranking diplomat in a recent speech to his colleagues: "We are going to have to acknowledge that our economic health and our ability to trade competitively on the world market may be the single most important component of our national security. . . . We must also become more activist in promoting American exports and in serving U.S. business interests overseas."

CHALLENGES TO NATION-STATES AND NATIONAL SOVEREIGNTY

Many of these transformations have led to another development: they increasingly appear to render the traditional borders and power of nation-states less meaningful or consequential than in the past. Ever since the emergence of the Great Powers in the seventeenth century, as we have seen, states—whatever their particular form—were regarded as the sole actors of international relations, as the only entities capable of mobilizing sufficient force to threaten the security of others, as the singular protectors and authority governing people within their own territories, and as the sole possessors of sovereignty whose leaders were immune from any responsibility beyond their own borders. Various features within the evolving international system, however, steadily challenged all of these features, assumptions, and claims.

Extraordinary advances in transportation, telecommunications, and the World Wide Web, global opinion, electronic commerce, and the international integration of goods, services, and capital, for example, all contribute to the surging process widely known as "globalization." The technological capacity in the digital era to immediately share nonstop, real-time coverage by organizations like Cable Network News (CNN) and the British Broadcasting Corporation (BBC) using orbiting satellites around the globe and the capabilities of Qatar's al-Jazeera television station literally transcend national borders and the ability of nation-states to control information or their own culture as they had in the past. "Nations once connected by foreign ministries and traders," notes the Center for Strategic and International Studies report entitled *Reinventing Diplomacy in the Information Age*, "are now linked through millions of individuals by fiber optics, satellite, wireless, and cable in a complex network without central control." The evolution of a worldwide market of trade and finance similarly creates vast networks of relationships and interests that often completely bypass nation-states and national divisions. More than four trillion dollars are exchanged every day in international money markets, for example, outside of any government control. Try as they may, nation-states simply cannot govern this process.

Other issues present still further challenges to the ability of nation-states to protect their own people and territory. These include effects of the proliferation of weapons of mass destruction, international terrorism, widespread epidemics like the HIV/AIDS virus, ethnic conflict, environmental pollution of the atmosphere and the oceans, migration and the flow of refugees, illicit drugs and transnational crime, collapsed or "failed" states, and "outlaw" or

"rogue" regimes. Under these circumstances it is not at all unusual to hear those knowledgeable about statecraft increasingly speak of broad "complex interdependence," "cooperative security," and the "indivisibility of security." Indeed, as political scientists Dan Caldwell and Robert Williams argue in their book, *Seeking Security in an Insecure World*, the security of individuals, states, and the international system has become so interconnected in our day that narrowly defined notions of "national security" are no longer relevant.

When facing these common threats, many states have realized that they can no longer "go it alone" and have sought greater security through cooperative and collective efforts. They have been willing to voluntarily surrender some of their national sovereignty to do so. Some have bound themselves to the regulations and requirements of regional organizations like the influential European Union, for example, believing that they could protect their interests best by joining with others rather than acting completely alone. Others have agreed to certain self-imposed restraints—including those regarding force and statecraft—by becoming parties to international legal agreements like the Non-Proliferation Treaty (NPT) dealing with nuclear weapons and its monitoring agency of the International Atomic Energy Agency (IAEA), the 1997 International Convention to Ban Land Mines, and the 1998 Rome Statute of the International Criminal Court designed to hold national leaders personally responsible for crimes against humanity, war crimes, or genocide. Still others have strongly believed that a correlation exists between respect for human rights and international peace and security, emphasizing the rights of individuals at the expense of the rights of states. They therefore have become parties to any number of international human rights treaties with treaty-monitoring mechanisms like the International Convention on the Elimination of All Forms of Racial Discrimination, International Covenant on Civil and Political Rights, and the International Convention Against Torture. All this presents a formidable challenge to traditional notions and claims of exclusive sovereignty. In fact, according to United Nations Secretary-General Kofi Annan, within the evolving international system there is an evolving redefinition of sovereignty itself:

> State sovereignty, in its most basic sense, is being redefined. States are now widely understood to be instruments at the service of their people, and not vice-versa. At the same time, individual sovereignty—by which I mean the fundamental freedom of each individual, enshrined in the Charter of the UN and subsequent international treaties—has been enhanced by a renewed and spreading consciousness of individual rights. When we read the Charter today, we are more than ever conscious that is aim is to protect individual human rights not to protect those who abuse them.

This can be seen in the increased willingness of the international community to ignore claims by leaders that national sovereignty grants them complete immunity from any kind of accountability. One need only consider the condemnation of dictators like Augusto Pinochet of Chile, the prosecution of war criminals like Slobodan Milosevic of Serbia, and the use of force to engage

in humanitarian intervention within the territory of other nations. As the International Commission on Intervention and State Sovereignty recently concluded in its report, tellingly entitled *The Responsibility to Protect*, the task at hand is to deliver "practical protection for ordinary people, at risk of their lives, because their states are unwilling or unable to protect them."

This constantly evolving meaning of national sovereignty within the larger evolving international system is unmistakable. It also is not without controversy or resistance. Whereas many states are willing to voluntarily surrender portions of their sovereignty on behalf of the larger system as a whole, others clearly are not. Indeed, some states are firmly opposed to this trend insofar as their own countries are involved and insist upon retaining the traditional prerogatives of their national sovereignty. These include, among others, China, Iran, Israel, North Korea, and the United States.

Despite this opposition, however, nation-states and national sovereignty continue to be challenged by other actors with claims to actively participate in global affairs. These include the international governmental organization of the United Nations and its many related specialized agencies, such as the International Labor Organization and World Health Organization, among many others, as well as supranational or regional organizations such as the European Union, Organization for Security and Cooperation in Europe, North Atlantic Treaty Organization, Organization of American States, the Arab League, African Union, and the Association of Southeast Asian Nations. Still other actors include the International Monetary Fund, World Bank, World Trade Organization, commodity cartels such as the Organization of Petroleum Exporting Countries, and the Group of Eight (G-8), an informal but exclusive body comprised of seven of the world's leading industrialized nations plus Russia. Although composed of nation-states, each of these organizations sometimes is more powerful than the sum of its parts, often challenging traditional attributes of national sovereignty itself.

Other international actors today do not represent nation-states at all. Among the most striking of these are global, or transnational, business corporations such as Microsoft, General Electric, International Telephone and Telegraph, Exxon Mobil, Mitsubishi, Royal Dutch/Shell, Nestlé, and Siemens, among others. They carry neither the burdens nor the limitations of governing, and their size, enormous wealth, and sophisticated ability to move goods, services, and capital worldwide often gives them significant global influence far beyond the control of specific national governments or international organizations. Indeed, some possess revenue that far exceeds the gross national products of many nation-states. For this reason, their chief executive officers and directors can have a much greater impact upon people and world events than many heads of governments. The same can be said to some extent about international crime syndicates (especially those in the drug trade), whose vast and unregulated wealth and global influence present security threats that exceed the ability of most states to protect even their own territory.

Still other actors in the evolving international system today are groups of private citizens seeking to challenge nation-states and national sovereignty

by influencing policies in particular directions and to extend citizen participation in the conduct of diplomacy by means of international NGOs. When the Economic Council of the United Nations first granted official consultative status to NGOs in 1948, the number was forty-eight. Today it is well over 2000. In recent years the number of these groups has expanded as never before in history. The authoritative Union of International Associations estimates that the total number of recognized international NGOs now exceeds 40,000. Particularly in the area of human rights, NGOs work to directly challenge national sovereignty and any of its corollary claims that government leaders can do whatever they wish to their own people without fear of being held responsible. It is estimated that there may be as many as 26,000 human rights NGOs operating in the world today. Some of these, such as Amnesty International, Human Rights Watch, and Médecins sans frontières, have an international influence. Others, such as the Afro-Asian Peoples' Solidarity Organization, Asian Coalition of Human Rights Organizations, or the Arab Organization for Human Rights, have a focus that transcends borders within regions. The impact of these organizations—greatly enhanced by communication technology—sometimes has been phenomenal. Human rights NGOs were largely responsible for mobilizing sufficient support to enact the International Convention Against Torture, the International Convention to Ban Land Mines, and the statute creating the path-breaking International Criminal Court. There are times when they and their highly motivated and Internet-connected members and cross-border networks can be mobilized long before governments can act or when political constraints prevent governmental action at all. Indeed, said one United Nations official recently, "Without the people of the NGOs, our program for human rights would be a mere shadow of itself."

If any doubts existed about the capacity of nonstate actors to challenge nation-states and national sovereignty, to threaten the ability of governments to protect the security and well-being of their own people, to present new kinds of opponents in the post–Cold War world, and to enormously influence contemporary global affairs in the evolving international system still remained after all these developments, they should have been irrevocably shattered by the premeditated terrorist attacks of September 11, 2001—a date now known simply as 9/11.

TERRORISTS AND THE "WAR ON TERRORISM"

Within less than two shocking hours on this single day, 3000 people were deliberately killed in New York City, Washington, DC, and rural Pennsylvania, starkly revealing the power of terrorist networks or cells to destroy human lives and wreck havoc. Osama bin Laden, a radical Islamic militant, and his nonstate terrorist organization known as al-Qaida, based in Afghanistan, claimed responsibility and called the actions "blessed attacks" against the "Great Satan" of the United States whom he accused of supporting Israel against the Palestinians, having a military presence in Saudi Arabia which served as the

home for Islam's holiest sites, and spreading a message of secularism and materialism that threatened the beliefs of more than a billion Muslim followers around the world. As a tool to bring about change by using violence and sowing fear, terrorism had a long history, and attacks had been made on American and other targets previously. But never before had a single episode captured so much global attention or made the world so painfully aware of its collective vulnerability. Although the main target had been the United States, eighty different countries lost citizens in the attack on the World Trade Center, and the international community reacted with outrage. Most nations in the world expressed their sympathy and support, with the leading French newspaper *Le Monde* declaring in a headline: "We are all Americans now." "All of us," continued Kofi Annan, "feel deep shock and revulsion at the cold-blooded viciousness of this attack. All of us condemn it and those who planned it—whoever they may be—in the strongest possible terms. . . . A terrorist attack on one country is an attack on humanity as a whole. All nations of the world must work together to identify the perpetrators and bring them to justice."

This terrorist attack and its aftermath—like other assaults and suicide bombings before and since, such as those of 2004 in Madrid and of 2005 in London—raised extremely difficult questions about peace, the relationship between international and national security, human rights, the effectiveness of the international system, the vulnerability of even the strongest of states, and force and statecraft. To begin a response, both the General Assembly and the Security Council condemned the attacks of September 11 in the strongest possible terms, reaffirmed their earlier conclusion that terrorism presented one of the most serious threats to peace and security, created the Counter-Terrorism Committee, and set about to develop specific, immediate, and far-reaching measures to combat international terrorist acts. Nearly all countries responded by taking immediate steps to combat terrorism within their own territories. But collective intelligence sources increasingly revealed the extensive and highly concealed network of terrorist cells in the world, and this persuaded most countries that national means alone could never adequately address the problem and that this global problem required a global response. NATO, for example, gave the United States its full support within twenty-four hours of the attacks, invoking Article Five of its founding treaty, stating that an attack on one of its members is an attack on them all, for the very first time in its history. Further diplomacy sought to build political will and support in a variety of ways, not the least of which was the use of twelve separate international counterterrorism conventions grounded in the rule of law. Simultaneous with this, there began to be a number of very specific efforts to achieve much greater cooperation in intelligence activities, increasing security measures and procedures, identifying and apprehending suspected terrorists, and freezing financial assets and prohibiting the transfer of funds or other material assets to those supporting terrorism.

But major issues of force and statecraft remained. Terrorist groups did not appear to be at all threatened or intimidated by the classical techniques

of deterrence or coercive diplomacy as used in the past against state actors. The United States therefore concluded that the use, rather than the threat, of force would serve as the best response. Less than one month after 9/11, it launched its initial cruise missile attacks and bombing raids on al-Qaida targets and the radical Taliban regime that had supported Osama bin Laden in Afghanistan. Ground forces followed immediately in an invasion. Within weeks, vast portions of territory once controlled by the Taliban were conquered and heavily fortified labyrinths of caves and tunnels destroyed, although hundreds of al-Qaida fighters managed to flee over the borders into neighboring Pakistan and Iran. In taking this military action, the United States received not only widespread domestic and international support, but also the actual contributions of many states willing to participate in one way or the other in a coalition to fight against those who engaged in terrorism.

Such remarkable and widespread support for the United States, however, did not last long. There began to be serious concerns about the escalation of the rhetoric about what Americans increasingly, broadly, and indiscriminately called "the war on terrorism," as well as deep worries that this conflict appeared to be rapidly expanding in terms of geography and nature. In his State of the Union speech in January 2002, for example, President George W. Bush said nothing about the Taliban or Osama bin Laden. Instead, he argued, "What we have found in Afghanistan confirms that, far from ending there, our war against terror is only beginning." Bush then went on in a moment of diplomatic infelicity to declare the existence of an "axis of evil," asserting that there was a connection between Iraq, Iran, and North Korea in their support of terrorism. His National Security Advisor, Condoleezza Rice, subsequently and ominously declared that these governments now had been "put on notice." By May this list was expanded to include Cuba, Libya, and Syria. Then, the Department of Defense announced a rapid acceleration of its transformation program to restructure and reposition combat brigades from their Cold War bases in Germany and South Korea to other parts of the world in order to increase its military presence and capacity to project force as a means of fighting a protracted struggle against terrorism.

More serious international concern and alienation came in the wake of a most important document released by the administration in September 2002 entitled *The National Security Strategy of the United States of America*. Among other things, this multifaceted and unusually combative statement enunciated the "Bush Doctrine," claiming the unique prerogative of using force preemptively and unilaterally. Armed force would no longer be considered as a last resort, it declared, for America now intended to act against threats "before they are fully formed." Therefore, asserted the critical operative sentence: "To forestall or prevent such hostile acts by our adversaries, the United States will, if necessary, act preemptively." Other nations reacted with outrage to these statements, arguing that such strident assertions of leadership and preeminence, preemption, and unilateralism not only violated the rule of law as embodied in the United Nations Charter's rules on collective security and the use of force, but in the context of ever-growing American

military capabilities that already far exceeded anyone else's, presented extremely serious threats to the peace and security of the entire evolving international system.

Their fears certainly were not relieved when Secretary of State Colin Powell attempted to persuade the UN Security Council in February 2003 that there existed a "nexus between Iraq and the al-Qaida terrorist network" and that Saddam Hussein possessed stockpiles of weapons of mass destruction that posed an imminent threat to world peace and security. The Americans and the British pressed the council for a resolution explicitly authorizing the use of armed force against Iraq, but most of the others believed that sufficient, credible evidence simply did not exist for these charges to be persuasive, and said so. The French and the Russians threatened to cast vetoes, as did the Chinese. Although they had participated in sanctions against Iraq and recently threatened serious consequences against Saddam for noncompliance with resolutions, the majority seriously doubted that a serious connection existed between terrorism and Iraq and wanted United Nations weapons inspectors to be given more time to actually find the alleged weapons of mass destruction. This, in turn, incensed President Bush, who lashed out, accusing the United Nations of making itself "irrelevant" and declaring that he did not need a "permission slip" to take military action. Knowing that it could not secure the necessary authorization from the Security Council for a mandate to specifically use force, the United States decided not to bring a resolution to a vote at all and launched a preventive war in March 2003 against Iraq.

PARTNERS OR RIVALS?

The members of every international system in history always have had to wrestle with the extent to which they were partners or rivals with each other. Historically, they generally balanced at some point along a scale of partnership and rivalry: at times readily agreeing on their shared interests and values, collective goods, and the fact that they needed each other in facing common dangers that threatened them, and, on other occasions disagreeing and competing with each other. Their particular position at any given time depended upon the circumstances of the specific case, and they rarely placed themselves at one extreme or the other over a wide range of issues. But with the end of the Cold War, the collapse of a bipolar world, the emergence of America as the sole superpower, and the evolution of a new system, careful observers wondered whether this balance between partnership and rivalry—or integration and fragmentation—would be placed in jeopardy. Questions started slowly, but took on a particular poignancy as leaders in the United States increasingly claimed special prerogatives, acted unilaterally, seemed unwilling to acknowledge that other states possessed legitimate interests as well, tried to thwart a number of major international treaties, and especially when they attacked Iraq.

When the Cold War ended, attention actually focused upon the theme of partnership in building a "New World Order." Indeed, President Bush the elder, who had considerable experience in working with the intelligence community and the United Nations, told the members of the General Assembly in a widely quoted 1991 speech that although "the United States is now the world's only remaining superpower," it

> has no intention of striving for a Pax Americana. However, we will remain engaged. We will not pull back and retreat into isolationism. We will offer friendship and leadership, and in short, we seek a Pax Universalis, built upon shared responsibilities and aspirations.

In many ways, his actions were consistent with his words. During the next year, when widespread starvation struck the African nation of Somalia, for example, Bush decided to send American troops to help with the international effort to distribute food and save lives, announcing that it could not ignore the shared global responsibilities and aspirations "even though the United States has no military, economic, or political interests at stake in such crises."

This pattern of working as partners with others was followed by Bill Clinton when he assumed the presidency in 1993. His administration actively participated in the international community's efforts to place sanctions on the regime of Saddam Hussein, develop international criminal law with the tribunals for war crimes by those responsible for genocide in the former Yugoslavia and Rwanda, establish global environmental protections, and sponsor the Partnership for Peace plan for expanding the membership of NATO to eventually include the former members of the Warsaw Treaty Organization and others once subjugated by the Soviet Union. Clinton hoped that this theme of international cooperation would be further enhanced in 1997 by naming former U.S. Ambassador to the United Nations Madeleine Albright as the first woman to ever hold the position of Secretary of State.

Even in the most challenging area of force and statecraft, the administration attempted to work in partnership with others and to avoid unilateral military action. This was not easy. One of the reasons involved serious differences of opinion over political-military doctrine and the use of force in humanitarian intervention. Should armed force be employed in gradually restricted and limited ways, it was asked, for example, or used overwhelming from the beginning on a huge scale in order to achieve a decisive outcome quickly? This was further complicated in the age of the diplomatic revolution by the emergence of an unusually hostile and partisan Congress. Still another reason had to do with the president's own personal weakness that brought scandal to his administration, and for which he had no one to blame but himself. Nevertheless, Clinton made great efforts to enlist Security Council support for the sending of American troops to Haiti to help restore democracy in 1994 and then to work in collaboration with the United Nations in Bosnia during 1995 and with NATO allies in Kosovo during 1999 to protect against genocidal "ethnic cleansing." The United States thus

agreed to actively participate with others in air attacks on military and communication sites, in a peacekeeping force to separate the parties and participate in reconstruction, and in the prosecution of Slobodan Milosevic in the name of human rights and international criminal law.

When the American administration changed hands upon the election of George W. Bush in 2001, it did not initially appear that there would be any drastic change of course. As a candidate, he frequently declared that he intended to work as a partner in cooperation with other nations and to pursue a more "humble" foreign policy. Indeed, during his inaugural speech he announced: "We will show purpose without arrogance." It very quickly became apparent, however, that partnership within a diplomatic system can mean different things to different people, and that failure to agree on basic principles can readily result in rivalry. Within a very short period of time, the new Bush administration deliberately removed itself from a number of international initiatives and agreements ranging from the environmental protections of the Kyoto Accord to the banning of land mines and restrictions on the spread of small arms and light weapons, withdrew from the treaty establishing the International Criminal Court, refused to participate in a conference to provide verification measures for the Biological Weapons Convention, and repudiated both the nuclear test-ban treaty and the ABM treaty prohibiting anti–ballistic missile systems.

The theme of partnership resonated loudly in the aftermath of 9/11 and during the war against the Taliban, al-Qaida, and Osama bin Laden in Afghanistan, but then seriously floundered again with the unilateralism of the *National Security Strategy of the United States*. The country's possession of "unprecedented—and unequaled—strength and influence in the world," it declared, presented "a time of opportunity for America." To take full advantage of this, the document announced that national security strategy would be based not on broad norms and restraints of international order but rather "on a distinctly °American internationalism that reflects the union of our values and our national interests," and, thus, that the United States intended "to lead." "In exercising our leadership," it went on to explain, "we will respect the values, judgments, and interests of our friends and partners. Still, we will be prepared to act apart when our interests and unique responsibilities require." Moreover, it asserted that the most critical instrument of statecraft would be armed force:

> The major institutions of American national security were designed in a different era to meet different requirements. All of them must be transformed. It is time to reaffirm the essential role of American military strength. We must build and maintain our defenses beyond challenge.

Such pronouncements about acting "apart" and armed forces "beyond challenge" provoked deep concerns among virtually all other nations in the world, but they marked only a prelude to the veritable chasm that would open in the intense debate when the United States invaded Iraq in March 2003. Steps leading to the outbreak of the war and its aftermath revealed extraordinarily

sharp differences over the nature of the threat posed by Saddam Hussein, the quality of intelligence and use of evidence, and the use of armed force to bring about a regime change, among many other issues. But it did much more that this, for the launching of what was in fact a *preventive* war against an uncertain and potential threat in the distance, rather than a *preemptive* war against a direct and imminent threat at hand that could not be averted by any means other than force, crossed a threshold of legitimacy for many and thereby created a crisis over the fundamental principles that should guide the evolving international system and its search for peace and security. No one posed the central question more directly that German Foreign Minister Joschka Fischer, who asked pointedly: "What kind of world order do we want?"

To some Americans, the answer to this question could be found in the *National Security Strategy of the United States* and its call for them to become the undisputed leader of the world with unprecedented and unsurpassed military superiority. They embraced the view expressed by President George W. Bush, Vice President Richard Cheney, Secretary of Defense Donald Rusmsfeld, and Deputy Secretary of Defense Paul Wolfowitz, among others, of the need to act apart from others when necessary and to use America's unparalleled power to full advantage, pursuing the national interest without the restraints imposed either by countervailing power or by international norms and collective decision making. They also welcomed the much-quoted opinion piece by David Frum and Richard Perle, American authors of *An End to Evil*, who argued that the United Nations had become "an obstacle to our national security," sliding "from irrelevance to oblivion," and boasted: "The U.N. member states know that the United States will in the end do whatever it has to do, regardless of what the United Nations says."

This particular vision of a world order and a unipolar system dominated by America produced enormous controversy and outrage. In fact, to the leaders of most other governments and to the hundreds of thousands of protestors who demonstrated around the world at the time of the Iraq War, as well as to critics within the United States itself, it demonstrated a sharp turn from partnership into rivalry and one that simultaneously rejected both the traditional balance of power and international security. Criticism from adversaries and extremists who bitterly detested America's powerful global influence could be expected, but now it came from close friends and allies. Long-time members of NATO began speaking openly of American "arrogance," "aggressive nationalism," "unilateralism," "hegemony," "self-indulgence," "bullying," and "imperialism." They referred to the United States as a "hyperpower" and "the new Rome," accusing it of being bent on domination and insistent upon refusing to restrain its own power as a part of the international order. Even British Prime Minister Tony Blair, who closely allied himself with the United States, felt compelled to openly warn before a joint session of the U.S. Congress: "What America must do is show that this is a partnership built on persuasion, not command." The normally friendly BBC began a series of critical broadcasts in 2004 on the subject of the American "Age of Empire," which concluded by stating that if things continued in this manner, the

United States could end up being "not only the most powerful country in the world but also the most distrusted country in the world."

Such attitudes only accelerated an already serious rift in the American-European alliance that had served as an anchor of international security for more than fifty years. Public opinion overwhelmingly opposed the American war in Iraq, and most governments told Washington that they had no intention of providing diplomatic, military, or financial support for its military campaign there. In this process, Europeans came to realize not only a widening strategic separation between themselves and the Americans, but also their own growing political and economic strength resulting from successful integration and the development and significant expansion of the European Union in 2004, which increased its membership to twenty-five nations, and thereby represented a population nearly twice the size of that of the United States. This was compounded by the aging of those Europeans who had emerged from the Second World War with considerable gratitude to the United States for saving them from tyranny and their replacement by a younger and more self-confident generation, who, according to opinion polls, increasingly viewed America as the country that posed the most dangerous threat to global peace. For all of these reasons, discussion steadily arose about the need for Europe to "rise as a counterweight to the United States."

Others discussed counterweights as a means to world order as well. The power of Russia, Japan, and India could not be discounted, nor could that of oil-rich countries in the Middle East. In addition, during a summit meeting in 2004 of the heads of state of all African governments, great attention was paid to the possibilities of what could happen to the international system if they combined their vast territory, resources of oil and diamonds, and population of the continent. As one spokesman declared: "We have the capabilities that would allow us to be as strong as the United States and the European Union, and this is a good thing, so there could be balance in the world. When there is no balance, there are wars and conflicts."

A more immediate and likely counterweight, however, appeared with the growing emergence of China. During the years of Mao Zedong, the country developed a reputation for pursuing a revolutionary foreign policy, strong opposition to both of the superpowers, a rejection of many international norms, an undertrained diplomatic corps, economic autarky, and isolation from the broader international community. With the rise of Deng Xiaoping and the end of the Cold War, however, China began to normalize or establish diplomatic relations with many countries, seriously train its diplomats, and accept many prevailing international institutions and rules. Especially after Jiang Zemin became president in 1993, it increasingly played a much more influential role in global affairs. Beijing started holding annual meetings, for example, with senior officials of the Association of Southeast Asian Nations (ASEAN) about matters of diplomacy and security. It then served as one of the founding members of the Asia-Europe Meeting to facilitate discussions between these two continents, signed the Comprehensive Nuclear Test Ban Treaty, and went on to ratify several major arms control and nonproliferation accords. China

became much more active on the Security Council when dealing with measures authorizing the use of force and participated in United Nations peacekeeping operations, including those in East Timor and Congo. It gained admission to the World Trade Organization in December 2001, proposed the establishment of a new security mechanism in Asia, launched a Web site within the Ministry of Foreign Affairs to explain its positions to a global audience, and actively inserted itself into the negotiations surrounding North Korea's nuclear program. In June 2003 President Hu Jintao became the first Communist Chinese leader to attend a meeting of the world's leading industrialized countries. All of this took place, of course, in the context of a rising self-confidence, enhanced by the knowledge of possessing the world's biggest population (1.3 billion people), fastest growing economy, and largest army, while at the same time developing a successful space program. Particularly with the emergence of the "war on terrorism" and American assertiveness, the writings of Chinese strategists have marked a critical shift in their view of the international system and China's role in it. Now they emphasize the need to adopt what they call "Great Power mentality" (*daguo xintai*) and to "share global responsibilities" as partners with other major actors within the evolving international system.

Serious discussions about the meaning of partnership and rivalry in the context of visions of world order and the international system continued within the United Nations itself. Here, member states watched with deep concern over the United States' unilateral and preventive use of force. When President George W. Bush spoke before the General Assembly in September 2003 after launching the war against Iraq, for example, he was greeted coldly and faced a barrage of criticism from the leaders of other nations. President Jacques Chirac of France described the war as "one of the gravest trials" in the history of the United Nations, saying that it "undermined the multilateral system." "In an open world," he continued, "no one can live in isolation, no one can act alone in the name of all, and no once can accept the anarchy of a society without rules. There is no alternative to the United Nations." In considering the whole issue of force and statecraft within the evolving international system, Kofi Annan delivered an unusually impassioned and sharp condemnation of American policy, declaring that "unilateralism" amounted to an assault on the "collective action" envisioned by Franklin Roosevelt and others who created the United Nations. He warned before all members of the General Assembly:

> This logic represents a fundamental challenge to the principles on which, however imperfectly, world peace and stability have rested for the last fifty-eight years. My concern is that, if it were to be adopted, it could set precedents that resulted in a proliferation of the unilateral and lawless use of force, with or without justification.

Annan concluded that "we have come to a fork in the road. This may be a moment no less decisive than 1945 itself when the United Nations was founded."

When faced with this intense debate, a number of governments responded by placing more of their energies and their hopes into the United Nations itself, which they saw as not being "irrelevant," but rather "indispensable." They renewed their commitment to the vision of global cooperation and security expressed in the Millennium Declaration of 2000, seeking to guide the evolving international system toward greater collective action. Many demonstrated their resolve by contributing billions of dollars and tens of thousands of military forces and civilian police to United Nations–mandated peacekeeping operations deployed in both interstate conflicts and intrastate civil wars in many troubled places in the world, including the Democratic Republic of the Congo, Sierra Leone, Liberia, the Syrian Golan Heights, Kosovo, East Timor, Ethiopia, and Eritrea, among others. They also actively participated in special missions for preventive diplomacy, employing techniques of early warning, fact finding, confidence building, and the establishment of good offices to help resolve disputes before they broke out in violence and in peacebuilding missions in Afghanistan and Iraq designed for reconstruction, drafting constitutions, organizing and supervising elections, establishing the rule of law, and helping to advance democracy and the protection of human rights. Some governments also sought to make the organization stronger by addressing issues of reforms, including the assessment of financial contributions and seriously discussing the politically charged issue of expanding or restructuring the permanent membership of the Security Council to reflect the growing influence of Germany, Japan, India, and Brazil, rather than being frozen in time with the five victors of the Second World War more than sixty years ago.

The area of greatest contention for partnership and rivalry within the United Nations and especially within the Security Council—as always—concerns force and statecraft. Here, many serious and difficult questions arise. Given the fact that since the Cold War ended the main threats to international security have derived more from developments within states than from external aggression by one state against another, for example, what should the members of the organization collectively do about using force to intervene within the domestic affairs of a country whose own national sovereignty is accorded special status under the Charter? When, exactly, is a threat judged to be "imminent" enough to justify preemption, and who makes that judgment? Who precisely decides what is a "last resort" and when diplomacy has been fully exhausted? Similarly, who makes the decision of whether "self-defense" is legitimately at stake when armed force is employed? Attempts to find answers to these questions and to devise both substantive rules and institutional arrangements to govern the use of force in the evolving international system make it clear that these tasks will not be easy.

Those seeking to develop greater international cooperation by means of strengthening the United Nations, of course, have cause for both optimism and despair. They know that the organization can never do more than its member states allow it do, that debate sometimes occupies more attention than action, and that the powerful and the wealthy cannot always be counted upon to be

partners. But they also know that the United Nations, despite all of the structural limitations and the political forces of rivalry aligned against it, has not only survived but in certain areas even prospered. Its contributions to peace-keeping and humanitarian intervention, peacebuilding, preventive diplomacy, mediation and conflict resolution, relief operations in the face of tragic disasters, advancement of human rights, promotion of democracy, extension of social and economic development, assistance to refugees, advancing international criminal law, and efforts to address globalization and complex interdependence all mark undeniable achievements. For these reasons, they view the United Nations as an imperfect but indispensable instrument in guiding the evolving international system toward peace and security in a dangerous world, taking hope from the observation made by Dag Hammarskjöld concerning slow but steady steps toward an ultimate goal, when he said: "The United Nations reflects both aspiration and a falling short of aspiration. But the constant struggle to close the gap between aspiration and performance now, as always, makes the difference between civilization and chaos."

Others look instead to the value of balancing rivalries in the world. They believe that peace and security are best served not by a conscious, grand design of cooperation, but more by considerations of geopolitics and countervailing power. Henry Kissinger argues, for example, that those responsible for statecraft need to avoid the collective security of internationalism and focus their attention instead on the competitive nature of nation-state behavior. The

"Aspiration and Performance": Efforts to Find Peace and Security Through the United Nations (UN Photo)

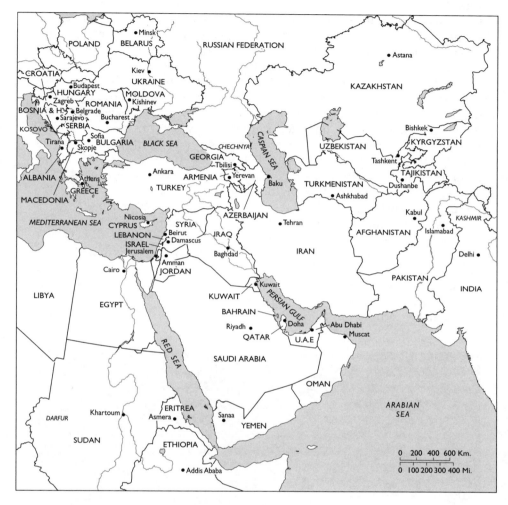

Turmoil in the Evolving System

United States, he writes, must be preoccupied with balance of power whether it likes it or not:

> Geopolitically, America is an island off the shores of the large landmass of Eurasia, whose resources and population far exceed those of the United States. The domination by a single power of either of Eurasia's two principal spheres—Europe or Asia—remains a good definition of strategic danger for America, Cold War or no Cold War. For such a grouping would have the capacity to outstrip America economically and, in the end, militarily.

Although starting from a very different premise, political scientist Charles Kupchan in *The End of the American Era* reaches a similar conclusion. He believes that due to the growing strength of Europe as a rival rather than a partner to the United States and the unwillingness of the American public to sustain foreign engagements and entanglements over time, the international system will again return to multipolarity and, thus, to competition and a balance of power. The prospect of such a balance emerging is greeted by some with enthusiasm. Others respond with deep concern and fear, as does Tony Blair, who warns: "There is no more dangerous theory in international politics than that we need to balance the power of America with other competitive powers, different poles around which nations gather."

The future direction of the evolving international system will depend, as it always has in the past, on the extent to which the participants view themselves as partners or rivals. Whether they choose to move toward broad-based collective security or toward a multipolar balance of power among only a few nation-states or regional groupings, the fact remains that no international system can possibly survive or function unless there is an essential agreement on fundamental goals and objectives. This is why a unipolar system dominated by a single state can not be sustained. The long-term maintenance of any system requires a foundation of shared aims among the major actors. One of the great insights of those who created and maintained the classical system of diplomacy, as we have seen, was the realization that a balance of power inhibits the capacity to overthrow an international system, but agreement on basic values inhibits the desire to do so. They reached the conclusion that realistic calculations rather than idealistic impulses made it essential for them to recognize the existence of each other and to regulate their rivalries by defining their own interests and *raison d'état* in terms of the larger, collective system that could preserve peace and security. But the lessons learned by one generation are not always accepted or understood by those who follow, the quality of leadership changes, and consensus on fundamental values is often extraordinarily difficult to achieve.

The participants of every international system in history have had to seriously wrestle with this challenge of choosing the extent to which they would pursue partnership or rivalry and how they would seek to reconcile the two. Just as those in the past had to confront the specific challenges of their time, so will those responsible for statecraft in our own time. In this endeavor, certain matters of globalization and complex interdependence will encourage

the participants to see that some threats are so widespread and so difficult that no single nation, however strong, can possibly solve them alone. They respect neither borders nor passports and call attention to the fact that global problems require global solutions. These include, among many others, the dangers of endemic violence, collective security and peace, terrorism, the proliferation of weapons of mass destruction, human rights abuses, indebtedness and development, infectious diseases, drugs, organized crime, poverty, population growth and migration, and environment degradation. Other issues instead will provoke division and exacerbate rivalries. Among these, one can point to the arguments over the necessity and legitimate use of armed force, conflicting claims of traditional national sovereignty and those of collective security, the roles to be played by the world's only superpower and that of the United Nations, the debate over the root causes and varieties of terrorism, the continuing conflict between the Israelis and their Arab neighbors and the Palestinians, fanaticism and xenophobia that perceive international cooperation as betrayal, economic competition and the growing worldwide divide between the rich and the poor, divisions of race and religion, and the clash of cultural and political differences at home and abroad.

Whether the evolving international system follows the path of misadventure and malice or that of peace and security, and whether it can find shared values in the midst of the diplomatic revolution or not will depend upon our ability to determine the extent to which we will be partners or rivals. In this regard, our future may well depend upon whether we can understand how and why others have succeeded or failed when dealing with the diplomatic challenges of force and statecraft in the past, and it is, consequently, to this matter that we now turn in Part II.

SUGGESTIONS FOR FURTHER EXPLORATION

Many accounts of, and broad prescriptions and strategies for, the evolving international system were raised at the end of the Cold War. Some of these include Alexander L. George, "The Role of Force in Diplomacy," in H. W. Brands et al. (eds.), *The Use of Force After the Cold War* (College Station, TX, 2003 ed.); John Mearsheimer, *The Tragedy of Great Power Politics* (New York, 2003); Paul Stern and Daniel Druckman (eds.), *International Conflict Resolution After the Cold War* (Washington, DC, 2002); Bruce Jentleson (ed.), *Opportunities Missed, Opportunities Seized: Preventive Diplomacy in the Post-Cold War World* (Lanham, MD, 2000); Karen Mingst and Margaret Karns, *The United Nations in the Post-Cold War Era* (Boulder, CO, 1999 ed.); George Bush and Brent Scowcroft, *A World Transformed* (New York, 1998); Center for Strategic and International Studies, *Reinventing Diplomacy in the Information Age* (Washington, DC, 1998); Samuel Huntington, *The Clash of Civilizations and the Remaking of the World Order* (New York, 1998 ed.); Charles Freeman, *The Art of Power* (Washington, DC, 1997); Boutros Boutros-Ghali, *Agenda for Peace* (New York, 1996 ed.); John Stremlau, "Antidote to Anarchy," *The Washington Quarterly*, 18 (Winter 1995): 29–44; Henry Kissinger, *Diplomacy* (New York, 1994); Gareth Evans, *Cooperating for Peace: The Global Agenda for the 1990s and Beyond* (St. Leonards, Australia, 1993); and Alexander L. George, "The Gulf War's Possible Impact on the International System," in Stanley Renshon (ed.), *The Political Psychology of the Gulf War* (Pittsburgh, 1993). The staggering impact of technology on communication,

transportation, armed force, and statecraft in general can be seen by consulting the wide variety of Web sites identified at the end of the Conclusion.

Challenges to the traditional state system and claims of national sovereignty are analyzed in Stephen Krasner, "Sharing Sovereignty," in *International Security*, 29 (Fall 2004): 85–120; Paul Gordon Lauren, *The Evolution of International Human Rights* (Philadelphia, 2003 ed.); T. V. Paul et al. (eds.), *The Nation-State in Question* (Princeton, 2003); International Commission on Intervention and State Sovereignty, *The Responsibility to Protect* (Ottawa, 2001); Royce Ammon, *Global Television and the Shaping of World Policy: CNN, Telediplomacy, and Foreign Policy* (New York, 2001); Charles Kegley and Gregory Raymond, *Exorcising the Ghost of Westphalia: Building World Order in the New Millennium* (Upper Saddle River, NJ, 2001); Richard Langhorne, *The Coming Globalization: Its Evolution and Contemporary Consequences* (New York, 2001); Joseph Nye, Jr. and John Donahue (eds.), *Governance in a Globalizing World* (Washington, DC, 2000); Martin van Creveld, *The Rise and Decline of the State* (Cambridge, 2000); Kofi Annan, "Two Concepts of Sovereignty," *The Economist*, September 18, 1999; and Jessica Mathews, "Power Shift," *Foreign Affairs*, 76 (January/February 1997): 50–66.

On terrorism and the "war on terrorism," see the annual, official reports entitled *Patterns of Global Terrorism* of the U.S. Department of State at www.state.gov; Michael Scheuer, *Imperial Hubris* (Dulles, VA, 2005); Richard Clarke, *Against All Enemies* (New York, 2004); David Frum and Richard Perle, *An End to Evil: How to Win the War on Terror* (New York, 2003); Peter Bergen, *Holy War, Inc.* (New York, 2002); John Esposito, *Unholy War* (New York, 2002); Richard Falk, *The Great Terror War* (New York, 2002); Charles Kegley, *The New Global Terrorism* (New York, 2002); and Bob Woodward, *Bush at War* (New York, 2002).

The always-present theme of partnership and rivalry has assumed much greater importance in the wake of American foreign and national security policy in the wake of 9/11 and the Iraq War, often generating considerable and heated debate. Interesting and sometimes provocative treatments can be found in Robert Jervis, *American Foreign Policy in a New Era* (New York, 2005); Stefan Halper and Jonathan Clarke, *America Alone: The Neo-Conservatives and the Global Order* (Cambridge, 2004); Andrew Bacevich, *American Empire* (Cambridge, MA, 2004); Zbigniew Brezezinski, *The Choice: Global Domination or Global Leadership* (New York, 2004); Barry Buzan, *The United States and the Great Powers* (Cambridge, 2004); John Lewis Gaddis, *Surprise, Security, and the American Experience* (Cambridge, MA, 2004); Robert Kagan, *Of Paradise and Power* (New York, 2004 ed.); Ivo Daalder and James Steinberg, "New Rules on When to Go to War," *Financial Times*, August 2, 2004; William Odom and Robert Dujarric, *America's Inadvertent Empire* (New Haven, 2004); Ivo Daalder and James Lindsay, *America Unbound: The Bush Revolution in Foreign Policy* (Washington, DC, 2003); Michael Hirsh, *At War With Ourselves* (New York, 2003); Charles Kupchan, *The End of the American Era* (New York, 2003); Joseph Nye, Jr., *Paradox of American Power* (New York, 2003); Clyde Prestowitz, *Rogue Nation* (New York, 2003); Andrew Bacevich, "Bush's Grand Strategy," *The American Conservative*, November 4, 2002; and United States, White House, *National Security Strategy of the United States, 2002* (Washington, DC, 2002). On the evolving strength of China, see Evan Medeiros and M. Taylor Fravel, "China's New Diplomacy," in *Foreign Affairs* (November/December 2003): 22–35; and David Lampton, "The Stealth Normalization of U.S.-China Relations," *The National Interest* (Fall 2003): 37–48. For broad trends, see the discussions in Dan Caldwell and Robert E. Williams, Jr., *Seeking Security in an Insecure World* (Lanham, MD, 2006); and Philip Bobbitt, *The Shield of Achilles* (New York, 2002).

PART TWO

HISTORY, THEORY, AND PRACTICE

─── 7 ───

Lessons of History and Knowledge for Statecraft

"Those who cannot remember the past," philosopher George Santayana once famously observed, "are condemned to repeat it." His thought-provoking statement is quoted so frequently because it seems to resonate intuitively with our own experience and understanding. We believe that we do and should learn from our past, trying to avoid previous mistakes and to duplicate behavior that brought success. It seems natural, therefore, to seek to apply this principle to the broader canvas of human experience as a whole, exploring whether and how people have gained insight from hindsight. With specific reference to issues of diplomacy and force and statecraft, for example, we want to know if leaders have learned any lessons from past failures and successes—or not. Almost every statesman and general has professed to having learned from history, but there are times when the evidence certainly suggests otherwise. There is often confusion and sometimes dispute about precisely how leaders learn, what they learn, how they deal with seemingly conflicting lessons, and whether the analogies that they take from the past are appropriate to specific problems at hand. With these factors in mind, it is important to explore in Part Two of this book how knowledge for statecraft might be gained in such a way as to address diplomatic challenges related to armed force and to consider the opinion of the distinguished historian of the Renaissance, Jacob Burckhardt, who once remarked that the true use of history should be not to make leaders more clever for the next time but to make them wiser forever.

CLASSICAL WRITERS ON THE IMPORTANCE OF HISTORICAL LESSONS

Virtually every writer who has ever seriously analyzed statecraft and international behavior has stressed the importance of learning historical lessons. They have strongly believed that whatever guides exist for survival in the present or future can be found only in the past, arguing that if we do not know where we have been, we cannot possibly know where we are or where we

are going. The study of history, they have maintained, can reveal invaluable insights about human behavior, the nature of diplomatic challenges, the range of choice and likely reactions to certain policies, the use or the threat of armed force, continuities and changes, the evolution of international systems, balances of power, the relationship between capabilities and intentions, and the role of ethical values and restraints on policy makers, among many, many other factors of statecraft. For this reason they have stressed time and time again the critical necessity for leaders to learn from history.

It is consequently not surprising that Thucydides would write his powerful, insightful, and path-breaking book, *The History of the Peloponnesian War*, with precisely this purpose in mind. He was not interested in simply recounting a story of the long life-and-death struggle between ancient Athens and Sparta, but rather in sustained inquiry into history as a means of discovering meaning and knowledge about human behavior to be used by policy makers. Thucydides took seriously the fact that the Greek word *historeo* meant to learn or gain knowledge through inquiry and thus sought to study the past in such a way as to move from the specific event to underlying patterns, or from the particular to the general. He analyzed the use of power by a demagogue like Cleon to gain knowledge of the larger nature of power politics and demagogues themselves, the instance of the negotiations with Argos to appreciate the more encompassing nature of negotiations as a whole, and the particular coercive threats like those in the Melian dialogue to understand the nature of force and statecraft itself. Indeed, as he wrote in his introduction, he wanted his words to be "judged useful by those who want to understand clearly the events which happened in the past and which (human nature being what it is) will, as some time or other and in much the same ways, be repeated in the future." In this regard, he wanted his work to provide wisdom and guidance for leaders who would face similar problems in the years that followed and thereby "to last forever."

This theme of the practical use of history as a guide for statecraft secured substantial reinforcement from Niccolò Machiavelli in the early sixteenth century. Indeed, as he wrote in the preface of *The Prince*, there was nothing "which I hold so dear or esteem so highly as the knowledge of the deeds of great men which I have acquired through a long experience of modern events and a constant study of the past." "With the utmost diligence," he continued, "I have long pondered and scrutinized the action of the great, and now I offer the results to Your Highness within the compass of a small volume." Machiavelli then presented his handbook for policy makers, drawing evidence from the historical experience of those who exercised power with failures and successes ranging from Moses of the Old Testament, Alexander the Great, and Severus of the Roman Empire to Cesare Borgia and other leaders of Renaissance Italy. From these he drew a number of conclusions, or lessons, designed to help leaders govern and advance the interests of their states. This matter became so important to Machiavelli that he returned to it again in his subsequent book, *The Discourses*, and concluded directly: "Whoever considers the past and the present will readily observe that all cities and all peoples

are and ever have been animated by the same desires and the same passions; so that it is easy, by diligent study of the past, to foresee what is likely to happen in the future."

Hugo Grotius reached similar conclusions and drew extensively from the past. As he argued early in the preface of his famous seventeenth-century *On the Law of War and Peace*, historical experience clearly reveals that people will "act in a similar way under similar circumstances." The two most important contributions to be gained from study of lessons of the past, he maintained, were examples of human behavior and a solid basis for judgment.

François de Callières echoed exactly this same theme in his masterful eighteenth-century *On the Manner of Negotiating with Princes*. The entire purpose for writing his book, he explained, was to develop the skills and the habits of thought necessary to deal with the critical issues of statecraft on which the whole fortunes, peace, and security of states depended. He worried that there had been "no discipline or fixed rules" by which "good citizens destined to become negotiators might instruct themselves in the knowledge necessary for this kind of employment." From his own considerable experience, astute observation, and careful reading of the past, de Callières believed that the conduct of diplomacy required very special kinds of skills: "It demands all the penetration, all the dexterity, all the suppleness which a man can possess. It requires a wide-spread understanding and knowledge, and above all, a correct and piercing discernment." The development of such understanding, knowledge, and discernment, he argued, could be found in studying alliances, military establishments, the interests and personalities of foreign leaders, the languages and customs of other countries, and "above all" and "of first importance," the study of history. Observed Frederick the Great a few years later, "What is the good of experience if you do not reflect?"

During the nineteenth century, Carl von Clausewitz's monumental and insightful *On War* focusing directly on force and statecraft reiterated and then further elaborated precisely the same theme. In fact, he opened his chapter on the use of history with these words: "Historical examples clarify everything and also provide the best kind of proof in the empirical sciences." He explained this by describing how history can assist policy makers by providing explanations of ideas, showing applications in the form of specific examples, offering support for various possibilities, and presenting evidence to deduce a particular doctrine or theory. Clausewitz's text on the relationship between means and ends, on war as a continuation of policy, consequently drew heavily upon historical evidence. He nevertheless cautioned that the use of history in this way required considerable effort and sophistication. In one of his most perceptive observations, Clausewitz warned against those who fleetingly look to find historical examples for quick answers for policy or the development of theory, who *"never rise above anecdote,"* and who draw vast lessons from only an individual case, "starting always with the most striking feature, the high point of the event, and digging only as deep as suit them, never getting down to the general factors that govern the matter."

These classical writers, who stressed the vital importance of historical lessons for statecraft, heavily influenced generations of successors. One thinks, for example, of Henry Kissinger, who wrote a thesis on the subject of "The Meaning of History," and whose first book, entitled *A World Restored,* focused on the experience of forming a successful coalition against Napoleon and holding the Congress of Vienna in 1814–1815 as a means of exploring larger and enduring issues of personalities, alliances, balances of power, legitimacy, national interests, peacemaking, and the nature of stability and security within an international system. As he wrote at the end, "No significant conclusions are possible in the study of foreign affairs . . . without an awareness of the historical context. For societies exist in time more than in space." Whether Kissinger actually or appropriately applied the historical lessons he wrote about as a scholar when he served as a policy maker, of course, will be debated for years to come, but there can be little doubt about his conviction in the value of history for the conduct of statecraft. One also thinks of political scientist Klaus Knorr, who introduced his influential book entitled *Historical Dimensions of National Security Problems* by writing that

> the understanding of past events and problems can be part of a learning process that assists us in understanding present events and problems. Without knowing how past societies coped with problems similar to our own, the options they considered, the choices they made, and the consequences entailed by these choices, we can only arrive at a flat, poorly constructed understanding of our present problems.

THE HISTORICAL HABIT OF MIND

Acknowledging the necessity of learning lessons from history, however, is not the same as understanding what it is that history actually teaches about the nature of statecraft. In seeking to address precisely this question, the Scottish historian D. P. Heatley decided in the aftermath of the upheaval of the First World War to write a book entitled *Diplomacy and the Study of International Relations.* He began his work by discussing the importance of learning historical lessons and then presented a direct proposition: "Political Science without History, it has been said, has no root; and History without Political Science has no fruit." With this in mind, Heatley argued that anyone who wanted to understand international relations must begin first with the study of how governments of earlier times attempted to solve their diplomatic problems, and this he regarded as the foundation and "training ground" of statesmanship. The best way to approach this task was not with some kind of simplistic memorization of names and dates, but rather with an exploration of important phenomena and problems from the richness of historical experience. He demonstrated what he meant by this with thoughtful treatments about such matters as the traditions and practices of diplomacy, references to the classical writers from Thycidides and Machiavelli to de Callières and Clausewitz, treaties and maps, the qualities required of diplomats, the conduct of negotiation, the challenges confronting persons charged with the

formulation and execution of foreign policy, the restraints imposed upon them by the nature of the international context of their work, the impact of ethical values, and the relationship between statecraft and that more drastic instrument of policy, armed force. With such an approach, Heatley believed, students of the past could avoid becoming mere chroniclers of what happened in international relations and instead become much more thoughtful interpreters and sophisticated analysts of how and why it happened. Fundamentally, he maintained that the study of history, more than anything else, could lead to reflection and wisdom by developing "the habit of mind that is required for appreciating questions of foreign policy."

It is exactly this habit of mind, of course, that helps to develop essential skills in understanding the world of diplomacy and the instruments of foreign policy by establishing perspective and a basis for judgment. Thinking in focused ways about history trains the mind to recognize certain patterns or reoccurrences in issues, problems, and human behavior; to identify important variables and causal mechanisms; to analyze both the similarities and the differences, or continuities and changes, between cases; and, especially, to appreciate the critical importance of context. It cannot at all pretend to provide a precise recipe book for action in every contingency that arises or detailed and highly accurate predictions about a specific outcome if a particular choice is made. Instead, the great value of such a habit of mind, or manner of reflection and sensitivity, or way of thinking, can be found in its power to provide vicarious experience and use broad and wide-ranging knowledge of the past in such a way as to focus thought and stimulate reflection about previous human experiences for the diagnosis and prognosis of current and future events.

Students of history seeking to gain knowledge for statecraft, for example, develop a habit of mind that realizes the critical importance of individual *people*. Nation-states, organizations, or groups of one kind or another do not make choices or take actions themselves—real people do. These are the leaders and their advisors, the ambassadors and strategic planners, the diplomats and intelligence officers, the generals and soldiers, the admirals and sailors, the negotiators and crisis managers, the politicians and bureaucrats, the business investors and human rights activists, and the local warlords and terrorists, among many other individuals. They do not behave as unitary or homogeneous actors, but instead sometimes cooperate as partners and sometimes compete with each other as rivals in ways that complicate calculations, reaching consensus, decision making, and conflict behavior. Yet, history demonstrates time and again that policies are determined and implemented—as they only can be—not by abstract entities, but by the human element of living men and women within their own contexts, each with his or her own personality, strengths and weaknesses, ability to handle stress, beliefs and ethical values, and casts of mind or perceptions. People determine the extent to which armed force is necessary and is dangerous. That force possesses bargaining influence in deterrence and coercive diplomacy only insofar as people are willing and able to use it, or others think they are willing and able. Ethical values and international norms have no power to restrain behavior unless

people feel bound to honor their obligations and make choices that protect the well-being of others. The whole concept of diplomacy itself is significant only insofar as it is put into practice by people. They may be wise or foolish, rational or irrational, able or incompetent, compassionate or vengeful, deliberative or impulsive, confident or frightened, flexible or rigid, and capable of seeing events from the perspective of others or not, but because of design or chance, office or character, people matter.

History also trains the mind to be attentive to *process*. Those who study the past tend to think processionally—of time passing. They view time as a stream, sometimes calmly meandering and sometimes cascading with force, but always aware not only of the present and future emerging from the past, but also in turn becoming the past. Historians analyze how events and developments evolve, as demonstrated in Part I when dealing with international systems and the diplomatic revolution, paying particular attention to cause and effect and to change and continuity. They examine those elements that change through time and those that stay the same, for example, exploring how the diplomatic challenges of our time are both similar and different from those of the past. This applies whether the discussion centers upon the advice of François de Callières or Kofi Annan, the international system-building efforts of Clemens von Metternich or Woodrow Wilson, or the use of force by Frederick the Great or George W. Bush. As David Trask, the former historian of the U.S. Department of State argues, such a habit of mind is indispensable for statecraft. "The policy maker," he observes, "has no alternative but to make use of historical information and historical thought simply because he [or she] is specifically concerned with process, the bread and butter of historians."

Reading and thinking about history similarly opens the mind to an extraordinarily wide range of *possibilities*. The systematic study of people and events over an extended period of time provides an enormously rich and varied array of imaginable or possible actions and strategies, and likely reactions, that far exceeds what any one person could ever haphazardly learn from personal experience in his or her own short lifetime alone. Knowing that certain things already have occurred affords a huge and available inventory or data base of information about human behavior replete with specific evidence, examples, variables, ideas, analogies, interpretations, patterns, benchmarks, and precedents that otherwise may have remained completely beyond a contemporary policy maker's imagination. History thus offers not only a spectrum of multiple choices, policy options, or range of alternative solutions that have been practiced and previously tried by others, but also some basis for judgment and diagnostic value about whether the strategies were appropriate or not and why they may have resulted in success or failure. This is precisely the point made by a 2005 RAND Corporation study prepared for the Department of Defense with reference to the insurgency in the war against Iraq. The report sharply criticized the tendency of American leadership "not to absorb historical lessons" and strongly recommended setting up some means "for exposing senior officials to possibilities other than those being assumed in their planning."

Historical study also creates a habit of mind that can develop a sense of *perspective and proportion*. In a brief but marvelous essay entitled "The Historian's Opportunity," Barbara Tuchman argued that the task of historians is to tell what history is about, what the forces are that drive us, and how we interact as humans. History, she wrote, "being concerned as it is with reality and subject as it is to certain disciplines," must see these various elements "in proportion to the whole":

> Distillation is selection, and selection . . . is the essence of writing history. It is the cardinal process of composition, the most difficult, the most delicate, the most fraught with error as well as art. Ability to distinguish what is significant from what is insignificant is *sine qua non*.

Study of the past involves not only making precisely these distinctions, but creating measuring rods against which actions are judged and establishing a contextual background against which people and events are viewed. One dimension of this entails developing a capacity to see the perspective of other actors and how they view their interests within the international system. Another element entails the perspective of time, or acquiring the ability to avoid the dangers of presentism by looking both backward and forward in such a way that a seemingly isolated event can be seen as a part of a larger pattern or process and given meaning beyond a mere immediate or single occurrence. These are precisely the tasks of those responsible for statecraft as well, who must be able to make intelligent, objective judgments about the relationship of specific parts to the whole, compare one case to others, and prudently determine what is important and possible—and what is not. It has been observed, for example, that one of the qualities that made Otto von Bismarck such a successful statesman was his extraordinary sense of perspective and proportion that enabled him to discern how specific problems were related to larger issues and to appreciate the range and the limitations of choice among human actors. The study of historical experience is excellent training for developing just such skills. Indeed, it was Bismarck himself who once said that fools learn from their experience, while the wise learn from the experience of others.

THE CHALLENGES OF LEARNING AND APPLYING LESSONS OF HISTORY

To emphasize the importance of learning and then applying lessons from history, nevertheless, is not the same as actually being able to do it in practice. The fact remains that many challenges confront those who seek to do so. Some of these involve the very process and nature of learning lessons themselves. In the first place, the study of history, although fascinating and often enjoyable, is nevertheless extremely challenging. It is complex and requires the time, effort, and ability to analyze the intricate interactions between people, the particular skills and personalities of leaders, forces of continuity and change, ideas and beliefs, domestic and foreign influences, and the state of technological

development, among many, many other factors and variables, and then to reach conclusions about meaning. Second, as a result of the inherent complexity, there is no such thing as a single, easily understandable *lesson* from history. Instead, history presents many faces and produces a variety of innumerable *lessons*. Third, these various lessons do not necessarily point in a single direction and at times appear to be ambiguous, inconsistent, or even contradictory. Certain cases from historical experience, for example, might indicate that diplomatic compromise serves the best course for preserving peace and security, whereas other cases might suggest that concessions only encourage further demands and aggression by opponents.

A fourth challenge stems from the fact that lessons are often selectively learned and disproportionally recalled, depending upon many factors that include different perspectives, different purposes, and the context of learning itself. Preconceived biases, ideology, operational codes, the psychological propensity to take mental shortcuts or to persist in holding beliefs about the past even in the face of contrary evidence, or the level of firsthand participation and associated trauma resulting from particular events can produce different results. Differences between people (including those between one generation and the next, or between one culture and another) affect how and what they learn. Studies in cognitive psychology, for example, reveal that people have a strong tendency to draw much more frequently and intensely on recent cases and on those they have personally experienced rather than those from another place or of a more distant past. It is understandable, therefore, why there can be different interpretations, conflicting conclusions, and passionate disagreements (even among historians) about the most appropriate lessons to be learned from particular historical cases.

These problems of learning are further compounded by the further challenge of application, or the realities and process of policy making. It often has been said that diplomacy is the art of the possible. All leaders face various kinds of restraints that necessitate trade-offs, as we shall explore in Chapter 12, and even those who have learned lessons from history are not always free to apply all that they may know. The desirable, in other words, is not always feasible. As a consequence, observes Kissinger, "Any statesman is in part the prisoner of necessity." He therefore concludes that every leader responsible for statecraft must face "a continual struggle to rescue an element of choice from the pressure of circumstance."

There is another difficulty of applying lessons of history to policy. Studies show that leaders frequently make serious mistakes due either to their ignorance of the range of possible choices based upon historical experience or to the related tendency to draw upon a lesson from a single historical case. Decision makers often possess a very limited and simplified knowledge of the past or prepare to fight the last war or deal with the previous crisis rather than the current one and, in doing so, incorrectly choose a case and misapply a lesson to a new situation that differs from the past in important ways. As historian Ernest May wrote in *"Lessons" of the Past: The Use and Misuse of History in American Foreign Policy*, leaders ordinarily do not take the time or make

the effort to seriously study the past or to analyze the full nature of their immediate international crisis or diplomatic problem. Instead, they resort to analogy and

> tend to seize upon the first one that comes to mind. They do not search more widely. Nor do they pause to analyze the case, test its fitness, or even ask in what ways it might be misleading. Seeing a trend running toward the present, they tend to assume that it will continue into the future, not stopping to consider what produced it or why a linear projection might prove to be mistaken.

May's subsequent study, written with his political science colleague Richard Neustadt under the title *Thinking in Time: The Uses of History for Decision Makers*, explores this problem even further. They observe that all too often leaders are seduced by simple and inappropriate analogies that make little or no effort to separate the *known* from the *unclear* and the *presumed* or to seriously compare the *likenesses* with the *differences* or the continuities with the changes between cases in history and those of the present.

The enormous dangers created for peace and security by this overly simplistic and careless approach have attracted the attention of other scholars as well. Among these are political scientist Yuen Khong's study employing insights from social psychology entitled *Analogies at War* and, most recently, security studies specialist Jeffrey Record's book, *Making War, Thinking History: Munich, Vietnam, and Presidential Uses of Force from Korea to Kosovo*. They reveal how American presidents and their advisors often made choices about whether or how to use force in statecraft based upon oversimplified and seriously inappropriate simplistic analogies and, therefore, misapplied lessons of history. These involved wars of choice, including Truman's decision to fight in Korea in 1950, Kennedy and Johnson's approach to military intervention in Vietnam, Reagan's decision to intervene in Lebanon and Grenada, the senior Bush's invasion of Panama and war against Iraq after the attack against Kuwait, and Clinton's use of military force in Somalia and intervention in Kosovo, among other cases. Time and time again, these policy makers chose one of only two analogies that they thought they knew best. One of these was "Munich," referring to the Munich Conference of 1938 and its role in bringing about the Second World War, which they believed taught that appeasement only encouraged aggression, that armed force was necessary, and that there should be "no more Munichs." Or, they used "Vietnam" as the analogy that taught the dangers of armed force without clearly defined missions and sufficient domestic support, and that there should be "no more Vietnams."

One of the most frequently misapplied historical analogies, for example, has been that of Munich. Reasoned compromise always had been part of classical diplomacy as a means of developing positive relations and lowering or eliminating the possibility of war. But the failed attempt to accommodate Adolf Hitler and his aggressive designs during the 1930s was subsequently etched into the consciousness of generations of policy makers and foreign policy specialists, who interpreted the experience as demonstrating the need to

always avoid being lulled by negotiation and to immediately and directly meet force with force. Although President Harry Truman wrote in his memoirs that he prided himself on his capacity "to look back in history for precedents," his historical knowledge was sketchy and his range was narrow, and he perceived that North Korean aggression in 1950 was "just like" Nazi expansion during the 1930s wherein aggression unchecked led to aggression unleashed. Rather than trying to determine under what conditions appeasement might constitute a viable strategy for avoiding war and under what conditions it might dangerously increase the likelihood of a worse war in the future, his impulsive fixation on what he regarded as a completely analogous situation to Hitler led him to send troops into Korea and thereby extended the American Cold War strategy of containment from Europe to Asia. British Prime Minister Anthony Eden used the same analogy during the Suez Crisis of 1956, arguing that Egyptian President Gamal Nasser was "the same as" Hitler and that if action were not taken in response to his seizure of the Suez Canal, it would be like the occupation of the Rhineland and would be followed by acts of aggression against all of his other neighbors. George Bush the elder invoked the analogy of Hitler and Munich when dealing with Saddam Hussein during the Persian Gulf Crisis of 1990–1991, as did Bill Clinton when confronting Slobodan Milosevic at the time of the Kosovo Crisis of 1999. More recently, and even though the cases were vastly different, when U.S. Secretary of Defense Donald Rumsfeld addressed Asian leaders in Singapore during 2004, he warned them against trying to make deals with terrorists. Any effort to do so, he said, would be "repeating the mistakes of the nations that tried to appease Adolf Hitler in the 1930s."

Although these misuses of historical analogy often appear to be the norm rather than the exception, there are occasional successes. Among these, the thoughtful deliberations and high quality of analysis demonstrated by the Kennedy administration during the intense Cuban Missile Crisis come to mind. When intelligence sources suddenly revealed that the Soviet Union was placing missiles in Cuba, only ninety miles off of their own shores and despite all promises to the contrary, the president and his advisors seriously debated and agonized about how they should respond. The records of their meetings indicate that, as a group, they were remarkably familiar with history and drew not upon one, but a range of historical cases during their deliberations. They spoke about the outbreak of the First World War in 1914, Franklin Roosevelt's "Quarantine Address" of 1937, the unfulfilled British and French deterrence guarantees to Poland in 1939, the Japanese attack of 1941, the Berlin Crisis of 1948, the Suez and Hungarian crises of 1956, and the decision to place American missiles in Turkey during 1957, among others. As Robert Kennedy records in his personal memoir of the crisis, *Thirteen Days*, the president's knowledge of history played a decisive role in his actual decisions. When the suggestion was made for a surprise military attack against Cuba, for example, it was met with rejection on the grounds that America could not possibly maintain a strong moral position at home or abroad if it became responsible for "another Pearl Harbor." As John Kennedy watched the crisis

escalate and the knot of conflict being pulled tighter and tighter, he similarly considered lessons from the disastrous mismanagement by leaders in 1914 who seized upon preexisting war plans, refused to create pauses or employ diplomatic alternatives, and issued demands upon opponents without thinking of the consequences. He had recently finished reading Barbara Tuchman's *Guns of August* and said to his brother Robert: "I am not going to follow a course which will allow anyone to write a comparable book about this time, *The Missiles of October*. If anyone is around to write after this, they are going to understand that we made every effort to find peace and every effort to give our adversary room to move."

This kind of reasoning by historical analogy is common, and the analogies selected matter. Sometimes they matter a great deal, particularly in the selection and rejection of policy options. Hard-pressed leaders under stress in the complex and uncertain environment of international politics quite naturally seek a mechanism or framework that will help them cope by interpreting where they and the problem confronting them fit into some comprehensible and meaningful context or pattern. As they try to process incoming information and engage in decision-making tasks, they look for guidance as to what should or should not be done and assume that the future in some way will resemble the past. Indeed, according to political scientist Yaacov Vertzberger in his stimulating book, *The World in Their Minds: Information Processing, Cognition, and Perception in Foreign Policy Decisionmaking*, it is not only natural but essential that policy makers responsible for major decisions—especially those dealing with force and statecraft—attempt to use analogies from previous experiences in history. When used critically, historical analogies help in the management and resolution of complexity and uncertainty by providing information and a diagnostic framework that offers a sense about the nature of the problem at hand and the issues at stake, concrete examples and illustrations, possible direction, and a sense of the dangers and prospects of alternatives that might otherwise be completely overlooked.

But, as he and other writers like political scientist Robert Jervis in *Perception and Misperception* observe, if the reasoning is unsound, this process can be notoriously inadequate and even hazardous. Some leaders posses detailed knowledge and a considerable data base of history, while others have only a rudimentary sense of the past and a superficial awareness of a very small number of cases. Some are capable of perceiving and comprehending historical perspective and making sophisticated judgments on the basis of evidence, while others clearly are not. Moreover, no event or situation is exactly the same in detail as another. Conditions change, and sometimes they change dramatically. It is risky, therefore, to assume that a particular outcome can be predicted with exactitude or that a past event can be quickly grasped as an accurate model for a present one. These dangers become particularly acute if policy makers draw hasty and unwarranted conclusions with little scrutiny from a sample of only one: a single and narrowly drawn case that most quickly comes to mind, that belittles significant contextual differences, that tends to confirm their own preconceived biases or preferred policies, and that gives them an

illusory sense of "knowing" history. In order to address this problem, it is critical to seek a much broader range of historical experiences and cases upon which one might draw and then to analyze and synthesize them in such a way as to develop a greater understanding of the international system and its actors as they confront the challenges of force and statecraft.

STRUCTURED, FOCUSED COMPARISONS

If it is hazardous for policy makers to rely, as they sometimes do, upon a single historical analogy in deciding what to do in a new situation, how then can experience from the past be utilized to deal effectively with a new situation that appears to bear a certain resemblance to previous cases but at the same time possesses some different features? The answer lies in developing the general historical habit of mind, broadening the range of cases from history to be examined, and then carefully and systematically focusing upon a phenomenon or problem that is repeatedly encountered in the conduct of statecraft over time, with different actors and in different settings. By comparing a particular strategy under different circumstances, one can identify more closely the conditions under which it is likely to work or fail. This, in turn, can lead to an identification and articulation of certain conditional generalizations, or lessons, regarding the efficacy of certain strategies or instruments of diplomacy. Without such an approach, whatever lessons from the past one might learn are acquired completely at random and often misapplied if not appropriate to fit particular circumstances.

In Part II of this book we attempt to demonstrate more specifically how lessons of history can be combined with theory and used to gain knowledge for statecraft. To do this, we indicate how individual historical cases of a particular problem can be systematically studied and analyzed within a well-defined framework that enables a systematic comparison and cumulation of the results in order to develop a more sophisticated appreciation of its uses and limitations. More specifically, we explore the especially important, instructive, and recurring phenomena of negotiation, deterrence, coercive diplomacy, and crisis management. In each chapter we analyze the nature of one of these strategies, the issues and problems that are likely to arise in attempting to implement it, as well as the conditions or causal mechanisms derived from historical cases that either favor success or contribute to failure.

The method that we have developed for this purpose is that of *structured, focused comparison*. Our many students over the years and readers of previous editions have told us that they have found this approach to be particularly helpful in providing an analytical framework to study history, articulate principles and concepts of theory, identify critical variables, and develop diagnostic skills in making judgments about the uses and limitations of strategies and the conditions on which their effective use depends. We therefore employ it in the chapters that follow with a wider range of cases than presented in earlier editions and with a number of more contemporary case studies.

The methodology of structured, focused comparison requires careful specification of the strategy to be studied, selection of historical cases in which it was employed, the variables of interest, and analysis of why it succeeded or failed in those cases. This approach requires that a systematic research protocol and structural format of analysis be developed that specifies the same set of issues to be addressed and the same questions to be asked of each case, thus providing a close and careful comparison of case explanations in such a way that they can be cumulated for broader knowledge.

Each chapter begins with an explicit delineation of a general *theory* or *conceptual model* that addresses a particular diplomatic challenge. These theories or models are constructed of basic principles that tell us much about the logic and intended purposes of policy. Although the theories are not strategies themselves, they do serve as valuable starting points for understanding and constructing them. Strategies derived from conceptual models tell us what must be done in general to achieve the desired objectives. But to actually do this in specific cases, the principles must be analyzed within a framework of *strategy variants* tailored to fit the situation at hand and likely to influence a particular actor. Thus, for example, while there is only one basic theory or model of deterrence or coercive diplomacy, there are a number of different strategies for each. The effectiveness of each, however, is highly *context dependent*; that is, the outcomes are influenced by many variables and the interactions between them. The choices of strategy variants, consequently, exhibit considerable uncertainty when dealing with the dilemmas of using force or threats of force as instruments of statecraft. This challenge is well understood by experienced policy makers and analysts. As George Bush the elder once observed, careful judgments have to be made about

> when the stakes warrant, where and when force can be effective, where no
> other policies are likely to be effective, when its application can be limited
> in scope and time, and where the potential benefits justify the potential costs
> and sacrifice. There can be no single or simple set of fixed rules for using
> force. . . .

To demonstrate the critical importance of context, and thereby avoid the limitations and hazards of mere abstractions, each chapter then presents three *specific historical case studies* of each theory or conceptual model. Each empirically-based case is selected for its intrinsic interest, its capacity to link theory with practice, and its insights that might assist in the elaboration, testing, and development of more differentiated theory. The first historical case is drawn from the classical system of diplomacy during the nineteenth century. The second comes from the twentieth century. The third is a more recent case taken from contemporary international affairs. We spread and compare the three cases in this way in order to provide evidence of how a given strategy was and is affected by both the continuities and the changes in the diplomatic revolution that constitutes a major theme of this book as a whole.

A *standard set of questions* is asked of each of these historical cases, as required of a structured, focused comparison. Such a controlled procedure or protocol

makes it possible to actually compare evidence in a systematic way. The three cases then are subjected to an *analysis*, and the comparison of the cases explains the outcomes in order to refine an understanding of when, judging from past experience, this strategy is or is not likely to be viable and how best to implement it. This results in the formulation of guides for thinking and conditional generalizations, which are not designed to be "decision rules" or substitutes for policy decisions, but serve rather as tools for diagnosing the nature of the problem and then determining what choices might be available and whether favoring conditions are present. In diplomacy, as in medical practice, accurate diagnosis must precede a determination for the best course of treatment in trying to solve a problem. Each analysis summarizes the major findings, draws upon additional research, and reiterates how the case studies can help us learn lessons of history and thereby contribute to knowledge required for statecraft.

SUGGESTIONS FOR FURTHER EXPLORATION

Among the many classic writers of statecraft and international behavior who stress the importance of learning lessons from history, one should consult Thucydides, *The Peloponnesian War*; Niccolò Machiavelli, *The Prince* and *Discourses*; and Hugo Grotius, *On the Law of War and Peace*, which are available in many modern editions. François de Callières, *De la manière de négocier avec les Souverains*, is also found in translation in many editions under the title of *On the Manner of Negotiating with Princes*. The best version of Carl von Clausewitz, *On War*, is the one translated by Michael Howard and Peter Paret (Princeton, 1976). On Henry Kissinger's efforts to find and use historical lessons, see his own *Diplomacy* (New York, 1995); *The White House Years* (Boston, 1979); and *A World Restored: Metternich, Castlereagh, and the Problems of Peace, 1812–1822* (New York, 1973 ed.); and the observations of John Lewis Gaddis, "Rescuing Choice from Circumstance: The Statecraft of Henry Kissinger," in Gordon A. Craig and Francis Loewenheim (eds.), *The Diplomats, 1939–1979* (Princeton, 1994); and Peter Dickson, *Kissinger and the Meaning of History* (New York, 1978). See also Klaus Knorr (ed.), *Historical Dimensions of National Security Problems* (Lawrence, KS, 1976); Kikujiro Ishii, *Diplomatic Commentaries* (Baltimore, 1936); and the perspectives provided in the journals *Diplomacy and Statecraft* and *Diplomatic History*.

Discussions about the historical habit of mind can be found in Gordon A. Craig, "The Historian and the Study of International Relations," *American Historical Review*, 88 (February 1983): 1–12; Paul Gordon Lauren, "Diplomacy: History, Theory, and Policy," Gordon A. Craig, "On the Nature of Diplomatic History: The Relevance of Some Old Books," and Samuel F. Wells, Jr., "History and Policy," all three in Paul Gordon Lauren (ed.), *Diplomacy: New Approaches in History, Theory, and Policy* (New York, 1979); David Trask, "A Reflection on Historians and Policy Makers," a speech released by the U.S. Department of State in 1976; Barbara Tuchman, "The Historian's Opportunity," *Saturday Review* (February 1967); Gordon A. Craig, *From Bismarck to Adenauer: Aspects of German Statecraft* (New York, 1965 ed.); and D. P. Heatley, *Diplomacy and the Study of International Relations* (Oxford, 1919). Reference to a recent RAND Corporation study can be found in "Pentagon Blamed for Lack of Postwar Planning in Iraq," *Washington Post*, April 1, 2005.

Insightful and thought-provoking treatments about the challenges of learning and then applying lessons of history can be found in a number of studies. Among some

of the most interesting of these, see Minxin Pei and Sara Kasper, Carnegie Endowment Policy Brief 24 (May 2003), "Lessons from the Past: The American Record on Nation Building"; Jeffrey Record, *Making War, Thinking History: Munich, Vietnam, and Presidential Uses of Force from Korea to Kosovo* (Annapolis, 2002); Stephen Rock, *Appeasement in International Politics* (Lexington, KY, 2000); Russell Leng, *Bargaining and Learning in Recurring Crises* (Ann Arbor, 2000); Wayne Bert, *The Reluctant Superpower* (New York, 1997); Jack Levy, "Learning from Experience in U.S. and Soviet Foreign Policy," in Manus Midlarsky et al. (eds.), *From Rivalry to Cooperation* (New York, 1994); William Jarosz with Joseph Nye, Jr., "The Shadow of the Past: Learning from History in National Security Decision Making," in Philip Tetlock et al. (eds.), *Behavior, Society, and International Conflict* (New York, 1993), pp. 126–189; Yuen Khong, *Analogies at War* (Princeton, 1992); Michael Howard, *The Lessons of History* (New Haven, 1991); Marc Trachtenberg, *History and Strategy* (Princeton, 1991); Yaacov Vertzberger, *The World in Their Minds* (Stanford, 1990); Richard Neustadt and Ernest R. May, *Thinking in Time: The Uses of History for Decision Makers* (New York, 1986); Robert Jervis, *Perception and Misperception in International Politics* (Princeton, 1976); Ernest R. May, *Lessons of the Past: The Use and Misuse of History in American Foreign Policy* (New York, 1973); Will and Ariel Durant, *The Lessons of History* (New York, 1968); and Francis Loewenheim (ed.), *The Historian and the Diplomat* (New York, 1967).

The methodology of structured, focused comparisons is most clearly articulated in Alexander L. George, "Case Studies and Theory Development: The Method of Structured, Focused Comparison," in Paul Gordon Lauren (ed.), *Diplomacy: New Approaches in History, Theory, and Policy* (New York, 1979). Greater elaboration of the broader issue of converting lessons of history into a more comprehensive, differentiated theory and the diagnostic use of theory and generic knowledge for policy making is discussed in Alexander L. George and Andrew Bennett, *Case Studies and Theory Development in the Social Sciences* (Cambridge, MA, 2004); Joseph Lepgold and Miroslav Nincic, *Beyond the Ivory Tower: International Relations Theory and the Issues of Policy Relevance* (New York, 2001); Alexander L. George, *Bridging the Gap: Theory and Practice in Foreign Policy* (Washington, DC, 1993); Alexander L. George (ed.), *Avoiding War: Problems of Crisis Management* (Boulder, CO, 1991); and James Cable, "The Useful Art of International Relations," *International Affairs* 57 (Spring 1981): 301–314.

8

Negotiation

"The art of negotiation," wrote François de Callières in the very first words of his classic *On the Manner of Negotiating with Princes*, "is so important that the fate of the greatest states often depends upon the good or bad conduct of negotiations and upon the degree of capacity in the negotiators themselves." A "single word or act" in negotiation, he emphasized, "may do more than the invasion of whole armies."

His insight has provided guidance to statesmen from the early eighteenth century when it was first written to the present, including those who guided the complex diplomatic negotiations that took place over the course of five years from 1958 to 1963 dealing with nuclear testing. By this time, the unimpeded arms race and the development of intercontinental ballistic missiles had made the possibility of mutual annihilation through nuclear war a reality. The Americans, the Soviets, and the British began to understand all too well the dangers associated with their continuation of nuclear testing. The fallout from their atmospheric tests, for example, dangerously elevated the level of the radioactive isotope, Strontium 90, that increasingly contaminated the earth and entered the food chain, becoming especially concentrated in milk. This set off considerable alarm about the safety of basic foods and the health of the planet and its inhabitants. Although these three states recognized that they had a common interest in addressing this problem, they all feared falling behind if they halted their own nuclear testing program while the others continued. In an attempt to resolve their mutual dilemma over the advantages and disadvantages of testing or not testing, the parties engaged in what political scientist P. Terrence Hopmann describes as "one of the most important negotiations of the second half of the twentieth century." Despite considerable political and bureaucratic resistance at home to any restrictions at all and enormous external disruptions caused by the shooting down of the American U-2 spy plane by the Soviet Union in 1960, the Berlin Crisis of 1961, and the Cuban Missile Crisis of 1962, the negotiators persisted. Finally, their long and difficult labors resulted in the watershed 1963 Limited Test Ban Treaty, allowing nuclear tests underground, but prohibiting all those in the atmosphere,

underwater, and in outer space. This agreement not only demonstrated the capacity of states to negotiate as partners in the midst of intense domestic opposition and international crises over profound issues of life and death, but marked the first breakthrough to slow the arms race with self-imposed restraints, the first arms control agreement between the Cold War rivals, and a major turning point in American-Soviet diplomatic relations as a whole.

Negotiation, as this case clearly illustrates, lies at the very core of diplomacy itself. Indeed, from the earliest evolution of diplomacy to our own time, as we saw in Part I, negotiations have characterized the way in which actors in the international arena collectively seek to solve their common problems, promote mutual interests, regulate their patterns of conflict and cooperation with one another, and thereby maintain their international system. By offering an alternative to the use of force and violence in the world, negotiations provide the means by which parties can coordinate their activities and develop mutually acceptable agreements. They are both promoters and products of the stability of the international system and cooperative relations among its members. As Cardinal Richelieu once wrote in a celebrated passage:

> States receive so much benefit from continuous foreign negotiations . . . that it is unbelievable. . . . I am now so convinced of its validity that I dare say emphatically that it is absolutely necessary to the well-being of the state to *negotiate ceaselessly, either openly or secretly, and in all places. . . .*

Diplomatic negotiations thus have been—and remain, especially today when the destructive power of modern weapons of mass destruction makes the resort to military force a highly dangerous option in all but the most desperate situations—the primary means for resolving conflicts by peaceful means. It is precisely for this reason that the *Oxford English Dictionary* actually defines diplomacy itself as "the conduct of international relations by negotiation."

PRINCIPLES OF NEGOTIATION

Negotiation and bargaining are closely related concepts. Sometimes there are elements of each in the other, and on occasion they semantically are used interchangeably. Both negotiation and bargaining involve an *interaction* and *interdependence* among actors, each seeking an outcome that will benefit its own interests, but nevertheless confronting a situation in which the positions and behavior of one influence the expectations, interpretations, counterpositions, and reactions of the other. In this dynamic, the actors consequently—and paradoxically—become both *rivals* and *partners* at the same time and joined into what has been called an "adverse partnership." Despite this similarity, however, it is useful to distinguish the differences between the two.

Bargaining in statecraft is normally regarded as a *contest* in which each side attempts to maximize its own gains at the expense of the other. This entails an open-ended and constantly changing process of manipulating or influencing an adversary's behavior by an exchange of verbal and nonverbal communication, offers and counteroffers, and threats and counterthreats of

power and military force designed to make the other back down or capitulate. Here the emphasis is on rivalry, competition, the conflicting issues that divide the antagonists, taking and holding firmly to fixed positions, and developing strategies to defeat an opponent. The greater the distance between the interests and positions of the parties, the more serious will be the extent of bargaining, or what strategic theorist Thomas Schelling describes as the threat or use of armed force to influence the behavior of others through "arms and influence" and "the diplomacy of violence," as we shall see in Chapter 9 on deterrence and Chapter 10 on coercive diplomacy.

Negotiation, by way of contrast, is the term usually employed in statecraft to describe *more formal discussions and structured procedures for collaborative problem solving*. It is normally characterized by explicit agendas, exchanged proposals, face-to-face meetings between diplomatic representatives in agreed-upon settings of time and place, rules of accommodation, and sometimes lengthy deliberations. Here there is a recognition of conflict, but a much greater emphasis is placed upon partnership and an appreciation of the fact the parties have a *shared* risk, a *mutual* desire to avoid the consequences of an enforced threat, and a *common* interest in solving problems. A premium is thus placed upon joint, rather than unilateral, action and finding a win–win solution. For these reasons, political scientist Fred Iklé succinctly observes in his book, *How Nations Negotiate*, "two elements must normally be present for negotiation to take place: there must be both common interests and issues of conflict. Without common interests there is nothing to negotiate for; without conflict there is nothing to negotiate about."

With this perceptive observation in mind, it is helpful to try to discern why some negotiations succeed and why others fail. Historical evidence and experience as well as considerable research on the nature of negotiation suggest that several important factors or conditions play vital roles.

1. One of these is a *shared interest in reaching an agreement*. Both sides (in cases of bilateral negotiations) or all sides (in cases of multilateral negotiations) must recognize that they share a common problem, admit the other's claim to participate in finding a diplomatic resolution, and agree that the issue of conflict between them is not so intractable as to prevent a genuine possibility of together forging a satisfactory solution. That is, they perceive that whatever it is that divides them, cooperation and joint problem solving on a particular issue or issues is in their best interest and is possible. Traditionally, and at its best, this has entailed the desire and the will among parties to accept certain rules of accommodation and enter into negotiations in good faith to try to reach a mutually acceptable, formal agreement that serves their interests.

2. Another important condition for negotiations to succeed is the ability to *ascertain and address each other's resistance points*. In negotiating over an issue of conflict, parties typically possess both maximum and minimum demands. At one end of the spectrum are their preferred outcomes, or all the things they ideally would like to obtain. These can be seen in the familiar practice of

parties in negotiations initially asking for more than they ever expect to get. At the other end is the minimum for which, at least at the beginning of negotiations, they are willing to settle, the benchmark or bottom line beyond which they expect to make no further concessions. This is frequently described as the *resistance point*. Reliable information about each side's resistance point and the set of interests, concerns, and attitudes that lies behind it, as one might imagine, is not always easily or quickly obtained. There may be a significant difference between a negotiator's "declared" and "real" resistance points, for example, and negotiators generally are very reluctant to reveal their minimal demands unless and until they are convinced that others are prepared to do the same. These factors emphasize the importance of patience in negotiations until some level of trust and a spirit of reciprocity and partnership can be established.

Once the respective resistance points can be more clearly ascertained, the negotiators are in a position to better assess the significance of the gap between their minimum demands and those of the other side and thereby determine how far apart they are from an agreement and whether there is space for negotiation. At this point the negotiators need to make a judgment about the value of agreement versus the value of no agreement, or what scholars Roger Fisher and William Ury describe in their book, *Getting to Yes*, as the *best alternative to a negotiated agreement* (and now widely known in the vocabulary of negotiation by its acronym, BATNA). An agreement will be acceptable only if it produces a better result than each party could obtain in the absence of an agreement. With this in mind, the negotiators may conclude that the distance between their resistance points is simply too great, that it is better to have no agreement than a poor one, that they have reached a stalemate, and, consequently, that it is useless to continue the negotiations at all. On the other hand, they may conclude that the other's minimal requirements may be weakened or changed or that there are ways of satisfying the other's irreducible demands without seriously jeopardizing their own interests. Most importantly, they believe that somewhere between their respective resistance points, as Figure 8-1 suggests, there exists a "settlement range" that would provide mutual benefits.

3. The shared interests and objectives among the parties to any negotiation are best discovered in that area between the resistance points known as the *settlement range*. It is in this space where the possibilities of partnership

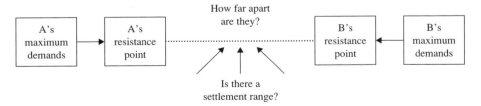

Figure 8-1

become most clearly evident and where negotiators seek some degree of convergence of their interests in reaching an agreement. The possibilities of finding settlement, of course, generally are easier in bilateral negotiations when there are only two parties involved as compared to highly complex multilateral negotiations in which there may be many actors, each with his or her own interests, preferred outcomes, initial maximum demands, and resistance points, and, therefore, a wide variety of possible coalitions and combinations. On occasion, the scope for a settlement may be increased if one party can strengthen the other's perception of their broader common interests, thus causing it to modify its minimum demands. This sometimes is attempted by means of the strategy of *linkage*, whereby one side encourages the other to be more conciliatory by persuading it that, depending upon how the current dispute is resolved, it stands to benefit or suffer in other issue areas. The final agreement may be a comprehensive settlement dealing with many issues or on other settlements dealing with more narrowly focused matters. In all cases, however, the parties secure benefits that they would not have been able to obtain on their own by peaceful means without negotiation.

4. For this reason, negotiations will not succeed unless there is a perception of *shared benefits*. Shared interests and objectives are in large part a function of whether the participants believe that an agreement will serve their fundamental interests and bring them some advantage that they otherwise would not be able to secure on their own or at a risk or prohibitive price. Each may secure gains in different ways and at different levels, depending upon their respective interests and asymmetries of power, influence, and alternatives—but they must benefit in one way or another. This is very much in keeping with the wisdom of de Callières, who advised that "the great secret of negotiation is to bring out prominently the common advantage to both parties" of any dispute. Any agreement that did not satisfy this condition, he warned, "is apt to contain the seeds of its own dissolution."

Such mutual benefits may take a variety of forms. Some of these include *extension agreements* designed to provide a formal ratification and continuation of existing arrangements, such as extending tariff agreements, renewing an alliance, or reaffirming access to overseas bases. Some may be *normalization agreements* devised to terminate an abnormal or dangerous situation, such as reestablishing diplomatic relations, terminating a trade war, or putting a cease-fire into effect. Others may be *redistribution agreements* that change territorial boundaries or divide market shares. Still others may be *innovation agreements* that set up new arrangements or undertakings that benefit the parties such as the creation of NATO or the IAEA, which serves as the inspection arm for monitoring compliance with the 1968 Nuclear Non-Proliferation Treaty. The types of agreements as well as the contexts of the negotiating process may differ, depending on which kind of shared benefits are being sought.

5. The final factor necessary for successful negotiations, of course, is the human dimension of *skilled negotiators*. None of the factors or conditions described thus far exists or operates on its own, but must be interpreted, shaped, and mobilized by people who possess the requisite skills for the art and the

science of negotiation. As Victor Kremenyuk writes in *International Negotiation*, "The center of gravity in this process of negotiation is the negotiator." This explains why writers from de Callières to contemporaries like Michael Watkins and Susan Rosegrant in their recent book, *Breakthrough International Negotiation: How Great Negotiators Transformed the World's Toughest Post-Cold War Conflicts*, despite their individual approaches, are consistent in stressing that negotiation requires certain kinds of skills.

Among these are the abilities to correctly diagnose the structure of the negotiating situation, evaluate the parties and their interests, assess the agenda, analyze the complexities, identify and try to minimize the barriers to agreement, ascertain and address the respective resistance points, determine the value of the best alternatives to a negotiated agreement, and, above all, to understand that the process of negotiation is both dynamic and interactive. Others include the capability to actually shape the negotiation process itself, offer incentives when possible, maintain flexibility on means and firmness on goals, build and sustain momentum, focus upon larger principles rather than personalities, foster productive working relationships with other negotiators, and find or create a viable settlement range. Still others entail the ability, as we shall explore in more detail in Chapter 11, to practice crisis management, avoid escalation, and defuse tensions. In the process of developing these skills, virtually all writers on negotiation agree upon the importance of understanding previous case studies, analyzing why negotiators in the past either succeeded or failed, and learning lessons from history.

These principles apply, in one degree or another, to all cases of international negotiation. The negotiations themselves may range widely over many different subjects, depending upon the interests of the actors and the problems they face in their particular historical context. Among some of the most challenging, serious, and far-reaching of these are those that seek to establish restraints on force and statecraft. As the eighteenth-century French writer Fortuné Barthélemy de Felice observed: "Without negotiation, armed force is an instrument that is both too fragile and too hard that will break in the hands of the one who employs it." It is thus to this matter that we now turn.

THE CONGRESS OF VIENNA, 1814–1815

One of the most famous of all cases of international negotiation occurred with the Congress of Vienna. The leaders of the Great Powers clearly realized that just as their military victory over Napoleon and his vast empire, which threatened them all, had been made possible only by close collaboration, so too peace and security would be completely dependent upon their ability to cooperate with one another. They understood, as we saw in Chapter 2, that all of them—including the defeated country of France—shared a vital interest in reaching mutually acceptable agreements about how best to create and maintain a viable international system that could regulate their patterns of conflict and cooperation with each other. For this reason, they all agreed to organize

a diplomatic conference that would enable them to participate together in formal, collective negotiations over their respective interests and positions. As Prussian Ambassador Wilhelm von Humboldt, who played a major role in devising the agenda and procedures, wrote just before the representatives arrived:

> The Plenipotentiaries of all the Princes and States that in some way or the other took part in the War were summoned to the same place. In this way, the risk of State-to-State negotiations producing dangerous misunderstandings can be avoided. It is also ensured that the arrangements that come out of the negotiations are not contrary to the general interest and also that they be provided with more force through general sanction or at least common recognition. Finally, it will be possible to agree on some general arrangements contributing to the peace and well-being of Europe.

To accomplish this challenging task, the Great Powers sent an unusually gifted and far-sighted group of negotiators to Vienna from September 1814 to June 1815. Chief among them was the host of the congress, Prince Clements von Metternich, a man who had become the Austrian foreign minister in 1806 at the age of thirty-six and continued to serve in that position until 1848, a term unequaled by any other European diplomat and one indicative of the uncommon talents that he possessed. Far from being narrow in his perspectives, he looked at the international system as a whole, believing that the conflicting interests of states should be reconciled for the common sake of general peace and stability, and showed a genius in conducting negotiations that made such reconciliation possible. He was joined in this broad outlook by the leading British delegate, Foreign Secretary Viscount Robert Castlereagh, who desired to create an equilibrium or balance of power in which all states played their appropriate role. Prince Charles Maurice Talleyrand-Périgord served as the chief representative of France, believing that his own country's best interests would be served by recognizing the legitimate interests of other and by maintaining relations with them on the basis of reciprocal respect. Prince Karl von Hardenberg, who as chancellor and foreign minister headed the Prussian delegation, was joined by the Russian Foreign Minister Count Karl Robert Nesselrode. Both possessed impressive negotiating skills, but constantly had to contend with the volatility of their sovereigns, Frederick William III and Alexander I, who insisted upon coming to Vienna. Delegates from some of the small powers were invited to attend as well, but not allowed to participate in meaningful negotiations.

Even though these delegates all shared a mutual interest in reaching an agreement, each started with extensive demands and with serious distances between their initial positions. Indeed, even before they formally assembled in Vienna, they began to assert all the things they wanted to obtain. Each of the Great Powers insisted upon securing territorial acquisitions that would benefit them the most. In some cases the demands of one conflicted directly with the demands of others, who wanted the same real estate for themselves. Serious differences emerged over the nature and political orientation of new or reconstituted governments as well as the agenda and the organization of

the negotiations themselves. Indeed, an indication of the degree of tension and distance between the apparent resistance points appeared so great at one stage that a temporary defensive alliance was signed by three of them against the other two, and armed conflict did not seem unlikely at all. The Russians, for example, made the mistake (repeated by other historical as well as contemporary negotiators) of assuming that military might would be sufficient for them to get their way. As one of their generals arrogantly boasted: "one does not need to worry much about negotiations when one has 600,000 men under arms."

Despite such attitudes and differences, however, over the course of several months of negotiations the parties began to reach a clearer understanding of their own genuine interests and to ascertain more accurately each others' minimal demands or actual resistance points. Although many of the most serious difficulties already had been resolved during their deliberations, the process nevertheless was enhanced considerably when Napoleon shockingly escaped from his imprisonment on Elba at the end of February and was not defeated at Waterloo until June. This experience forced them to be reminded of their shared interest in reaching an agreement and to realize that they could create a settlement range in which their respective interests might be successfully accommodated. In this regard, the negotiators came to learn that such a range could be increased if they paid less attention to specific details or annoying personalities and focused instead upon larger principles of settlement. For those at Vienna, three major principles emerged: compensation (for costs incurred in the effort to defeat Napoleon), legitimacy (respect for the prerogatives of pre-Napoleonic rulers and the restoration of their thrones), and balance of power (an equilibrium of armed force between the Great Powers so as to discourage unilateral aggression on the part of any of them). Another principle emerged as well, which was one of ethics and human rights, for they all agreed to condemn the international slave trade as "repugnant to the principles of humanity and universal morality."

Once the range of settlement was developed, the negotiators then could proceed to create the actual terms of a formal agreement or agreements that would provide them with specific benefits. Although the principles were not always uniformly followed, all of the Great Powers secured concrete gains in the distribution of territory. Britain retained Heligoland in the North Sea, Malta in the Mediterranean, Cape Colony in South Africa, Ceylon in the Indian Ocean, and several islands in the Caribbean seized during the war. Austria obtained valuable possessions on the Italian peninsula, along the eastern coast of the Adriatic Sea, and in Poland. Prussia gained almost half of Saxony, parts of Poland, and extensive holdings in the Rhineland. Russia received Finland, vast Polish provinces, and some possessions along the Black Sea formerly belonging to the Ottoman Turks. Although France was forced to pay a war indemnity, it remarkably was allowed to restore the Bourbon monarchy and to keep most of its original territory.

These individual gains were enhanced by the larger benefit to them all of securing a balance of power and what the negotiators hoped would be a larger

international system based upon compromise and consent that would bring them peace and security after years of nearly continuous and convulsive war. In this regard, they were very mindful of issues of force and statecraft. They agreed to a combination of a significant reduction in the size of their standing armies, mutual restraint, and the inclusion of a number of specific military provisions within their final settlement. This included creating buffer zones and neutralizing those areas most likely to provoke competition between themselves. Fearing that French, Prussian, and Austrian rivalries might all intersect at the common point between them and explode, for example, they promised to guarantee the neutrality of Switzerland. Similarly, to prevent rival claims of the Russians, Prussians, and Austrians that converged precisely at Cracow from the danger of escalating into war, they agreed that the city and its surrounding territory not only would become neutralized but also demilitarized by formally pledging that "no armed force shall be introduced upon any pretense whatever." Around France, however, the negotiators wanted to station troops or to have them close by. The armies of the Dutch and the Prussians thus were positioned on the northern borders that they shared with France, and the armed forces of Austria and the Royal Navy of Britain were not far away should they become necessary. Moreover, during November 1815, the parties reached two related agreements. In the Second Peace of Paris they agreed to deprive France of several strategic fortresses in the north and east and to maintain an army of occupation for three to five years, depending upon the country's progress in the reestablishment or order and tranquility. At exactly the same time in the Quadruple Alliance they agreed to constitute themselves as the Concert of Europe and hold diplomatic conferences "for the purpose of consulting upon their common interests" and, as we shall explore more fully in the next chapter, to use their armed forces as a deterrent for collective security to enforce their settlement. Now, for the first time in a quarter century, statesmen could turn their collective attention to problems of peace rather than preparations for war.

THE CONFERENCE ON SECURITY AND COOPERATION IN EUROPE, 1972–1975

For students of negotiation, the landmark Conference on Security and Cooperation in Europe (CSCE) stands out as one of the most intricate, innovative, and interesting cases in modern diplomacy. It emerged as a result of the dissatisfaction generated by the failure to hold a general peace conference following the Second World War and the dangerous tensions created by the continued division of Europe during the course of the Cold War, as we saw in Chapter 5. In seeking to address a number of the resulting security issues through negotiation, however, the conference actually set into motion forces that would grow to be of revolutionary importance.

The negotiating marathon began in November 1972 after the government of Finland invited a number of states to participate in preparatory talks about principles and procedures for a wide-ranging security conference. It took them

months to reach any agreement, but once they did, it paved the way for the foreign ministers of the participating nations to meet in Helsinki July 1973 to launch the formal negotiations for CSCE. They understood that this would mark the first postwar gathering of all of the states of Europe (except for Albania, which chose not to attend), the United States, and Canada; the first meeting of the two military alliances of NATO and the Warsaw Pact along with the neutral and nonaligned states; the first time for both Germanies to openly and jointly take part in an international conference; and the first time among these many participants, both large and small, that each would have an equal vote in the negotiations. As the Finnish President Urho Kekkonen observed: "This is no meeting of the victors of war; nor is it a meeting of the Great Powers. Our Conference is the common endeavor of all concerned governments on the basis of mutual respect and equality to reach solutions on vital questions concerning all of us."

With these thoughts very much on their minds, thirty-five separate delegations gathered together in Geneva to formally and officially conduct serious and substantive negotiations from September 1973 to July 1975. Given this long period of time, the need to have widespread collaboration among so many participants, the rotation of committee chairs, and the impact of numerous government agencies along with domestic politics, there was little opportunity for a single individual negotiator to stand out in name or reputation above the rest. The tasks at hand, however, required extraordinary levels of negotiating skills. For this reason, all delegations (with the single exception of the United States, which eventually was pressured to change) arrived headed by diplomats of ambassadorial rank.

The delegations at CSCE hoped to reach an agreement that would improve security and cooperation in Europe, but they all initially wanted something very different. The Soviets, who had pushed for such a conference for several years and attached great significance to it, demanded that the negotiators deal with borders only, insisting that official recognition be accorded to the territorial and political order that they had imposed by the force of arms on Eastern Europe at the end of the Second World War. For their part, the Communist governments of Eastern Europe wanted to gain legitimization as normal members of the international community, guarantees of nonintervention (their memories of the Soviet invasions of Hungary in 1956 and Czechoslovakia in 1968 remained strong), and access to Western technological advances and economic opportunities. The Western Europeans who were members of NATO and the European Union, and considerably encouraged by human rights NGOs, declared their most important objective at the conference was to bring about peaceful change by means of greater freedom, and thus insisted that security could not be considered without respecting human rights. Neutral and nonaligned countries like Austria, Finland, and Switzerland, among others, also took a firm stand on the necessity of advancing human rights, particularly behind the Iron Curtain, and on promoting *détente* by defusing the acute tension between the superpowers and their allies. In sharp contrast, the United States government, guided by Secretary of State

Henry Kissinger, remained skeptical and largely uninterested in the negotiations at all.

It took almost two years of protracted and complex negotiations in Geneva to determine the respective resistance points of the participants and to find some range of settlement. Achieving consensus among *all* thirty-five delegations representing their own interests and sometimes those of a bloc or alliance to which they belonged on an agreement seeking to address the multifaceted and vital issues of security in Europe presented an enormous challenge. Their common interests and issues of conflict were seen in both broad principles and subjects. The principles involved those of sovereign equality, which entitled the participants to act and be treated as states in their own right, the inviolability of borders, the territorial integrity of states, the peaceful settlement of disputes, and respect for human rights, among others. The negotiators decided to organize specific subjects into different categories or "baskets": security affairs; cooperation in economics, science and technology, and the environment; human rights; and follow-up meetings to monitor compliance. Various texts were submitted to small working committees in order to try to narrow the differences and find a settlement range. It became very clear to all the negotiators in this process that there would be linkage between the principles and the subjects, and that in order to secure what they wanted in one or more areas they would have to make concessions in others. This generated great frustration, particularly among the Soviets and their premier, Leonid Brezhnev, who had staked his personal prestige on the outcome, as they watched what they hoped would be a simple and quick conference about borders turn into a lengthy negotiation about the whole meaning of comprehensive security and cooperation.

In the end, the terms of the Final Act of CSCE, signed by all the heads of state in a concluding ceremony in Helsinki in August 1975, depended upon the relative balance between these principles and baskets and the concrete benefits that they bestowed upon the parties. As one of the participants cogently observed: "The principles are valueless without the practice." All agreed upon what they called "the indivisibility of security" and their common responsibility to settle their disputes by peaceful means and fulfill their obligation under international law in good faith. Of particular importance to force and statecraft, they believed that they would all benefit by mutually pledging themselves to lessen military confrontations, to develop confidence-building measures by such means as providing advanced notification of major military maneuvers and exchanging military observers, and, most significantly, to

> refrain in their mutual relations, as well as in their international relations in general, from the threat or use of force against the territorial integrity or political independence of any State, or in any other manner inconsistent with the purposes of the United Nations and the present declaration. . . .

"No consideration," they emphatically stated, "may be invoked to serve to warrant resort to the threat or use of force in contravention of this principle."

The final agreement provided other benefits as well. All parties anticipated that they would gain from their promise to increase economic cooperation by expanding trade and business opportunities, to share scientific and technological knowledge and to conduct joint research projects, and to take measures that would help protect their shared environment. The Soviet Union obtained the one major objective that it regarded as essential to its security and so desperately had sought: formal recognition of the existing borders of Eastern Europe. A number of critics in the West responded by accusing the negotiators of "selling out" and "capitulation" by conceding this provision. What they failed to appreciate, however, is that in order to secure this benefit, the Soviet Union had to grant major concessions, both of which would play unanticipated and profound roles in the near future. One of these was to refrain from any form of armed intervention or threat of such intervention against another participating state as it had done in the past against Hungary and Czechoslovakia. The other was a pledge to respect human rights, thereby making its domestic conduct a matter of international scrutiny.

Despite strong and determined resistance from the Soviet Union, which described the whole subject as "interference in internal affairs" and an "unjustified waste of time," other participants insisted on making human rights an integral part of their negotiations. They argued that peace and security in their broadest and most meaningful sense are composed of many different and interrelated dimensions. In this regard, they insisted that a strong link existed between genuine international security, national security, and the security of individuals. In fact, they described this connection as an "essential factor" for security and cooperation in Europe and refused to budge on other matters unless this was acknowledged and given practical effect. The final agreement consequently contained what has been called "the most spectacular innovation of the Helsinki process" and one "nothing short of revolutionary": explicit provisions linking respect for human rights with international security. The text boldly declares that the participating states "will act in conformity with the purposes and the principles of the Charter of the United Nations and with the Universal Declaration of Human Rights," recognizing civil and political rights, freedom of thought and conscience, and the right of individual citizens "to know" about these rights and to "act" accordingly.

Armed with this highly publicized agreement declaring that how sovereign states treat their citizens is a legitimate matter of international scrutiny, individuals trapped under oppressive Communist regimes began to organize NGOs for the purpose of monitoring compliance with the promises. The Final Act proved to be a beginning rather than an end, for it gave them both hope and legitimacy, and they seized upon it. Noted Soviet dissidents like Yuri Orlov, for example, immediately formed the Moscow Helsinki Group and began to speak out at great personal risk—but with the knowledge that others could help. "We do not have the means by which to reach our [own] government," he explained. "My appeal to Brezhnev probably got as far as the regional KGB office." "The crucial question," however, was now with the CSCE agreement, Soviet officials could be reached "through the governments of other countries."

164 HISTORY, THEORY, AND PRACTICE

Others realized this fact as well, including activists who instituted Helsinki Watch (eventually Human Rights Watch) in Poland, dissident (and future president) Václav Havel, who created Charter 77 in Czechoslovakia, and those who established the larger International Helsinki Federation for Human Rights to draw public attention to any violations that might occur. Although persecuted, arrested, broken at labor camps and psychiatric hospitals, and exiled by their own governments, fearful of losing power, they courageously persisted and watched as these seeds sown at CSCE began to assume political importance and change the world that they had known, playing powerful roles in eventually leading to the outbreak of the Velvet Revolution, the fall of the Iron Curtain, the collapse of the Soviet Union and its empire, and the end of the Cold War itself.

NEGOTIATIONS OVER NUCLEAR WEAPONS IN NORTH KOREA, 1993–2006

Ever since the isolated and highly secretive Communist and feudal family-based government of North Korea first began developing its nuclear program in the mid-1950s, other nations worried deeply about the implications of proliferation. Various international and regional efforts attempted to halt this development of nuclear capabilities, but nothing seemed to work and suspicions ran deep. Tensions began to spiral dramatically in early 1993 when U.S. intelligence photos revealed hidden storage tanks, the IAEA demanded special inspections on suspected nuclear sites, and North Korea, in a fit of anger, announced its intention to withdraw from the regulations of the NPT in ninety days. When the United Nations Security Council began to discuss the possibility of attempting to use sanctions, North Korea announced that it would regard any such actions as "acts of war" and respond accordingly. Then, in 1994, the unpredictable regime of Kim Il Sung decided to unload the core of its five-megawatt nuclear reactor, removing enough plutonium-rich fuel rods to provide the raw material for several nuclear weapons. This provocative action not only revealed that North Korea had no intention of participating in efforts to control worldwide proliferation, but possessed the capacity to quickly produce weapons of mass destruction, which, in turn, could escalate an arms race in Asia, seriously threaten South Korea and American troops stationed there, and perhaps be sold to states like Iran and Libya. As the rhetoric became more bellicose and preparations for possible war intensified, U.S. Secretary of Defense William Perry declared that the situation "poses the greatest security threat to the United States and the world today."

The newly installed Clinton Administration first tried to respond to this crisis by considering the use of coercive diplomacy, a strategy that we will explore in Chapter 10. But it quickly became apparent that provocative threats would be completely counterproductive and might well push North Korea over the edge. The Americans consequently reached the conclusion, in the words of one official, that it was "best to engage in dialogue." The question, however, was how could serious negotiations be started? The answer came

in a rather unconventional way that demonstrated once again the impact of individual people. Kim Il Sung invited former U.S. President Jimmy Carter to visit North Korea to intervene in the dispute, open a channel of communication, and help to find a way to bring the parties together. The reaction of American officials ranged from vague hope to skepticism to horrified alarm, but in the end Clinton made the controversial decision to let him go not as a government representative but as a private citizen. Carter quickly established a relationship of trust and created a breakthrough that allowed both sides a face-saving way out of their impasse and thus send their skilled negotiators back to the negotiating table with a new seriousness of purpose. The Americans selected Assistant Secretary of State for Political-Military Affairs Robert Gallucci, a man with two decades of nonproliferation experience to lead their delegation. The North Koreans sent Vice Foreign Minister Kang Sok Ju to head their negotiating team. Then, suddenly, just as the delegations were beginning their new round of talks in Geneva, Kim Il Sung, who had controlled his country with an iron fist since 1948, died at the age of eighty-two. The negotiators hoped that this, too, would facilitate their work.

Not surprisingly, the two sides began with opening positions that were very far apart and, at times, diametrically opposed. As one of the American negotiators describes it:

> We played hard initially, hoping that the North Koreans would come around, and we sat there and we butted heads. We'd make our points, they'd make their points, we'd go back [and] the interagency would say, 'No, we don't want to change our position.' So we'd go back . . . say the same thing, they'd say the same thing, and we'd go back to our country and say, 'We're still butting heads,' but the principals would say, 'No, we're still not going to give in.'

In this process, both sides gradually came to a serious assessment of their own interests, realizing that no military solution presented a credible option, that there were few viable alternatives, that they shared an interest in reaching an agreement, and that they needed to adjust their initial resistance points in order to find a range of settlement. One State Department official recalled:

> I can remember one of their guys, as we were breaking for lunch, saying to me, 'Please look very carefully at what we said.' And we went back and looked at it, and the message that came out of it was, 'If we're willing to take some steps, you have to take some steps as well.' That took us a while to figure out—what we could do and how far we could go.

With the cautious approval of Washington and Pyongyang, Gallucci and Kang were able to craft an agreement known as the Agreed Framework of 1994 that they hoped would bring them shared benefits. To do this, they attempted a strategy of what we will call "conditional reciprocity." That is, they sought to overcome a lack of mutual trust by creating coupled reciprocal conditions over a period of time. Mutual adherence to the conditional actions called for in the early and middle phases of the agreement, they believed, would improve confidence in order to encourage continued adherence to the

remaining set of actions. The United States, for example, would secure the substantial gain of limiting nuclear proliferation because North Korea agreed to immediately shut down and eventually dismantle its particularly dangerous gas-graphite nuclear program, including its existing reactor and plutonium reprocessing facility. In exchange, and to compensate North Korea for energy lost from its closed reactor, the United States agreed to provide shipments of heavy fuel oil and to oversee construction of two proliferation-resistant, light-water reactors. Before the delivery of any of the sensitive nuclear components for these new power plants, however, North Korea had to submit to any inspections deemed necessary by the IAEA and, as the components began to arrive, to begin shipping the dangerous spent fuel rods out of the country. Benefits, in other words, would be conditioned by reciprocity, and both sides—not insignificantly—thereby could avoid war.

Despite the celebration that followed the negotiations and Gallucci's observation for force and statecraft that "it was a wonderful mating of the military instrument being ready and the diplomatic instrument being used," the Agreed Framework nevertheless suffered from a number of problems. The text, for example, failed to provide specific schedules for coordinated and reciprocal moves and gave the United States an usually long period of time ("by the target date of 2003") to fulfill its obligation to provide the new and much safer reactors. In addition, it did not provide for any body to monitor compliance, to supervise implementation with the provisions of conditional reciprocity, or to make mid-course adjustments that might become necessary. Given the historical context of distrust, these flaws simply magnified the probability that each side would be keenly sensitive to any signs, real or imagined, that the other might not be meeting its commitments. Sharp criticism also emerged from those states with vital interests in the question of nuclear weapons in North Korea who nevertheless had been excluded from the negotiations such as South Korea, Japan, the People's Republic of China, Russia, and the IAEA itself.

Further and very serious problems emerged from domestic politics. Shortly after the Agreed Framework was signed, the Republican Party gained control of both houses in Congress and announced its intention to undermine the agreement. Such pronouncements and the subsequent U.S. failure to construct the light-water reactors probably encouraged North Korean leaders to believe that they must take steps to safeguard against the increasing likelihood that the agreement eventually would collapse. They therefore decided to initiate a clandestine nuclear weapons program, develop their ballistic missile capabilities, and fire a test missile over Japan. These actions, in turn, contributed to George W. Bush's determination to isolate rather than engage the regime, to accelerate national missile defense to protect against threats from "rogue states" like North Korea, and then, in his 2002 State of the Union Address, to accuse it of being in league with Iraq and Iran as part of what he called the "axis of evil." This highly provocative statement, coupled with the Bush Administration's proclamation of the doctrine of preemption, could not help but contribute to North Korea's perception that it might be the victim

of an attack by the United States and that it should pursue other ways of providing for its security. Consequently, North Korea withdrew from the NPT, restarted its nuclear reactor, forced the IAEA inspectors to leave the country, and accused Bush of being a hypocritical, "shameless charlatan." The Bush Administration subsequently decided to invade Iraq in 2003 and announced that it was formally abandoning the Agreed Framework. The standoff reached a new low in early 2005 when U.S. Secretary of State designate Condoleezza Rice described North Korea as "an outpost of tyranny," prompting the government of Kim Jong Il to claim that it possessed nuclear weapons to defend itself against any attack and that it would not negotiate at all in the face of such "hostile" American policy.

Despite this intense level of rhetoric and hostility, the parties realized through time, as many other diplomats have in the past, that it was in their mutual interest to negotiate and thereby try to avoid the risks and dangers of miscalculation, escalation, and possible war. As a consequence, six-nation negotiations resumed in Beijing during 2005 and continued into 2006 in an effort to find ways of restraining North Korea's nuclear weapons program.

ANALYSIS

These historical cases certainly reveal the central role that negotiation plays in diplomacy and confirm the observation of de Callières that the very fate of nations can hinge upon the success or the failure of negotiations involving force and statecraft. In addition, a focused comparison of these cases can help us to more fully understand the broader principles of negotiation, to consider some lessons that might be drawn, and to appreciate how recent transformations in history have affected the tasks of negotiation in our world today.

It is clear, for example, that negotiations cannot succeed unless there is a shared interest in reaching an agreement. All parties must recognize that they have an interest in jointly finding a diplomatic solution to a problem or issue of conflict that they share in common. Those who gathered at the Congress of Vienna in 1814–1815 understood this. They realized that despite their intense competition over the distribution of territory and different visions of the roles that they should play to maintain peace and security, they most certainly shared a vital interest in creating a viable international system and in preventing another Napoleon from arising in their midst. Although they entered into the negotiations with many diverse interests that drove them apart, the thirty-five delegations at the Conference on Security and Cooperation in Europe also fully appreciated the fact that it was in their mutual interests to reach a formal agreement to safeguard their future. Similarly, even the vast chasm that existed in the conflict between the North Koreans and the United States could not obscure the fundamental realization that unchecked nuclear proliferation would be in the interest of neither side.

These cases from history also demonstrate that negotiations will fail if the participants are unable to see beyond the initial and often posturing demands and to correctly ascertain and address their respective resistance points. All

negotiators must determine what they are—and are not—willing to concede and assess their best alternative to a negotiated agreement. Despite a number of outrageous opening positions and the opinion of the Russians that since they possessed such formidable military power they did not even need to negotiate at all, for example, the delegates assembled at Vienna eventually came to understand what they and their fellow participants regarded as their barest minimums, or bottom lines beyond which they were unwilling to grant further concessions in order to reach an agreement. The same process occurred during the Helsinki and Geneva negotiations for CSCE, as it became evident that the Soviet Union would not be granted the recognition of borders it so desperately sought unless it addressed the resistance point of the West that human rights provisions be included in the Final Act. In the negotiations that led to the Agreed Framework, the United States made it clear that they would not make concessions unless the North Koreans agreed to halt their nuclear program, while the North Koreans stated that the negotiations would collapse unless they received a commitment from the United States to provide oil shipments and two new reactors to compensate for energy lost from their closed nuclear reactor.

Successful negotiations also require the ability to discover shared interests and objectives that exist in a settlement range somewhere between the respective resistance points. The negotiators must be able to find or create an area where their interests converge and where they might become partners rather than simply rivals. Diplomats at the Congress of Vienna discovered that their settlement range expanded considerably when they agreed that they genuinely needed each other and that they should focus less upon specific details and more upon the larger principles of compensation, legitimacy, and balance of power. Those involved in the negotiations over CSCE came to learn the same lesson, although it took almost two years do so. Agreement was facilitated when the delegates ultimately realized their common interests in the broader principle of what they called "the indivisibility of security" and the linkage among its various elements, such as the inviolability of frontiers, the peaceful settlement of disputes, refraining from the threat or use of force, and respect for human rights. Similarly, although the settlement range between the United States and North Korea was very narrow due to the wide gap between their positions and their mutual lack of trust, the negotiators managed to find enough common ground to result in the Agreed Framework.

Both individually and collectively, these cases also show that negotiated agreements will not be reached unless all sides perceive that they have secured some advantage that they otherwise would not have been able to obtain peacefully without negotiation. That is, there must be shared benefits. In the final settlement of 1814–1815, for example, all of the Great Powers benefited from their new collective security arrangement, and each of the victors obtained significant gains of territory that they had not possessed previously. CSCE was even more remarkable in this regard, for thirty-five separate delegations needed to be convinced that they would gain from the agreement. By 1975 all participants came to believe that they would benefit from the

provisions reaffirming the principles of the United Nations and international law, military confidence-building measures, and increased economic opportunities, among others addressing comprehensive security and cooperation. More specifically, the Soviets secured recognition of existing borders, the Eastern Europeans attained guarantees against armed intervention, and the West, along with neutral and nonaligned countries, gained provisions about human rights. Similarly, in the Agreed Framework, the United States obtained a limitation on nuclear proliferation in East Asia, North Korea secured the promise that it would receive oil supplies and two new and much safer reactors, and both avoided war.

The critical importance of skilled negotiators is also demonstrated in each of these cases. None of the issues of conflict between the parties resolved themselves. Final agreements were reached because there were extremely able human negotiators with the skills to find common interests, ascertain resistance points, formulate settlement ranges, and create mutual benefits. These include, among other factors previously described, the abilities to identify and minimize the barriers to agreement, to evaluate the parties and their interests, to shape the process of negotiation, and to build and sustain momentum. Those responsible for guiding the Congress of Vienna to reaching an agreement, for example, included Metternich and Castlereagh, two of the most impressive negotiators in the annals of Europe diplomacy. The complex and intricately interconnected provisions of the Final Act of CSCE, which provided benefits of security and cooperation for all parties, could only have been produced by very skilled negotiators. Similarly, even the detractors of the Agreed Framework agreed that Gallucci and Kang possessed remarkable negotiating skills to reach any agreement at all in an atmosphere characterized by great hostility and an almost total lack of trust.

Finally, one of the great advantages of analyzing cases of negotiation ranging from the beginning of the nineteenth century to our own time is that it helps to reveal the impact of what we have called, beginning with Chapter 3 and continuing throughout the book, the diplomatic revolution. Part of this phenomenon has been the expanding number of actors who have demanded active participation in important international negotiations. At the Congress of Vienna, the opinions of only the five Great Powers made any serious difference. Although other parties sometimes had intense interests at stake in the negotiations, they either played little role in the deliberations or were not invited to participate at all. In sharp contrast, and indicative of the expansion of the diplomatic community, at the Conference on Security and Cooperation in Europe, not only did a total of thirty-five delegations participate (including two from North America), but each, regardless of size or level of power, demanded an equal vote. Since the rules of accommodation required consensus, this gave even the smallest of states extraordinary influence. This proved to be of great frustration to the superpowers, who discovered that they could not simply dictate to others and that their vast arsenals of sophisticated nuclear weapons and armed force could not advance their national interests in this kind of setting. The impact of the number of actors was also seen in

the negotiations over nuclear weapons in North Korea. Part of the weakness in both the substance and the legitimacy of the Agreed Framework resulted from the fact that others with vital interests in the outcome had been excluded from the formal deliberations, including all of those parties to the NPT represented by the IAEA, which worried about proliferation not only in East Asia, but in places such as Iraq and Iran.

Numbers, of course, do not tell the whole story of the growing complexities in negotiations; yet another change in the diplomatic revolution has been major transformations in the types of actors. In traditional diplomacy, such as that of 1814–1815 at the Congress of Vienna, the only meaningful actors in international negotiations were nation-states. Those called upon to negotiate on behalf of the national interests of their countries did not have to worry about influences outside their immediate and closed circle known as the "inner ring." By the time of CSCE, much had changed dramatically, for as one observer noted, "it involved not only governments and their representatives talking behind closed doors but also citizens and their organizations hammering on those same doors." Transnational corporations interested in trade opportunities, labor associations advocating jobs, NGOs and religious bodies promoting human rights, and scientists urging increased research cooperation, among many other interest groups, all mobilized their energies in such a way as to make a profound impact upon the Final Act. The impact of thousands of NGOs can hardly be exaggerated, especially when they have worked with small and medium-sized countries on issues directly concerning force and statecraft, as demonstrated by their role in helping to create the Mine Ban Treaty prohibiting antipersonnel land mines (an accomplishment that won a share of the 1997 Nobel Peace Prize for NGO leader Jody Williams from the United States) and to establish the International Criminal Court. Other important actors of our time include the European Union and the World Trade Organization. As scholars Fen Osler Hampson and Michael Hart observe in their book, *Multilateral Negotiations*, these many different types of actors "see themselves as direct stakeholders and thus seek to affect outcomes by bringing pressure to bear on their national government. Many of these groupings also have an international constituency . . . enabling them to mount effective campaigns at the national and international levels." They conclude, therefore, that negotiation today "is, in essence, a coalition-building exercise involving states, nonstate actors, and international organizations." When such coalitions are not built, some nonstate actors can seriously thwart or even destroy negotiations entirely, as indicated in 2005 by the challenges of militant groups like Hamas and Hezbollah to the efforts of the Palestinian leader Mahmoud Abbas and Israeli Prime Minister Ariel Sharon.

Additional complications for international negotiations have been presented by the growing impact of domestic politics. The negotiators at the Congress of Vienna gave little thought to political opposition that might arise to challenge their deliberations and decisions. In fact, Castlereagh condemned even the prospect of public opinion influencing the negotiations, describing it as a dangerous element "to force . . . upon the nations, at the expense of their honor

and of the tranquility of the world." The situation began to change dramatically by the time of the Paris Peace Conference of 1919, when the negotiators constantly confronted the pressures of what they called the "New Diplomacy" and "public diplomacy," not the least of which was the influence of public opinion and domestic politics in their own countries. Delegates at CSCE similarly found their deliberations widely covered by the press and heavily influenced by political and bureaucratic factors at home. To the frustration of Henry Kissinger, several members of Congress paid very careful attention to the deliberations, and some even insisted upon going to Geneva to attend the negotiations in person. In the case of North Korea, the new majority of Republican members of Congress determined that they would sabotage the Agreed Framework negotiated by the Democratic Clinton Administration, and new instances of negotiation often brought hardline protestors into the streets of South Korea.

Technological developments and the growing complexity of security issues also have characterized the diplomatic revolution and challenged negotiations. Delegates at the Congress of Vienna conducted their deliberations slowly, with few written communications from their capitals, and with rather straightforward conceptions of security based upon a balance of power defined largely in terms of territory and military forces armed with relatively simple weapons. Those who negotiated at the CSCE, by comparison, were constantly in contact with their foreign ministries and political leadership by electronic (and sometimes encrypted) means. They also worked mightily to understand the various dimensions of "complex interdependence" and what they described as "the indivisibility of security," exploring the many interconnections between military force, economic strength, technological advances, environmental health, and human rights. During the negotiations involving nuclear weapons in North Korea, even more advanced technology was used for communication and for the gathering of intelligence, particularly the use of spy satellites. The sheer complexity of the issues at stake is revealed by the fact that on the American side alone, highly trained specialists were taken from the Department of State, Department of Defense, National Security Council, Central Intelligence Agency, National Reconnaissance Office, and Department of Commerce, among other agencies. Overshadowing all of their efforts, of course, was the stark realization that they were dealing with deadly nuclear materials and weapons of mass destruction.

The whole process of international negotiation has also been enormously affected by the transformation of cultural values and norms. Those negotiators who assembled at the Congress of Vienna shared many of the same traditions, characteristics, and basic goals and objectives for their international system. Diplomats of this classical era agreed upon and generally adhered to reasonably well-defined rules of procedure and accommodation, appreciated the need for mutual respect and self-restraint, and felt obligated to reciprocate concessions. They quite literally spoke the same language. Such cultural homogeneity greatly facilitated consensus and diplomatic negotiations by making it possible to find accord on the time, place, agenda, the level of

Public Opinion Attempting to Influence Negotiations: Protestors in the Street (Getty Images)

representation, and other modalities of conference arrangements all designed to address the first principle of negotiation in reaching a mutually acceptable, formal agreement.

In sharp contrast, there has been a vast increase in cultural heterogeneity in today's world. The many differences in politics, religion, ideology, perceptions, assumptions, patterns of communication and decision making, language, normative values, and the passions that they arouse in recent times have had a profound impact upon human negotiators and their negotiations. It is not unusual, for example, to find highly divergent negotiating styles and different conceptions of negotiation itself. This can be seen on those occasions when certain actors demonstrate little self-restraint, do not show respect for others, regard negotiation as another form of combat rather than an instrument for moderating or resolving conflict, and do not fear being unreasonable or abusive. There also are times when the parties cannot even agree on rules of accommodation or when one side or the other argues tenaciously over

seemingly minor procedural matters. The agenda setting and procedural arrangements surrounding the Korean War truce, the Vietnam peace talks, and the conference following the Arab-Israeli War of 1973, to illustrate, were all plagued by prolonged and bitter wrangling over such trivial subjects as the shape of the table and placement of the participants. Other manifestations of difference, particularly in an age of public opinion and mass media, occur when nations enter into negotiation not because they either expect or desire an agreement, but rather for show or "side effects." They may conclude that a refusal to begin deliberations might be politically damaging at home or present an image of inflexibility abroad that may harm relations with allies or neutrals, as indicated by the reluctant agreement of the United States to even participate in CSCE. Or, nations may enter into negotiations to size up an opponent, to acquire information, to deceive by stalling for time or to delay the possible use of force, to "maintain contact," to extract propaganda advantages, to demonstrate toughness, or to extract concessions, as indicated by the on-and-off-again talks, high level of rhetoric, and often "nonnegotiable" policy positions surrounding nuclear weapons in North Korea.

Such an analysis of historical cases thus reveals much about the critical importance of negotiation to diplomacy, the principles of negotiation in partnership and rivalry, and a number of valuable lessons that might be learned. It also demonstrates not only the impact of the expansion and heterogeneity of the international community, the increased influence of public opinion and domestic politics, and the dramatic transformations in communication and weapons technology, but also the serious challenges that these factors present to negotiating matters of force and statecraft during the diplomatic revolution of our time.

SUGGESTIONS FOR FURTHER EXPLORATION

Many new studies have appeared that focus upon the importance, theory, and practice of negotiation. These include Harvey Langholtz and Chris Stout (eds.) *The Psychology of Diplomacy* (New York, 2004); Christer Jönsson, "Diplomacy, Bargaining, and Negotiation," in Walter Carlsnaes et al. (eds.), *Handbook of International Relations* (London, 2002); Victor Kremenyuk (ed.), *International Negotiation* (New York, 2002 ed.), I. William Zartman and Jeffrey Rubin (eds.), *Power and Negotiation* (Ann Arbor, MI, 2002 ed.); Michael Watkins and Susan Rosegrant, *Breakthrough International Negotiations* (San Francisco, 2001); Fen Hampson with Michael Hart, *Multilateral Negotiations* (Baltimore, 1999 ed.); Brigid Starkey et al., *Negotiating in a Complex World* (Lanham, MD, 1999); P. Terrence Hopmann, *The Negotiating Process and the Resolution of International Conflicts* (Columbia, SC, 1998 ed.); Raymond Cohen, *Negotiating Across Cultures* (Washington, DC, 1997 ed.); the prescriptive theory of negotiation presented in Roger Fisher, William Ury, and Bruce Patton, *Getting to Yes* (New York, 1991 ed.); Martin Patchen, *Resolving Disputes Between Nations* (Durham, NC, 1988); I. William Zartman and Maureen Berman, *The Practical Negotiator* (New Haven, 1982); and Howard Raiffa, *The Art and Science of Negotiation* (Cambridge, MA, 1982). Very recent scholarship can be found in the *Journal of Conflict Resolution*, *International Negotiation*, and *Negotiation Journal*; books in the series "Negotiation, Diplomacy, and Foreign Policy" published by the U.S. Institute of Peace; and the work of the Process of International

Negotiation (PIN) project of the International Institute for Applied Systems Analysis at www.iiasa.ac.at.

Earlier, but still very valuable, analyses can be found in Charles Lockhard, *Bargaining in International Conflicts* (New York, 1979); Glenn H. Synder and Paul Diesing, *Conflict Among Nations* (Princeton, 1977); Daniel Druckman (ed.), *Negotiations: Social Psychological Perspectives* (Beverly Hills, CA, 1977); I. William Zartman, *The Fifty Percent Solution* (New York, 1976); Richard Walton and Robert McKersie, *A Behavioral Theory of Labor Negotiations* (New York, 1965); Fred C. Iklé, *How Nations Negotiate* (New York, 1964); Thomas Schelling's seminal "Essay on Bargaining" in *The Strategy of Conflict* (Cambridge, MA, 1960); Cardinal de Richelieu, *Testament politique*, Louis André (ed.), (Paris, 1947 ed.); Fortuné Barthélemy de Felice, "Négociation," in *Code de l'Humanité*, vol. 9 (Yverdon, 1778); and, of course, de Callières and others as cited at the end of Chapter 1 and Chapter 2.

For the Congress of Vienna, see Henry Kissinger, *A World Restored: Metternich, Castlereagh, and the Problem of Peace, 1812–1822* (New York, 1973 ed.); Harold Nicolson, *The Congress of Vienna: A Study in Allied Unity, 1812–1822* (London, 1945); and those listed under the appropriate suggestions at the end of Chapter 2 and Chapter 9.

Studies that deal with the Conference on Security and Cooperation in Europe include Paul Gordon Lauren, *The Evolution of International Human Rights: Visions Seen* (Philadelphia, 2003 ed.); Daniel Thomas, *The Helsinki Effect: International Norms, Human Rights, and the Demise of Communism* (Princeton, 2001); Vojtech Mastny, *The Helsinki Process and the Reintegration of Europe* (New York, 1992); the eyewitness account by an American diplomat who participated in the negotiations, John J. Maresca, *To Helsinki: The Conference on Security and Cooperation in Europe, 1973–75* (Durham, NC, 1985); the documentary materials in Igor Kavass et al. (eds.), *Human Rights, European Politics, and the Helsinki Accord*, 6 vols. (Buffalo, NY, 1981); Luigi Ferraris (ed.), *Report on a Negotiation*, Marie-Claire Barbere (trans.) (Alphen a/d Rijn, 1979); and *Yearbook of Finnish Foreign Policy, 1975* (Helsinki, 1975).

Excellent discussion about the development, implementation, and demise of the Agreed Framework as well as the subsequent crisis can be found in the book by several key U.S. participants, Joel Wit, Daniel Poneman, and Robert Gallucci, *Going Critical* (Washington, DC, 2004); Victor Cha and David Kang, *Nuclear North Korea* (New York, 2003); Michael O'Hanlon and Mike Mochizuki, *Crisis on the Korean Peninsula* (New York, 2003); Jonathan Pollack, "The United States, North Korea, and the End of the Agreed Framework," *Naval War College Review*, LVI (Summer 2003): 11–49; Selig Harrison, *Korean Endgame* (Princeton, 2002); the discussion in *Breakthrough International Negotiation* (2001) as cited above; Robert Litwak, *Rogue States and U.S. Foreign Policy* (Baltimore, 2000); Ashton Carter and William Perry, *Preventive Defense* (Washington, DC, 1999); and Leon Sigal, *Disarming Strangers* (Princeton, 1998).

The study of diplomacy is filled with cases of negotiation. For some of those that deal specifically with matters of force and statecraft, see the London Conference on Belgian Neutrality (1831), Convention on the Dardanelles and Bosphorus (1841), Paris Peace Congress (1856), Hague Peace Conferences (1899 and 1907), Paris Peace Conference (1919), Washington Naval Conference (1921–1922), Test Ban Treaty (1958–1963), United Nations Disarmament Conference on the Non-Proliferation Treaty (1967–1968), Strategic Arms Limitation Talks I and II (1968–1972 and 1977–1979), Mutual Balanced Force Reduction (MBFR) in Europe (1973–1990), Camp David Accords (1978), Strategic Arms Reduction Treaties I and II (1991–1993), Oslo Accords (1992–1993), and the Ottawa Conference on the Mine Ban Treaty (1996–1997).

9

Deterrence

In the dangerous standoff of the Cold War, each of the superpowers greatly feared that its adversary might somehow be tempted to launch an attack against them, their allies, or their interests. To prevent such a frightening event from ever occurring became their highest priority, and they consequently engaged in acquiring weapons that dramatically increased their capacity to inflict serious damage on the other. Each calculated that the very threat of using armed force would be sufficient to deter the other from ever attacking in the first place. Nothing, of course, could generate more fear than weapons of mass destruction. It is for this reason that as early as 1952 the leading Republican spokesman for foreign affairs, John Foster Dulles, wrote an impassioned article entitled "A Policy of Boldness," in which he called for going beyond the limitations of conventional weapons and drawing upon the power of new nuclear weapons. The nation, he said, "must develop the will and organize the means to retaliate instantly against open aggression by Red armies, so that, if it occurred anywhere, we could and would strike back where it hurts, by means of our own choosing." Dulles argued that this hopefully would create such tremendous fear in the minds of adversaries that it would "stop open aggression before it starts." To fail to do so, he warned, could create a "catastrophe" and "it will be because we have allowed these new and awesome forces to become the ordinary killing tools of the soldier when, in the hands of the statesmen, they could serve as effective political weapons in defense of peace." When Dulles became secretary of state, he put his strategic plan into practice, ominously warning the Soviet Union and all other Communist regimes in a highly publicized speech that any aggression would be met by the "massive retaliatory power" of nuclear weapons from the arsenal of the United States. He and others proudly described this threat as "the ultimate deterrent."

This strategy, known as "Massive Retaliation," was not the first, or the last case of using threats of force as instruments of statecraft to deter opponents. Indeed, deterrence is as old as the arts of diplomacy and warfare themselves. Throughout history, city-states, kingdoms, empires, and nation-states all

have sought to prevent or deter the actions of rivals they found dangerous to their interests. In his *History of the Peloponnesian War,* for example, Thucydides recounted how leaders mobilized troops and positioned fleets to make others "think twice before attacking," and thus deter them from aggression. Machiavelli wrote similarly about "shows of force" as being economical means of persuading an adversary that the costs and risks of launching an attack might be too high. The balance-of-power system of the nineteenth century was designed to keep the peace by deterring any overt aggression in the same way.

These long-standing practices of deterrence in statecraft, however, were not accompanied by any explicit conceptual framework or analyses of principles. Statesmen and generals in the past simply based their actions on historical lessons that they had learned and on the belief that if they presented a credible threat of using armed force, an adversary might fear the consequences, "think twice," and therefore be persuaded not to launch an attack in the first place. This rather basic approach was reinforced by at least two factors. In the first place, if threats proved to be an insufficient deterrent, war was considered to be a perfectly legitimate instrument of foreign policy that resulted in limited rather than catastrophic costs. Second, it was difficult to elaborate a sophisticated theory of bargaining with threats of force when limited technological capabilities prevented any sharp distinction from being made between the power to hurt and the power to destroy. From the time of the ancients to the first half of the twentieth century, it was virtually impossible to hurt an enemy seriously—to burn cities, ruin crops, seize property, and inflict pain—without first having defeated its military forces.

This situation changed with the advent of strategic bombing. For the first time, military technology made it possible to hurt an opponent terribly before, or even without, destroying their armed forces. With the development of this possibility, the *threat* to hurt could be separated—in fact as well as in theory—from the threat to engage and destroy their military capabilities. This particular distinction, when coupled with the differentiation between the threat and the use of armed force, appeared all the more critical with the emergence of nuclear weapons and sophisticated delivery systems. The new extent of potential devastation convinced many strategists that war no longer could be considered a rational policy option as it had been in the past. A prescient book entitled *The Absolute Weapon* confirmed this attitude at a very early stage. In the words of its editor, Bernard Brodie: "Thus far the chief purpose of our military establishment has been to win wars. From now on its chief purpose must be to avert them. It can have almost no other useful purpose."

Many scholars and policy makers alike thus increasingly began to believe that, given the destructiveness and the unacceptable costs of modern weapons of mass destruction, the first task of diplomacy and strategy must be *to prevent rather than wage war.* How to do this through deterrence and yet maintain security in the context of the Cold War, then the post-Cold War world, and then global terrorism thus became a matter of absolutely vital concern to policy makers and scholars alike. This acute problem has elevated the role of

deterrence strategy to a preeminent position in the study of international relations and, therefore, has resulted in a great deal of serious thinking about the fundamental principles of deterrence.

PRINCIPLES OF DETERRENCE

Deterrence consists essentially of an effort to persuade an opponent to refrain from taking certain action, such as an armed attack, that is viewed as being highly dangerous to one's interests by making them fear the consequences of such behavior. It tries to convince an adversary that the costs and risks of a given course of action that they might undertake will far outweigh any possible benefits that they hope to gain. "To deter," write political scientists Robert Art and Kenneth Waltz in *The Use of Force: International Politics and Foreign Policy*,

> literally means to stop someone from doing something by frightening him
> . . . dissuasion by deterrence operates by frightening a state out of attacking, not because of the difficulty of launching an attack and carrying it home, but because the expected reaction of the opponent will result in one's own severe punishment.

In this kind of persuasion, or bargaining with threats of force, the relationship between the adversaries is clearly *psychological rather than physical*. Deterrence attempts not to destroy an opponent or to physically restrain them, but to affect their motivation or *will*. The key, therefore, lies in the minds of people. The strategy seeks to persuade them that their interests would be served best by not embarking upon a particular course of action at all. In this sense, it is largely designed to defend the status quo and attempts to end wars before they ever begin.

By directing threats against an opponent's will, therefore, deterrence attempts to influence their future behavior. The adversary is warned in advance that if they initiate action contrary to the interests of the state practicing deterrence, they will suffer unacceptable consequences. In this situation of shared risk, the opponent thus is told that any pain or suffering is contingent upon *their* behavior, and that *they* are the ones who must make the agonizing decision to proceed toward a clash. If they act, then the threats will be carried out. If they do nothing, then they can avoid the threatened punishment indefinitely. As strategic theorist Thomas Schelling colloquially described it in *Arms and Influence*, one state basically says to another:

> If you cross the line we shoot in self-defense, or the mines explode. . . . If *you* cross it, *then* is when the threat is fulfilled, either automatically, if we've rigged it so, or by obligation that immediately becomes due. But we can wait—preferably forever; that is our purpose.

To accomplish this objective, a number of factors must be taken into account.

1. The formulation of a strategy of deterrence must begin by weighing the genuine *interests* of one's country that are engaged in the area that may be

threatened by hostile action and to assess just how important they are. Vital interests call for unambiguous defense, while less important ones might suggest various levels and forms of protection.

2. The next step is to create and convey to the opponent a *commitment* to defend those interests. This is done when the deterring power backs its commitments by making *threats of punishment* if the opponent acts. In this process of bargaining with threats of force, communication is essential to convince an opponent of one's resolve and strength to enforce the threats. Some states attempting deterrence may prefer to do this by formal diplomatic notes, public speeches, or personal messages between heads of government. Others may rely largely on nonverbal means of communication such as the existence of historical patterns of defense, alliances, troops stationed along a border, ships deployed in nearby waters, or strategic superiority in weaponry.

3. To be effective, it is important to observe, such *threats must be both credible and sufficiently potent in the eyes of the opponent.* That is, they must pose a level of costs and risks that the opponent regards as of sufficient magnitude to overcome their motivation to challenge the defending power's position. Deterrence, in other words, is not simply a matter of announcing a commitment and then issuing threats. In order to successfully operationalize this strategy, the threats must be credible. When the potential power to hurt is used as bargaining power, the threat will deter an aggressor only if it is persuasive by being believable and does not sound like inflated bluster or mere bluff generated by rhetorical flourish.

There are two interdependent dimensions that provide credibility to threats. First, the deterring power must possess the *ability or capabilities* to inflict considerable harm and/or to prevent the adversary from accomplishing its objective by mounting an effective and punishing defense. A state must actually possess—and be able to persuade an opponent that it possesses—the strength and usable capabilities to do what it threatens to do, otherwise it will not be believed and the threat will have no persuasive force at all. When Bismarck set out to deter France from launching any attack for revenge after 1871, decision makers in Paris had every reason to believe that the powerful Germany army possessed the necessary ability to back up or enforce his threats. Similarly, when Nikita Khrushchev wanted to establish credibility for his country's own deterrent, he declared in his famous 1960 speech to the Supreme Soviet:

> The Soviet Army today possesses such combat means and such firepower as no army has ever had before. I stress once again that we already have enough nuclear weapons—atomic and hydrogen—and enough rockets to deliver them to the territory of a possible aggressor, and that if some madman should cause an attack on our state or on other socialists states, we could literally wipe out the country or countries that attack us off the face of the earth.

Coming in the wake of the successful launch of the Sputnik satellite, few doubted that the Soviet Union possessed such capabilities in their arsenal. But having even weapons of mass destruction does not ensure credibility. Indeed, one of

the basic flaws of Mutual Assured Destruction was the nagging belief that nuclear weapons simply were not usable in any practical sense. This explains why President Kennedy declared in a 1961 message to Congress on the subject of force and statecraft: "Our weapons systems must be usable in a manner permitting deliberation and discrimination as to timing, scope, and targets in response to civilian authority."

Second, a state implementing a strategy of deterrence must convey to the opponent that it has the *will or resolution* to defend the interests in question and to carry through on its threats if necessary. A leader may possess considerable and perhaps even overwhelming military power that they are willing to threaten as a deterrent, but they may be unwilling to actually use it.

That is, if a crisis begins to intensify well beyond its verbal stages and it becomes clear that the deliberate use of provocative threats and manipulation of risks is resulting in dangerous and unwanted escalation and perhaps even inadvertent war, as we shall see in Chapter 11 on crisis management, the increased probability of considerable costs might well erode the original motivation to enforce deterrent threats and thereby reduce credibility. Or, it may appear after reflection that the interests at stake are not as important as originally thought, and thus not worth the price that might have to be paid for their defense.

4. In this regard, it is important to recognize that *the validity and credibility of a given commitment is directly related to its possessing a demonstrable or reasonable relationship to the deterring state's appropriate or vital national interests.* The credibility of will is in large part a function of the determination of just how serious a challenge to the status quo might be. Here it is important to make a distinction. Few would doubt the determination of a state to employ *strategic deterrence* to defend its vital and central interests against an invasion of its own borders or those of its closest allies if attacked. But what about *extended deterrence*, or the willingness to honor a commitment to weaker allies, neutral states, peripheral or questionable interests? In these cases, is an ally's well-being part of one's own vital national interest, and thus worth the costs of war, or not? If such doubts arise in the mind of an opponent, they seriously compromise the credibility of the commitment. The policy of "Massive Retaliation" suffered from exactly this problem, for although no doubts existed over the awesome power possessed by the United States, few believed that it would be willing to risk nuclear holocaust and its own destruction to defend territory thousands of miles from their own shores, say, in Korea or Vietnam.

5. *Finally, any analysis of the principles of deterrence must also take into account what is demanded of—or, more appropriately, denied—an opponent and how this influences their motivation to refrain from initiating action.* A strategy designed to deter may seek to deny an adversary something that they consider to be extremely important. This might include strategic strongholds, territory for expansion, access to mineral wealth or oil, or vague but nevertheless important notions of domestic prestige or international reputation. A leader highly motivated to obtain such things by changing the existing order may calculate

that to be denied these objectives is, for whatever reason, too high a price to pay. The threat may well be communicated clearly and credibly but, at the same time, be insufficient to deter. An aggressor may calculate, as did the Japanese in 1941, when they determined that to be denied the opportunity for expansion would be tantamount to "national suicide," that although the costs of launching a campaign might be relatively high compared to the prospective benefits, they are worth the risk. This concept is very important for deterrence in revealing that it is the initiator's "utility calculation"—not that of the defender—that determines whether or not a challenge will be made against the status quo and the maintenance of the international system.

The historical cases chosen for analysis in this chapter help to explain these principles more clearly and offer perspective on deterrence in action. All illustrate the fact that deterrence does not take place in isolation, but in a broader context. The diplomatic revolution introduced new complications, as we shall see moving from our oldest case to the most recent one.

Collective Security for the Post-1815 Settlement

Those leaders who led the struggle to defeat Napoleon understood that they could win neither the war nor the peace that would follow unless they worked together as partners. They calculated that the strong and seasoned French forces could not possibly be defeated unless confronted with a successfully mobilized military coalition. At the same time, they wisely looked beyond the immediate task toward the future and believed that whatever peace settlement and postwar order they might establish could be sustained only if they simultaneously created a system of collective security to serve as a deterrent against any possible resurgence of French aggression. They seem to have been convinced by Thomas Hobbes's observation a century and a half before in *Leviathan* that armed force could deter aggression by creating "a fear of the consequences" and by providing the power to frighten men into "the performance of their covenants by the terror of some punishment greater than the benefit they expect by breach of their covenant."

For this reason, Britain, Austria, Russia, and Prussia agreed in 1814 to sign the Treaty of Chaumont. Here they agreed to establish a system of collective security. Their clearly communicated text provides a classic example of deterrence:

> The High Contracting Powers, reserving to themselves to concert together, on the conclusion of a peace with France, as to the means best adapted to guarantee to Europe, and to themselves reciprocally the continuance of the Peace, have also determined to enter, without delay, into defensive engagements for the protection of their respective States in Europe against every attempt which France might make to infringe the order of things resulting from such Pacification.
>
> To affect this, they agree that in the event of one of the High Contracting Parties being threatened with an attack by France, the others shall employ their most strenuous efforts to prevent it. . . .

If any doubts existed about the wisdom of their thinking about the need to deter renewed French aggression, they quickly vanished when in March 1815 Napoleon escaped his exile on Elba, announced before adoring and tumultuous crowds that he would again raise an army to secure fresh victories, and then launched a new campaign against Europe.

The fact that they had to renew military operations and finally defeat Napoleon in June once and for all at Waterloo vastly increased the motivation of the victorious powers to make sure that this did not happen again. They therefore renewed their commitment to implement a strategy of deterrence by means of collective security with even greater determination. Toward this end, they wanted to convey the credibility of their will, and thus in November openly pledged for all to see in the formal Quadruple Alliance of 1815 that they would collectively protect their new international system against aggression from France. According to the text, they sought "to fix beforehand by a solemn treaty the principles which they propose to follow, in order to guarantee Europe from the dangers by which she may still be menaced." They thus formally threatened that should they be attacked, they would be "obligated to place themselves on a war establishment against that Power."

Interestingly enough, statesmen like Metternich and Castlereagh saw the wisdom of combining force and statecraft. They believed that deterrent threats of armed force often were necessary in international relations, but they also wisely understood that exclusive reliance upon such threats in the absence of consensus on basic principles and a sense of responsibility to the system as a whole would only bring dangers. For this reason, they simultaneously stated in the text of the Quadruple Alliance itself their determination to actively employ diplomacy as well. They pledged to hold periodic conferences and congresses to discuss any threats that might emerge and thereby act together in concert "for the purpose of consulting upon their common interests, and for the consideration of the measures which . . . shall be considered the most salutary for the repose and prosperity of Nations, and for the maintenance of the Peace of Europe."

This important combination was evident in other ways as well. The leaders of the Great Powers understood that solemn and explicitly conveyed words and treaty commitments can greatly increase the credibility of deterrent threats. But they also appreciated that whereas verbal and written communications can communicate a certain level of resolve and intention, they are rarely sufficient to give credibility to the actual ability to enforce or carry out threats. Consequently, those who were determined to establish and maintain their post-Napoleonic international system made every effort to carefully create and orchestrate the collective military strength of the members of the Concert of Europe. The purpose of these forces, wrote Metternich with considerable insight, was to possess a "strong union of States" to deter "the storm" of possible aggression and revolution against the system as a whole. Few doubted the strength of the Austrian army or the British navy at this time or that of the other Great Powers. Indeed, it was the criteria of armed force that allowed them to use the designation of "Great" in the first place.

These capabilities of the *individual* Great Powers, however, represented only part of the equation for deterrence. Perhaps the most critical feature was the fact that credibility was enormously enhanced whenever threats designed to deter aggression could be made and enforced by *collective* security. After their terrifying experience in defeating Napoleon, the statesmen assembled at the Congress of Vienna, as we saw in Chapters 2 and 8, strongly believed that their safety and peace and security could only be obtained by creating a balance of power. They consequently designed a structure and a strategy that would inform any potential aggressor in advance that any attempt to impose hegemony would be met forcefully by the collective military might of the others aligned or balanced against them. They further understood and appreciated that this could be enhanced even more by avoiding rigid alliances against seemingly permanent enemies and creating maximum flexibility that could enable weight to be shifted in one direction or the other depending upon circumstances. The fact that France was restored to its Great Power status as early as 1818 and invited to play its appropriate role as the fifth member in the equilibrium, for example, indicated that this strategy of deterrence was not designed for vengeance or directed against one particular state, but against any state that might endanger the international system as a whole. A strong France, they reasoned, could help guard against an expanding Prussia to the north or assist others in checking Russia to the east. This warning of countervailing power was given in advance to deter: to create a fear of the consequences by means of a credible threat that would convince any leader tempted to launch a war that the costs would far outweigh any possible benefits.

Deterrence by collective security is always difficult, for both the common and conflicting interests of all states must constantly be taken into account, and these vary according to time and circumstance. The Great Powers after 1815 certainly experienced their own share of disagreements about how best to threaten and to use their armed forces. Significant arguments emerged, for example, over the meaning of Czar Alexander I's so-called "Holy Alliance," what they should do about revolutions in Naples and Spain, the legitimacy of intervening in the internal affairs of other states, or the dangers posed to foreign affairs at the time by the dynamic forces of liberalism and nationalism. These were to be expected. Nevertheless, the statesmen of the time remarkably managed to overcome their differences and act together as the Concert of Europe whenever serious threats to the system emerged. Indeed, their strategy of deterrence through collective security, when combined with other features such as the balance-of-power structure and the shared goals among the major actors within the system, proved to be so impressively successful that not one war occurred between the Great Powers for forty years.

BRITISH AND FRENCH ATTEMPTS TO DETER HITLER'S ATTACK ON POLAND, 1939

Well before he even came to power, Adolf Hitler had written in his venomous autobiography *Mein Kampf* that if he were ever placed in a position of power,

he would seek to build a powerful German state based upon armed force that could be used to crush domestic enemies at home and foreign enemies abroad. Among the latter, he focused his attention upon those nations that stood in the way of his expansionist dream of *Lebensraum*, or living space, including Czechoslovakia and Poland. Rather than causing alarm, however, these dangerous positions were largely dismissed or discounted for a variety of reasons by those who practiced a policy of appeasement, as we explained in Chapter 3. Political leaders in Britain and France hoped that if they gave Hitler what he wanted he would be satisfied and therefore would refrain from any aggressive moves that might threaten the international system as a whole. For this reason Prime Minister Neville Chamberlain returned from the Munich Conference in September 1938 and told cheering crowds that he had secured "peace in our time." It was true, he acknowledged, that the partition of the Sudetenland from Czechoslovakia had been given to Hitler as a sacrifice, but said that it was a small price to pay for peace. What he had secured in return, he announced as he waved the agreement triumphantly in the air, was Hitler's solemn word and actual signature on paper that this was his "last territorial claim in Europe."

Hitler was true to his word for almost six months. Then, suddenly and in flagrant violation of the Munich Agreement, he ordered German troops in March 1939 to invade and completely subjugate the rest of Czechoslovakia. This not only eliminated Czechoslovakia as an independent state and member of the League of Nations, but ominously placed the armed forces of Germany all along the southern as well as the western borders of Poland, which Hitler had identified years before as one of his major targets for future expansion. Winston Churchill, who had been warning against the acute dangers of appeasement since its inception, consequently declared simply but accurately: "We are in the presence of a disaster of the first magnitude."

With the invasion of Czechoslovakia, the scales fell from the eyes of Chamberlain. "Is this the last attack upon a small state," he asked publicly, "or is it to be followed by another? Is this in fact a step in the direction of an attempt to dominate the world by force?" Chamberlain now came to realize that Hitler could not be trusted at all and that without credible force to back them up, any negotiations or agreements with him had no permanent value whatsoever. This called for a complete and abrupt reversal of policy if war was to be averted. He found himself joined by the French government in this conviction. Both Britain and France consequently determined to attempt a new strategy of deterrence. Toward this end, they belatedly began to build what they hoped would be a bulwark against further German aggression by increasing the size and the state of readiness of their armed forces, introducing conscription, concluding a mutual assistance pact with Turkey, and promising support and protection for Greece and Romania. The most important effort by far, however, was the deterrent threat that they issued to Germany by pledging to guarantee the integrity of Poland. On March 31, 1939, Chamberlain delivered what he hoped would be a critically important speech, declaring in Parliament:

> In order to make perfectly clear the position of His Majesty's Government
> . . . I now have to inform the House that . . . in the event of any action which
> clearly threatened Polish independence and which the Polish Government
> accordingly considered it vital to resist with their national forces, His
> Majesty's Government would feel themselves bound at once to lend the Polish
> Government all support in their power. They have given the Polish
> Government an assurance to this effect.

In an effort to try to enhance the credibility of the threat, Chamberlain said,
"I may add that the French Government have authorized me to make it plain
that they stand in the same position in this matter as do His Majesty's
Government."

Hitler was both surprised and angered by this declaration and its threat
to thwart his plans. When the news came from London, he flew into a rage,
hammered his fist on a table top, stormed up and down his office, and
shouted at those who witnessed the whole spectacle. As the French *chargé
d'affaires* in Berlin reported to his superiors in Paris:

> For the first time the Third Reich has come up against a categorical no; for
> the first time a country has clearly expressed its determination to oppose
> force by force, and to reply to any unilateral movement with rifles and guns.
> This is the kind of language that is understood in Germany. But they have
> not been used to hearing it for a long time.

Yet, he added with some noteworthy unease in a sentence at the end of his
dispatch, "It has also been difficult for them to believe their ears. . . ."

Difficult to say the least. Given the previous years of appeasement, was
this threat to be believed or not? The British and French attempt to deter Hitler
from attacking Poland, of course, could have been greatly enhanced if it had
been a part of a larger system of credible collective security, like that of the
Great Powers during the post-1815 settlement. But where were the others?
The Italy of Mussolini saw only advantages in aggression and actually signed
the Pact of Steel with Germany for future military adventures. Japan was busy
planning its own attacks in Asia and the Pacific and similarly drew closer to
Nazi Germany. The United States remained immobilized in isolation and stubbornly refused to join the League of Nations or become involved in partnership with others in global affairs at all. China continued its descent into domestic
chaos and weakness, rendering itself unable to play any significant role. This
left only the Soviet Union as a potential source of military strength for deterrence, and certainly no effective opposition to Germany could be mounted in
Eastern Europe without it. The threat of the countervailing power of Britain,
France, and the Soviet Union, whose military forces outnumbered those of
Germany—and its prospect of a serious two-front war to both the west and
the east—could have produced highly realistic fear in Hitler.

Yet, all of the efforts by the Soviets to do precisely this by seeking collective security arrangements against possible German aggression throughout the
1930s had been rebuffed by a West intensely distrustful of any Communist
regime. Moreover, Poland had every reason to be suspicious of Soviet

motives and to question whether Joseph Stalin's "protection" or Adolf Hitler's threats presented the greatest danger. In sharp contrast, Stalin found Hitler particularly eager to strike a deal. If the Soviet Union would promise not to go to war against Germany if he attacked Poland, Hitler would pledge not to wage war against the Soviet Union and, in a secret protocol, would agree to let it take vast swaths of territorial spoils in the eastern half of Poland, Finland, the Baltic States, and the Romanian provinces of Bessarabia and northern Bukovina. Stalin, seeking to delay any military clash with Germany as long as possible while at the same time grabbing as much land as he could, took the bait. The two dictators therefore struck the ruthless bargain in the Nazi-Soviet Pact of August 1939.

With this agreement in hand, Hitler calculated that he had little to fear, at least in the short run. There would likely be no war in the east against the Soviet Union until he decided to launch one himself. There might be a war in the west against the British and the French, but who could tell? The British continued to try to clearly convey their intent to carry through on their promise to defend Poland. Even as late as the end of August, Chamberlain drew upon the historical lesson of what could happen with unclear signals and tried to make this deterrent threat as credible as possible. "It has been alleged that if His Majesty's Government had made their position more clear in 1914 the great catastrophe would have been avoided," he wrote with urgency to Hitler. "Whether or not there is any force in this allegation, His Majesty's Government are resolved that on this occasion there shall be no such tragic misunderstanding." In order to make sure that Hitler knew precisely where the British stood, he warned as explicitly as he possibly could that "they are resolved, and prepared, to employ without delay all of the forces at their command."

This was a clear warning communicated directly, but neither the British nor the French had taken any meaningful action to stop Hitler's aggression since he came to power. At the last minute, when the disastrous prospect of war confronted them directly, their will might falter again and they might even renege on their pledge and abandon the Poles as they had the Czechs. After all, there were still plenty of people in both London and Paris who asked openly in letters to the editor why they should have to die to save far away Danzig. But if for some reason they did honor their commitment, Hitler reasoned, they would have great difficulty in rendering any significant military support in time to actually save Poland. If this occurred, he could likely present them a *fait accompli* and simply force a settlement upon them. Moreover, he reasoned that no other nation in the world could or would mount any significant collective security against Germany in defense of the Poles. Hitler therefore determined to continue his string of conquests by the force of arms and resolved to crush Poland without delay. "We have nothing to lose," he told his generals, "we have everything to gain." At dawn on September 1, 1939, German guns opened fire against Poland. This marked not only the complete failure of deterrence for the British and the French but, once they decided to fight, the beginning of the Second World War.

Contemporary American Deterrence Over Taiwan

A BBC newscast of July 2004 ominously ran under the headline: "Beijing Warns of War with Taiwan." This followed an earlier RAND study of security affairs that concluded:

> Critical differences between Mainland China and Taiwan about the future of their relations make the Taiwan issue the most intractable and danger-ous East-Asian flashpoint and the one with the greatest potential for bring-ing the United States and China into confrontation in the near future.

To prevent such an outcome is the task of contemporary American deterrence over Taiwan.

This deterrence began with the surprise onset of the Korean War in late June 1950. Fearing that the new Communist government of Mao Zedong and the People's Republic of China (PRC) would see the war as an opportunity to crush the U.S.-supported and rival Republic of China (ROC) government of Chiang Kai-shek on the island of Taiwan and force it to unify with the main-land, President Harry Truman ordered the Seventh Fleet into the Taiwan Strait. The purpose of such a move, he declared, was to deter Beijing by threaten-ing that any aggression against Taiwan would be met by armed force and thereby to "prevent the conflict from spreading." This threat was made more serious and given greater credibility when the United States formally signaled its intention to defend Taiwan by signing the bilateral Mutual Defense Treaty in 1954. Together, the fleet and the treaty constituted the beginning of the difficult and often changing American commitment to defend Taiwan by attempting to develop and maintain an acceptable and credible strategy of extended deterrence.

Some of the difficulties and complications of this strategy became readily apparent during the two Taiwan Strait crises of 1954–1955 and 1958. Both of these began when the PRC decided to probe the extent of the American commitment far from its own shores by initiating heavy artillery barrages against ROC forces on the offshore islands of Quemoy and Matsu. When this occurred, considerable domestic political pressure was exerted upon Congress and the White House by supporters of Chiang Kai-shek known as the "China Lobby" to strengthen the deterrent threat even further. For this reason, President Dwight Eisenhower in a press conference felt obliged to threaten that the United States would use tactical nuclear weapons against the Chinese Communists if war should break out. Chiang simultaneously expanded the size of his own armed forces and increasingly tried to push American leaders far beyond the mere defense of Taiwan into supporting any effort that he might make to invade the Chinese mainland and to "liberate" China from Communist rule. That he attempted to bind the United States more firmly to his own aspirations in this way is understandable, but it served to demonstrate that extended deterrence can create serious dangers when it provides tempting opportunities for a weak ally to manipulate and embroil the much stronger deterring power in struggles that may not be their best interests.

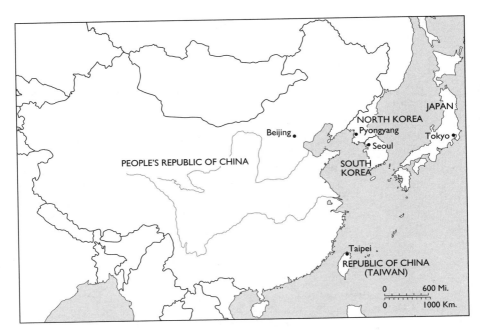

Asia

In June 1962, for example, Chiang once again threatened harassment or invasion of the Chinese mainland, prompting the PRC to undertake military precautions and deployments. In this escalating situation, President John Kennedy feared that the United States could well be pulled into a wider conflict that it did not want and therefore employed diplomatic channels to assure the Chinese Communist leaders that his country would not support any such ROC action. At the same time, however, he felt it necessary to remind them of America's commitment to defend the offshore islands and Taiwan. These positions, especially when combined with subsequent U.S. and Communist Chinese support for opposing sides during the Vietnam War, continued to exacerbate American relations with both the PRC and Taiwan for years.

A major transformation of America's deterrence strategy occurred when President Richard Nixon and his National Security Advisor Henry Kissinger concluded that the dramatic shifts in the geopolitical world of the Cold War necessitated that the United States and the People's Republic of China reduce tension and strive to normalize their relations. The first major indication of this change occurred with the signing of their 1972 Shanghai Communiqué, in which Nixon and Kissinger agreed with Beijing's highly motivated insistence that there could no longer be "two Chinas," that it alone represented the sole legal government of China, and that Taiwan must be considered an integral part of the People's Republic of China. This commitment was repeated and reinforced six years later under the Carter Administration in a joint U.S.-PRC communiqué that finally established formal diplomatic relations between the

two states. At the same time, however, the United States announced that it would "maintain cultural, commercial, and other unofficial relations with the people of Taiwan."

Yet, the deliberate vagueness of some of the provisions in these agreements and what appeared to supporters of Taiwan within the United States to be a diminution of deterrence provoked domestic political forces that prompted members of the U.S. Congress to pass the Taiwan Relations Act in 1979 opposing the use of force by the PRC to regain Taiwan. According to the text, the key to maintaining relations in the area would rest "upon the expectation that the future of Taiwan will be determined by peaceful means" and that anything other than this would be "a threat to the peace and security of the Western Pacific area and of grave concern to the United States." The act sought to strengthen the credibility of the deterrent threat by announcing that America would engage in arms sales and provide "defense articles and defense services in such quantities as may be necessary to enable Taiwan to maintain a sufficient self-defense capability." Continuing, the act stated that the president and Congress would determine "appropriate action by the United States in response to such danger." Thus, although the Taiwan Relations Act asserted a deterrence commitment of some kind to oppose the use of force against Taiwan, it left unclear exactly how the United States might respond if this actually occurred. The resulting uncertainty of this particular formulation came to be called "strategic ambiguity."

Further complications arose from domestic changes from within Taiwan itself. A general election in 1992 of a national legislature, a direct presidential election in 1996, and constitutional reform led to the emergence for the first time of a democratic government for the Republic of China. To this was soon added a growing assertion of the claim, especially by the leaders of the Democratic Progressive Party, that Taiwan should be regarded as a sovereign independent state in its own right, and one no longer encumbered by Beijing's demand for its eventual absorption into the PRC. Chinese Communist leaders became enraged and in the spring of 1996 initiated a war-threatening crisis with military exercises that rehearsed a missile attack and invasion of Taiwan. President Bill Clinton responded by signaling both resolve and capability with the sending of two U.S. aircraft carrier battle groups into the area (the largest display of U.S. military power in Asia since the Vietnam War), but at exactly the same time dispatched National Security Advisor Sandy Berger and Undersecretary of State Peter Tarnoff to Taiwan to bluntly warn its leaders that U.S. support was not a blank check and that America would not defend them if they unilaterally declared their independence. Secretary of State Madeleine Albright reiterated the same point at a news conference shortly thereafter in Beijing.

All of these developments and their implications for security in the East Asia–Pacific region have created a new and difficult problem for the United States to explicitly differentiate and then make credible what has come to be a strategy of dual deterrence over Taiwan. The first objective still remains to deter an armed invasion by the PRC against Taiwan (at the same time that

Beijing seeks to practice counterdeterrence to prevent America from intervening into what it regards as internal Chinese affairs). The second objective is to deter Taiwan from asserting a claim to be a separate sovereign state and making a unilateral declaration of independence that would trigger military attack from the mainland, and thereby force the United States to decide whether it is willing to go to war with a nuclear power of more than 1 billion people. The American commitment to aid in the defense of Taiwan thus must tread a very fine and precarious line and make an extremely careful distinction between deterring *an unprovoked PRC attack on Taiwan* and the possibility of PRC military action *in response to a declaration of independence by Taiwan*. This, in turn, presents a very difficult security dilemma: how to dissuade one side without encouraging the other. Too much pressure against Beijing might encourage the Taiwanese to take greater risks in incrementally seeking what is described as "creeping independence," whereas too much pressure against Taiwan might encourage the PRC to harden its own position. In seeking to deter both sides, the United States runs the risk of deterring neither.

Such a policy of dual deterrence would be challenging even in the best of times, but it is rendered even more complicated by changing circumstances. As we have seen, leaders and conditions change through time and international developments are always being transformed. Certain changes appear to represent an escalation of conflict, such as the growing popularity of Taiwan's President Chen Shui-bian's rhetoric about sovereignty, the ambitious nuclear modernization program of the PRC, and the strident warning issued from Beijing that it may attack Taiwan before the 2008 Olympics if the pro-independence agenda is not halted. Fears also increased when President George W. Bush described the People's Republic of China as a "strategic competitor," sent National Security Advisor Condoleezza Rice to Beijing to issue tough warnings, and appeared to endorse arms acquisitions by Taiwan that would enable them to strike urban population centers and high-value targets like the Three Gorges Dam deep within the PRC. At the same time, the Bush Administration warned Chen Shui-bian against taking any action that might alter the status quo, stressed that the growing economic ties between the United States and China should not be placed at risk, and worked with the PRC on common strategic interests in trying to restrict the nuclear weapons program of North Korea, all of which could be signs that deterrence can sometimes weaken in stages rather than collapsing all at once. Commitments in deterrence are complex political-diplomatic-military phenomena, given to protect an ally or client against some dangers, under some circumstances, for some time, and each of these can change. As such, the evolving case of deterrence over Taiwan, like the others, serves as a valuable reminder that events do not take place in a vacuum but in a particular historical context.

ANALYSIS

Inherent in the calculus of deterrence, as seen in all of these cases, lies the assumption of a unitary, "rational" opponent—that is, one who can be

deterred from taking a particular course of action by carefully calculating that the costs and risks of pursuing it clearly outweigh any benefits to be gained. But there are grave dangers lurking in oversimplification here. The adversary may be, in fact, a small group of several individuals, who differ from each other, who must share power, and who strike compromises with each other. Similarly, although some leaders, past and present, appear to have a much better ability than others to make rational calculations about unacceptable costs and potential benefits, not all actors see the world or calculate the value of gains and losses in the same way. Differences in beliefs, culture, ethical values, attitudes toward risk taking, knowledge of history and international politics, ability to handle stress, perceptions of logic, and views of themselves and others, among other factors, can vary greatly. There is no substitute for knowledge of a specific actor's mind-set and preferred way of behaving and how these might correspond or conflict with one's own, and this is often difficult to obtain, interpret, and apply correctly in assessing intentions or predicting responses.

The efforts at collective security after 1815, for example, were constantly challenged by the seemingly irrational desires of Czar Alexander I to suppress "liberal" regimes, of the British to support them, and of the French to extend revolutionary fervor and renew the glory that was once theirs under Napoleon. Chamberlain's policy of appeasement rested upon a seriously incorrect image of Hitler and wishful thinking and foundered for the most part of the rocks of Hitler's completely insatiable appetite for conquest and his willingness to go to war to get what he wanted. U.S. deterrence policy over Taiwan similarly had to confront an extremely hostile and highly ideological Communist regime in Beijing, which constantly condemned America for its capitalism, imperialism, racism, and support for archrival Chiang. Although some of the more bombastic rhetoric has changed today, many Chinese leaders still exhibit simultaneous characteristics of paranoia, victimization, and entitlement and have repeatedly said that they would be willing to risk defeat in war rather than allowing China to be permanently divided.

Any power seeking to deter another also must consider the critical issue of weighing its own and its opponent's interests in an area of conflict in order to calculate the utility of various policy options. It is often difficult to determine one's own national interests, let alone those of an opponent, but failure to do so can result in the disintegration of even the best deterrence strategy. This can be readily seen in the way in which the balance of power and the congress system sufficed to deter French or any other aggression after 1815, but started to show signs of strain as the divergent interests of the Great Powers began to manifest themselves on the Continent and in the New World. Likewise, the British and French attempt to deter Hitler's attack on Poland was hampered by the highly divergent interests between the Soviet Union seeking to expand its influence, on the one hand, and those trying to obtain its participation in the security agreement while at the same time limiting its penetration of Eastern Europe, on the other. Last, as the expressions of "strategic ambiguity" and "dual deterrence" imply, the United States has had

great difficulty establishing and articulating its own tangible national interests in its relations with Taiwan and the People's Republic of China.

After assessing its own and the other party's interests, the deterring power
must then make an explicit or implicit commitment to defend the ally, territory, or interest it perceives as being threatened. This, too, is often not as
simple a task as it might first appear. To be sure, in the first case the members of the Quadruple Alliance clearly demonstrated their commitment to prevent further French military action outside of France by articulating from the
start both in the terms of the alliance treaty and in the pledging of a specific
quantity of troops in the event of any violation. Their determination to maintain the system by using the countervailing weight of the post-1815 balance
of power, by way of contrast, was certainly serious, although it remained
much more general in its expression and was not directed against any particular country. Chamberlain's attempt to practice deterrence suffered from
many problems, as we shall soon see, but an explicit communication was not
among them, for he repeatedly made his pledge to Poland as clear and
unambiguous to Hitler as he possibly could. The articulation of a clear commitment thus is neither a simple nor a sufficient means of implementing
a successful deterrence policy. By contrast, the deliberate American policy
of "strategic ambiguity" toward Taiwan may afford the United States maximum flexibility, but at the same time it creates considerable uncertainty and
presents more questions than answers about the actual extent of its deterrent
commitment.

As discussed earlier in this chapter, the deterring power must back up its
commitment with threats that are both credible and sufficiently potent in the
eyes of the aggressor to prevent them from attempting the undesired course
of action. The credibility of a threat is comprised of two components, the first
of which is the ability or capabilities to inflict considerable damage upon
an opponent. In this regard, the members of the Quadruple Alliance were
demonstrably capable of actually doing what they threatened to do. The combined strength of the Great Powers acting in concert with their countervailing military and naval might could defeat France or another state that might
endanger the maintenance of the international system. The United States similarly possesses significant armed force to defend Taiwan against an all-out
Chinese attack, if necessary. In the case of the attempt to deter Hitler in 1939,
by way of contrast, the British and the French had significant military and
naval forces, but without the support of the Soviet Union these were
insufficient to create a fear of unacceptable losses within Germany in the short
run or to render timely assistance to their ally of Poland. Thus, the issue
of a deterring power's capability can be seen as a critical element in the
development of a successful strategy.

The possession of vast capabilities, however, sometimes presents its own
dangers. That is, it can easily create the illusion among the most powerful
leaders that simply threatening to use their armed forces will get them what
they want. Where capability fails is in those instances where the force possessed by the deterring power is either inappropriate or unusable in a given

situation. All of Britain's vaunted sea power of the Royal Navy could not prevent France's 1822 intervention in Spain to restore the Bourbon monarchy if the other great land powers approved of the action. In examining other historical cases, it can be seen that the superpowers were continually frustrated throughout the Cold War by the fact that their powerful nuclear weapons appeared to have so little impact upon preventing lower intensity wars in the Third World and, as we shall see in Chapter 11 on crisis management, found much to their surprise in 1973 that even supplying large quantities of arms to their respective Arab and Israeli allies was not sufficient to deter assaults. Similarly, there are many in today's world who find it difficult to understand why America's huge and unparalleled arsenal of military might cannot fully deter terrorist attacks.

The second component of credibility comes from the will and resolution of the deterring power to defend the interests in question. In the successful examples of deterrence among the case studies, it is evident that there exists a strong correlation between the demonstration of firm resolve and the success of the policy. The validity of a given commitment, of course, is directly related to the degree to which it is related to the nation's vital interests. Metternich, Castlereagh, and other statesmen who met in 1814 and 1815 strongly believed that their interests would be best served by peace and security and thus were firmly resolved to not allow France or any other country to involve Europe in another set of wars. They manifested their determination by their use of occupying troops and commitments in international treaties to enforce the terms of their settlement. In sharp contrast, in 1939 the will and resolve of the Allied powers was seriously in doubt in Hitler's mind as a result of their previous policy of appeasement. As Churchill described it in *The Gathering Storm*, whatever credibility the British and the French once possessed to enforce their threats had been "squandered and thrown away." Whether the United States will view its interests as requiring the resolve to defend Taiwan in the event of an unprovoked Chinese invasion with its consequent likelihood of very significant costs and losses, of course, remains an open question that will be answered only through time and circumstance.

But using force and statecraft together in deterrence is difficult, and even capabilities and resolve are not fully sufficient to guarantee success. An analysis of efforts to deter also must take into account what is being denied to an opponent and how this influences their motivation to seriously challenge and change the status quo. Here the level of the opponent's motivation is the key. The newly restored monarchy in France was not inclined toward adventurism and had no motive for starting another series of disastrous wars in Europe after 1815, and thus submitted willingly to the restrictions placed on it by the Quadruple Alliance and then the Concert of Europe. Although the People's Republic of China is highly motivated for nationalistic and security reasons to seek unification, it nevertheless appears to be content to bide its time and not risk a military confrontation with the United States as long as Taiwan does not unilaterally declare its independence. When the British and the French announced that they would defend Poland, on the other hand, Hitler

declared that his motive for territory was too strong to be denied and that he had no intention of being deterred from his course. "I am determined," he shouted after receiving the threat, "to continue to march on this path!" It can be seen, then, that a sufficiently potent deterring force must exist not only in reality but, perhaps more importantly, in the mind of the potential aggressor as well.

Having examined these three cases within the framework of general principles, it is now possible to build upon this foundation and further explore what other lessons, insights, or features of deterrence might be discerned from historical experience.

One of the most important observations that we can make is that, *despite its attractions, the strategy of deterrence possesses a number of serious limitations and dangers*. When compared with military strategies, bargaining with threats is understandably alluring. Threats are infinitely more palatable than the actual use of force. If successful, they can achieve policy objectives with much less money and bloodshed, fewer psychological and political costs, and less risk than strategies that rely directly or exclusively upon the actual use of force to influence international behavior. But these encouraging features cannot be allowed to distract from the fact that bargaining with threats of force is inherently dangerous and comes with high risks. No policy maker in the world likes to be threatened with harm and punishment. Historical experience demonstrates again and again that intimidation can easily provoke anger, pride, suspicion, frustration, or a highly emotional rather than a carefully calculated response and might actually encourage a desire for retaliation or revenge in the form of a response in kind, counterthreats, an arms race, or even preemptive war, among other undesired consequences. Although deterrent threats are designed to discourage and *intended as defensive*, they often are *perceived as offensive* and therefore provoke. Each of these features is escalatory by its very nature and, as we saw in Chapter 8 and shall see in Chapter 11, can quickly violate the requirements of both negotiation and crisis management. Given these dangers of deterrence, political scientist Patrick Morgan warns that we may want to seriously "reconsider our willingness to continue trusting our fate to our capacities for violence."

For all these reasons it is critical to appreciate that deterrence is most effective when it is employed in conjunction with other instruments of statecraft, that is, when it is used as one among several means of foreign policy and not as a substitute for creative diplomacy. The Allied powers of 1815 clearly recognized this fact when they allowed for the rapid rehabilitation of France in the international system and established their deterrence commitments accordingly. By reintegrating France, providing incentives, and establishing the Concert of Europe, the members of the Congress of Vienna laid the groundwork for a system that prevented a major war in Europe for four decades. This was truly a successful application of the strategy of deterrence in conjunction with other diplomatic means. Similarly, while maintaining its deterrent threat over Taiwan, the United States has worked to establish many diplomatic, economic, and cultural incentives to avoid war with the People's

Republic of China. The same cannot be said for the period after the First World War, for in their efforts to deter Germany from aggression and to isolate the Soviet Union to prevent the spread of Communism, the victorious powers employed only threats and thereby created two "pariah" nations that would later combine to thwart the deterrent provisions of the Versailles Treaty and eventually conclude the 1939 Nazi-Soviet Pact.

Research on the successes and sobering failures of deterrence also demonstrates that an exclusive reliance upon negative threats precludes any possibility of using positive reassurance, incentives, or inducements to help resolve serious differences. Similarly, if the power to hurt is seen only in terms of armed force, military might, or physical punishment, all other nonmilitary or nonlethal instruments become completely dismissed. International disputes arise over many different and complex issues, but not all problems are military problems that can be solved by military means. It is therefore instructive to consider the possibilities of nonmilitary threats short of force. Lessons drawn from the richness of statecraft in the past would suggest that these might include such actions as withdrawing from negotiations, recalling ambassadors, terminating commercial relations, or imposing economic sanctions, among many other possibilities. A recognition of these gradual and differentiated measures may encourage leaders to consider a more flexible, careful, and specific tailoring of threats to fit the unique circumstances of each bargaining situation, rather than an automatic and exclusive reliance upon military might alone. Such refined distinctions may become increasingly important, for as some forms of armed force become less and less usable in certain cases, other kinds of threats in combination with diplomatic efforts become all the more critical.

This theme of the need for greater differentiation and sophistication brings us to our final conclusion that, like all other strategies, *deterrence is heavily dependent upon the historical context*. Each case occurred within a time, a place, and with particular people that condition the possibilities and the constraints under which the principles of deterrence operate. Moreover, deterrence cannot possibly compensate for a deficient foreign policy ill adapted to the specific challenges at hand. This is why it is so critical to understand the particular context of each of the cases of collective security for the post-1815 settlement, the British and French attempts to deter Hitler from invading Poland in 1939, and contemporary American deterrence over Taiwan. The same applies to all other historical and contemporary cases of deterrence.

The particular circumstances of each case, however, must also be seen within the broader context of what we have called the diplomatic revolution, or those dramatic changes that have transformed certain features of diplomacy and the evolving international system through time. Moving from the more distant to the most recent of the three cases studied in this chapter, for example, one can see the increasing impact of public opinion. Although it had minimal influence upon the statesmen gathered at the Congress of Vienna, public opinion greatly influenced governments in 1939 and certainly continues to do so in the contemporary American deterrence policy over Taiwan. Similarly, although neither Metternich nor Castlereagh paid much attention to economic

factors as an element in either deterrent threats or incentives, extensive commercial transactions play an especially powerful role in Chinese-American relations today. The shared culture and norms of diplomacy among the Great Powers that made collective security possible after 1815 were shattered at the time of Hitler, Stalin, and Mussolini. One of the most dramatic transformations, of course, can be readily seen with the profound impact of technology. Advances in transportation and communication certainly played their role in moving people and messages from one capital to another, but this has been overshadowed by those revolutionary changes in weapons technology that transformed the threats of war with smooth-bore muskets after the Napoleonic wars into contemporary threats of war with weapons of mass destruction.

Indeed, it is precisely this revolution in weapons technology—and the dangers that it possesses—that leads some foreign policy specialists, and even some officials, to sharply challenge the efficacy of much of the dominant American strategy of deterrence. They point particularly to today's inherent dangers of threat-based strategies, the possibly of incalculable damage and loss of lives, and the hair-trigger problems and high risks caused by launch-on-warning alert systems, vulnerabilities in command and control, and the acute dangers that new developments in weapons of mass destruction pose to their owners as well as to their targets. In addition, some critics also argue that deterrence during the Cold War may have provoked as much as it restrained the Soviets and actually prolonged superpower tensions by a "balance of terror" dependent upon "nuclear blackmail." Moreover, they observe, at the time of the Cold War there was an assumption by Americans that Soviet and Chinese leaders would behave rationally and prudently in the face of threats of severe punishment if they challenged the vital interests of the United States. But times and adversaries have changed, argue these critics, and this fact requires a reassessment and a much more careful and sophisticated analysis of a particular opponent's thinking, beliefs, and approaches to risk calculation and risk acceptance. In our contemporary world there may well be those who are completely insensitive to deterrent threats.

One of the most significant features of the diplomatic revolution, for example, is the emergence of nonstate actors in international relations and, even more specifically, of terrorists and suicide bombers. As the attacks of September 11, 2001, against the World Trade Center and the Pentagon revealed with shocking clarity, some adversaries calculate costs and benefits in very different ways and are not at all deterred by threats of military action. These actors are intensely motivated—indeed, they are willing to sacrifice their lives—to achieve their objectives. Some do not fear force as punishment, but believe that it actually enhances their legitimacy and increases their support. Other difficulties stem from the fact that terrorists often lack many identifiable assets, such as massed armies in the field or territory with specific borders, that can be located and targeted in order to deter them and generally lack developed decision-making structures, well-defined and reliable lines of authority, and effective command and control over operational

units. Each of these factors, among others, complicates or defeats efforts to employ deterrence against them. The implications of these new problems for strategies of deterrence presented by terrorism and the increasing impact of nonstate actors will be discussed in the Conclusion dealing with ongoing and future challenges for force and statecraft.

SUGGESTIONS FOR FURTHER EXPLORATION

The general theory of deterrence can be found in Alexander L. George and Richard Smoke, *Deterrence in American Foreign Policy: Theory and Practice* (New York, 1974). Many other stimulating treatments also exist. Among these, see Lawrence Freedman, *Deterrence* (Boston, 2004); Patrick Morgan, *Deterrence Now* (New York, 2003); Keith Payne *The Fallacies of Cold War Deterrence and a New Direction* (Lexington, KY, 2001); Robert Art and Kenneth Waltz, *The Use of Force* (New York, 1999 ed.); Paul K. Huth and Bruce M. Russett, "Testing Deterrence Theory," *World Politics* (July 1990): 466–501; Paul Stern et al. (eds.), *Perspectives on Deterrence* (New York, 1989); Richard K. Betts, *Nuclear Blackmail and Nuclear Balance* (Washington, DC, 1987); Robert Jervis, Richard Ned Lebow, and Janice Gross Stein, *Psychology and Deterrence* (Baltimore, 1985); Paul K. Huth and Bruce M. Russett, "What Makes Deterrence Work?: Cases from 1900 to 1980," *World Politics* (July 1984): 496–526; Paul Gordon Lauren, "Theories of Bargaining with Threats of Force," in Paul Gordon Lauren (ed.), *Diplomacy: New Approaches in History, Theory, and Policy* (New York, 1979); Patrick M. Morgan, *Deterrence: A Conceptual Analysis* (Beverly Hills, CA, 1977); Thomas C. Schelling, *The Strategy of Conflict* (Cambridge, MA, 1960); Nikita Khrushchev, "Khrushchev's Supreme Soviet Report," *Current Digest of the Soviet Press,* February 10, 1960; John Foster Dulles, "A Policy of Boldness," *Life,* XXXII (May 19, 1952); and Bernard Brodie (ed.), *The Absolute Weapon: Atomic Power and World Order* (New York, 1946).

Deterrence and collective security during the post-Napoleonic period is discussed in Paul Schroeder, *The Transformation of European Politics* (Oxford, 1994); Alan Sked, *Europe's Balance of Power* (London, 1979); Henry Kissinger, *A World Restored* (New York, 1973 ed.); Paul Schroeder, *Metternich's Diplomacy at Its Zenith* (New York, 1962); G. De Bertier de Sauvigny, *Metternich and His Times* (London, 1962); Clemens von Metternich, *Mémoirs: documents et écrits divers,* Alfons von Klinkowström (ed.), 8 vols. (Paris, 1881–1886); and Edward Hertslet (ed.), *The Map of Europe by Treaty,* vol. 1 (London, 1877).

Treatments of the failure to deter Hitler can be found in Frank McDonough, *Hitler, Chamberlain, and Appeasement* (Cambridge, 2002); Richard Davis, *Anglo-French Relations Before the Second World War: Appeasement and Crisis* (New York, 2001); Keith Robbins, *Appeasement* (London, 1997); D. C. Watt, *How War Came* (London, 1989); Larry Fuchser, *Neville Chamberlain and Appeasement* (New York, 1982); Anna Cienciala, *Poland and the Western Powers, 1938–1939* (London, 1968); Allan Bullock, *Hitler: A Study in Tyranny* (New York, 1962 ed.); Winston Churchill, *The Gathering Storm* (Boston, 1948); and the multivolume collections from the British Foreign Office under the title of *Documents on British Foreign Policy, 1919–1939* (London, 1946–1985) and from the French Foreign Office as *Documents diplomatiques, 1938–1939* (Paris, 1939) and the *Commission de publication des documents relatifs aux origines de la guerre, 1939–1945* (Paris, 1963–1986).

The case of Taiwan is studied in Nancy Bernkopf (ed.), *Dangerous Strait: The U.S.-Taiwan-China Crisis* (New York, 2005); "Beijing Warns of War with Taiwan," BBC News, July 30, 2004; David M. Lampton, "Is Pentagon Fueling Tensions in Taiwan Strait?,"

Straits Times, July 22, 2004; Donald S. Zagoria (ed.), *Breaking the China-Taiwan Impasse* (Westport, CT., 2003); Douglas McCready's 2003 Strategic Studies Institute report entitled, "Crisis Deterrence in the Taiwan Strait"; Robert S. Ross, "Navigating the Taiwan Strait: Deterrence, Escalation Dominance, and US–China Relations," *International Security*, 27 (Fall 2002): 48–85; Pan Zhongqi's 2001 Stimson Center report entitled "The Dilemma of Deterrence: U.S. Strategic Ambiguity Policy and Its Implications for the Taiwan Strait"; the 2000 RAND report entitled "Taking Charge" written by Frank Carlucci et al.; Chapters 9 and 12 of Alexander L. George and Richard Smoke, *Deterrence in American Foreign Policy* (New York, 1974); and Harry Truman, *Memoirs* (New York, 1956). Evolving developments can be followed by exploring "Taiwan Confrontation" at www.comw.org and comparing the websites of the U.S. Department of State at www.state.gov, the Foreign Ministry of the People's Republic of China at www.fmprc.gov.cn, and the Foreign Ministry of the Republic of China at www.mofa.gov.tw.

The history of international relations abounds with many cases of deterrence for those interested in further exploration. Among some of the more suggestive are America's Monroe Doctrine against Europe (1823), Britain and France against Russia (1853), the North's efforts to deter British intervention in the American Civil War (1862–1865), Bismarck against Austria (1870), Germany against France after 1871, the Anglo-German naval arms race prior to 1914, the United States and others against Japan prior to 1941, the Berlin Blockade (1948), the United States and NATO against the Soviet Union after 1949, Chinese Communist intervention in the Korean War (1950), the Eisenhower Doctrine in the Middle East (1957–1958), the Berlin Crisis (1961), outbreak of the Cuban Missile Crisis (1962), outbreak of the October War (1973), Operation Desert Shield to deter Saddam Hussein from attacking Saudi Arabia and Israel (1990–1991), and the creation of no-fly zones over Iraq by the United States, Britain, and France to protect Shi'a Muslims in the south and Kurds in the north from attacks (1991–2002).

— 10 —

Coercive Diplomacy

Saddam Hussein's well-armed Iraqi troops suddenly invaded and quickly overran Kuwait in August 1990. This blatant act of aggression imperiled security throughout the Middle East, threatened oil supplies, and shocked world leaders and peoples alike as they contemplated what would happen if they acquiesced to this action and thereby passively allowed the strong to conquer weak neighbors at will. A remarkable international consensus rapidly emerged, therefore, to demand that Iraqi forces pull completely out of Kuwait. In accordance with the provisions of the UN Charter, members of the Security Council of the United Nations authorized the application of coercive diplomacy against him. They began by imposing sanctions, instituting an embargo, and freezing financial assets to hurt him economically, keeping the threat of resorting to military force in the background. When this gradual turning of the screw failed to erode his motivation, they dramatically escalated their level of coercion. After working closely with other countries as partners to gain their consensus and support, President George Bush the elder secured Security Council support for an explicit ultimatum backed by the threat of force. They demanded a complete withdrawal from Kuwait and threatened "to use all necessary means" unless compliance was forthcoming by the deadline of January 15, 1991. To enhance the credibility of this threat, more than 500,000 troops, highly sophisticated weapons, and massive supplies were deployed to the Persian Gulf. As U.S. Secretary of State James Baker described it: "Iraq must either comply with the will of the international community and withdraw peacefully from Kuwait or be expelled by force." Despite this threat and the overwhelming military power poised against him, Saddam Hussein refused to comply. His motivation to retain his conquest was greater than his motivation to avoid war. Coercive diplomacy consequently failed and the Persian Gulf War began.

This case, of course, was but one in a long line of efforts to employ diplomatic coercion. For centuries, thoughtful practitioners and observers have recognized that in an uncertain and precarious world in which military force,

violence, and ambition were seemingly always present, intimidation designed to change behavior occurred frequently. They came to learn long ago that although dangers and limitations certainly existed, attempts to gain objectives by threatening—as compared to actually using—punishment might be accomplished with fewer costs and less bloodshed than was the case with war. Sun Tsu, who wrote his famous *The Art of War* in China 2300 years ago, for example, observed the value of threatening to use force to influence an adversary's will. Thucydides, who wrote his *History of the Peloponnesian War* at approximately the same time, described how the Greek city-states frequently engaged in making threats in order to secure their objectives. He recounted how in one of the most famous cases of coercive diplomacy, the powerful Athenians issued demands to the much weaker Melians, threatening that failure to comply would result in great punishment. "You, by giving in," they declared, "would save yourself from disaster . . . [for] your actual resources are too scanty to give you a chance of survival against the forces that are opposed to you at this moment." Other suggestions about ways to employ threats also were given by Machiavelli in the *Art of War* and *The Prince*, and Hobbes in his *Leviathan* emphasized the importance of "coercive power to compel." Even the refined and restrained François de Callières maintained that every diplomat must understand the significance of pressure to be effective in persuasion and bargaining.

Statesmen of the classical period of diplomacy possessed a general knowledge of these writings and, through time, increasingly made coercive diplomacy an integral part of their conventional wisdom and practice of statecraft. They never systematically articulated the principles of the strategy, however, or explicitly identified its various characteristics. Instead, they simply observed through their own successes and failures that it was a political-diplomatic strategy of bargaining that provided a valuable alternative to an exclusive reliance upon military action by attempting to persuade opponents by means of threats. They learned through time, for example, that strong threats could sometimes persuade an opponent to stop an invasion or give up territory. They also learned that coercive diplomacy could be a seductive strategy that held hidden dangers and limitations, for sometimes threats could backfire and quickly escalate to dangerous levels or even to unanticipated war.

These broad and rather simple generalizations about coercive diplomacy, like those about deterrence, as explained in the previous chapter, prevailed until military technology made it possible to distinguish the power to hurt from the power to destroy. Once this occurred with strategic bombing during the Second World War, the threat to inflict harm could be separated, in fact as well as in theory, from the threat to destroy military capabilities. With the increased dangers made possible by nuclear weapons and sophisticated delivery systems during the Cold War, it became critical to make a distinction between threats and the actual use of armed force in statecraft. As a consequence, many theorists and strategists began to devote serious and sophisticated attention to identifying and understanding the principles of coercive diplomacy.

Principles of Coercive Diplomacy

In his pioneering study entitled *The Strategy of Conflict*, theorist Thomas Schelling concluded that "most conflict situations are essentially *bargaining* situations." For this reason, he argued with considerable insight that statecraft should be concerned not "with the efficient *application* of force but with the *exploitation of potential force*." In *Arms and Influence* he further discussed how nations use threats of their capacity for violence as bargaining power:

> To inflict suffering gains nothing and saves nothing directly; it can only make people behave to avoid it. The only purpose, unless sport or revenge, must be to influence somebody's behavior, to coerce his decision or choice. To be coercive, violence has to be anticipated. And it has to be avoidable by accommodation. The power to hurt is bargaining power.

With this in mind, he therefore concluded, "There is a difference between taking what you want and making someone give it to you. . . . It is the difference . . . between action and threats."

These particular observations, in addition to the work of many other theorists, help us to understand that the strategy of coercive diplomacy, or forceful persuasion (or *compellance*, as some prefer to call it), employs threats to persuade an opponent to do something. It seeks to convince an adversary to call off or undo some encroachment, such as removing troops or weapons from a particular area, halting an invasion in progress, or giving up territory that has been occupied. To do this, coercive diplomacy—like deterrence, with which it is frequently compared—generally bargains with threats of force. But unlike deterrence, which attempts to dissuade an opponent from undertaking action that *has not yet been initiated*, coercive diplomacy attempts to reverse actions that *are already occurring or have been undertaken* by an adversary. Deterrence tries to *inhibit* behavior by fear of the consequences. To deter, a state incurs an obligation to defend or digs in and waits—in the interest of inaction. Coercive diplomacy, by contrast, tries to *initiate* behavior by fear of the consequences. To coerce, a state puts into motion a policy to make the other move—in the interest of action. It is the opponent who must act in order to avoid a collision.

Another distinction between deterrence and coercion lies in the difference of purpose. Although each attempts to influence behavior, deterrence is basically a defensive strategy, while coercive diplomacy can be either defensive or offensive in nature. Defensive coercion may be attempted by a single nation, a collective group or alliance of states, or the United Nations to persuade an opponent to stop or undo an encroachment viewed as highly dangerous to the maintenance of the status quo or the international system, and it is often employed when deterrence has failed. Offensive coercion, on the other hand, may be attempted in order to blackmail adversaries to give up something that they already possess rather than having to forcefully take it.

Coercive diplomacy thus is different from the crude use of military force, for it seeks to *persuade* an opponent to stop their aggression or change course rather than physically bludgeoning them into doing it. Like deterrence,

coercive diplomacy tries to employ threats not to harm an adversary physically or negate their capabilities, but to affect their motivation or *will*. It attempts to convince an opponent that their interests would be best served by changing the direction of their behavior and thereby avoiding the threatened punishment, giving them the opportunity to stop or back off before employing force or escalating its use. They are told that it is *they* who must turn aside if catastrophe is to be avoided. As such, the behavior of one is contingent upon the behavior of the other—and neither one is capable of having full control of the other. Coercive diplomacy, therefore, is essentially a *diplomatic* strategy backed by the threat of force. The volatile nature of the bargaining, when coupled with the employment of threats and perhaps the demonstration of just enough exemplary military force to emphasize one's determination to use more if necessary, thus requires careful and appropriate diplomatic communication and signaling, bargaining, negotiating, and crisis management with the opponent.

The strategy of coercive diplomacy offers the possibility of achieving one's objective economically, with little bloodshed, fewer political and psychological costs, and often with much less risk of escalation than does traditional military strategy. For this reason, it is often a dangerously beguiling strategy. Leaders of militarily powerful countries are sometimes arrogantly tempted to believe that they, with little risk to themselves, can issue demands and make threats that easily intimidate weaker opponents. But most people do not like to be threatened or have demands made against them, and even a superpower can fail to coerce a weak opponent and find itself drawn into a costly and prolonged conflict. If a recalcitrant opponent refuses to comply and, in effect, calls the bluff of the coercing power, the latter then is faced with two stark choices: backing down and thereby risk the loss of face and future bargaining power, or waging war and thereby risk loss of life and military defeat. Because both outcomes are possible, leaders should never undertake coercive diplomacy without the greatest of care.

Given the obvious dangers and high risks of this strategy, it is therefore important to identify the conditions that favor its success, or by their absence, mitigate against it. Comparisons of historical cases suggest that five are of critical importance.

1. Since coercive diplomacy is directed toward an opponent's will, a coercing power must, in order to be successful, *convey that it is more highly motivated to achieve its stated demands than the adversary is to oppose them*. It must, in other words, communicate the message that there is an asymmetry of motivation: that, for whatever reason, its own propensity for creating and tolerating risks is by far the higher of the two. In this regard—and like we saw with deterrence—the motivation of a state attempting coercive diplomacy becomes more convincing if it can demonstrate that its appropriate or vital national interests are genuinely at stake and that these are acknowledged by strong domestic and international support. But motivation is affected by many psychological, political, and cultural factors, and these can

be influenced by what is demanded, what is threatened, what is offered, and what amount of time is offered for consideration.

2. Careful attention, for example, must be given as to *what is demanded of an opponent*, for this can greatly affect the balance of motivation. The demand that an adversary *stop* a particular course of action requires appreciably less than a demand to *undo* whatever has already been gained at the cost of time, money, and perhaps even lives. This distinction is extremely important for an obvious reason: if one demands a great deal, the opponent's motivation to not comply will likely be strengthened. But if the coercing power can carefully restrain or limit its demands to what is essential to itself without thereby humiliating or engaging vital interests of the opponent and is clear about the precise terms of settlement, then it is more likely to create an asymmetry of motivation that favors the success of the strategy as a whole.

3. Motivation also is affected by fear. In this regard, coercive diplomacy—like deterrence—requires *threats that are both credible and sufficiently potent in the mind of the opponent to create a fear of unacceptable punishment if there is noncompliance with the demands*. To do this, the coercing state must demonstrate that it has both the *ability or capabilities* and the *will or resolution* to inflict unacceptable damage on something that the opponent values more than the object of dispute, and thereby to persuade them to overcome their natural reluctance to comply with demands and to take the kind of action that will avert punishment. These threats might involve economic sanctions, the severance of diplomatic relations, increasing the exemplary and limited use of force, limited invasion, declaration of war, or escalating the targets or the types of weapons used in a war already in progress, among many other possibilities. Regardless of the precise nature of the threat, however, the potential power to hurt is used as bargaining power to induce adversaries to avoid it.

4. The *offer of positive incentives* by the coercing power can have a profound impact upon motivation as well. Practitioners of coercive diplomacy often mistakenly rely solely on threats of punishment and thereby completely overlook the often critical importance of offering incentives. Yet, there are times when diplomatic objectives can be achieved only if one offers genuine and even substantial concessions. Coercive diplomacy thus is best conceived as a flexible strategy in which the "carrots" of incentives are combined with the "sticks" of threats in such a way as to facilitate bargaining and possible compromise.

5. Finally, those practicing the strategy of coercive diplomacy need to decide *how much of a sense of urgency to create in the adversary's mind to achieve compliance with the demands*. In crisis situations, time is not unlimited and resolution is normally sought at an early rather than a later stage. On some occasions, states adopt what has been called the "try-and-see" approach. In this variant of the strategy, a coercing power makes modest threats and waits to see whether they will suffice to persuade the opponent before escalating and taking the next step into further action. This approach is consistent with the principles of crisis management, for it attempts to slow the momentum, provide time for communication and thoughtful decision making, and gradually turn the

screw of coercion by an incremental progression of pressure if necessary. When, on the other hand, states wish to deliberately create an acute sense of urgency, they go to the other extreme and employ a full-blown ultimatum, complete with a demand, a threat, and the characteristic short time limit for compliance. Historically, such limits have ranged from a few weeks or days down to only a few hours. The 1939 British ultimatum to Hitler after he invaded Poland demanded a positive rely within two hours, for example, and the American ultimatum to Germany in 1916 demanded compliance "immediately." Since they are designed to speed up the pace of bargaining, it is not at all uncommon for ultimata to announce that "the clock is ticking toward a showdown" or that "time is running out."

As our historical cases will reveal, these five components are not always fully present or tailored to fit the context and unique circumstances of each situation. This fact makes coercive diplomacy fraught with risks and much more difficult and problematic than is often thought to be the case. The motives and interests at stake in the conflict may be vague or incorrectly perceived, the demands made on the opponent may lack clarity or specificity, the threat of punishment for noncompliance may be ambiguous or of insufficient potency or credibility, a coercing power may not fully convey a sense of just how urgently it wants to find a solution to the conflict at hand, or the target of coercive diplomacy may engage in unjustified wishful thinking. Moreover, people normally do not respond well to coercive demands and threats made against them. They may lash out in an emotional response, launch a preemptive strike, or dig in their heels, creating a response completely opposite of what was desired. Unlike deterrence, in which a target easily can comply while claiming that it never intended to change its behavior in the first place, coercion requires that the target visibly alter its behavior in overt submission with a great loss of face. All this helps to explain why success in the application of coercive diplomacy is not easy to achieve, why the strategy so often fails, and why disaster can be just a single decision or mistake away.

American "Gunboat Diplomacy," 1852–1854

The expression "gunboat diplomacy" came into general usage during the nineteenth century as maritime powers increasingly reached the conclusion that in conspicuous demonstrations of armed force, navies often lent themselves better than land-based armies to being used as instruments of coercive diplomacy. Warships mounted with heavy guns could be easily dispatched and withdrawn, displayed and moved about in various combinations with other vessels, flexibly tailored to incrementally adjust the amount of armed force required by particular circumstances, and generally able to be controlled for purposes of crisis management. They could project armed force and make highly credible threats over great distances, particularly if there were significant asymmetries of power and technological capabilities, as the Americans and Europeans discovered in Asia, Africa, Latin America, and the islands of the

Pacific. For all these reasons, as one naval officer observed, navies could "best unite force with persuasion."

With this in mind, the U.S. government determined in 1852 that its navy would make an excellent tool to coerce the Japanese into changing their long-standing closed-door policy that thwarted American interests and influence in the Pacific. Japan had deliberately and successfully secluded itself from other powers for two centuries, refused to engage in international trade, and forcefully resisted any efforts by foreigners to penetrate their country. In 1852 President Millard Fillmore determined that this policy stood in the way of his dreams of expansion, and therefore ordered the stern-looking Commodore Matthew C. Perry, who had considerable personal experience with "gunboat diplomacy" in Africa and Mexico, to cross the ocean with a squadron of ships and to demand that the Japanese "open" their country. American leaders sought to entice them with trade and to frighten them with a credible threat to inflict harm. Naval superiority and technological sophistication, they believed, could demonstrate capabilities better than anything else and would be able to simultaneously show the leaders of Japan "both the emblem of peace and the cannon's mouth."

The instructions issued to Perry provide a most interesting and classic case of coercive diplomacy. The Department of State warned him that in bargaining situations like this, "it is manifest, from past experience, that arguments or persuasion addressed to this people, unless they be seconded by some imposing manifestation of power, will be utterly unavailing." He was therefore instructed to begin with a friendly and conciliatory approach to the Japanese, but in words that deserve to be quoted directly:

> If, after having exhausted every argument and every means of persuasion, the commodore should fail to obtain from the government any relaxation of their system of exclusion . . . he will then change his tone, and inform them in the most unequivocal terms that it is the determination of this government to insist. . . .
>
> Do everything to impress them with a just sense of the power and greatness of [the United States] and to satisfy them that its past forbearance has been a result, not of timidity, but of a desire to be on friendly terms with them.

Thus, when Perry sailed his squadron including four men-of-war, two of which were impressive steam frigates that carried eight-inch guns and were among the fastest ships in the world at the time, into the Bay of Yedo (later called Tokyo) in July 1853, he sought to inspire fear and thereby gain psychological advantage. It worked. According to firsthand accounts, as the Japanese, who had never before seen steamships, watched them come belching smoke, actually moving against a strong wind, and displaying power in their own harbor, they became terrified. As historian Arthur Walworth writes in *Black Ships Off Japan*, to the rice farmers watching from the shore "the ships seemed sullen, masterful, full of pent-up force," and many wondered whether the Americans had succeeded in "floating volcanoes" to use against others. To drive the point home further, Perry eventually landed on

shore with a thirteen-gun salute, nearly 400 officers and men, two heavily armed black bodyguards, and a band playing "Hail, Columbia!" Here he delivered a letter from Fillmore boasting about the power of the American navy and demanding that Japan revise its laws to permit trade and access to shipwrecked seamen and coaling stations. If the Japanese refused to comply, Perry threatened menacingly, he could not "hold himself accountable for the consequences."

In their initial response, the Japanese replied that the impertinent letter and its demands were contrary to their laws and their interests and ordered Perry to leave. Although somewhat taken aback, the commodore had studied as much about the history of Japan as he could in advance, and this led him to conclude that a positive answer would require time and thoughtful deliberation in which the Japanese leaders carefully weighed the consequences of noncompliance. He could play on the fact that they were internally torn at the time between the traditionalists, on the one hand, and those who favored progressive change, on the other, and that these groups would debate both the advantages of incentives and the disadvantages of punishment coupled within his coercive diplomacy. The incentives, or inducements, could be found in the benefits that might flow from the offer for commercial trade and access to advanced Western technology. The punishment for noncompliance also had to be considered, for they already had seen the success of Western "gunboat diplomacy" in Asia and had the object lesson of China's earlier humiliation at the hands of the British navy before them. Perry consequently sailed away in ten days, but did so only after using forceful language in combination with his gunboats, pointedly threatening that he would give them several months for an answer and would return if necessary with even more force. As he wrote in a personal letter to the emperor:

> Many of the large ships-of-war destined to visit Japan have not yet arrived in these areas, though they are hourly expected; and the undersigned, as an evidence of his friendly intentions, has brought but four of the smaller ones, designing, should it become necessary, to return to Yedo in the ensuing spring with a much larger force. But is it expected that the government of your imperial majesty will render such a return unnecessary. . . .

Perry's second arrival in Japan in March 1854 sought to rachet up the level of coercion, for he wanted to intimidate by demonstrating beyond any reasonable doubt both the will and the capability of the United States to use armed force if the Japanese did not comply with his demands. This time he came with even more naval power, including three modern steamers out of a total of nine warships. As one of his crew members described the scene, there was a "long line of boats crowded with men glittering with bayonets, the brass . . . guns blazing in the sun ready to vomit forth death and destruction." He also brought gifts, particularly a miniature railroad train and telegraph designed to impress the Japanese with American technological prowess and superiority. For added effect, Perry presented a copy of a published history of the American war with Mexico, which included dramatic sketches of the results of the devastating bombardment by the U.S. fleet against Veracruz.

Not surprisingly, the leaders of Japan engaged in serious and often agonizing debate about how best to respond to these threats. Some argued that they should never give in and meekly comply with the outrageous and arrogant American demands, whatever the cost, for it would be a "disgrace" to national prestige and "honor." Others, like advisor to the Shōgun, Naosuke Ii, rationally and pragmatically calculated that the Americans possessed sufficiently potent will and ability to harm them and, consequently, that the Japanese had reason to fear the consequences if they failed to comply. As he wrote in his revealing memorandum:

> Since 1609 . . . we have had no warships capable of opposing foreign attack on our coasts with heavy guns. . . . There is a saying that when one is besieged in a castle, to raise the drawbridge is to imprison oneself and make it impossible to hold out indefinitely; and again, that when opposing forces face each other across a river, victory is obtained by that which crosses the river and attacks. It seems clear throughout history that he who takes action is in a position to advance, while he who remains inactive must retreat.

To avoid disaster, he therefore proposed a tactical retreat:

> Even though the Shōgun's ancestors set up seclusion laws, they left the Dutch and the Chinese to act as a bridge [to the outside world]. Might this bridge not now be of advantage to us in handling foreign affairs [with the Americans], providing us with the means whereby we may for a time avert the outbreak of hostilities and then, after some time has elapsed, gain a complete victory?

With these rather carefully calculated thoughts in mind, the leaders of Japan determined that they would reluctantly comply with the American demands.

The result took the form of the 1854 Treaty of Kanagawa. Here, the Japanese accepted the incentives that were offered and agreed to open two ports for obtaining coal and other supplies, establish consular privileges in these locations, and assist shipwrecked American crews. Beyond these concessions, however, they refused to do more or open up their entire country. Perry wisely understood that he could not achieve anything else without risking extended war far from American shores, and thus accepted the terms. He returned home triumphantly declaring that his success was but a foretaste "that the people of America will, in some form or other, extend their dominion and their power, until they shall have brought within their mighty embrace the islands of the great Pacific, and place the Saxon race upon the eastern shores of Asia." The Japanese, in sharp contrast, viewed their concessions as merely a temporary expedient designed to avoid immediate disaster and buy time for modernization until, in the words of Naosuke, the circumstances changed in their favor such that they might secure "complete victory."

U.S. POLICY TOWARD JAPAN, 1938–1941

The memory of "gunboat diplomacy" lasted for decades, with the Americans believing that they could again successfully intimidate Japan whenever

necessary and the Japanese vowing that they would never allow themselves to be coerced in such a way again. These contrasting views became particularly evident between 1938 and 1941, when Japanese military expansion into China proceeded in earnest and became increasingly worrisome to the United States. At first the United States responded with a policy of deterrence designed to dissuade Japan from any further encroachments. When it became clear that this strategy was failing, however, Washington escalated its pressure and attempted a very strong variant of coercive diplomacy in an effort to reverse previous Japanese advances. In the end, this strategy failed as well.

Militarists and extreme nationalists in Japan had dreamed for years of creating a vast empire in Asia. They argued that destiny had selected them as the superior "Yamato race" and called them to create and rule a "Greater East Asian Co-Prosperity Sphere." Toward this end, they began as early as 1931 to carve out territory in China and set up a puppet government in Manchuria. Aggression continued, and the so-called "China Incident" of 1937 brought even more Japanese troops to the mainland, where they continued to insist that conquest was absolutely fundamental to realizing their destiny. In sharp contrast, U.S. interests in China were minor in comparison and lacked the driving force that characterized Japanese actions. Moreover, the strength and the credibility of the American government to signal its displeasure and make effective warning to Japan were severely limited by any number of factors, including the refusal of the United States to participate in the League of Nations, its lack of power and influence in Asia, and the domestic popularity of its policy of isolationism.

Despite these constraints, the United States nevertheless tried to coerce Japan into halting its course of expansion by imposing an embargo on certain military goods, canceling credits, and abrogating a commercial treaty in 1939. These measures were meant to force Japan into moderating its policies in Asia. However, this strategy of coercion through economic punishment was not sufficiently potent and did not make clear to the Japanese what was expected of them. Cordell Hull, the American secretary of state, was reluctant to stop all trade with Japan in order to maintain at least some measure of leverage, but would not specify how he expected to use this weapon in the future. Despite these early pressures, clear communication of a firm U.S. commitment to back its rhetorical demands on Japan was lacking, and the Japanese leaders believed that they were much more strongly motivated to resist American demands than U.S. leaders were to enforce them. The stake in the conflict of interests in Asia thus was clearly greater for the Japanese than for the Americans. Japan therefore continued its policy of military expansion and by taking full advantage of the chaos caused by Hitler's aggression in Europe, tightened its grip on China and began to threaten the Dutch East Indies and French Indochina.

To rachet up the level of coercion, the Roosevelt Administration clamped an embargo on aviation fuel and top-grade scrap iron sought desperately by Japan in July 1940. Instead of forcing the Japanese change their policies, however, this only aggravated them more. They consequently determined to

draw even closer to the other aggressors and quickly signed the Tripartite Pact with Germany and Italy, thereby providing a counterwarning to the United States to refrain from interfering in Asia. This, in turn, provoked the Roosevelt Administration into seeing an even broader global threat to peace and security. They therefore sent five submarines to reinforce the U.S. naval base in Manila and extended the economic embargo against Japan to include all scrap metals. Having been presented with few concrete demands, and not completely sure whether the United States was trying to deter them from future conquests or to force them to undo the ones they had already gained, the Japanese were somewhat startled by the avalanche of new economic hardships that now faced them. Rather than make compliance more attractive, however, the new American policy of stepped-up pressures boomeranged, making the government of Japan only more determined to acquire secure and independent sources of raw materials and weakening the moderates within the Japanese cabinet. The new U.S. threat to escalate pressures confirmed Tokyo's worst fears about the future and prompted a faster pace of expansion. The embargo of vital materials was interpreted not as a warning, but as a provocation.

A critical turning point that severely escalated the diplomatic confrontation occurred in July 1941 when the United States decided to freeze Japanese assets in American banks and, in effect, impose a total embargo on oil. As one cabinet member described Roosevelt's increased resolve: "He thought that it might be better to slip the noose around Japan's neck and give it a jerk now and then." This, in turn, greatly increased the danger of confrontation, for the Japanese imported approximately 80% of their oil from the United States, and they knew that without these supplies of "life blood" fuel, their empire would collapse. Each day that passed without oil imports weakened their military strength, and thereby made the time pressure relentless. Civilian leaders like Prime Minister Konoye Fumimaro argued that diplomatic negotiations should be continued and that concessions should be made to the United States, if necessary, to avoid war. Military leaders like War Minister and General Tojo Hideki, on the other hand, adamantly opposed buckling under to the Americans. "If we yield to the United States at this time [they] will become more arrogant and more overbearing," he declared, insisting that any withdrawal of troops from China "would not be in keeping with the dignity of the Army."

The Japanese decision about how to respond to American coercive diplomacy was not impulsive, but evolved as a result of months of careful deliberation and serious debate between civilian and military authorities in Tokyo. Throughout this process, the tightening restrictions on oil intensified pressure for adopting a military option. Supplies diminished at the same time that Japan's daily requirement for 12,000 tons of oil continued, and the chances that its military operations could be sustained until new sources of fuel could be obtained from British and Dutch possessions in Southeast Asia grew smaller with each passing day. Those present at the Imperial Conference in September consequently decided that they would go to war with

the United States if the strangling embargo on strategic materials was not lifted by October 15. Then, in mid-October, the Konoye cabinet fell, and General Tojo became prime minister. Although the deadline had been reached and their armed forces were massing for a possible attack, the new government decided to continue to try to find some alternative to what would certainly be a devastating war. The Japanese cabinet therefore resolved to stake everything on their last set of proposals, which they presented to U.S. Secretary of State Cordell Hull.

These eleventh-hour proposals offered very little, for the Japanese had no desire to dismantle their newly acquired empire. The United States, for its part, saw little reason to negotiate. Hard-liners like Secretary of War Henry Stimson fostered incorrect images that prevented a more precise and calculated application of coercive diplomacy by arguing that the Japanese were "notorious bluffers" who would back down when confronted firmly. On November 26, Hull thus presented not a counterproposal, but a new set of demands in an uncompromising note described by one historian as "one of the most fateful documents in American history." He offered the incentives of removing the freeze on Japanese assets and a nonaggression treaty, but these were hardly potent enough to encourage compliance with a series of severe demands. Completely disregarding the principles of crisis management, Hull then muttered, "I have washed my hands of it, and it is now in the hands of . . . the Army and Navy."

In Tokyo, this news of escalated coercive diplomacy was seen as unacceptably provocative. Japanese leaders viewed these new demands as nothing short of an ultimatum, a sign that the basic hostile intentions of the United States had now been fully revealed and that the Americans had completely rejected what Tokyo had considered the last hope for peace. It simply confirmed their previous analysis of costs and benefits. Even in the face of highly credible and potent threats, they had no motivation at all to comply with American demands if it meant completely dismantling ten years' worth of investment in effort, resources, and prestige. Thus, when the Imperial Conference met on December 1, Tojo declared:

> The United States demanded complete and unconditional withdrawal of troops from China, withdrawal of our recognition of the Nanking Government, and the reduction of the Tripartite Pact to a dead letter. This not only belittled the dignity of our Empire and made it impossible to harvest the fruits of the China Incident, but also threatened the very existence of our Empire. . . . Under the circumstances, our Empire has no alternative but to begin war . . . in order to resolve the present crisis and assure survival.

With these thoughts in their minds, and despite their own calculations that the United States was far superior to them in military and industrial strength and that the likelihood of long-term victory was exceedingly remote, Japanese leaders refused to be coerced and made the fateful decision to go to war. Their naval task force already at sea therefore received confirmation of the final destination for a surprise attack: Pearl Harbor.

The Cuban Missile Crisis, 1962

When the American intelligence community discovered in October 1962 that the Soviet Union was in the process of secretly deploying medium- and intermediate-range ballistic missiles into Cuba, the world suddenly faced the most dangerous crisis of the entire Cold War. The discovery immediately produced a reaction of stunned surprise and anger among American leaders. Once it was realized that as soon as the missiles became operational they could strike almost any city within the United States, anger turned to an acute sense of danger. Members of the Joint Chiefs of Staff immediately and unanimously advised that the use of armed force was "essential," declaring that "military steps were the only ones the Soviet Union would understand." President Kennedy rejected their advice, for he believed that even surgical air strikes against the missile sites alone would lead to war. He perceived Khrushchev as ultimately an intelligent man who would retreat if opposed resolutely and given sufficient time to calculate his interests. Rather than employing military force in the first instance, therefore, Kennedy decided instead to first seek a peaceful outcome, if possible, by trying the strategy of coercive diplomacy in an effort to induce Khrushchev to undo his action by removing the missiles himself.

To begin this process, Kennedy determined that the United States would impose a naval blockade around the island of Cuba. This would be short of armed combat and provide dramatic, forceful, and highly credible coercive pressure that the Soviets could easily understand. Moreover, such a blockade could be more easily controlled than troops on the ground in an invasion force and could be quickly increased if the circumstances warranted. Although the naval blockade could prevent additional Soviet missiles, warheads, and military equipment from reaching Cuba, it obviously could not remove the missiles that had already arrived and were being made operational. It was Kennedy's hope, however, that the blockade and preparations for a possible air strike or invasion of Cuba would demonstrate his resolution, give Khrushchev time to consider that he had greatly miscalculated the likely American reaction, and exert sufficient bargaining leverage and coercive pressure to induce Khrushchev to remove the missiles.

There was no assurance, however, that coercive diplomacy was a viable strategy or that it could be applied without setting into motion developments that would lead to a war that neither side wanted. In an age of weapons of mass destruction, the risks of catastrophe were enormous. What would happen if Khrushchev, who immediately denounced the blockade as an "act of war," ordered Soviet vessels and submarines to smash through it and test Kennedy's resolve? Might this lead to actual shooting on the high seas or Soviet retaliation elsewhere that could set into motion uncontrollable escalation to a major war—perhaps even a thermonuclear war? Would Khrushchev, who had invested so much in the missile deployment, be capable of such a public retreat before the eyes of the world? What if neither Kennedy nor Khrushchev could create pauses to slow down the tempo of the crisis or select a course of action

that signaled a desire to negotiate rather than seek a military solution? Or, what if neither of the leaders could maintain top-level civilian control of his own military forces as instruments of statecraft?

It is precisely these kinds of questions that reveal a striking tension between coercive diplomacy and the principles of managing a crisis in order to avoid triggering unwanted escalation and possibly war. This is why Kennedy exercised deliberate restraint and initially chose to ignore the advice from his military hawks to use force immediately, employing instead the relatively weak "try-and-see" variant of coercive diplomacy at the outset. During the first five days of the confrontation, for example, the president deliberately avoided issuing Khrushchev a time limit for compliance with his demand for removing the missiles or explicitly threatening him with an air strike or invasion for noncompliance. As for Khrushchev, even though he blustered and issued coercive threats of his own in an effort to undermine Kennedy's resolve, he nonetheless went to great lengths to avoid a clash at sea. Within hours after Kennedy announced the blockade, to illustrate, Khrushchev chose to resist his own hardline military advisors, whom he described as "maniacs" interested only in using armed force, and directed Soviet vessels carrying missiles and other military equipment to Cuba to turn back immediately. Both Khrushchev and Kennedy appreciated the risks associated with the use of force, and thus behaved with sober prudence and reasonable skill to avoid escalation and to extricate themselves from the war-threatening crisis.

Once the danger of a clash on the high seas was safely managed, however, American and Soviet cooperation in managing the crisis began to break down. On Saturday morning, October 27, both leaders suddenly experienced disturbing new challenges to their ability to control events. A startling lack of synchronization in the interaction between the two sides emerged. The context and meaning of possibly critical moves and communications became confusing; deciphering the intentions and calculations behind specific moves of the opponent became difficult. Policy makers in Washington puzzled over the discrepancy between Khrushchev's personal and more accommodating private letter of Friday evening, in which he hinted at a deal for withdrawal of the missiles in return for an American pledge of noninvasion of Cuba, and his more formal and hard-lined letter of the next day advancing new demands. Other disturbing events occurred on Saturday. A U-2 spy plane was shot down over Cuba by Soviet military officers without an explicit order from Moscow to do so, two other U.S. aircraft were fired upon by Cuban air defense forces as they swooped low over the missile sites, an American reconnaissance plane wandered by mistake over Siberia, aggressive antisubmarine activities by the U.S. Navy dangerously forced all Soviet submarines in the area to the surface, and ominous reports arrived that Soviet consulate personnel were burning classified papers. Any of these developments could have triggered escalation into war. Policy makers in the White House anxiously speculated that the Kremlin was now taking a harder line and determined to test U.S. resolution, that perhaps Khrushchev was no longer in charge, or that Moscow was trying to extract a higher price for removal of the missiles. Moreover, each

passing day of work by Soviet technicians in Cuba brought the missiles closer to becoming operational.

A new sense of urgency now gripped Kennedy and his advisors, and they determined to make two drastic changes in their strategy of coercive diplomacy. The first of these was to convert the try-and-see approach into the more serious variant of the ultimatum. To do this, the president sent his brother Robert to verbally deliver a much more potent threat and a time limit of twenty-four hours to Soviet Ambassador Anatoly Dobrynin, telling him:

> We had to have a commitment by tomorrow. . . . He should understand that if they did not remove those [missile] bases, we would remove them. . . . Time was running out. We had only a few more hours—we needed an answer immediately from the Soviet Union. I said we must have it the next day.

Kennedy thereby focused his demand on the limited objective of the removal of the missiles rather than the broader and more extensive matter of changing the Communist regime of Fidel Castro. He wanted to convince Khrushchev that the United States was more highly motivated by what was at stake than the Soviet Union—that is, that it was more important to the United States to get the missiles out of Cuba than it was to the Soviet Union to keep them there—and that he had the resolution to achieve that objective. The credibility of the urgent threat was enhanced by the fact that preparations for an armed invasion of Cuba by the United Sates had been completed on the same day and that Soviet and Cuban intelligence sources warned Moscow that American military action was imminent.

The second important change was the decision to couple this additional coercive pressure with inducements to make it easier for the Soviet leader to agree to remove the missiles. That is, Kennedy determined that he would create a carrot-and-stick approach, coupling the ultimatum with certain concessions that he had earlier refused to discuss. He offered a significant concession, promising that he would call off the naval quarantine and that the United States would pledge to not invade Cuba if the Soviets removed their missiles under appropriate United Nations observation and supervision. He also secretly agreed to remove U.S. Jupiter missiles stationed in Turkey next to the Soviet Union. The combination of this quid pro quo, mutual reassurance, and growing fear generated by urgency and the image of thermonuclear war created powerful incentives on both sides to prevent unacceptable escalation. Within just a few hours, therefore, Khrushchev accepted Kennedy's formula and the crisis was settled.

ANALYSIS

Coercive diplomacy is an attractive, indeed sometimes a beguiling, strategy because it offers strong powers the possibility of achieving their objectives without war. But, like deterrence, it typically assumes a type of simple, uncomplicated rationality on the part of the opponent. If the opponent is "rational," they will surely see that it is in their interest to comply with the demands

made against them and back down. This assumption, however, oversimplifies the psychological, political, and cultural roots of motivation and the considerations that may influence those who are the targets of coercive diplomacy. Governments are not unitary actors, and there is frequent competition among various bureaucracies, military branches, interests, and personalities that may have very different perceptions, values, ideas about what constitutes the "national interest" or "honor," and calculations of possible benefits or "unacceptable" costs. Moreover, there is no way to confidently or successfully predict what leaders will do when subjected to the harsh demands, threats, and time limit of an ultimatum. An opponent's reluctance to undertake a humiliating retreat, as cognitive psychology repeatedly and persuasively emphasizes, can activate psychological tendencies to engage in wishful thinking, to discount evidence that challenges their existing preconceptions, and distort the ability to correctly anticipate the behavior of others, thereby leading to critical miscalculations. Historical cases reveal that the outcome of coercive diplomacy entails a complex and sometimes quite subjective matrix of psychological, cultural, and political variables.

Those Japanese leaders who complied with the demands of Admiral Perry's "gunboat diplomacy," for example, did so in part because they held a much longer perspective of history than did the Americans and believed that their action was a mere tactical move to buy time until circumstances changed in their favor, which ultimately would bring them victory. When the United States began to coerce Japan again in 1938, neither the Americans nor the Japanese believed that their disagreements would or should lead to war. But, as the United States ambitiously escalated its demands and tightened its credible and highly potent oil embargo, misperception and miscalculation increased, as did Japanese intransigence. Then, when the United States issued an ultimatum, it did not instill a fear of unacceptable punishment as hoped, but instead produced just the opposite reaction: it completely boomeranged and provoked the Japanese into making a very difficult and desperate decision to actually initiate war. At the onset of the Cuban Missile Crisis, Khrushchev initially and mistakenly perceived Kennedy as a young, inexperienced leader who could be pushed around. Moreover, as the crisis escalated, it revealed that Soviet policy makers subjected to days of stress, sleep deprivation, and decisions made under pressure easily became emotional and erratic. Even among "the best and the brightest" American leaders, wrote Robert Kennedy from firsthand experience, there were those "of the highest intelligence" who "because of the pressure of events . . . appeared to lose their judgment and stability."

Coercive diplomacy, by its very nature, is a strategy that induces stress. Unlike negotiation, it shifts attention away from common interests and focuses instead on conflict. It can trigger shock, anger, and a sense of desperation that easily can exacerbate rather than resolve a crisis and thereby actually provoke the very kind of behavior it seeks to avoid. Acute stress can seriously degrade performance by creating decisional pathologies among fatigued leaders forced to make critical decisions under the pressure of time

when the costs of failure are high. Crisis-induced stress can easily provoke emotional outbursts and increase cognitive rigidity, impairing the ability to accurately process new information that challenges existing beliefs, reducing creativity and the ability to improvise, narrowing the range of perceived alternatives or options, and limiting the degree of toleration for ambiguity. One would like to believe that fateful decisions of war and peace are not influenced by such factors, but they often are.

An analysis of these historical cases also reveals the absolutely critical importance of motivation or will—for both sides—and how the asymmetry of motivation can be deliberately enhanced or diminished by the coercing power. Success is more likely if the state practicing coercive diplomacy can convey that it is more motivated to achieve its objectives than the adversary is to oppose them and that this calculation can be influenced by the nature and the extent of what is demanded. The quite natural motivation of the Japanese to resist American coercion in the nineteenth century, for example, was significantly reduced by the fact that the United States did not demand any more than a relatively modest opening of a few ports for trade and assistance for shipwrecked American sailors. Similarly, during the Cuban Missile Crisis, Kennedy's limited demand, confined to the objective of removing the missiles alone, greatly helped to persuade Khrushchev that he could comply without threatening the wide-ranging and vital national interests of the Soviet Union. In sharp contrast, and contrary to conventional wisdom, which holds that the strength and credibility of threats is *the* critical factor on which successful coercion depends, the Pearl Harbor case demonstrates something quite different. Even though its threats were strong and credible, when the United States failed to clarify and refused to limit policy objectives and then demanded in 1941 that the Japanese suddenly reverse long-held beliefs and undo or give up what they had acquired over the course of ten years, it actually strengthened Japan's motivation not to comply at all. When confronted with this choice, Japanese leaders made the decision to inflict damage of their own upon the coercer by launching a preemptive war rather than accept the terms for avoiding it.

All three of these cases present examples of credible and potent threats. None of the states employing coercive diplomacy lacked either the will or the ability to carry through with the punishment that they threatened in the event of noncompliance. Each attempted to convey that they meant what they said and create in the mind of their opponents a fear of unacceptable costs. They thus sought to use their potential power to hurt as bargaining power to make their opponents act in order to avoid it. Admiral Perry's use of "gunboat diplomacy" effectively threatened to use American superiority in military technology to inflict punishment on Japan. When the United States employed coercive diplomacy against Japan prior to the Second World War, it clearly presented a highly credible and potent threat of cutting off all vital oil supplies. When Kennedy threatened Khrushchev in 1962, he focused very specifically on the potential use of armed force to attack the missile sites in Cuba in order to destroy the weapons before they became operational. The greatest danger in

this case, however, was that if the threat was carried out, neither side would be able to control the consequences, that is, an American attack would likely kill Soviets on the ground in Cuba and that this, in turn, would rapidly lead to retaliation and uncontrollable and unacceptable escalation. Both Kennedy and Khrushchev thus greatly feared that if they failed to manage the crisis, the result would be thermonuclear war.

The existence of incentives can also play a particularly significant role in the success or failure of coercive diplomacy. Few international problems are ever resolved by simply making threats. But, as these historical cases reveal, incentives—like threats—must be credible and have sufficient potency in order to affect the motivation of opponents to comply with demands made against them. When attempting to coerce Japan in the nineteenth century, the United States effectively coupled inducements with its threats. Perry offered to extend the benefits of commercial trade and access to Western technology, and this possessed considerable appeal, at least to the progressives in the Japanese court. When employing coercive diplomacy in 1941, Secretary of State Hull offered to remove the freeze on Japanese assets and to sign a nonaggression treaty. But these incentives were hardly potent enough to encourage the leaders of Japan to alter their balance of motivation and comply with the otherwise severe American demands, and they refused to be coerced. In contrast, Kennedy offered substantial inducements: a promise to call off the naval quarantine, to not invade Cuba, and to remove the U.S. Jupiter missiles from Turkey. These concessions played a profound role in altering Khrushchev's balance of motivation to comply and thus in resolving the missile crisis.

Yet another factor that can influence the success or failure of coercive diplomacy is the level of urgency. In one way or another, states determine how much time they will give an opponent to reflect on the costs that are likely to follow if the threats of punishment are carried out and to comply with the demands made against them. They can vary their choices between a mild try-and-see approach or a much more extreme ultimatum that dramatically escalates the pressure by setting a definite time limit for compliance. American "gunboat diplomacy" in 1853 and 1854 utilized the former, actually giving the Japanese eight months for what they hoped would be ample time for thoughtful deliberation. In 1941, the leaders in Japan believed that, given their rate of oil consumption, the practical effect of the ultimatum from the United States required some form of compliance within a few weeks. During the Cuban Missile Crisis, Kennedy's ultimatum gave the Soviet Union twenty-four hours to remove the missiles. Soviet compliance in this particular case, however, appears to have much more to do with the asymmetry of motivation, enormous fear of war, and the existence of potent incentives rather than the press of time. Indeed, extensive research on other historical cases suggests that ultimata with short time limits easily can add unnecessary stress and provocation to already dangerous confrontations and may not be successful in facilitating resolution by peaceful means.

Finally, these cases, ranging from Japan to the Soviet Union, from the Pacific to the Caribbean, from the nineteenth century to the twentieth, and from

gunboats to missiles, all provide invaluable reminders of the fact that coercive diplomacy, like all strategies of force and statecraft, is highly dependent upon the historical context. Each occurred with particular leaders making decisions within the range of possibilities and restraints afforded by their own time and place. Moreover, each was affected by the broader diplomatic revolution that changed many features of diplomacy and the international system itself.

Public opinion and the media, for example, played a relatively small role in shaping the agenda or influencing international priorities in the nineteenth-century case of American coercion against Japan. There was little knowledge or even interest among either the American or the Japanese public in the other, and Perry was specifically instructed to refrain from any communication with the press, lest failure arouse public criticism of government policy. On the eve of the Second World War, by way of contrast, Japanese leaders had deliberately whipped their populace into a nationalistic frenzy that they then found difficult to control. Roosevelt, for his part, had to contend with serious restraints imposed by domestic political opinion. Polls showed overwhelming support for the Chinese and against any "appeasement" of Japanese aggression, for example, but at the same time strong resistance to any coercive diplomacy that might escalate and thereby violate America's strong isolationist sentiment. In an age of extensive television coverage, Kennedy and his advisors were forced to devote considerable effort during the Cuban Missile Crisis to calculating the impact of their decisions upon domestic opinion at home, fearing the severe political consequences of appearing to be "weak" on the eve of an election. In addition, they regarded global opinion to be particularly important and thus worked hard to present a favorable impression among allies in Latin America and Europe, whose support they sought, and at the United Nations before what they called "the courtroom of world opinion."

Part of the effectiveness of this American presentation before the United Nations in 1962 came as a result of technological developments to collect and communicate intelligence. The advanced technology of U-2 spy planes flying miles above the earth made it possible to show dramatic photographs of the Soviet Union placing missiles in Cuba and thereby convincingly counter Khrushchev's claims to the contrary. Such intelligence also had the enormous advantage of providing warning of pending danger and allowed the Americans to discover the missiles before they became operational, and thus design their coercive diplomacy accordingly. No such technology existed for Admiral Perry or anyone else in the 1850s when, in the words of one observer, information was gathered and shared by "mouth-to-mouth" communication and "rumor." Although the signals were either unclear or misinterpreted, the United States had discovered how to use technological means to break the diplomatic code of Japan prior to the outbreak of the Second World War. Each advance in technology, however, also increased the pace of events, forcing statesmen to make decisions in ever-shorter periods of time. The months available for prudent judgment and decision making in the nineteenth century, for example, had turned into days and then hours by the time of the Cuban Missile Crisis.

The number of actors in the international system further demonstrated the growing challenges and complexities of diplomacy. When America employed "gunboat diplomacy" against Japan in 1853 and 1854, it knew for all intents and purposes that it needed to calculate only the relatively isolated interests and reactions of itself and Japan. When the United States attempted to coerce Japan from 1938 to 1941, however, Roosevelt and Hull understood that their decisions would have implications for all those nations in Asia and the Pacific, as well as Britain, France, and the Netherlands. During their confrontation of 1962, both Kennedy and Khrushchev were painfully aware of the fact that their decisions—made all the more complicated by the ideological contest of the Cold War—would affect the entire planet. As Robert Kennedy ominously explained, the crisis "was my life—and for Americans and Russians, for the whole world, it was their life as well."

The reason for this horrifying fear, of course, came from the fact that weapons technology by the time of the Cuban Missile Crisis included nuclear weapons of mass destruction. If coercive diplomacy by the United States against Japan had failed in 1854, it would have taken months to mobilize additional force across the vast ocean, and, even then, the amount of damage that could have been inflicted by weapons at the time remained very small. Such limitations changed dramatically in the next century, as evident when the Japanese refused to be coerced and destroyed much of the strength of America's Pacific fleet within just a few minutes during their surprise attack against Pearl Harbor. The existence of nuclear weapons and sophisticated delivery systems in 1962 and the radioactive fallout that would have resulted immediately from their use, in the words of one of the leading decision makers, meant that the failure of coercive diplomacy would likely lead to "the abyss of nuclear destruction and the end of mankind."

These potential extraordinary costs resulting from the deliberate manipulation of the risks of war through the use of demands and threats, especially in our own time, have led any number of scholars and policy makers alike to become acutely aware not only of the uses of this strategy but also of its difficulties, limitations, and dangers. A broad-ranging and insightful new study entitled *The United States and Coercive Diplomacy*, edited by Robert Art and Patrick Cronin, to use but one example, explores several post–Cold War cases. The book focuses on coercive diplomacy's more recent targets, ranging from Serbia and Afghanistan to Haiti and North Korea, from nonstate actors like warlord Mohammed Farrah Aideed in Somalia and terrorists like Osama bin Laden to regional powers like Iraq. The authors point out that policy makers are not always well schooled in matters of force and statecraft, are often insufficiently sensitive to the risks of coercive diplomacy, and do not fully appreciate the complexities of how difficult it is to apply abstract principles to actual policy in particular circumstances or to predict outcomes. They observe that possession of military superiority over an opponent is not sufficient for success, that targets may refuse to back down for reasons such as honor or prestige and develop "countercoercion" techniques of their own, and that this strategy is more difficult in the case of nonstate actors like

terrorists or suicide bombers, who are intensely motivated to resist and who possess few tangible assets that can be threatened with punishment. After carefully exploring these cases and analyzing the evidence, they conclude that coercive diplomacy has sometimes worked—but more often has failed.

All systematic analyses of case studies of coercive diplomacy reveal that this strategy, perhaps even more so than deterrence, is highly context-dependent. It does not take place in a vacuum, and thus must be tailored in an exacting way to fit the unique configuration of each situation and to take into account the particular behavioral characteristics of a specific adversary. But the many details of a crisis in which coercive diplomacy may be employed are seldom clearly visible to any policy maker, miscalculations and unintended consequences are likely, and, as a result, the strategy can easily fail. Efforts to engage in coercive diplomacy therefore rest heavily upon skill at understanding the nature of the conflict, correctly assessing the adversary and empathizing with them, providing reassurances, adjusting to ever-changing circumstances, and relying more on diplomatic communication rather than military signals alone. The actors employing coercive diplomacy must continually evaluate the risks of what they are doing and must slow the momentum of events as necessary in order to give the opponent time for sober reflection. They must choose and time their actions carefully to make them compatible with the opponent's ability to appraise the evolving situation and to respond appropriately. Moreover, they must always leave the adversary with a way out of the crisis that avoids the extremes of either war or abject humiliation. As all of these observations suggest, coercive diplomacy includes some of the important requirements of crisis management, a topic to which we now turn in the next chapter.

SUGGESTIONS FOR FURTHER EXPLORATION

The general theory of coercive diplomacy presented here draws from Alexander L. George and William E. Simons (eds.), *The Limits of Coercive Diplomacy* (Boulder, CO, 1994 ed.); Alexander L. George, *Forceful Persuasion* (Washington, DC, 1991); and Alexander L. George, David Hall, and William Simons, *The Limits of Coercive Diplomacy* (Boston, 1971 ed.). Other very helpful discussions are available in Robert J. Art and Patrick M. Cronin (eds.), *The United States and Coercive Diplomacy* (Washington, DC, 2003); H. W. Brands et al. (eds.), *The Use of Force After the Cold War* (College Station, TX, 2003 ed.); James A. Nathan, *Soldiers, Statecraft, and History* (Westport, CT, 2002); Daniel Byman and Matthew Waxman, *The Dynamics of Coercion* (Cambridge, 2002); Kenneth Schultz, *Democracy and Coercive Diplomacy* (Cambridge, 2001); Lawrence Freedman (ed.), *Strategic Coercion* (Oxford, 1998); Peter Jakobsen, *Western Use of Coercive Diplomacy After the Cold War* (New York, 1998); Alexander L. George, "The Impact of Crisis-Induced Stress on Decision Making," in Frederic Solomon and Robert Marston (eds.), *The Medical Implications of Nuclear War* (Washington, DC, 1986); Russell J. Leng, "When Will They Ever Learn," *Journal of Conflict Resolution* (September 1983): 379–419; Richard Ned Lebow, *Between War and Peace* (Baltimore, 1981); Paul Gordon Lauren, "Theories of Bargaining with Threats of Force: Deterrence and Coercive Diplomacy," in Paul Gordon Lauren (ed.), *Diplomacy: New Approaches in History, Theory, and Policy* (New York, 1979); Charles Lockhart, *Bargaining in International Conflicts* (New York, 1979); Barry Blechman and Stephen Kaplan, *Force Without War*

(Washington, DC, 1978); Glenn H. Snyder and Paul Diesing, *Conflict Among Nations* (Princeton, 1977); Glenn H. Synder, "Crisis Bargaining," in Charles Hermann (ed.), *International Crises* (New York, 1972); Paul Gordon Lauren, "Ultimata and Coercive Diplomacy," *International Studies Quarterly*, 16 (1972): 131–165; Oran Young, *The Politics of Force* (Princeton, 1968); and Thomas Schelling *Arms and Influence* (New Haven, 1966) and *The Strategy of Conflict* (New York, 1960).

The case of "gunboat diplomacy" in Asia is treated in Thomas Patterson et al., *American Foreign Relations* (Boston, 2005 ed.); Akira Iriye (ed.), *Mutual Images: Essays in American-Japanese Relations* (Cambridge, MA, 1975); Roger Pineau (ed.), *The Japan Expedition of 1852–1854: The Personal Journal of Commodore Matthew C. Perry* (Washington, DC, 1968); Samuel Eliot Morrison, *"Old Bruin"* (Boston, 1967); William Neumann, *America Encounters Japan* (Baltimore, 1963); William G. Beasley (trans. and ed.), *Select Documents on Japanese Foreign Policy, 1853–1868* (London, 1955); Henry Graff, *Bluejackets with Perry in Japan* (New York, 1952); Arthur Walworth, *Black Ships Off Japan* (New York, 1946); and Francis L. Hawks (ed.), *Narrative of the Expedition of an American Squadron to the China Seas and Japan* (Washington, DC, 1856). For broader discussion of navies as instruments of coercive diplomacy, see Robert Mandel, "The Effectiveness of Gunboat Diplomacy," *International Studies Quarterly*, 30 (1986): 59–76; James Cable, *Gunboat Diplomacy, 1919–1979* (New York, 1986 ed.); and Edward Luttwak, *The Political Uses of Sea Power* (Baltimore, 1974).

For American-Japanese relations leading to the outbreak of World War II, see Gordon Prange et al., *Pearl Harbor: The Verdict of History* (New York, 2001); Scott Sagan, "From Deterrence to Coercion to War," in George and Simons (eds.), *The Limits of Coercive Diplomacy*; Gordon Prange, *At Dawn We Slept* (New York, 1991); Charles Neu, *The Troubled Encounter* (New York, 1975); Richard Dean Burns and Edward M. Bennett (eds.), *Diplomats in Crisis* (Santa Barbara, CA, 1974); Dorothy Borg and Shumpei Okamoto (eds.), *Pearl Harbor as History* (New York, 1973); Chihiro Hosoya, "Miscalculation in Deterrent Policy: Japanese-U.S. Relations, 1938–1941," *Journal of Peace Research*, 5 (1968): 97–115; and Nobutaka Ike (ed.), *Japan's Decision for War* (Stanford, CA, 1967).

Much has been written about the Cuban Missile Crisis, including James Blight, Bruce Allyn, and David Welch, *Cuba on the Brink* (New York, 2002 ed.); Ernest May and Philip Zelikow, *The Kennedy Tapes: Inside the White House During the Cuban Missile Crisis* (Cambridge, MA, 1998); Richard Ned Lebow and Janice Gross Stein, *We All Lost the Cold War* (Princeton, 1994); James A. Nathan (ed.), *The Cuban Missile Crisis Reconsidered* (New York, 1992); Michael Beschloss, *The Crisis Years* (New York, 1991); Raymond L. Garthoff, *Reflections on the Cuban Missile Crisis* (Washington, DC, 1989 ed.); McGeorge Bundy, *Danger and Survival* (New York, 1988); and Robert Kennedy *Thirteen Days* (New York, 1969).

Many other cases of coercive diplomacy exist in the annals of statecraft. Some of the more suggestive of these include the Great Powers of Europe against Mehemet Ali of Egypt (1840); Britain against Greece in the Don Pacifico Affair (1850); Britain against the United States in the *Trent* Affair (1861); the French ultimatum against Siam (1893); Italy against Turkey (1911); the whole series of ultimata leading to the outbreak of the First World War (1914); Britain and France against Hitler following the invasion of Poland (1939); the United States against Laos (1961–1962), North Vietnam (1965), Nicaragua and Libya (1981–1989), Somalia (1992–1994), Haiti and North Korea (1994), Saddam Hussein and Iraq (1990–2002), Bosnia (1995), Kosovo (1999), and terrorism (1993, 1998, and 2001–2006).

— 11 —

Crisis Management

During the tense days of the Cuban Missile Crisis when the two super-powers stood at the very brink of possible annihilation, the deeply worried Soviet leader Nikita Khrushchev sent a personal letter to President John Kennedy warning that if they both continued to escalate their actions against each other, the result would be global disaster. "The more the two of us pull," he warned, "the tighter the knot will be tied." In this process, Khrushchev poignantly observed,

> a moment may come when that knot will be tied so tight that even he who tied it will not the have the strength to untie it, and then it will be necessary to cut that knot, and what that would mean is not for me to explain to you, because you yourself understand perfectly of what terrible forces our countries dispose. Consequently, if there is no intention to tighten that knot, and thereby doom the world to the catastrophe of thermonuclear war, then let us not only relax the forces pulling on the ends of the rope, let us take measures to untie that knot. We are ready for this.

Because both leaders came to understand that they were not only rivals, but also partners in their common interest to avoid the frightening consequences of an inadvertent war, they sought to take urgent and deliberate steps to actively manage or control the crisis in such a way as to prevent it from escalating. They succeeded in this effort. But the experience had been harrowing, and shortly thereafter Secretary of Defense Robert McNamara remarked soberly: "Today there is no longer any such thing as military strategy; there is only crisis management."

His words, of course, were an overstatement and a simplification of the lessons to be learned; but they serve to emphasize the critical importance in statecraft of keeping war-threatening situations under control. The history of relations among states is studded with innumerable international crises that resulted when negotiation, deterrence, and/or coercive diplomacy all failed. Some of these were managed peacefully, but others ended in war that neither side wanted. In each crisis, policy makers were called upon to make high-stake and delicate diplomatic and military decisions under great stress. They

knew that their decisions could have resulted not merely in success or failure for their own nations, but in the preservation or the destruction of the existing international order itself. With the current existence of weapons of mass destruction, a nearly overwhelming volume of information in an age of instantaneous communications, and the intense pressure of time and events, crisis management becomes even more essential. Indeed, this explains not only the creation of the independent and nonpartisan Crisis Management Initiative based in Helsinki, but also the fact that the highly secure Operations Center in the U.S. Department of State maintains a twenty-four hour Crisis Management Support team to alert, brief, and advise the secretary of state on how to manage dangerous international crises in our world of today.

PRINCIPLES OF CRISIS MANAGEMENT

Leaders responsible for major decisions about force and statecraft from the historical past to the present have understood that crises provide one of the most fascinating and most frightening features of international affairs. They generally break out suddenly, present serious threats to vital interests, demand quick decisions under intense stress, and stand on the threshold of war or peace. There are times when they are be resolved or defused and other times when they result in armed conflict. If one state deliberately intends to launch a premeditated, preemptive, or preventive war to achieve its objectives, of course, there is little that another can do to prevent it. But what about those cases that escalate into an inadvertent war that neither side wants or

Crisis Managers and Crisis Management: The Cuban Missile Crisis (Getty Images)

expects at the outset of a diplomatic crisis but that nonetheless occurs? In comparing the outcomes of international confrontations, how does one account for the fact that some end peacefully and some result in war? To what extent does the ability or failure of the adversaries to apply principles of crisis management explain whether crises of this kind end up in inadvertent war? And, more basically, what exactly are these principles of crisis management?

As a tool for resolving conflicts and avoiding inadvertent war, crisis management was a familiar phenomenon during the classical system of diplomacy. Its techniques and modalities were tacitly developed through time by trial and error with a certain level of prudence, self-restraint, and good judgment, coupled with the advantages of limited armed force and the shared norms of cultural homogeneity, but never with any explicit theory or clear articulation of principles to guide policy makers who wanted to protect the national interest without becoming involved in a war. There were accounts of the kinds of mistakes that statesmen had made at moments of high crises, but certainly never a systematic effort to articulate lessons from the past or any handbook of how to actually manage a crisis once it broke out. This began to change with the frightening Cuban Missile Crisis, the experience of which created an infinitely greater sense of urgency about managing crises in the age of weapons of mass destruction. Scholars and policy researchers thus actively studied the nature of crisis management in considerable detail. As a result, we now know much more about problems of information processing and decision making under crisis conditions, the special requirements of command and control, the means of coordinating diplomatic and military actions, the problems of communication with opponents during crises, and the tasks and requirements for practicing crisis management.

1. Analyses of historical cases, for example, quickly reveal that *it is only because neither side is willing to back down that a perceived conflict of interest results in a crisis* in the first place. Confrontations between adversaries can easily be managed and terminated—in fact, avoided altogether—if one side is willing to back away. In fact, in many situations it requires a deliberate policy decision to transform a misunderstanding or a genuine conflict of interest between states into an actual crisis. President Truman, for example, was urged by important advisers not to take action to oppose the Soviet blockade of land access to West Berlin in 1948 based on the grounds that it would be highly disadvantageous for the United States to become involved in military operations to defend a military outpost lying well inside East Germany. He ignored that advice and decided to accept this challenge from the Soviet Union to change the status quo in their favor. This marked the beginning of the Berlin Crisis.

2. Once a crisis is set into motion, *each side feels compelled to do what is needed to protect or advance what it perceives as its most important interests.* At the same time, however, *these very interests force it to recognize the necessity for self-restraint and avoiding actions that could trigger unwanted escalation* of the crisis. It is the tension between these two objectives—the protection of one's interests and, at the same time, the avoidance of measures that could trigger undesired

escalation and possibly war—that creates the essential policy dilemma that all policy makers must resolve if they hope to successfully practice crisis management.

3. The resolution of this dilemma at a time of a war-threatening crisis requires leaders *to develop a careful political-military strategy* that combines force and state-craft in a way *appropriate to the situation at hand*. They need to be particularly sensitive to both diplomatic and military considerations, balancing the two in such a way as to avoid the extremes of relying either exclusively on weapons or exclusively on words. In this regard, they need to be aware that military preparations and threats of force are often indispensable for supporting diplomatic efforts in crisis situations, but that the logic of military operations— even logic based upon sound military doctrine—can conflict with the logic and requirements of diplomacy. The immediate deployment of troops or naval assets may make perfect sense as a means of conveying resolve or of getting ready to fight if war should erupt, for example, but at the same time may present grave dangers by working against the political and diplomatic necessities of proceeding slowly and building in pauses for thoughtful deliberation and communication. Successful crisis managers need to combine both of these factors but must understand that threats and movements of military forces, as Clausewitz observed many years ago, must be commensurate with limited objectives and carefully employed as instruments of policy, not as substitutes for policy.

4. In developing such a strategy, it is of considerable importance to recognize that careful analyses of crises in the past reveal that management is greatly facilitated if both sides resist the temptation to inflict a damaging and humiliating defeat on the other and instead *carefully limit the objectives they pursue in the confrontation*. Why is this self-restraint important? The more ambitious or "offensive" the strategic aims intended to alter the existing situation at the expense of the adversary, the more strongly motivated the other will be to resist. Less demanding or "defensive" aims designed to prevent or reverse serious alterations in the status quo, by way of contrast, tend to provide lesser threats to vital interests and thereby increase the probability of accommodation. In the end, all parties must recognize each others' legitimate interests and strive to find a mutually acceptable formula for terminating the crisis.

5. In addition, the *limitation of the means employed* to achieve those ends may also be necessary for successful crisis management. A power such as the United States, for example, has unparalleled military forces for attacking and destroying any number and variety of targets. What may be described as "gross military capabilities" of this character, however, do not necessarily provide a president with what may be called viable "usable options" in a diplomatic crisis or low-level military conflict in which armed forces need to be carefully tailored to the peculiarities of a particular situation. The use or threatened use of excessive force during the critical opening stages of a diplomatic crisis laden with dangerous escalation potential might well signal that the country bluntly sought to impose its will on an adversary by military means alone rather than to actually manage the crisis through the means of diplomacy.

During the Cuban Missile Crisis, to illustrate, Kennedy managed to limit both ends and means. He rejected the advice that he aim at a regime change or the removal of Fidel Castro and confined the objective to the removal of the immediate danger of the missiles themselves. Similarly, he rejected the recommendation from the Joint Chiefs of Staff that he launch air strikes against the missile sites or an armed invasion against Cuba itself, deciding instead to combine the means of a naval blockade with those of diplomacy for crisis management.

6. Studies of historical cases indicate that *all* sides in an international confrontation must understand, create, and adhere to other *operational principles and conditions that favor crisis management* as well. That is, the limitation of objectives and means alone will not ensure control over the danger of escalation and inadvertent war. Leaders also must seek to maintain control by consciously avoiding stress-induced decisional pathologies such as cognitive rigidity, feelings of desperation, or passive resignation with its notions of "inevitability," and instead create conditions that favor managing a crisis well enough to avoid war. Such favoring conditions are highly context dependent, and the importance of each varies from one crisis to another, and although none guarantees success, they all have been found likely to make a difference and affect outcomes. Each arises, in one way or another, from the necessity of policy makers to deal with the inherent dilemma of force and statecraft that we have examined throughout: the need on occasion to use both even though there is a tension that often exists between the military and the diplomatic measures that they employ in a crisis.

These favoring principles and conditions include the following: (1) *Maintain top-level civilian control of military institutions and actions.* Of surpassing importance for crisis management is civilian control at the highest levels over the selection and timing of military options. This may extend even to control over specific tactical maneuvers and operations such as alerts, deployments, and low-level moves that might lead to an undesired clash with the opponent's forces. (2) *Create pauses in the tempo of military actions.* The momentum of military movements may have to be deliberately slowed down in order to provide adequate time for the two sides to exchange signals and communications, to engage in diplomacy, and to assess the situation, reflect, make decisions, and respond to proposals. (3) *Coordinate diplomatic and military moves.* Whatever military moves are undertaken must be carefully coordinated with political-diplomatic actions and communications as part of a carefully integrated strategy for terminating the crisis acceptably without war. (4) *Confine military moves to those that constitute clear demonstrations of one's resolve and are appropriate to one's limited crisis objectives.* Extraneous or confusing "noise" that might lead to misperception, in other words, must be avoided or minimized. (5) *Avoid military moves that give the opponent the impression that one is about to resort to large-scale warfare and, thereby, force them to consider preemption.* (6) *Choose diplomatic-military options that signal a desire to negotiate rather than seek a military solution.* (7) *Select diplomatic-military options that leave the opponent a way out of the crisis that is compatible with their fundamental interests.*

Effective adherence to these principles and conditions thus requires, among other things, an appropriate political-miliary strategy with necessary capabilities, effective command and control, intimate interaction between civilian and military planners in order to design and apply usable options, and skill and flexibility in adapting to unexpected developments as a crisis unfolds. Such qualities, however, are not easy to obtain during war-threatening crises of intense pressure and acute stress, where rationality and objectivity can easily give way to confusion, shock, fear, anger, cognitive rigidity, and impulsiveness. Individual leaders, for example, may or may not possess the necessary skills. Some may rise to the occasion and become successful managers, while others may become completely overwhelmed by events and fail disastrously. Similarly, appropriate crisis management often imposes stringent constraints on the use of military force, and this can easily lead to serious tensions that strain the experience, imagination, and patience of diplomatic and military professionals alike. Civilians may have imperfect control over their military forces, or those forces may have been designed and structured in ways that rob them of the flexibility needed in a crisis. Moreover, efforts by leaders to use armed forces in the service of offensive and assertive foreign policy may well find that they lose their capability to be used when needed as highly refined, discriminating instruments for crisis management.

Utilizing these broad principles of crisis management, it is possible to compare the relative performance of policy makers in different historical crises in such a way as to come to a deeper understanding of the nature of such management, the importance of context and the impact of what we have called the diplomatic revolution on managing crises, and the more far-reaching issue of how success or failure in crisis management can result in the preservation or destruction of the international system itself.

BISMARCK AS AN "HONEST BROKER" IN THE CRISIS OF 1878

The origins of the Crisis of 1878 lay in the slow disintegration of the Ottoman Empire, violations of human rights, and Great Power ambitions in the Balkans. Sensing a unique opportunity to expand its influence and territory, Russia declared war on the Ottoman Turks the previous year and sent its army marching south. When the Turkish resistance finally collapsed, General Nicholas Ignatiev sought to exploit the temporary military advantage to the fullest. He therefore deliberately disregarded his instructions from civilian authorities to do everything possible to avoid any foreign suspicion that might lead to intervention, and instead recklessly imposed the Treaty of San Stefano with seemingly unlimited objectives that would virtually destroy Turkey in Europe and unilaterally expand Russian territory and influence in the Balkans, the Black Sea, and the Straits. These provisions not only directly violated previous agreements, but granted advantages only to Russia that, if implemented, would completely upset the balance of power throughout the region and the eastern Mediterranean. The other powers consequently concluded that

the treaty was completely unacceptable. France and Italy announced that the provisions threatened their national interests, and Austria mobilized troops in its southeastern provinces, declaring that it would oppose any Russian expansion by war if necessary. The Turks began assembling more troops in and around their capital and erecting earthworks. Britain also threatened war, called up its reserves, issued orders for its navy to be sent through the Straits into the Sea of Marmara, and brought several thousand Indian troops to strategic stations in the Mediterranean as a demonstration, all while crowds in London began to sing the belligerent chant that gave the word "jingosim" to the world:

> We don't want to fight, but by jingo if we do,
> We've got the men, we've got the ships, we've got the money too!

At exactly the same time, Russian troops were only one day's march from the very gates of Constantinople, poised to attack if necessary. It thus appeared as though a very localized conflict easily could escalate into a much larger inadvertent war involving Europe as a whole. The situation became so tense, in fact, that one British commentator in retrospect ominously observed: "If even a midshipman had lost his temper, he might have run the country into war." Indeed, as historian William Langer concludes, "peace hung by a hair."

In this crisis situation, German Chancellor Otto von Bismarck saw the possibility that any war involving several powers would bring catastrophic consequences upon the entire international system he had been trying to construct since the unification of Germany. He was never particularly bothered by international competition and rivalry, but wanted to avoid general war at all costs. Bismarck understood that the maintenance of peace and stability would not just happen on its own, but would require serious and deliberate efforts at crisis management. Of particular importance, he viewed the crisis itself as the real enemy. He saw the task of management in this case as one not of advancing one's own power at the expense of an opponent in which a gain by one side amounted to a loss for the other, but rather of convincing all the antagonists that they were partners in shared risk and had a common interest to avoid escalation that could lead to inadvertent war. In response to the suggestion of the Austrian foreign minister, and in keeping with the earlier norms and practices of the Concert of Europe, Bismarck consequently offered the hospitality of Berlin for an international conference and reluctantly announced that he would attempt to serve as an "honest broker" to help manage the crisis.

The Congress of Berlin thus assembled in the German capital in June 1878. In addition to Bismarck, the representatives included most of the leading statesmen and foreign ministers of Europe, including the Earl of Beaconsfield (Benjamin Disraeli) and Lord Salisbury of Britain, Prince Gorchakov and Count Shuvalov of Russia, Count Andrassy of Hungary, William Waddington of France, and Count Corti of Italy, in addition to representatives of Turkey and observers from the Balkans. It lasted one month and was easily the most distinguished diplomatic gathering between the Congress of Vienna of 1814–1815 and the Paris Peace Conference of 1919. In fact, the knowledge that

the congress would even be held and that they would have to actually face each other greatly encouraged the antagonists to work toward negotiating at least some agreements in advance.

In accordance with diplomatic custom, the delegates elected Bismarck, as the head of the government hosting the Congress of Berlin, to be its president. But he was the leader in more than name. Bismarck became the vital crisis manager, dominating the meetings, setting the pace and tone, rigorously insisting that the most serious issues of dispute be addressed with the greatest dispatch, variously employing both incentives and threats, working sometimes in formal sessions and sometimes in private, and constantly reminding all parties of what was necessary for crisis management, particularly on those occasions of great tension and strain when it appeared as though the congress might collapse. His success as an impartial "honest broker" cannot be better illustrated than by the fact that afterwards he was accused by all sides of having favored their opponents. Indeed, in the end, all of the participants of the congress agreed that without Bismarck and his personal skills, the effort would have ended in failure.

The key, of course, was adhering as closely as possible to the operational principles of crisis management. Delegates at the Congress of Berlin, for example, worked to maintain civilian control over their respective military forces. Bismarck—who had far more experience than he ever wanted in constantly struggling to insist that the German General Staff be an instrument rather than a maker of foreign policy—hardly needed to be convinced of the critical importance of this requirement. No troops or naval forces were allowed to threaten others during the course of the diplomatic deliberations, military commanders (like General Ignatiev, who had done so much to precipitate the crisis in the first place) found themselves kept under strict control, and military experts were invited to participate only as consultants during certain stages of the congress. This meant that diplomatic and military moves were coordinated and that armed forces were used to signal resolve and limited crisis objectives rather than creating impressions of large-scale warfare. Neither the Russians nor the British were willing to withdraw their forces from existing positions, for example, but both deliberately refrained from sending them any closer to Constantinople or using them in any way that might encourage the other to escalate. All parties desired to avoid what they called an "untoward event" like a midshipman losing his temper or some other incident that could trigger unwanted war.

As we have seen, it is not uncommon in crisis situations like this where the antagonists employ a combined political-military strategy for coercive diplomacy to be used simultaneously with crisis management, even though the requirements of each might actually conflict with each other. In this case, the evacuation of Russian troops from the boundaries of Bulgaria and the issue of who would replace them became a major point of contention between Russia and Britain. When it appeared that negotiations had failed, the British issued an ultimatum and spread the rumor that they would abandon the congress entirely if a solution could not be found. Rather than concluding that the

situation was beyond control or that there was nothing he could do, Bismarck remained determined not to have the conference collapse and labored indefatigably to secure a last-minute Russian concession on this matter.

Bismarck also used other techniques of crisis management throughout the congress. He constantly built in pauses in order to give all sides adequate time to communicate with each other and to assess the situation, make decisions, and respond to proposals. When progress began to stall over the highly contentious issues of Bulgaria or the lines of military occupation, to illustrate, he engineered the postponement of discussion for a few days. In addition, he and his fellow delegates selected diplomatic-military options that both signaled a desire to negotiate rather than seeking a military solution and to leave opponents a way out of the crisis that was compatible with their fundamental interests. They came to understand the necessity of mutual restraint, of recognizing each other's interests, and of having limited objectives. The final settlement of the Treaty of Berlin consequently was based on reciprocal compensation in which none of the powers received everything they desired, but all obtained something that they wanted. Britain gained Cyprus, France received permission to take Tunis, Austria obtained authorization to occupy Bosnia and Herzegovina, the Turks were relieved of the excessive terms imposed by San Stefano and perhaps of another war that might result in the total dismemberment of their country, religious minorities within the Ottoman Empire received a level of international recognition and sanction for the protection of certain human rights, and although Russia was forced to give up its original grandiose aims, it nevertheless secured control over a new Bulgaria, the mouth of the Danube River, and several strategic strongholds at the eastern end of the Black Sea. The Italians and Germans obtained no additional territory, but were spared the agony and the costs of having to choose sides between the other powers and thereby further fracture the international system if armed conflict had broken out. In this way, the crisis was successfully managed and an inadvertent war that easily could have engulfed all of Europe avoided.

The "Guns of August," 1914

If the Congress of Berlin provides evidence of skillful leaders practicing successful management, the crisis of 1914 that led to the outbreak of the First World War reveals a tragic instance of inept mismanagement. Several years of imperial rivalries, economic competition, arms races, war plans, and a bipolar alliance system of "two armed camps" that pitted the Triple Entente of Britain, France, and Russia against the Triple Alliance of Germany, Austria, and Italy had contributed to a series of crises. But each of these had been controlled, or at least localized, and many observers assumed that this would continue with nations going to the brink of war and then resolving the crisis through diplomacy at the last moment. What they did not fully realize, however, was how their peril had been vastly compounded by the cumulative effect of these heightened tensions, which made each succeeding crisis more difficult to

control, the implications of their countries assuming severe levels of risk unwarranted by national interests or rational long-term strategic objectives, or the consequences of their military chiefs increasingly becoming autonomous of civilian control and creating inflexible war plans that emphasized military rather than political requirements and speed rather than reflection. Of particular importance was the fact that the leaders of the time were more interested in not appearing weak than in keeping the peace and quite frankly possessed neither the understanding nor the skills necessary to conduct effective crisis management.

All of this began to be painfully evident in the decisions that were made and the events that transpired after the assassination of the Austrian Crown Prince Franz Ferdinand at the hands of Serbian-sponsored terrorists on June 28, 1914. This assassination was not, as the popular metaphor would have it, a match thrown onto a powder keg that automatically, and in a deterministic way, resulted in war. In fact, one of the more curious features of the crisis is that it started out very slowly and evolved over the course of six weeks. The Austrians, for example, took nearly one month to decide how to respond, and many of the troops were on harvest leaves to gather crops rather than preparing for war. Prior to taking any serious action, they carefully sought to learn whether their ally Germany would support them or not. Rather than carefully assessing his nation's vital interests at stake in the Balkans, or urging a diplomatic rather than a military solution, or insisting upon some measure of control, however, the German Kaiser William II impulsively granted the foolhardy "black check" to their Austrian ally on July 5, telling them that he would support whatever they decided to do. In doing so, wrote historian Sydney Fay, the Kaiser and his advisors were "putting a noose around their necks and handing the other end of the rope to a stupid and clumsy adventurer who now felt free to go as he liked." Insensitive as ever to the international implications of his decisions, Wilhelm II then simply abandoned his responsibilities and left for a holiday cruise.

With this unqualified support in their hands, the Austrians then dramatically escalated events by issuing a forty-eight-hour ultimatum to the shocked Serbs with demands so deliberately harsh that they were sure to be rejected. British Foreign Secretary Edward Grey said that he had never seen one government send another government "a document of so formidable a character." When the Russian Foreign Minister Sergei Sazonov saw the text of the ultimatum, he was aghast and shouted out to the Austrian ambassador: "This means European war. You are setting Europe alight!" The Serbians composed a masterful reply that acceded to most of the Austrian demands. In fact, when Wilhelm II read the reply, he wrote happily, "Every reason for war now disappears!" But by this time the Austrians were not interested in compromise. They rejected the Serbian response as unacceptable, dismissed a British proposal for a diplomatic conference that might have helped to manage the crisis, and declared war on Serbia on July 28, 1914.

Rather than building in pauses in the tempo, or avoiding military moves that give an opponent the impression that one is about to escalate, or choosing

diplomatic-military options that signal a desire to negotiate rather than seeking a military solution—as required by crisis management—in order to keep the war localized between the Austrians and the Serbs alone, Russia decided to support Serbia by immediately ordering partial mobilization against Austria. At this point, Czar Nicholas II was shocked to discover that the only plan his military staff had readied was for mobilization against both Germany and Austria and to hear his commanders insist that restraint would only lead to disaster and that they must be given authorization for full mobilization. To make matters worse, instead of carefully coordinating diplomatic and military moves, at the same time that Russian forces were moving west toward the border with Germany, Russian diplomats were telling the Germans that they had nothing to fear. The Germans, however, perceived that actions spoke louder than words. They consequently engaged in the extreme variant of coercive diplomacy by issuing an ultimatum demanding that if Russia did not stop its mobilization within twelve hours, Germany would follow suit. The Russians refused, and Germany declared war on Russia on August 1, thereby expanding the conflict exponentially. This occurred, remarkably, without a single serious political discussion between St. Petersburg and Berlin about the substance of the crisis or the need for diplomacy and in the absence of any major, tangible dispute between the two countries.

This pattern of mobilization with its resulting escalation was repeated by others, and each successive step made the crisis more difficult to manage. Within only days of the Austrian declaration of war against Serbia, every one of the major European powers had called up its armed forces. Each claimed that their military mobilization was a defensive measure only, designed for deterrence and taken merely as a response to the dangers posed by others. They all feared that disastrous consequences would occur if a potential adversary gained even a momentary advantage in mobilizing its forces. This encouraged them to see the military incentives of moving as quickly as possible rather than the diplomatic advantages of building in pauses for thoughtful deliberation and negotiation. They also hoped that their own mobilization might serve as a deterrent, warning others against taking similar action. But in a context of fear, misperception, and seemingly total lack of empathy for the perceptions of others, this produced exactly the opposite reaction. Every mobilization, in turn, especially since they were not accompanied by serious efforts of diplomatic negotiation, gave all the others the overwhelming impression that large-scale warfare might be imminent and that they should consider countermeasures and possibly preemption in order not to be placed at a serious disadvantage.

Crisis management, of course, requires the firm determination to actually manage or maintain control over events. Thus, the most serious mistake that any leader can make is to believe that there is nothing they can do to prevent war or that management is not possible. In a crisis situation, therefore, anyone seeking to manage must avoid falling prey to the dreaded word, "inevitable." Yet, this is precisely what the leaders of 1914 failed to do. Time and time again, and even at early stages of the crisis, they concluded that they were helpless and passively resigned themselves to whatever fate awaited them.

Paul Cambon, the French ambassador in London, for example, stated that he saw "no way of halting the march of events." Arthur Nicolson, the British Permanent Under Secretary for Foreign Affairs, wrote: "I am of the opinion that the resources of diplomacy are, for the present, exhausted." In a telling comment written in his own hand, William II declared in despair, "My work is at an end!" Similarly, one of the leading generals in Russia advised the foreign ministry that "war had become inevitable."

As the inflexible Russian war plan severely limited the options for civilian crisis managers, so too did the German counterpart known as the von Schlieffen Plan, which called for an attack on France first and then an attack on Russia. The French, seeing an opportunity for revenge for their loss of territory during the Franco-Prussian War, had no interest in urging restraint upon their ally Russia and instead actually encouraged her to resist German demands and promised unconditional support in doing so. Nevertheless, the kaiser now began to fear a two-front war and tried to persuade his Chief of the General Staff, General Helmuth von Moltke, to change the plan in such a way as to divert German attention away from France and toward the more immediate threat of Russia alone. Barbara Tuchman in *The Guns of August* captures the memorable scene with these words:

> Moltke was in no mood for any more of the kaiser's meddling with serious military matters. . . . He saw a vision of the deployment crumbling apart in confusion, supplies here, soldiers there, ammunition lost in the middle, companies without officers, divisions without staffs, and those 11,000 trains, each exquisitely scheduled to click over specified tracks at specified intervals of ten minutes, tangled into grotesque ruin of the most perfectly planned military movement in history.
> "Your Majesty," Moltke said to him now, "it cannot be done. The deployment of millions cannot be improvised. If Your Majesty insists on leading the whole army to the East it will not be an army ready for battle but a disorganized mob of armed men with no arrangements for supply. Those arrangements took a whole year of intricate labor to complete"— and Moltke closed upon that rigid phrase, the basis for every major German mistake, the phrase that launched the invasion of Belgium and the submarine war against the United States, the inevitable phrase when military plans dictate policy—"and once settled, it cannot be altered."

In fact, it could have been altered and, in accordance with the operational principles of crisis management, should have been altered. These plans were made by men and could have been changed by men. But Kaiser Wilhelm II, like Tsar Nicholas II, was not wise enough or strong enough to exert and maintain civilian control over military options or the military machinery that he had done so much to create, and both simply acquiesced to their generals who insisted that an all-or-nothing war plan must determine policy and that priority should be given to military necessity over political consequences.

The principles of crisis management were further violated in other ways. Little effort was made to coordinate diplomatic and military actions or communications as part of a carefully integrated strategy. On the very day that

the German Chancellor Bethmann-Hollweg sent a telegram to the Austrian Cabinet stressing the necessity of "urgently and impressively" exercising restraint and accepting mediation in the conflict with Serbia, for example, Moltke sent his own telegram to the Austrian chief of staff Conrad von Hötzendorf urging him to mobilize his army at once. These completely contradictory messages not only signaled confusion to leaders in Vienna, but made them quite naturally ask whether civilians or military commanders were really in control in Berlin. Similarly, instead of confining military moves to those that were appropriate to limited crisis objectives or selecting diplomatic-military options that would leave opponents a way out of the crisis that was compatible with their fundamental interests, the leaders foolishly plunged their countries and the world ever-closer toward full-scale war—and catastrophe. Germany, to illustrate, issued an ultimatum to France demanding neutrality in the event of war and sent another ultimatum to Belgium that demanded free passage for German troops. When both were rejected on the basis of vital national interests, Germany declared war on France and launched an invasion of neutral Belgium on August 3, revealing a complete disregard for international law, a preference for a military solution over any negotiations at all, and a strong indication of unlimited objectives. In response, Britain issued an ultimatum to Germany, demanding that all troops be withdrawn from Belgium within less than one day. The demand was met with refusal, and Britain declared war against Germany. With this, the great storm broke.

The leaders of the Great Powers had failed to adhere to any of the principles of crisis management, and thereby allowed a secondary conflict to escalate completely out of control. As a result of their failure, a local dispute in the Balkans led to the invasion of Belgium and the dispatch of British troops on the other side of Europe with a war everywhere between—one that eventually drew in the United States, China, and Japan. Their monumental mismanagement resulted not only in the unanticipated horrors of the First World War, but with it the collapse of several of their own governments and the entire international system they had known.

MANAGING THE 1973 ARAB-ISRAELI WAR

It is important to understand that local wars do not—and need not—break out into widespread general inadvertent wars if crisis management can be practiced successfully. This can be seen in any number of cases, not the least of which are those that have occurred between Israel and its neighbors. The crises, and then the wars, of 1948–1949 with the creation of Israel, 1956 with the Sinai campaign during the Suez Crisis, 1967 with the Six Day War and Israeli occupation of significant territories, and 1969–1970 with the War of Attrition between Egypt and Israel, all involved deep and violent passions, seemingly unreconcilable differences, and high stakes for many parties, but never resulted in large-scale wars involving other countries beyond the region. This pattern of success was placed in serious jeopardy, however, when the Egyptians and Syrians decided to reverse their previous losses by the force

of arms, attacking Israel on October 6, 1973, with a carefully coordinated offensive and thereby launching the Yom Kippur, or Arab-Israeli, War. The Arab forces engaged in the fiercest tank battles since the Second World War and, in sharp contrast to their past military humiliations and defeats, scored surprising victories in the Golan Heights and the Sinai, forcing the heavily favored Israelis to abandon their myth of invincibility as well as strategic positions such as the Bar-Lev fortified line along the Suez Canal.

It was at this precise point that the dangers of escalation—and thus the challenges for crisis management—began to emerge. Buoyed by the initial successes of Arab forces, Iraq and Jordan decided to supply troops for the Syrian front, and Saudi Arabia and other oil-rich states imposed an oil embargo to coerce their customers into supporting the Arabs. More ominously, each side in the war possessed an outside superpower patron. Neither would have been able to wage this kind of war, in fact, if it had not been for outside military and financial assistance. As the battles ranged and fortunes changed, President Anwar Sadat of Egypt turned to the Soviet Union and Prime Minister Golda Meir of Israel turned to the United States, frantically appealing for ever-higher levels of support. They did so with the full understanding that both of the Cold War rivals had much to gain and much to lose in this war. To refuse the requests for aid would jeopardize their entire respective interests in the Middle East, whereas to grant them would be to risk escalation of the conflict and the very real possibility of a war between the superpowers.

The two superpowers had feared exactly this kind of a problem for several years. They each supported client states that they could not fully control and that were certainly capable of ignoring their advice and drawing them into inadvertent wars at a time when they themselves possessed enough weapons of mass destruction to destroy the planet. Indeed, it was in anticipation of just such a situation that they had signed the Agreement on the Prevention of Nuclear War just four months before in the spirit of *détente*, promising that if any crisis threatened to risk escalation into nuclear war between them, they would "immediately enter into urgent consultations with each other and make every effort to avert this risk."

Despite this agreement, however, neither the Soviets nor the Americans were prepared to abandon either their rival clients in the Middle East to catastrophic defeat or their own hopes of securing unilateral advantages at the expense of the other, if possible. Thus, when Israeli forces began to reverse the military tide in this fast-moving war, on October 10 the Soviets initiated a massive airlift and sealift of arms to Egypt and Syria to enable them to improve their performance on the battlefield. Within four days the first C-5 cargo planes arrived from the United States to provide new weapons and supplies for Israel, and the risks of this local war escalating into a larger global war began to increase dramatically. The situation grew much worse when it became clear that neither superpower could restrain their determined and at times reckless respective clients and make them observe a cease-fire agreement brokered on October 22. When the Israeli army crossed the Suez Canal and began an

offensive against Egypt, the Soviets accused the United States of failing to restrain the Israelis, placed their Air Force and Strategic Rocket Forces on full alert, ordered transport planes to their embarkation points, positioned eighty-five ships in the Mediterranean, and threatened that it would intervene militarily if necessary to prevent an Egyptian defeat. On October 24, Soviet leader Leonid Brezhnev emphasized to President Richard Nixon: "I will say it straight that if you find it impossible to act jointly with us in this matter, we should be faced with the necessity urgently to consider the question of taking appropriate steps unilaterally." Within only six hours, the United States placed its military forces on a worldwide, just-short-of-war DEFCON III alert, issued new orders to the Strategic Air Command (SAC) and the North American Air Defense Command (NORAD), sent another aircraft carrier at full speed into the eastern Mediterranean, and warned the Soviets that any intervention would produce "incalculable consequences." This was the only time since 1962 that strategic forces had been alerted during a crisis between the superpowers, a fact acknowledged by Nixon when he later described the situation as the "most serious threat to U.S.-Soviet relations since the Cuban Missile Crisis."

The crisis now reached its most critical stage. To manage it in such a way as to keep it from escalating into a major, inadvertent war now required serious effort on both sides. Each had clearly used the threat of armed force to signal its resolve not to let its respective client be humiliated in defeat, and each had employed both deterrence and coercive diplomacy, but now was the critical time to act in accordance with the operational principles of crisis management. At this stage, both the United States and the Soviet Union appear to have finally reached the conclusion that half-hearted efforts could not control the crisis and that whatever ambitious objectives they originally had sought now had to be significantly modified. This applied particularly to Nixon and his secretary of state, Henry Kissinger, who initially and grandiosely had wanted to use the confrontation to expand American influence by weakening Soviet alliances in the area, making both Israel and Egypt more pliable to the interests of the United States, advancing America's own approach to the Arab-Israeli conflict, and perhaps providing some distraction from the domestic woes of the Watergate scandal. As the possibility of a larger inadvertent war escalated, however, they realized that the crisis itself was the most dangerous adversary and needed to be resolved before it careened completely out of control.

To manage the crisis, therefore, they joined with their counterparts in Moscow to confine military moves to alerts and maneuvers that signaled resolve, but indicated the new and more limited objective of ending the crisis itself. They simultaneously maintained strict civilian control of military options, created pauses in the tempo, maintained open channels of communication, and coordinated diplomatic and military moves designed to terminate the crisis without war. In the interests of crisis management, for example, the U.S. Sixth Fleet was instructed to remain in small, fixed operating areas to avoid any movements that might give the impression to the Soviets that America was about to resort to large-scale warfare, even though this was at odds with sound

military logic to reduce the vulnerability of the ships in the event of a Soviet preemptive strike. By the same token, when Soviet military officers requested that Egypt be allowed to use R-17 missiles to attack the air base where United States supplies to Israel were being unloaded, Foreign Minister Andrei Gromyko refused to give his authorization. At the same time, in an attempt to control military actions, Kissinger strongly rebuked the Israelis and demanded in the strongest possible language that they halt their offensive against Egypt and abide by the terms of the cease-fire, and the fighting stopped.

Of particular importance, both sides sought to choose diplomatic-military options that signaled a desire to negotiate rather than seek a military solution and that left the opponent a way out of the crisis that was compatible with their fundamental interests. During an important press conference shortly after noon on October 25, Kissinger reiterated his opposition to sending any American or Soviet forces to the Middle East, but carefully suggested to the Soviet Union a way out without loss of prestige. He declared that the United States was not asking the Soviets to pull back from anything they had done and that it did not consider that the Soviet Union had taken any irrevocable action. "We are not yet prepared to say," he announced, "that they have gone beyond their limits." Kissinger then offered to turn to the United Nations and work with the Soviets as partners on the Security Council in passing a resolution that would authorize the introduction of United Nations forces into the area. Brezhnev immediately accepted this offer. As a consequence of their joint cooperation, the Security Council passed Resolution 340 on the afternoon of October 25, calling for an immediate cease-fire, a return of combatants to earlier lines, and the dispatch of an international peacekeeping force to police the agreement. This resolution, the American pressure on Israel, and the decision to jointly participate in sending observers to monitor the cease-fire satisfied the Soviets that their client Egypt would be protected, and they announced that they saw no reason to contemplate intervention and therefore stood down from their alerts. Once this was accomplished, the United States began to relax its own alert, and the crisis ended without a disastrous war between the superpowers.

ANALYSIS

By exploring these three cases in light of the principles discussed at the beginning of this chapter, we now can understand the nature of crisis management more clearly, see why some efforts succeed and others fail, consider what lessons might be drawn, and have a greater appreciation for the impact of historical context or, more specifically, the way in which the diplomatic revolution has affected crisis management in our own day.

There can be little doubt, for example, that an appropriate political-military strategy for crisis management cannot possibly succeed unless there is skilled, top-level civilian control over military institutions and actions. In this regard, modern policy makers enjoy many technological advantages

over their predecessors. Improvements in communications and transportation allow leaders to exert much more personal control over military forces than ever before. One has only to compare the relative inaccessibility of a crisis area like the Balkans from European capitals in the nineteenth century with Kissinger's ability in 1973 to fly to the threatened region in a matter of hours or the capabilities of today's U.S. State Department's Crisis Management Support team and Department of Defense's National Military Command Center for rapid worldwide communications, which enable policy makers to be in instant contact with their military forces, even though they may be half a world away.

But the vast growth in the size and complexity of a modern world power's internal political and military bureaucracies has created new problems for the exercise of top-level civilian control. This becomes magnified if allies or client states, each with their its complex organizations, are involved. Bismarck's tasks of management were infinitely easier when compared to those of his successors in 1914, who could not coordinate or control their own military organization, foreign ministry, or principal ally. How much more difficult, then, the task of the superpowers in 1973, who had to control not only their own forces but those of their often reckless client states as well! Indeed, had the United States and the Soviet Union been able to exert better control, the Egyptians and Syrians might not have started the war in the first place, and the Israelis might not have brought about the resulting nuclear confrontation.

Having observed the need for civilian control, however, it is also important to acknowledge that the mere existence of civilian leaders is no guarantee that the requisite skills will be present or that successful management will result. The 1914 case certainly confirms this. Evidence strongly suggests that at the beginning of both the American war in Vietnam and the 2003 invasion of Iraq, strong willed civilians, who thought they knew best, deliberately rejected the more prudent—and accurate—advice provided by professional military commanders.

With regard to the need to slow down the tempo of military actions, crisis managers in the contemporary world are likely to encounter greater difficulties than did statesmen in the nineteenth and early twentieth centuries. With events driven at an ever faster pace by sophisticated improvements in communication, transportation, and weapons technology, political leaders are under extraordinary pressure to make critical decisions in shorter and shorter time intervals. This becomes evident when one compares the duration of the three crises above. The crisis surrounding the Congress of Berlin was drawn out for months. The crisis leading up to the outbreak of World War I was of little more than a few weeks in duration, and those leaders forced to make decisions spoke constantly of their fear that "time was running out." The critical period in the 1973 Arab-Israeli War lasted less than one week, with the serious management taking place in the course of only forty-eight hours. It is difficult, indeed, to create pauses when the momentum of events is so pressing.

Moreover, the increasing impact of public opinion and pressure groups on decision making has complicated the managers' task of slowing down or "freezing" a crisis. Those leaders who met at the Congress of Berlin began to

experience the early impact of domestic politics and the press on their de-liberations, but, by comparison with later cases it was minimal. This is why Disraeli could boast about the delegates issuing a few statements for public consumption and then going behind closed doors and doing whatever they wanted. By 1914, public opinion could be whipped up by highly national-istic organizations wanting to confront adversaries, a sensational press, and those politicians seeking to use the crisis for their own agendas, and this proved to be a phenomenon of great significance in European capitals in the last days before war broke out. In attempting to manage the Arab-Israeli War of 1973, Kissinger needed to contend with the same kinds of problems, including groups and lobbyists at home exerting pressure to support Israel at all costs, polit-ical opponents resisting any *détente* with the Soviets, and various economic interests and angry motorists vehemently complaining about long lines at gas stations, all demanding policies that would end the Arab oil embargo.

The requirement for coordinating diplomatic and military moves in a cri-sis encounters both advantages and disadvantages under the impact of the diplomatic revolution. Successful coordination requires accurate and timely information and effective communication. In this regard, the sophisticated means of collecting and analyzing intelligence in the modern age, such as satellite detection from space and computer-generated imaging and analyses of vast amounts of information, can (if used properly) give contemporary policy mak-ers in times of crises many advantages in command and control completely unknown to their predecessors. More sophisticated communication and transportation technology, as evident by the use of the American-Soviet "hot-line" and of aircraft that carried Kissinger to Moscow and Soviet Premier Alexei Kosygin to Cairo for face-to-face meetings, certainly assisted in managing the 1973 crisis. At the same time, the United Nations played an important role, especially in its use and timing of peacekeeping forces, in coordinating the activities of diplomats and military personnel.

But, given the potential scale and level of destructiveness in contemporary warfare, the decisions that shape the capabilities and doctrines of modern mili-tary forces do not always take into sufficient account the task of using these same forces as instruments of management in times of crises. This is the prob-lem created when armed forces are viewed only in terms of "gross military capabilities" to fight large-scale warfare, thereby severely restricting the ability of leaders to find "usable options" and to fine-tune and coordinate mili-tary and diplomatic moves. In the case of the First World War, for example, the opposing sides possessed mass armies, inflexible plans for mobilization, and intricate war plans, which contained no options other than full-scale military conflict. Thus, the attempts of Germany and Russia at coercive diplomacy became de facto declarations of war once mobilization was instituted. This situation contrasts unfavorably with events during the 1973 crisis, in which leaders in both the United States and the Soviet Union in the end were able to coordin-ate their diplomatic efforts with selective military alerts and deployments.

In addition, with the substantial increase in the number of individuals and departments that participate in a modern government's foreign policy, as well

as an array of international institutions with culturally heterogeneous members, special efforts must be made to successfully coordinate diplomatic moves with overall policy and military actions. Bismarck's role as an "honest broker" was made considerably easier by the fact that he only had to deal with representatives of the five Great Powers, who could control their military institutions and who already shared a remarkable degree of homogeneity among themselves. It was not nearly as simple in 1914 when, for example, no one knew who spoke for Germany or what its policy actually was. The contrast becomes even greater when one compares 1878 with the 1973 crisis in which Nixon, Kissinger, Brezhnev, Meir, and Sadat shared few common values, had to contend with their own strong-willed bureaucracies and constituencies, and found themselves having to deal with the Organization of Petroleum Exporting Countries sponsoring economic coercion and conflicting sympathies with the General Assembly of the United Nations.

The diplomatic revolution also has both aided and complicated the ability of statesmen to confine military moves in a crisis to those that constitute clear demonstrations of their resolve and are appropriate to limited objectives. As already noted, as a result of more sophisticated intelligence collection and analysis, such demonstrations often can be more easily verified by technical means. Those leaders gathered at the Congress of Berlin, for example, were completely dependent upon reassuring words and fragmented information that came slowly and from far away. This is no longer the case. Similarly, the flexibility and multiple uses of some—but not all—modern military forces makes them capable of conveying resolve and, at the same time, appropriateness for limited objectives. But not all forces or military moves can do this. The full-scale mobilizations of 1914 signaled that war was imminent and, with it, the strong likelihood of unlimited objectives. The alerts and deployments of 1973 could have conveyed either limited or unlimited objectives, depending entirely upon how they were perceived by the opponent.

This matter of perception is particularly important when considering the operational requirement to avoid military moves that give the opponent the impression that large-scale warfare is about to be initiated. The key factor here is "impression," for as we have seen with a variety of historical and contemporary cases, and as recent studies of human crisis behavior reveal, actions are not always perceived as they are actually intended, and this can lead to mistaken images with unintended consequences. This places a particular premium upon the ability *to see the situation from the perspective of the adversary* and *to consider how they might view one's own behavior.* Misperceptions can be a source of serious miscalculations, and these can lead to major errors in policy, missed opportunities, and avoidable catastrophes.

Advances in military technology, for example, have made it vastly more difficult to avoid giving the wrong impression or perception, for the nature of some weapons in our time has provided capabilities for a belligerent to rapidly launch a devastating first strike. The limited forces possessed at the time of Bismarck effectively precluded anyone from immediately overwhelming another. By 1914, however, leaders perceived that the large armies

of the major powers made the delay of mobilization by even a single day an almost fatal mistake. In the contemporary world of weapons of mass destruction, the situation is even graver. If a policy maker hesitates for even an hour when confronted with a nuclear threat, for example, total destruction of his or her state could result. Thus, when the Soviets and the Americans placed their armed forces on alert and sent fleets into the Mediterranean in 1973, the critical question was whether these actions signaled a tactical move to support their respective clients in the Middle East or a strategic one designed to position them to attack the other superpower. This challenge will repeatedly confront modern policy makers who struggle with force and statecraft.

The very destructiveness of modern weaponry, with its capacity to annihilate not only military forces but civilization as well, paradoxically has greatly strengthened the incentives to choose diplomatic-military options that will signal a desire to negotiate rather than to seek a military solution. Here, fear can play a critical role. In today's world of weapons of mass destruction, leaders are acutely aware of the horrors of modern war. For this reason, most rational policy makers are much more eager to explore avenues of negotiation and compromise rather than employ force and less likely to indulge in widespread belligerent nationalism or fatalistically believe in the "inevitability" of war, as so many did in 1914. This explains why Nixon and Brezhnev invested so much effort to carefully signal each other during the 1973 crisis, for neither one wanted to place the other in a position similar to that of the German kaiser and risk the thermonuclear exchange that might follow. Nevertheless, any international system—including our own—must struggle with the problem of how to deal with those leaders who do not share this fear and who are willing to recklessly resort to armed force to accomplish their goals.

As a result of the increase in the ideological nature of many international disputes, however, it has become more difficult to select diplomatic-military options that leave an opponent a way out of the crisis compatible with his or her fundamental interests. The conflict between the interested parties in 1878 was about classic power politics, and management took place in the context of many shared values, and thus could be settled relatively quickly as long as the major actors received reciprocal compensation. By 1914, however, nationalism and imperialism had combined forces to add a more complicated dimension to the international situation, and ideology played an extremely volatile and important role in the 1973 crisis. This trend appears likely to continue. Consequently, separating an opponent's fundamental interests from the rhetoric—whether it rings with slogans about "the axis of evil," "holy war," "infidels," or "jihad"—is one of the truly difficult challenges for those seeking to practice crisis management today.

Beyond the theoretical and operational principles demonstrated by the three specific cases treated above, our analysis of these and many other historical and contemporary cases of crisis management and mismanagement also indicates that not all diplomatic crises lend themselves equally to manageability by leaders. In fact, some crises are peculiarly resistant to even the best

efforts of some statesmen to avoid war because of either the structure and dynamics of the international system, balance-of-power considerations, domestic and alliance restraints on the parties to the dispute, the unpredictable behavior and decisions of others, the characteristics of modern technology, or because the interests of the two sides are so fundamentally antagonistic that they cannot be easily reconciled. An inadvertent war may occur, for example, because one or the other side reaches the conclusion during the crisis that no other alternatives exist to secure its objectives or to avoid an unacceptable diplomatic outcome, or because one or the other side decides to embrace more ambitious objectives than it entertained at the outset of the crisis and is willing to accept the risk of war or resort to armed force for this purpose.

Comparisons of successes and failures in avoiding inadvertent war consequently reveal the relevance and importance of three additional variables in assessing the scope and efficacy of crisis management: (1) the *incentives* to avoid war, (2) the *opportunities* for constructive crisis management, and (3) the *level of skill and capabilities* for crisis management. If there is a pronounced desire or high motivation to genuinely avoid inadvertent war, for example, leaders are much more likely to look for, create, and utilize opportunities for managing a crisis. The converse is also to be expected. There are times, of course, when alliance structures or domestic pressures, among other factors, make it very difficult to see incentives or to seek opportunities; and when this happens, the likelihood of a crisis escalating into an inadvertent war is high.

But the lessons of history would indicate that much of crisis management depends on the skill and the capabilities of individual people. Indeed, the whole concept of management itself is significant only as it is interpreted and implemented by men and women within their own particular context of time and place. Incentives and opportunities will not suffice to avoid war if individual leaders lack the intelligence to understand the nature of crisis management and diplomacy or the ability to function under great stress, to exercise self-restraint, to adhere to the operational principles of crisis management and apply them, to see the situation from the perspective of others, or have some ethical sense of responsibility for the larger international system as a whole. This applies to policy makers on all sides during a crisis, for management requires partnership in the midst of intense rivalry, in which the behavior of one dramatically influences the other in a dynamic interaction. One lesson remains clear from all cases: crisis management does not passively happen on its own, but requires the necessary skills and capabilities among leaders to make it happen. As political scientist Phil Williams observes, success requires "the traditional qualities of statesmanship—wisdom, diplomatic skills, and incisive judgment—[which] can prove decisive, either through their presence or through their absence." When, in the words of Winston Churchill, "the balance quivers" and the stakes are high, the lack of ability, the failure to reflect or empathize, poor judgment, or even momentary carelessness on the part of single individuals can easily transform a crisis into an inadvertent war.

SUGGESTIONS FOR FURTHER EXPLORATION

For a detailed analysis of the principles of crisis management and its requirements, modalities, and problems, see Alexander L. George (ed.), *Avoiding War: Problems of Crisis Management* (Boulder, CO, 1991). Other important analyses also can be found in Arien Boin et al., *The Politics of Crisis Management* (Cambridge, 2005); Chester Crocker et al. (eds.), *Turbulent Peace* (Washington, DC, 2001); Joseph Bouchard, *Command in Crisis* (New York, 1991); Gilbert R. Winham (ed.), *New Issues in International Crisis Management* (Boulder, CO, 1988); Richard Ned Lebow, *Nuclear Crisis Management* (Ithaca, NY, 1987); Scott D. Sagan, "Nuclear Alerts and Crisis Management," *International Security*, 4 (Spring 1985): 99–139; Richard Smoke and William Ury, *Beyond the Hotline* (Cambridge, MA, 1984); Alexander L. George, "Crisis Management: The Interaction of Political and Military Considerations," *Survival*, 26 (September–October 1984): 323–334; Paul Bracken, *The Command and Control of Nuclear Forces* (New Haven, 1983); Arthur N. Gilbert and Paul Gordon Lauren, "Crisis Management: An Assessment and Critique," *Journal of Conflict Resolution*, 24 (December 1980): 641–664; Paul Gordon Lauren, "Crisis Management: History and Theory," *International History Review*, 1 (October 1979): 542–556; Richard Smoke, *War: Controlling Escalation* (Cambridge, MA, 1977); Phil Williams, *Crisis Management* (New York, 1976); Ole Holsti, *Crisis, Escalation, War* (London, 1972); Coral Bell, *The Conventions of Crisis: A Study in Diplomatic Management* (London, 1971); and Oran Young, *Politics of Force* (Princeton, 1968).

The Cuban Missile Crisis stimulated considerable thinking about the principles of crisis management, and continues to do so today. Consequently, it is useful to consult those references provided at the end of Chapter 10 on coercive diplomacy, as well as Sheldon Stern, *Averting "The Final Failure"* (Stanford, 2003); Graham Allison and Philip Zelikow, *Essence of Decision* (New York, 1999 ed.); and Alexander L. George, "The Cuban Missile Crisis," in Alexander L. George (ed.), *Avoiding War: Problems of Crisis Management* (Boulder, CO, 1991).

More discussion of the case of Otto von Bismarck, his colleagues, and the larger context of the Congress of Berlin in 1878 can be found in Norman Rich, *Great Power Diplomacy, 1814–1914* (New York, 1992); Paul Gordon Lauren, "Crisis Prevention in Nineteenth-Century Diplomacy," in Alexander L. George (ed.), *Managing U.S.-Soviet Rivalry* (Boulder, CO, 1983); Edward Crankshaw, *Bismarck* (New York, 1981); Immanuel Geiss, *Der Berliner Kongreß 1878* (Boppard am Rhein, 1978); William L. Langer, *European Alliances and Alignments, 1871–1890* (New York, 1964 ed.); W. N. Medlicott, *The Congress of Berlin and After* (London, 1963 ed.); B. H. Sumner, *Russia and the Balkans, 1870–1880* (Hamden, CT, 1962 ed.); and Edward Hertslet (ed.), *The Map of Europe by Treaty*, Vol. 4 (London, 1891).

Probably no crisis has been studied more extensively than that of 1914. Stimulating places to start further reading include David Stevenson, *Cataclysm* (New York, 2005); Richard Ned Lebow, "Contingency, Catalysts, and International System Change," *Political Science Quarterly*, 115 (Winter, 2000–2001): 591–616; Henry Kissinger, *Diplomacy* (New York, 1994); James Joll, *The Origins of the First World War* (London, 1992 ed.); Jack Levy, "The Role of Crisis Management in the Outbreak of World War I," in Alexander L. George (ed.), *Avoiding War* (Boulder, CO, 1991); Ole Holsti, "Theories of Crisis Decision Making," and Samuel R. Williamson, Jr., "Theories of Organizational Process and Foreign Policy Outcomes," both in Paul Gordon Lauren (ed.), *Diplomacy: New Approaches in History, Theory, and Policy* (New York, 1979); Paul Kennedy (ed.), *The War Plans of the Great Powers* (Boston, 1979); Fritz Fischer, *Germany's Arims in the First World War* (New York, 1967); Barbara Tuchman, *The Guns of August* (New York, 1962); Sydney Fay, *The Origins of the World War*, 2 vols.

(New York, 1930 ed.); and "London Times Sees War Inevitable," *New York Times*, August 3, 1914.

For treatments of the Arab-Israeli War of 1973, see John Stoessinger, *Why Nations Go to War* (Belmont, CA, 2004 ed.); Henry Kissinger, *Crisis* (New York, 2003); Barry Blechman and Douglas Hart, "Nuclear Weapons and the 1973 Middle East Crisis," in Robert Art and Kenneth Waltz (eds.), *The Use of Force: Military Power and International Politics* (New York, 1999 ed.); Richard Ned Lebow and Janice Gross Stein, *We All Lost the Cold War* (New York, 1994); Yaacov Bar-Siman-Tov, "The Arab-Israeli War of October 1973," in Alexander L. George (ed.), *Avoiding War* (Boulder, CO, 1991); Henry Kissinger, *Years of Upheaval* (Boston, 1982); Richard Nixon, *RN: The Memoirs of Richard Nixon* (New York, 1978); and Amos Perlmutter, "Crisis Management: Kissinger's Middle East Negotiations," *International Studies Quarterly*, 19 (September 1975): 316–343.

Many fascinating historical cases exist for further exploration of crisis management and mismanagement. These include, among others, the crises of Spain (1822–1823), Belgium (1830), the Near East (1852–1854), Fashoda (1898), Bosnia (1908–1909), Agadir (1911), Ethiopia-Italy (1935–1936); Munich (1938), Iran (1945–1946), Berlin (1948–1949 and 1958), the U.S.-China crisis over Korea (1950), Suez (1956), Quemoy and Matsu (1958), the Congo (1960), the Middle East (1967), Sino-Soviet border crisis (1969), the American hostage crisis in Iran (1979–1980), Persian Gulf Crisis (1990–1991), Kosovo (1998–1999), and India-Pakistan (2002–2003).

PART THREE

RESTRAINTS AND REFLECTIONS

— 12 —

Ethics and Other Restraints
on Force and Statecraft

For centuries in a world where competition and violence seemed to be always present, thoughtful and frightened men and women have wrestled with the extremely difficult problem of how to restrain their worst excesses. They have understood that at times their very survival depended upon their ability to control their rivalries and to contain the brutal destruction and loss of human life caused by the use of armed force. It is for this reason that the search to find some kind of restraints often has preoccupied the thoughts of those as divergent as political and religious leaders, diplomats, philosophers, generals, strategic theorists, theologians, international lawyers, investors, scholars, students, human rights activists, and pacifists, among many others vitally concerned about force and statecraft.

PRACTICAL, STRUCTURAL, AND POLITICAL RESTRAINTS

Diplomacy, it has often been said, is "the art of the possible." This insightful description comes from lessons learned from long and sometimes painful historical experience and serves to remind us that statesmen rarely can do exactly what they would like to do. Instead, they generally are compelled to settle for the least harmful of a number of unpleasant alternatives because they are confronted with any number of practical, structural, and political constraints or restraints that limit their freedom of choice and action.

Some restraints occur as a result of very practical limitations. Geographical distance and terrain, limited information and time to make decisions, inertia, and even the weather, the crops, momentary state of health, or condition of the roads can present constraints. In addition, every state has a finite resource base. Each possesses only a certain amount of territory and assets for their bases or port facilities, only so much population to provide soldiers for their armies or sailors for their navies, and only so many weapons for their arsenals. The amount of funding for military expenditures (even for those who engage in deficit spending) is ultimately limited by their natural resources, economic strength, and industrial capacity. Each faces limitations upon the

level of education of its inhabitants, the degree of technological sophistication, the effectiveness of its transportation and communications systems, the cohesiveness and morale of its people, and the number of leaders knowledgeable and skilled in the practice of statecraft. Some states—like the Great Powers during the classical system of diplomacy or the United States, Russia, and China today—obviously possess more of these resources than others, but none has an unlimited supply on which they can draw without end.

Restraints also are imposed by the power, capabilities, and interests of other states, each claiming its own prerogative of national sovereignty. The extent to which one country can pursue its objectives is based in large part on the relative strength of other countries at any given time. The power and capabilities of others, allies and adversaries alike, in other words, can place severe restrictions upon any state's freedom of action in the use of force by creating a fear of unacceptable consequences, and thereby make it refrain from doing something that it wants to do or do something that it otherwise would not choose to do. Indeed, this is the feature that undergirds the strategies of both deterrence and coercive diplomacy, as we saw in Chapters 9 and 10. The traditional balance of power helped to keep the peace in part because it restrained leaders who feared that aggression on their part would result in unacceptable costs from a coalition of countervailing forces. It is thus in any state's prudent self-interest to make some level of accommodation with others and thereby to accept certain restraints.

In this regard, it is essential to remember that capabilities are measured in people as well as things. States, as observed in Chapter 7, do not make and implement decisions in international relations—people do. This is why de Callières and others who followed him spent so much time stressing the importance of developing a knowledge of history and the professional skills necessary for the conduct of statecraft. Negotiation, deterrence, coercive diplomacy, and crisis management, as seen in Part II, cannot possibly succeed unless leaders possess the requisite wisdom and skill to make them work.

The sheer complexity of international relations itself imposes restraints. At any given point in time, many issues and problems are competing for attention, and some of these may be inextricably linked in complicated ways. A conflict in one part of the world may have dangerous consequences for another crisis elsewhere, or a major commitment of armed forces in one region may limit the ability to deploy them quickly to another area should the need arise. During the Cuban Missile Crisis, for example, Kennedy and his advisors were deeply worried about how their actions in the Caribbean might impact the precarious arrangement of Berlin and the status of American forces in Europe, South Korea, and Japan. As a consequence, those responsible for statecraft are restrained from devoting their full energies or resources to a single crisis that may involve the threat or the use of armed force.

Practical restraints also are presented by the unknown and the unpredictable. Those responsible for statecraft never fully know all that they need to know. They operate in partial darkness because of the complexities of the world, the uncertainties and sometimes the irrationality of human behavior, ignorance

and the capacity for self-delusion, and the incomplete and often ambiguous nature of intelligence information and analysis. There can be unforeseen and unintended consequences, and sometimes things go wrong even in the best of plans. These are the factors insightfully described by Bismarck as the "imponderabilia" of diplomacy and by Clausewitz as the "fog" and "friction" of war.

Limitations likewise are presented by the creation of structures or systems. Some of these may be international in nature. During the classical system of diplomacy, as we explored in Chapter 2, the structure of the balance between the five Great Powers operating as the Concert of Europe placed significant limits upon what states could and could not do. In the words of one nineteenth-century statesman, its purpose was to "neutralize and fetter the selfish aims of each." The founders of the United Nations, as seen in Chapter 4, hoped that they might create a binding system or structure of collective security that would impose constraints upon how states behaved toward each other and thereby severely restrict the use of armed force in the world. Similarly, the International Atomic Energy Agency, World Trade Organization, and other multilateral bodies are all structured as they are in order to provide some limitations upon sovereignty and thereby restrain any single member state from acting unilaterally in pursuit of its interests alone. Systems of international law, treaties, and legal conventions also are specifically designed to provide checks upon unrestrained behavior by states.

Domestic structures also create restraints upon making and implementing decisions involving force and statecraft. Any large, modern state possesses complex government bureaucracies organized to conduct its business and composed of thousands of civil servants and those who lead them. These many individuals rarely, if ever, act in a monolithic way or speak with a common voice. Indeed, where they stand on a given issue often depends upon where they sit. The vested interests, personalities, perspectives, and cultures of their particular departments or units or missions easily can determine what policy options they generate, what positions they take, how they protect their autonomy and use their capabilities, and how they engage in what is often described as "turf battles" or "bureaucratic politics." It is not at all uncommon when dealing with issues of force and statecraft, for example, to see sharp differences and even severe competition between "hawks" and "doves" and between foreign ministries and military establishments and thereby to appreciate, as discussed in Chapter 11, why successful crisis management requires the ability to keep them under control. Bismarck and his immediate successors constantly found themselves caught in contests between the German Foreign Office and the General Staff that worked so hard to establish itself as a "state within the state." The impassioned, acrimonious, and highly public disputes between Secretary of State George Shultz, on the one hand, and Secretary of Defense Caspar Weinberger and the Joint Chiefs of Staff, on the other, during the first Reagan Administration presented serious restraints to direction and consistency in whether and how American military forces should intervene in the world. More recently, the sharp differences between

Secretary of State Colin Powell and Secretary of Defense Donald Rumsfeld manifested themselves over the inspection of suspected weapons of mass destruction purportedly held by Saddam Hussein, whether or not to seek United Nations authorization for military action, and the American invasion of Iraq in 2003 itself.

Politics and structures combine to present restraints in other ways as well. This occurs particularly in democratic regimes characterized by free elections, multiple parties, constitutions and the rule of law, and the division of power among different branches of government authority. The founders of the United States, for example, believed that history had taught them to be wary of authoritarian governments where, in the absence of genuine checks and balances, a king and his immediate advisors alone and in secret could make the major decisions of war and peace. For this reason, they deliberately created a structure of divided government designed to provide restraints on the use of force. The U.S. Constitution thus entrusts the president with the authority to conduct the nation's foreign affairs and to serve as commander-in-chief of the armed forces, but, at the same time, gives to the Senate the power to ratify treaties and appoint ambassadors and to Congress the sole power to raise and support armies, to provide and maintain a navy, to call forth the militia, and to declare war. The Constitution of Japan provides even greater restrictions by explicitly stating: "Aspiring to an international peace based on justice and order, the Japanese people forever renounce war as a sovereign right of the nation and the threat or the use of force as a means of settling international disputes."

Whether these constitutional provisions actually restrain, of course, is a matter of political will. Facing unilateral presidential decisions to commit troops to Korea and Vietnam and to invade Cambodia in the clear absence of any serious consultation or declarations of war, for example, the U.S. Congress determined to pass, over the veto of President Richard Nixon, the War Powers Act of 1973. The stated purpose of this legislation, in the words of its authors, was

> to fulfill the intent of the framers of the Constitution . . . and insure that the collective judgement of both the Congress and the President will apply to the introduction of United States Armed Forces into hostilities, or into situations where imminent involvement in hostilities is clearly indicated by the circumstances, and to the continued use of such forces in hostilities or in such situations.

Toward this end, the act requires the president to consult with Congress "in every possible instance" where armed force might be employed abroad, to provide written notification within forty-eight hours of any military action in a hostile area, and to explain its "estimated scope and duration of the hostilities or involvement." If Congress does not approve of the action through either a declaration of war or specific statutory authorization, the armed forces must be removed within sixty to ninety days. Every president from the time of Gerald Ford to the present has chafed under these imposed restraints, however, and

the controversies raised by the War Powers Act are renewed whenever American forces are sent into combat overseas. This could be vividly seen in the decisions to deploy troops to Panama in 1989, Kuwait and Iraq during the Persian Gulf War in 1991, Haiti in 1994, Bosnia in 1995, Kosovo in 1999, Iraq in 2003, and to a variety of other countries as a part of the larger "war on terrorism."

In each of these cases it was political will that determined whether constitutional, legislative, or legal restraints would be imposed upon the use of armed force by the United States or not. But such will is ever-changing and is subject to a wide variety of factors. There are times when it appears as though clashing partisan interests of political parties play a heavy role. When Democrats controlled Congress, for example, they passed the 1984 Boland Amendment in a deliberate attempt to prohibit Republican President Ronald Reagan from providing military support to the Contra rebels in Nicaragua. When the Republicans gained the majority, they in turn were eager to restrain Democratic President Bill Clinton when he thought it necessary to send forces to Bosnia. The political will of leaders also can be influenced by election cycles, the media, various pressure groups, economic interests, financial contributors, or others with access to power. Especially during the period of the diplomatic revolution, political will can be affected dramatically by public opinion, whose level of support for military action and wars can range (and sometimes quickly change) from strong enthusiasm to intense opposition with accompanying peace protests, or from those who would impose virtually no restrictions at all to those who would impose severe restraints upon when and how armed force is used in the world. Such contested opinions among voters also can be found among government leaders, diplomats, and military personnel themselves, as they struggle to determine what kinds of restraints they are willing and unwilling to observe. These individual and collective opinions can be influenced by many different factors, including perceived interests, fears, aspirations, and values. Among the latter, perhaps the most complex and challenging is that of moral values or ethics.

ETHICS AND INTERNATIONAL POLITICS

Living life requires that we make choices among alternatives about what we will and will not do. Such choices are unavoidable. Normally these decisions involve matters of daily life, but for those bearing heavy responsibilities for statecraft, they can require momentous decisions about war and peace. Regardless of their scope, however, when these choices have an impact upon other people, they involve ethics. This is due to the fact that ethical reasoning centers upon *judgments about the relationship between human conduct and the well-being of others made on the basis of normative standards.* These standards, in turn, are usually comprised of three elements:

1. The first of these is the essential and distinctive feature of ethical *limit*, or restraint. It maintains that there exists a limitation, or restriction, or

a boundary drawn around our behavior that provides a restraint on how we should conduct ourselves in relation to other people. Not everything, in other words, is permissible. Certain behavior is acceptable and certain behavior is unacceptable—hence, the moral values of right and wrong, good and bad, just and unjust.

2. There also is a recognition that there are *consequences* of our behavior upon the well-being of others. Intentions are not sufficient, for what we do—and do not do—affects other people. They may be protected and the value of their human rights affirmed, or they may be harmed or even killed because of our conduct. Ethics thus proscribe that we take the interests, rights, and points of view of others beyond ourselves into account.

3. Finally, ethical standards maintain that we bear *responsibility* for our conduct. We have an obligation or duty to honor the established limits. Thus, in one way or another, and sooner or later, we are held accountable for our actions and inactions.

These elements apply to all ethical standards, but herein lies a serious problem. There is not one standard of ethics on which every person can agree. There are many standards and traditions. This plurality results in part from the fact that what we regard as right or wrong is shaped by a multiplicity of different sources or foundations. Parents, teachers and schools, peers, religion, states, society, customs and tradition, institutions, prevailing culture, various groups or organizations, law, philosophy, exemplars whose qualities and behavior we admire, the standards of particular professions, and personal experiences and intuition all play roles in developing normative values that shape our "moral compass" or conscience.

Sometimes these different standards can reach agreement at a point of overlapping consensus that reinforces the same or similar ethical values. Many times they do not. The customs of different countries are not always the same. The values promoted by a state are often determined by a particular leader or a majority of voters in democratic societies, and these can be contested and changed through time within particular historical contexts. Sharp differences occur between a sense of responsibility to broad-based humanity as compared to one's own country, or to the good of the world community as a whole rather than to its separate parts. Religious traditions vary greatly and at times can produce sharp disagreements between liberal and conservative believers about core ethical values. Even within the area of moral philosophy there are different schools of thought ranging from the ethics of Aristotle based on personal character and virtue, of Immanuel Kant founded on universal principles, or of John Stuart Mill based on utilitarian calculations of the greatest good for the greatest number.

There thus are times when these different approaches actually compete with each other in their efforts to nurture, to persuade, or to impose certain ethical values. In the area of force and statecraft, the most intense and serious competition between values most often occurs between those of religion and those of the state. Faith-based religious values tend to center upon beliefs in

enduring, transcendent, and universal principles, ultimate responsibilities to the divine, and ways in which these beliefs are faithfully held and expressed in the way that we live our lives and conduct ourselves toward humankind. For this reason, and when at their best, they look both at the world and beyond the world, seeing it and its people in spiritual terms as they *should be*. State values, on the other hand, normally focus upon ascribing moral worth to a particular nation or government, emphasizing responsibilities and loyalty to it, and placing a priority on conduct that will best serve its own interests, leaders, and/or people. They thus tend to look at the here and now and the exercise of earthly power over discernable stakes, seeing the world and its people in secular terms as they *are*. As a consequence, religions and states can provide quite different—and sometimes contesting—answers to questions about appropriate limits, those whose well-being should benefit from our conduct, and the ultimate point of reference for our allegiance and responsibilities.

The existence of these deep contrasts, the powerful impact and decidedly mixed record of religions and states in the world, and the fact some people regard their beliefs about ethics so intensely, helps to explain why individuals have wrestled so long and so hard with the challenge of ethical restraints in statecraft and why they have reached such extremely different conclusions throughout history and up to the present.

Some observers, for example, have decided that because the distance between the spiritual soul and the secular state is so far that it can never be bridged, it is necessary for political leaders to cast their lot unequivocally with the state and its emphasis upon *raison d'état* and *Realpolitik*, insisting that ethical values based upon religious belief have little or no place at all in statecraft. This was the conclusion reached by Machiavelli when he wrote in *The Prince* that "the gulf between how one should live and how one does live is so wide that a man who neglects what is actually done for what should be done learns the way to self-destruction." He contended that religious restraints may be applicable to the conduct of individuals as they live their personal lives—but rarely to states whose interests always must take precedence over any moral scruples. When possible, leaders should act "good"; but, when necessary, their responsibility to the state requires that they "know how to do evil" and be prepared to behave "contrary to good faith, charity, humanity, and religion." Toward this end, he sought to elevate the interests of one's own country to the status of a supreme ethical norm of its own, declaring in his *Discourses* that in conducting state policy, "no considerations of justice or injustice, humanity or cruelty, nor glory or shame, should be allowed to prevail."

Others carried this argument even further, maintaining that in the world of international politics, only "might makes right" and virtually *any means* can be used to secure *any ends* that benefit the state as long as they are efficient and promise success. This explains why Thucydides had the militarily powerful Athenians contemptuously scoff at the weak appeal of the Melians for what was "fair and right." Thomas Hobbes maintained in the same vein that in a world of constant and vicious struggle, self-imposed moral restraints are either

simplistically naive at best or dangerous at worst. Political scientist Hans Morgenthau also emphasized these arguments in a modern age of nationalism even further, contending in *Politics Among Nations*:

> a world society and . . . a universal morality do not exist. . . . The nation fills the minds and hearts of men everywhere with particular experiences and, derived from them, with particular concepts of political philosophy, particular standards of political morality, and particular goals of political action. Inevitably, then, the members of the human race live and act politically, not as members of one world society applying standards of universal ethics, but as members of their respective national societies, guided by their national standards of morality. In politics the nation and not humanity is the ultimate fact.

Such statements most certainly do not go unchallenged, for there are those who do see humanity and not the nation as the ultimate fact. Many strongly object to the proposition that ethics somehow stop at national borders. Instead, they argue strongly that ethical principles focused upon humanity must serve as standards for judging the ends, the means, and the likely consequences of policy. "National interests" are heavily dependent upon the broader values upheld by an international system, and the "necessities" of world politics, rather than being beyond the realm of ethical choices and moral judgment, ultimately rest upon them. As scholar Stanley Hoffmann maintains in his thoughtful book, *Duties Beyond Borders: On the Limits and Possibilities of Ethical International Politics*, ethical choices are inherent in virtually all major decisions of statecraft, for individual people do not cease to be responsible as moral agents just because they act as public officials in the name of collective groups or wear a military uniform. "We must remember," he writes, "that states are led by human beings whose actions affect human beings within and outside: considerations of good and evil, right or wrong, are therefore both inevitable and legitimate."

But even among those who believe that ethical restraints should play a role in statecraft, there still are vast differences of opinion as to how this might be accomplished. There certainly have been times when individuals have claimed that the values of their religion and the values of their state were not different at all, but rather one and the same. It is not at all difficult to find cases of political or military leaders who have built support for their own agendas by manipulating the language and fervor of religion, or theocratic leaders who have placed a higher priority on secular rather than spiritual objectives and used the power of a state to advance their own interests. Their words of explanation may be genuine expressions of sincere personal belief, or they may be nothing more than calculating statements of religiosity designed to deceive others into thinking that the exercise of power is somehow ethically justified or divinely ordained. It is difficult to know precisely the motives of Bismarck, the very epitome of *Realpolitik*, for example, when he received his first diplomatic appointment as an ambassador and wrote: "I am God's soldier, and where he sends me there I must go." "I believe that I am obeying God," he said on another occasion, "when I serve my King." More

recently, U.S. Deputy Undersecretary of Defense for Intelligence General William Boykin asserted that since America was "a Christian nation," its terrorist enemies "will only be defeated if we come against them in the name of Jesus." He further declared: "We in the army of God, in the house of God, kingdom of God, have been raised for such a time as this."

Such a deliberate melding of the values of religion with the values of the state, however, leaves many other observers and practitioners alike deeply worried. To them, the idea that one is a chosen instrument of God can be, and often has been, a dangerous concept that can all too easily lead to moralistic self-righteousness, hubris, and megalomania. They view the simultaneous embrace of two often conflicting normative standards that pull in different directions as too seductively simplistic, too much like trying to square a circle, and too self-serving. As one of Bismarck's critics once bitingly observed, the chancellor conveniently "believes firmly and deeply in a God who has the remarkable faculty of always agreeing with him." They fear that such a mixture can provide the means to cloak reprehensible actions with the mantle of virtue, to convince citizens that they can remain true to their religious beliefs while being loyal and patriotic to their state, or to arouse fanaticism about battles between "good" and "evil." This, they argue, encourages confrontational and uncompromising crusades and "holy wars" against "heathens," *jihads* against "infidels," or intolerant extremism that completely destroys any sense of limit or self-restraint.

For this reason, many have agonized over the question of how they should apply ethics and act when faced with a genuine dilemma or crisis of conscience: when their religious and moral convictions clash with actions in the service of their government that they find to be deeply repugnant. Thus, sincere Buddhists sometimes have asked how they can possibly seek things of the spirit or follow the teachings of nonviolence while working on behalf of a state engaged in extending its power by military means. Dedicated Muslims similarly have inquired on occasion how Islam, which teaches compassion and mercy toward others, can be used to justify the expansion of a state by the sword or terrorist attacks against innocent civilians. In the same way, there have been times when earnest Christians have asked how they could faithfully follow the commands of Jesus to "love your enemies and pray for those who persecute you," to "turn the other cheek if someone strikes you," and to honestly acknowledge that "no one can serve two masters . . . you cannot serve God and mammon" and yet at the same time support the deliberate launching of wars of choice, torture, or the use of "shock-and-awe" violence.

The incompatibility of these positions has led some devout religious believers to conclude that they must answer to a "higher law" whereby their responsibilities to their religious faith must transcend whatever obligations they might have to any human government. They therefore believe that, when necessary, they should reject the values of the state and completely remove themselves from any kind of action that might assist its quest for political power. They have decided that *the ends never justify the means*. Some individuals in this situation have resigned from office, like Lord John Morley, who

immediately submitted his resignation from the British Cabinet in 1914 when it was announced that his country would go to war. Others have become conscientious objectors. As Franz Jägerstätter, an Austrian who refused to perform military service in the German army during the Second World War, expressed it:

> For what purpose, then, did God endow all men with reason and free will if, despite this, we have to render blind obedience [to the state] . . . ? What purpose is served by the ability to distinguish between good and evil? . . . Now anyone who is able to fight for both kingdoms and stay in good standing in both communities (that is, the community of the saints and the Nazi folk community) and who is able to obey every command of the Third Reich— such a man, in my opinion, would have to be a great magician. I for one cannot do so. And I definitely prefer to relinquish my rights under the Third Reich and thus make sure of deserving the rights granted under the Kingdom of God.

In this case, the consequences of such faith-based ethical restraints presented too great a threat to the state. After writing these words, Jägerstätter was taken to another room and beheaded.

Most people have no desire to suffer this kind of punishment for their beliefs or to take one absolutist position or another in the tension between religious values and those of the state or between individual and group behavior. Instead, they often find themselves struggling to avoid having to choose between being described as either a secular amoralist or so-called vulgar, political "realist," on the one hand, or a spiritual idealist or so-called "perfectionist," on the other. They therefore seek some way to navigate through the thicket of competing demands that confront them in a complicated world of imperfect human beings in which they exercise limited control, trying to reconcile the desirable of what *should* be done with the possible of what *can* be done. It is for this reason that theologian Reinhold Niebuhr concluded in his book *Moral Man and Immoral Society: A Study in Ethics and Politics*: "Politics will, to the end of history, be an area where conscience and power meet, where the ethical and coercive factors of human life will interpenetrate and work out their tentative and uneasy compromises." After reflecting on this thought-provoking statement, historian and veteran diplomat E. H. Carr felt compelled to add: "The compromises, like solutions to other human problems, will remain uneasy and tentative. But it is an essential part of any compromise that both factors [conscience and power] shall be taken into account."

The challenges of actually making these compromises and applying ethics in statecraft are often profound. There is not always a simple, black-or-white distinction, for example, between conscience and power. Conscience, as we have seen, can be pulled in different directions, and general ethical principles do not provide clear-cut rules or policy directives that tell decision makers exactly what to do in specific situations. Similarly, and as we shall explore in the Conclusion, it is essential to recognize that power is not confined to military force alone, but is composed of many different elements that also include skillful diplomacy, knowledge and information technology, economic

strength, reputation, culture, ideology, and what is widely described as the "moral force" of ethical values themselves. In international relations, these factors are further complicated by the fact that there are a multiplicity of philosophical and religious traditions, that an overzealous commitment to a particular ethical principle may be inappropriate or even dangerous in certain circumstances, and that leaders in a world of ambiguity where decisions are made with incomplete information can never fully know all the consequences of their actions or inactions. All this helps to explain why it is often so agonizing for those who seek to avoid absolutist extremes and abstractions and instead genuinely attempt to make reasonable ethical judgments about *what ends* and *what means* are justified in *what situations* or particular contexts.

But in this endeavor those concerned with statecraft are not completely alone and not without guidelines to help them find their way through the dilemmas of making ethical choices. In fact, as a result of many historical experiences and individual and collective efforts, there has emerged a substantial body of consensual, normative standards developed to help regulate behavior in the international system by establishing ethical restraints for foreign policy in general and, more specifically, ethical restraints for threats and uses of armed force.

ETHICAL RESTRAINTS FOR FOREIGN POLICY

Even the earliest practitioners of statecraft came to understand that, for reasons of both necessity and conviction, they could avoid international anarchy only if they kept their conflicts and competition within bounds by developing certain restraints in the form of norms of behavior. Some, like the theologian Cornelius Jansenius, as seen in Chapter 1, explicitly stressed that foreign policy must be governed not just by practical self-interest, but also by religious faith-based ethical values. After witnessing the horrors of the Thirty Years' War, the jurist and diplomat Hugo Grotius stressed that relations among states simply must be governed by rules and laws based upon moral principles. François de Callières wrote in the same way about the need for diplomats to be honest, love truth, and be of good character, to practice "plain and fair dealing," to be "good Christians" and persons "of peace," and to be faithful to their states while recognizing that "such obedience cannot be held to cover any action against the laws of God or of justice."

Many of the successes of the classical system of diplomacy, as we explored in Chapter 2, can be attributed to the restraints and rules of accommodation that derived from a common set of diplomatic norms and the fact that statesmen of the time placed a value on their reputation for honoring them. Metternich was particularly skilled in establishing the foundation for a new international system by inducing other countries to submit their disagreements to this larger sense of shared values. Even Talleyrand, who certainly was no stranger to political manipulation, admitted the necessity of having ethical restraints for foreign policy, declaring that in the end any balance of power could "only last so long as certain large States are animated by a spirit of moderation and justice." The case of William Gladstone, who served as British prime

minister during the nineteenth century, is particularly well known as a example of a statesman with strong religious convictions who believed that he had a larger duty to frame his diplomacy in terms of the call from the Sermon on the Mount for compassion, humility, and peacemaking. Still others proposed that only genuinely praiseworthy objectives should be pursued in foreign policy, that morally dubious means should not be employed when other means were available, that statesmen should choose a course of action least likely to cause damage to things of value, and that the selection of means should be proportional to the ends pursued.

These principles and general guidelines, among others, served to contribute to a slow but nevertheless progressive evolution of international ethical norms designed to provide restraints on the behavior of states with one another within the international system. They were handed down from one generation to another and further developed with various degrees of compromise and changes through time. Sometimes they clearly were honored more in the breach than in the observance. But on other occasions, they were taken very seriously, especially in those cases of efforts to alleviate suffering by promoting justice, peacemaking, conflict prevention and resolution, human rights, reconciliation, and humanitarian relief. Indeed, as political scientist Robert McElroy argues in his book, *Morality and American Foreign Policy: The Role of Ethics in International Affairs*, such norms often enter the consciences of state decision makers, members of the domestic public, and those comprising global opinion, thereby influencing their perceptions of issues and their actions. For this reason he maintains that it is not hard to find times when ethical principles based upon the broader sense of responsibility to the well-being of humanity appear to have taken precedence over narrowly defined state interests.

One of his historical cases explores the interesting choice faced by the U.S. government when confronted with an event inside the Soviet Union in 1921. At the time, the administration of Warren G. Harding viewed the Soviet Union as a major threat to American interests due to its repudiation of pre-war debts, its confiscation of foreign property, and its propaganda against capitalism. Consequently, the United States tried to diplomatically isolate the Soviets from the world and economically cut off all trade with them in the hope that such actions would seriously weaken their government and lead to its eventual collapse. Suddenly, in the spring of 1921 the Soviet government faced the very type of threat to its existence that the Americans had desired: the outbreak of massive famine. The situation became so desperate that even Lenin concluded that if no way could be found to feed the peasants, the Soviet regime and its experiment with Communism would perish. Yet, within days of a Soviet appeal for help, Secretary of Commerce Herbert Hoover, a man strongly committed to his Quaker religious beliefs, began to mobilize a massive American relief effort to avert starvation in Russia. He, the president, and members of Congress, according to McElroy's analysis, internalized the international norm that held nations responsible for helping other countries devastated by disaster regardless of their political orientation. In conscience,

they could not sit by and watch tens of millions of Russians starve to death, even if providing famine relief meant thwarting their own political, strategic, and economic interests by stabilizing the detested Soviet regime.

The strength of the perceived need for the creation and maintenance of such international ethical norms and restraints can be seen in the fact that so many of them have emerged precisely at a time when values themselves were—and are—seriously contested as a result of the diplomatic revolution. The rise of highly ideological regimes in Communist Russia, Fascist Italy, and Nazi Germany that demanded much in the name of the state, as we saw in Chapter 3, seriously challenged many previously accepted ethical standards and norms from the classical system of diplomacy. The expansion of the international community with actors from around the entire globe, as explored in Chapter 4, brought the values of other cultures and religious faiths other than Christianity to the fore. The escalation of the Cold War, as discussed in Chapter 5, exacerbated this breakdown of shared values even further when leaders of the superpowers framed their relations in terms of the "running dog lackeys of capitalistic imperialism" versus "Godless Communism" and the "Evil Empire." This trend toward severe heterogeneity has continued more recently, as observed in Chapter 6, with those who view international relations as nothing short of "the clash of civilizations," with those Americans who detest certain countries as "the axis of evil" or those elsewhere who hate the United States as "The Great Satan," and with the intense arguments among different denominations of Christianity and different sects of Islam as to how their respective believers actually should behave in the world. The sheer magnitude of these challenges and contests of values makes the efforts and the achievements in establishing consensual, international ethical norms for foreign policy all the more remarkable.

Customary international law and international treaty law provide some of the most notable examples of this progressive development of ethical restraints. Here, whether we explore the writings of early legal scholars as discussed in Chapter 1 or the more recent judgments of the International Court of Justice within the United Nations system, the very concept of legitimacy within a society of states is established and conferred by agreement among governments upon normative values, or what they regard as acceptable—and unacceptable—behavior. As parties to treaties or conventions, they explicitly agree by mutual consent to accept certain norms, rights, and responsibilities designed to regulate and restrain their relations with one another. These, in turn, provide rules of law and standards of legitimacy against which state behavior is judged.

Such normative standards are particularly striking in the area of international human rights. Indeed, it is here that the consequences of action without limit or restraint—and of inaction—upon the well-being of others becomes so evident and so shocking. For centuries, the leaders of states understood that they could treat those under their control as they wished, as matters of exclusive domestic jurisdiction, without outside scrutiny, criticism, or intervention. They could engage in various forms of abuse including discrimination,

exploitation, segregation, enslavement, persecution, and even genocide in the knowledge that they could hide behind the cloak of national sovereignty. Victims had nowhere to run and nowhere to hide and found themselves forced to remain objects of international pity rather than subjects of international law.

The transformation from the traditional culture of impunity toward one of accountability seriously began to change once the horrors of the Holocaust became known to the world. Many government leaders, individual activists, and NGOs (including those representing many religious faiths) reacted by arguing that this experience demonstrated as nothing else could the relationship between human rights and international peace and security. They said, with a particularly revealing choice of words, that this barbarous event had "outraged the conscience of mankind" and convinced them that they had a responsibility to those who suffered from abuse, irrespective of nationality, race, gender, or religion. Consequently, they announced their determination to challenge the claims of national sovereignty when necessary and to establish meaningful and viable international human rights norms. These began with the landmark 1945 United Nations Charter in which all member states pledged to hold themselves responsible for promoting and encouraging respect for human rights and the path-breaking and standard-setting Universal Declaration of Human Rights. The majority of governments in the world, along with NGOs like Amnesty International, then worked to create a whole series of binding human rights treaties formally recognized by a vast majority of nations and peoples of the world, including those dealing with racism, apartheid, civil and political rights, social and economic rights, discrimination against women, rights of the child, and the prohibition of torture. Indeed, as Eleanor Roosevelt who served as the American representative on the United Nations Commission on Human Rights described it, the whole process of promoting human rights itself reflects "the measure of mankind's evolving ethical sense."

Some indication of the degree to which these norms for human rights have been accepted and internalized by the international community can be seen in the reaction produced when it is perceived that they have been egregiously violated. Widespread moral outrage ensued, for example, over revelations about the cruelty against dissidents in psychiatric wards and the gulag of the Soviet Union, the murder of black activist Stephen Biko and the imprisonment of Nelson Mandela by the white minority regime of South Africa, the brutality of the dictatorships of Augusto Pinochet in Chile and Pol Pot in Cambodia, the 1989 attack against students in Tiananmen Square and continued suppression of political and religious freedom in China, the Taliban's blatant discrimination against women, or the beheading of captives by terrorists.

These same kinds of ethical values focused upon the well-being of others can be seen in the growing international sense of responsibility for the consequences of unrestrained economic competition and the resulting disparity between the rich and the poor in the world. Many thoughtful observers regard this as one of the most serious problems of our time. They see the

enormous gap between affluence and poverty as a glaring case of economic and social injustice whose chronic deprivation not only causes untold suffering, but also serves as a breeding ground for discontent that easily can manifest itself in war and terrorism. In this way, destitution threatens both the human person as well as peace and security. It is not surprising, therefore, that a number of nation-states and NGOs have worked to create normative restraints on economic behavior and to coordinate policies that address matters of what is known as distributive justice. The results of their efforts can be found in the United Nations Development Program, World Health Organization, Food and Agricultural Organization, and World Bank and International Monetary Fund, among many others, as they seek to establish an international human poverty index (HPI), develop the Norms on the Responsibilities of Transnational Corporations and Other Business Enterprises, and conduct programs focused upon famine and disaster relief, foreign aid, debt and investment policies, health care, working conditions, and development assistance.

Ethical values have also played an important role in the development of international normative restraints designed to address the suffering that results from environmental degradation. It has become increasingly evident that the continued misuse and overuse of scarce and shared resources creates severe consequences for life throughout the planet. As a consequence, serious questions of ethical responsibility arise. Are we only responsible for the health and well-being of those people within our particular nation, or to others beyond our borders as well who might suffer as a result of our action or inaction? Are we only responsible to ourselves and those currently alive or, given the finite nature of many resources, to future generations as well? Do we have any responsibilities to other forms of life? It is exactly these kinds of questions that have prompted significant efforts to establish ethical norms that create restraints to protect endangered animal and plant species and to reduce land, water, and air pollution. The 1992 United Nations Conference on Environment and Development, widely known as the "Earth Summit," proved to be the largest international conference held in history. It brought together more than 25,000 participants, including 172 official governmental delegations and the representatives of 2400 environmental NGOs. Together they negotiated the Convention on Biological Diversity and the UN Framework Convention on Climate Change, which in turn led to the 1997 Kyoto Protocol calling for a reduction of greenhouse gas emissions for the well-being of the planet as a whole. When the United Nations Climate Change Conference subsequently was held in 2005, and it became clear that certain nations refused to participate in this endeavor by accepting restraints, the prime minister of Canada Paul Martin publicly called upon them to heed "the conscience of the world."

Not all endeavors to establish ethical restraints for foreign policy have such a broad global perspective or result from consensual international efforts. There are times when states deliberately impose limits upon themselves alone. That is, they make choices from within about what they are willing and unwilling

to do to advance their interests in the world. One of the most striking examples of this occurred when the United States began to seriously investigate the Central Intelligence Agency in the wake of the Watergate scandal. Although fully aware of the necessity of having an effective intelligence service, congressional committees discovered shocking accounts of unrestrained covert action during the Cold War conducted in the name of national security that entailed destabilization campaigns, the overthrow of democratically elected governments, plots to assassinate foreign leaders, use of illegal drugs on unsuspecting victims, and insurgency and counterinsurgency, with many accompanying violations of human rights. The revelations prompted widespread public outrage and led Senator Frank Church to describe the CIA as a "rogue elephant out of control." Congress responded by establishing select committees to oversee and restrain covert operations, while presidents Ford, Carter, and Reagan issued executive orders explicitly prohibiting political assassinations by any agent of the United States under their administrations, declaring that such deliberately targeted murder in statecraft was completely contrary to basic ethical values.

ETHICAL RESTRAINTS FOR ARMED FORCE

The challenges that exist in creating ethical restraints for foreign policy are rendered even more difficult when dealing with armed force. It is here that choices about whether, under what circumstance, and how to use force as an instrument of policy have perhaps the most severe consequences on the well-being of others, including intense suffering and death. It also is here that universal values about the sanctity of all life and prohibitions against doing harm to others often come into such direct conflict with those values of the state when violence is employed or killing is ordered. As Stanley Hoffmann observes, war is where people are most obviously torn between humanity and country—between their conscience as moral beings, whose thoughts and feelings about responsibilities transcend borders, and their loyalties as citizens of a particular nation-state. History demonstrates that wars provide the greatest opportunities for national self-righteousness, for loosening standards and denying the well-being of others, and for political leaders and military commanders to plead necessity and argue that they really have no choice but to respond to the wartime imperatives forced upon them. It is therefore important to appreciate that in these particular matters of force and statecraft, the stakes are high, the consequences severe, and the arguments intense.

At one end of the spectrum, for example, are pacifists, who argue that any threat or use of military force at all is intrinsically evil. They believe that violence only begets more violence and seek strength in moral force rather than physical force. They argue that killing—for any reason—is wrong and can never be justified. For this reason, dedicated pacifists unambiguously embrace nonviolence, oppose the possession of weapons as instruments of war, and reject war itself, even in self-defense. This position has a tradition extending over many centuries, often finding inspiration from Buddhism, the teachings of Jesus

and practices of the early Christian church, Bertha von Suttner's book *Lay Down Your Arms!*, the examples of Mohandas Gandhi and Martin Luther King, Jr., and the Peace Testimony of the Quakers from 1660 declaring: "We utterly deny all outward wars and strife, and fightings with outward weapons, for any end, or under any pretense whatever; this is our testimony to the whole world."

In sharp contrast to this argument is that of militarists, who glorify the state without reservation and who view violence and war not only as necessities but as morally good. Such a position is given expression by the philosopher G. W. F. Hegel, who contended that war transcends the mediocrity of everyday life, enhances domestic cohesion, creates fear and respect abroad, and provides the ultimate test for the virtue of citizens and states. The Bolsheviks also embraced violence rather than turning away from it, for as Leon Trotsky explained:

> We were never concerned with the Kantian-priestly and vegetarian-Quaker prattle about the 'sacredness of human life.' To make the human life sacred we must destroy the social order which crucifies him . . . and this problem can be solved only by blood and iron.

This idea that war and violence are ennobling and that the end justifies whatever means are necessary is echoed by others, including historian Heinrich von Treitschke in *Politics*, naval officer and strategist Alfred Thayer Mahan in "The Moral Aspect of War," front-line soldier Ernest Jünger in *Battle as an Inner Experience*, Adolf Hitler in *Mein Kampf*, any number of extreme nationalists, and those terrorists who seek glory by taking the lives of others in order to achieve their own martyrdom.

But most statesmen in history and in our own day, it is probably safe to say, have tried to avoid being pushed into either the pure pacifist or the rabid militarist position. Instead, they have attempted to navigate their way through conflicting demands and responsibilities, competing ethical values, the pressures of domestic and foreign politics, and the various practical, structural, and political restraints of their own time and place. They have reached the conclusion that armed force has its defensive and peacekeeping as well as aggressive uses, and that when leaders fail to avail themselves of the former, they are likely to find themselves at the mercy of those skilled in the latter. This has led many of them to keep armed force as a necessary instrument of statecraft, but at the same time recognizing its dangers and seeking ways of keeping it within certain limits. In such a process they have tended to be nonperfectionist practitioners rather than dogmatic theoreticians, making many compromises along the way in their choices among all the variations of conscience and power and of what they could do and what they should do.

The results, as one would expect, thus often appear to be inconsistent, incomplete, and a peculiar mixture of self-interests and ethical values. Nevertheless, in their own incremental ways they have helped to create a variety of normative restraints for armed force, including the legitimate uses of force and acceptable kinds of threats, the numbers and types of weapons, arms control, weapons testing bans, demilitarized zones, and disarmament.

Some of these ethical norms can be seen in the persistent efforts over time to develop international treaty law establishing restrictions or prohibitions on certain kinds of weapons considered to cause excruciating pain or traumatic suffering to others. Religious leaders of the twelfth century, for example, worked to place restrictions on the use of crossbows, which they described as "barbaric" and "unchristian." In the Hague Convention of 1899, statesmen from all of the major countries in Europe and Asia banned the use of soft-nosed dum-dum bullets, which tore savage wounds in the human body, on the grounds that they were "uncivilized," "inhumane," and "against the laws of humanity." More than 120 nations signed the 1925 Geneva Protocol prohibiting asphyxiating or poisonous gasses, declaring that such weapons were "justly condemned by the general opinion of the civilized world" and thereby sought to bind alike "the conscience and the practice and nations."

Similar values influenced subsequent negotiations, as we discussed in Chapter 8, and produced a variety of restraints in other arms control agreements. A particularly notable example of the impact of ethical norms on statecraft is provided by the pressures brought to bear upon the United States to conform with the prohibitions concerning chemical and biological weapons. Widespread domestic opinion within the United States and global opinion abroad viewed these ghastly weapons as morally "abhorrent," and on this basis, as McElroy observes, sufficient political pressure was mounted to eventually compel the Nixon administration to reverse course and make substantive changes in American military doctrine and force structure. Over the strong objections of the Joint Chiefs of Staff, the president therefore announced in 1969 that the United States would unilaterally destroy its stockpiles of biological weapons, formally renounce the first use of all lethal chemical weapons, and begin the process of ratifying the legal restraints of the Geneva Protocol. Ethical values similarly drive much of the effort to establish restraints and prohibitions on antipersonnel land mines and weapons of mass destruction today, including the 2005 review conference of the Non-Proliferation Treaty on nuclear weapons which remains the most widely adhered-to arms control treaty in history.

These norms also play a role in how threats of armed force are perceived. Because of its defensive nature, designed to prevent aggression, as seen in Chapter 9, deterrence normally does not produce ethical problems as serious as those of other strategies. The one notable exception, of course, is the threat of nuclear annihilation. Some ethical critics of nuclear deterrence, for example, argue that because it threatens to do what is morally reprehensible (namely, to inflict staggering mass destruction), it cannot possibly be justified, whereas others contend that such catastrophic damage can be threatened as long as it is never actually done if deterrence fails. Coercive diplomacy in its offensive variant, which seeks to extend control through intimidation and fear, as explored in Chapter 10, also raises significant ethical questions that challenge internationally established norms. This explains why the texts of the United Nations Charter and the Helsinki Final Act provide explicit restraints on coercive threats of force.

But history indicates that armed force all too frequently moves beyond the possibility of violence in threats to the actuality of violence and death in warfare. Since it is in war that the greatest harm is inflicted upon people and their human rights, it is in war where the greatest ethical conflicts arise. From the time of the ancients to the present, and in virtually all cultures for which we have written records, there have been individuals who have been deeply concerned about this aspect of force and statecraft and have argued that because war is a human activity that involves human choices, it cannot escape moral argument and judgment. They thus have given much thought to creating ethical standards for judging the legitimacy of recourse to violence: how wars between states might be both permitted and restrained in when and how they are fought. In this process, they have sought to avoid the two extremes of believing either that *nothing* is justified in war—or that *everything* is. The resulting principles are collectively known as just war tradition.

Whether the use of armed force is ethically justified or not, according to the theory of just war, depends upon compliance with particular restraints in both ends and means and is comprised of two parts. The first of these is *jus ad bellum,* or the justice *of* war. Traditionally, the norms for restraining any choice of going to war or not have included the following criteria:

1. *Just cause.* The only ethical justification for the resort to war is to stop aggression and to defend against armed attack. This is a necessary, but not a sufficient condition. That is, even if a state has received an injury constituting a just cause, it cannot go to war unless the other requirements are met as well.

2. *Right intention or purpose.* A war is just only if it seeks to provide self-defense or to protect others from grievous harm if attacked and to create peace by restoring conditions as they existed before the aggression took place. Wars of conquest designed to acquire territory, subjugate, or annihilate thus do not qualify, nor do preventive wars.

3. *Legitimate authority.* The use of force is ethically permissible only when it is authorized by a legitimate, responsible, and duly constituted authority. Violence initiated by dissident groups, terrorist cells, or private individuals therefore is not justified.

4. *Public declaration.* There must be a formal, public declaration of war in order to open to public debate the judgment of whether the injury received warrants a resort to arms and to provide the offending state the opportunity to offer redress in lieu of violence.

5. *Limited objectives and proportionality.* A war is ethically warranted only if its objectives are limited to a specific political end and if the good towards which the war is aimed is proportional to the original offense and to the harm that the war will cause.

6. *Reasonable chance of success.* Given the destruction, pain, and death that it will cause, the use of force in war is ethically justified only if it is likely that it will succeed in achieving the limited objectives for which it is fought. Good intentions and grandiose plans, in other words, are not sufficient. This

condition, like the one that precedes it, is designed to avoid a crusading or "holy war" mentality and to protect against the pointless use of military forces by leaders who would recklessly steer a nation into armed conflict.

7. *Last resort.* A state can resort to war only if all of the other conditions have been met and it has made every effort to resolve the dispute first by nonmilitary means (such as diplomatic negotiation, arbitration, or various forms of persuasion).

The second component of just war theory is that of *jus in bello*, or justice in war. This emerged to deliberately counter any argument that a noble end justifies whatever means are necessary. The decision to resort to war in a particular case might be just, but this does not mean that it can be fought in unjust ways. As a result of the deep concern over this issue, two principal criteria have been designed to restrain the actual conduct of war:

1. *Protection of innocents.* Armed force can only be justified if it is used against an adversary's political leadership and military forces. Every effort, consequently, must be made to distinguish between combatants and innocent civilians or noncombatants. Noncombatants must be immune from attack. Indiscriminate mass destruction of populations or violence against civilian targets thus is ethically impermissible.

2. *Proportionality.* The means used in the prosecution of a war must be proportionate to the limited ends for which the war is being fought. Leaders therefore must avoid any profligate use of force in overkill that will inflict more loss of life and more damage than is necessary or congruent with what is at stake. Military actions, in other words, must use the minimum level of force necessary to achieve the limited objectives of the war.

It is important to acknowledge that these normative values of the just war tradition do not come without difficulties. In fact, they can be fraught with theoretical, practical, and political problems when being operationalized within specific contexts. What role should prudence play, for example, in determining what is truly "the last resort" in a given situation? Or, given the fact that modern weapons of mass destruction could annihilate a significant part of any state's population, can one engage in anticipatory self-defense instead of waiting until actually attacked? Or, under what circumstances is it legitimate to use force against a state in the name of humanitarian intervention to protect human rights abuses, even if that state has not launched an attack against another state?

Despite the difficulties, however, these norms have an impact upon force and statecraft. They now are regularly taught at any number of military academies, including West Point. Of particular significance, they have been highly influential in establishing many legal limitations, including international "laws of war," "rules of engagement," and formal treaties creating restraints in the use of violence. One thinks of the Geneva Conventions, first signed in 1864 and modified several times thereafter, in which almost every nation in the world has accepted responsibility for the humane treatment of prisoners

of war, the protection of civilians, and the care of the sick and the wounded, and explicitly do so in the name of "the laws of humanity and the dictates of the public conscience." In addition, the extent to which these ethical restraints have been widely internalized is evident by the sense of moral outrage elicited when it is perceived that flagrant violations have occurred. One can see this in the widespread public condemnation resulting from such cases as the deliberate bombing attacks against unprotected civilian populations during the Second World War, the My Lai massacre in Vietnam, Saddam Hussein's use of chemical weapons against the Kurds, "ethnic cleansing" in Bosnia and Croatia under orders from Slobodan Milosevic, and terrorist attacks whose victims indiscriminately (and sometimes deliberately) include women and children in order to increase the extent of fear. It is also evident by the nearly universal condemnation of preventive war, the extraordinary rendition of "enemy combatants" to clandestine "black sites" in other countries for interrogation outside the rule of law, and the documented and graphically photographed abuse and torture by Americans of detainees in Afghanistan, at the naval base of Guantanamo Bay in Cuba, and at Abu Ghraib prison in Iraq.

On occasion these ethical norms and their broader sense of limits and responsibilities become so powerful that they influence the consciences of military personnel to the extent that they refuse to obey direct orders from their state. German Field Marshal Erwin Rommel, for example, chose to burn rather than follow Hitler's written command that all Allied soldiers found behind German lines immediately be killed. More recently, one thinks of the more than 600 Israeli soldiers who have joined the "Courage to Refuse" movement, as well as a number of elite commandos and fighter pilots, who have refused to participate in missions in populated areas of the West Bank and Gaza. "In the past we fought for a just cause," they declared in a written statement, "[but today] we have reached the boundary of oppressing other people." Moreover, they argue, attacks in these occupied territories must be regarded as "illegal and immoral" because they so often violate human rights and cause death among innocent civilians.

It is exactly these kinds of ethical judgments and normative values that have motivated so many statesmen and citizens in recent years to work toward the development of international criminal law. They have believed that the lessons of history are sufficiently convincing when it comes to atrocities perpetrated by unscrupulous leaders who are allowed to hide in a culture of impunity behind the shield of national sovereignty. For this reason they have argued that peace and security can best be maintained by establishing a rule of law that holds those who violate widely accepted ethical restraints personally responsible for their actions. Decisions rendered at the International Military Tribunal at Nuremberg and again at the International Military Tribunal for the Far East in Tokyo following the Second World War set important legal precedents in this regard by declaring that "just following orders" would no longer serve as a sufficient or legitimate defense for ethically reprehensible actions that violated what the prosecution described as "the moral sense

of mankind." The Security Council of the United Nations explicitly cited these same principles when it established criminal tribunals for the former Yugoslavia in 1993 and then for Rwanda in 1994. As these norms became even more widely accepted, a larger and larger number of states and their leaders began to work seriously toward creating a permanent international tribunal. This explains the major motivation for those representatives of more than 150 nations who negotiated the treaty creating the first permanent and independent International Criminal Court (ICC) to try those accused of gross violations of these normative standards in the form of war crimes, crimes against humanity, and genocide. These particular atrocities, they revealingly stated in the preamble to the text, "deeply shock the conscience of mankind."

This search for limits and prohibitions against crossing unacceptable thresholds emerges with particular starkness with the element of technology that forms such an important component of what we have called the diplomatic revolution. One of the reasons why modern weapons of mass destruction generate so much debate about ethical issues is the fact that they have lost their traditional capacity to remain limited instruments of policy by other means. Their horrifying capabilities violate the restraints of protecting innocents and proportionality. Nuclear, biological, and chemical weapons simply cannot be controlled, cannot discriminate between combatants and noncombatants, and cannot maintain any rational relationship between massive annihilation and limited political objectives. Thus, concludes scholar Michael Walzer in his influential book *Just and Unjust Wars*: "Nuclear weapons explode the theory of just war. They are the first of mankind's technological innovations that are simply not encompassable within the familiar moral world." It is for this reason that there are individuals today who strenuously work to go beyond the familiar and establish new norms for precisely these kinds of weapons.

The existence of the many ethical restraints that we have discussed, as well as those currently being developed, of course, most certainly provides no guarantee that they will be consistently honored over the demands of national policy or that decision makers will give them conscientious attention and adequate weight when determining their foreign policies and military actions. Historical experience indicates that competition and violence are never easy to restrain and international relations do not always lend themselves to simple moral verdicts. Adversaries exist, agreements can be violated, self-imposed restraints can be exploited, and some individual leaders have a very poorly developed sense of conscience or moral responsibility. Wars continue to be fought, ethical quandaries among competing values persist, complexities and ambiguities remain, and perhaps more questions of ethics are raised than are answered.

Nevertheless, the very fact that such standards have been created—and continue to be developed—in the face of these enormous challenges bears remarkable testimony to the longstanding and enduring human desire to find limits and to appreciate their value in restraining destructive competition and violence. There are times, as we have seen, when they possess a power

of their own and provide genuine restraints on the conduct of foreign policy and war. Yet, even when they do not, their very existence provides valuable reminders of how leaders should act and what kind of an international community might be created. They remind us of the necessity and the legitimacy of asking serious questions about ends, means, and consequences of policy in the world and give us a basis of judgment that can serve as a safeguard against the tendency to engage in convenient rationalizations, hypocrisy, or moral self-deception. In this regard, and as we shall see in the Conclusion that follows, there are reasons to believe that ethical restraints on force and statecraft—particularly in an age of weapons of mass destruction and terrorism —may become even more important in the future than they ever have been in the past.

Suggestions for Further Exploration

The fascinating, but challenging, matter of ethics in statecraft is discussed in Mark Amstutz, *International Ethics* (Lanham, MA, 2005 ed.); "General Casts War in Religious Terms," *Los Angeles Times*, October 16, 2003; Leslie Gelb and Justine Rosenthal, "The Rise of Ethics in Foreign Policy," *Foreign Affairs*, 82 (May/June 2003): 2–7; Douglas Johnston (ed.), *Faith-Based Diplomacy: Trumping Realpolitik* (New York, 2003); the special issue of *Orbis*, 42 (Spring 1998) on "Faith and Statecraft"; Gordon Graham, *Ethics and International Relations* (Oxford, 1997); Cathal Nolan (ed.), *Ethics and Statecraft* (Westport, CT, 1995); Joel Rosenthal, "Private Convictions and Public Commitments," *World Policy Journal*, 12 (Summer 1995): 89–96; Douglas Johnston and Cynthia Simpson, (eds.), *Religion: The Missing Dimension of Statecraft* (New York, 1994); Robert W. McElroy, *Morality and American Foreign Policy* (Princeton, 1992); Dorothy Jones, *Code of Peace* (Chicago, 1992); Kenneth Thompson (ed.), *Moral Dimensions of American Foreign Policy* (New Brunswick, NJ, 1984); National Conference of Catholic Bishops, *The Challenge of Peace* (Washington, DC, 1983); J. E. Hare and Carey Joynt, *Ethics and International Affairs* (London, 1982); and Stanley Hoffmann, *Duties Beyond Borders* (Syracuse, NY, 1981). Recent scholarship appears in the journal *Ethics and International Affairs* and on the Carnegie Council on Ethics and International Affairs's Web site at www.cceia.org.

Some earlier studies still remains highly relevant to contemporary problems, including Hans Morgenthau, *Politics Among Nations* (New York, 1978 ed.); Hedley Bull, *The Anarchical Society* (London, 1977); Ernest W. Lefever, (ed.), *Ethics and World Politics* (Baltimore, 1972); E. H. Carr, *The Twenty Years' Crisis* (New York, 1964 ed.); Arnold Wolfers, "Statesmanship and Moral Choice," in his book *Discord and Collaboration* (Baltimore, 1962); Reinhold Niebuhr, *Moral Man and Immoral Society* (New York, 1932); and Niccoló Machiavelli, *The Prince*, Chapters XV and XVIII, and *Discourses*, Part III, Chapter 41 in various editions.

For particular aspects of ethics and foreign policy, see the Human Development Reports at www.undp.org; the journal *Human Rights Quarterly*; Ian Clark, *Legitimacy in International Society* (New York, 2005); Glen Stassen (ed.), *Just Peacemaking* (Cleveland, OH, 2004 ed.); Paul Gordon Lauren, *The Evolution of International Human Rights* (Philadelphia, 2003 ed.); W. M. Reisman and James E. Baker, *Regulating Covert Action* (New Haven, 1992); Paul Gordon Lauren (ed.), *The China Hands' Legacy: Ethics and Diplomacy* (Boulder, CO, 1987); Paul Gordon Lauren, "Ethics and Intelligence," in Al Maurer et al. (eds.), *Intelligence* (Boulder, CO, 1985); Alexander L. George,

"Domestic Constraints on Regime Change in U.S. Foreign Policy," in Ole Holsti (ed.), *Change in the International System* (Boulder, CO, 1980); and Gordon A. Craig, *From Bismarck to Adenauer* (New York, 1965 ed.).

The specific issue of ethical restraints in war is treated in Larry May, Eric Rovie, and Steve Viner, *The Morality of War* (Upper Saddle River, NJ, 2006); Mary Ellen O'Connell, *International Law and the Use of Force* (New York, 2005); Franklin Eric Wester, "Preemption and Just War," *Parameters* (Winter 2004–2005): 20–39; the though-provoking Jean Bethke Elshtain, *Just War Against Terror* (New York, 2004); Michael Walzer, *Arguing About War* (New Haven, CT, 2004); Mark Danner, *Torture and Truth* (New York, 2004); Paul Christopher, *The Ethics of War and Peace* (Upper Saddle River, NJ, 2004 ed.); Paul Gordon Lauren, "From Impunity to Accountability," in Ramesh Thakur and Peter Malcontent (eds.), *From Sovereign Impunity to International Accountability* (Tokyo, 2004); Chris Hedges, *War Is a Force That Gives Us Meaning* (New York, 2003 ed.); "Ariel Sharon's Pilot Problem," *Time*, December 15, 2003; Terry Nardin (ed.), *The Ethics of War and Peace* (Princeton, 1998 ed.); Geoffrey Best, *War and Law Since 1945* (Oxford, 1994); David A. Welch, *Justice and the Genesis of War* (New York, 1993); Michael Walzer, *Just and Unjust Wars* (New York, 1992 ed.); Joseph S. Nye, Jr., *Nuclear Ethics* (New York, 1986); Donald Wells, *War Crimes and the Laws of War* (Lanham, MD, 1984); Gordon Zahn, *In Solitary Witness* (New York, 1965); Roland Bainton, *Christian Attitudes Toward War and Peace* (Nashville, TN, 1960); and Kenneth Waltz, *Man, the State and War* (New York, 1954). See also "Laws of War" at the Avalon Project at www.yale.edu/lawweb; and the "Courage to Refuse" movement at www.seruv.org.il.

Those interested in exploring cases from history that demonstrate some of the challenges of ethical restraints in statecraft will find much material in the Treaty of the Holy Alliance (1815), Lieber's Code of Military Conduct (1863), efforts to create the International Red Cross and international humanitarian law (1864), the Declaration of St. Petersburg (1868); the foreign policies of William Gladstone (1868–1874, 1880–1885, 1886, and 1892–1894), Woodrow Wilson (1913–1921), Jimmy Carter (1977–1981), and Nelson Mandela (1994–1999); and the diplomacy of U Thant as United Nations Secretary-General (1961–1971). Some of the ethical dilemmas of humanitarian intervention can be seen in the United Nations–sanctioned military action in Somalia (1992–1995) and the NATO campaign against Serbia on behalf of Kosovo (1999). Those interested in rival moral claims will find intense arguments surrounding America's decisions to drop nuclear bombs on Hiroshima and Nagasaki (1945), to engage in the Vietnam War (1961–1973), and whether to go to war in Iraq in 2003 and then how to wage it.

Conclusion: Reflections on Force and Statecraft and the Diplomatic Challenges of Our Time

Those responsible for statecraft, as discussed throughout this book, have struggled since the earliest evolution of diplomacy with the challenges of finding ways to survive and to realize their foreign policy objectives by appropriate means. Most have reached the conclusion that efforts to deal with international conflicts and competition solely by peaceful means of rational persuasion do not always succeed, and that sometimes the threat or the use of force appear to be the only language that certain leaders seem to understand. In these circumstances, force becomes a necessary instrument of policy. Yet, on the other hand, they also have come to realize that such threats or uses of force at times have not only been ineffective, but seriously aggravated disputes between states and even triggered wars that might otherwise have been avoided. Caught in this fundamental dilemma between necessity and danger, policy makers have experimented over time as partners in creating a wide variety of diplomatic means and international systems to keep their rivalries within certain bounds and devised ways of restraining and controlling armed force. Their experiences, their successes, and their failures not only provide ways to understand the past, but instructive lessons as to what we might expect in the diplomatic challenges of force and statecraft that confront us in our time.

Statesmen throughout history, for example, have been forced to learn—sometimes through painful personal experience—that diplomacy is indeed the art of the possible; and what is possible is dependent upon the particular conditions of the time, or historical context. That is, the skills and personalities of individual leaders, the relative power and interests of other states, the structure of the international system, and prevailing ethical norms, among other factors at any given point in time, play absolutely critical roles in determining what can and cannot be done. This is one of the reasons why it is so important for those interested in and/or responsible for foreign affairs to carefully study history in such a way as to learn about continuities and changes and

to develop the ability to analyze the role of people, process, possibilities, perspective, and proportion. There are valuable lessons to be gained thereby; some of these may be remarkably applicable to a situation or case that arises, and some may not, depending upon the context.

This context-dependent feature of the lessons of history also applies to theories or conceptual models of statecraft. Theoretical principles generally are developed in order to explain and understand those behavioral characteristics demonstrating patterns, or continuities, that appear to be valid across cases. The delineation of these principles for such important subjects as negotiation, deterrence, coercive diplomacy, crisis management, and ethical restraints thus provides extremely useful tools of analysis and diagnois. In fact, at times such principles may offer considerable assistance, insights, and policy-relevant guidance to decision makers—on other occasions, the usefulness of these principles may be less so. They cannot simply be taken off a shelf and superimposed upon each and every circumstance and somehow assumed to be policy. As we saw in our discussions of structured, focused comparisons, each case study possesses both similarities and differences with the others. The task is to develop the skills necessary to make discerning judgments about continuity and change and to appreciate that the degree of relevance for theory in any given case is again dependent upon context.

In this regard, there is no broad or sweeping context more critical to statecraft than the continuities and the changes in the diplomatic revolution. Some elements of statecraft have remained relatively constant in history, such as human nature, the basic strategies and issues of diplomacy, the debate between partnership and rivalry among members of the international system, and the central dilemmas involving the necessities and the dangers of armed force. But others have changed dramatically. As we explored in some detail, at the very end of the nineteenth and beginning of the twentieth centuries, certain forces began to transform features of the classical system of diplomacy. Through time, they became even more pronounced, creating some changes that made statecraft easier and others that made it infinitely more complicated. These dynamics continue to this day and, for this reason, will greatly shape the challenges ahead.

One of these changes appears with the number and nature of actors within the international system. At one time, only five states known as the Great Powers of Europe, roughly equal in strength and arranged in a balance of power, made and enforced the decisions for all the rest. As a result of the upheaval of two world wars, the whole process of decolonization, and the breakup of the Soviet Union, that number vastly increased. Today, there are nearly 200 nation-states conducting diplomacy, each with its own interests and perspectives, each claiming the prerogatives of national sovereignty, and each demanding to participate in global affairs. These are not at all equal and vary greatly in size, strength, and influence, ranging from the smallest of countries to the world's only superpower, the United States, with no peer competitors.

But the number of nation-states does not tell the whole story. During the seventeenth and eighteenth centuries there were no administrative mechanisms designed to manage diplomatic relations, and during the nineteenth century

the Concert of Europe existed with a mere five members. But today nation-states belong to a vast array of intergovernmental organizations, alliances, or associations that also play roles as actors in their own right in international relations. Every state, for example, is a member of the United Nations and its specialized agencies. Most hold membership in the World Trade Organization and are parties to monitoring bodies created by human rights treaties. Many participate in elaborate alliance systems stretching from the North Atlantic to Latin America and Southeast Asia. Some participate in regional groups like the European Union, Organization of American States, Shanghai Cooperation Organization, or the African Union, or partnerships like the G-8. The collective interests of the members and participants of these various organizations and groupings enable them to leverage their power, with the result that the whole often becomes greater than the mere sum of its parts.

At the same time, challenges will continue to be presented by the expansion in the number of nonstate actors. During the classical system of diplomacy, only nation-states were recognized as the actors within the international arena with sufficient power to influence the security of the others. This is no longer the case. Indeed, there are many actors that are not states at all, but who actually distrust states, are capable of challenging traditional claims of national sovereignty, and have the ability to create an enormous impact upon global affairs. There are transnational corporations today, for example, that possess far greater financial resources than many national governments and are certainly able to make their influence felt in economics and in politics. Added to these are a growing number of privatized military firms (PMFs) that provide training, logistics, intelligence, and even combat support under contract to the highest bidder. Virtually thousands of NGOs with worldwide objectives continue to expand in numbers, size, and influence, particularly in the areas of human rights and environmental protection. Moreover, there are the particularly dangerous, transnational nonstate actors of terrorist networks like al-Qaida, who, although possessing relatively minor material capabilities, can cause great damage, inflict pain, sow fear, and thereby seriously challenge even the most powerful of nation-states.

The impact of nonstate actors on international relations is also a reflection of yet another feature of the diplomatic revolution: the growing role of domestic political pressures and public opinion. Diplomacy in the time of the classical system was regarded as the exclusive domain of government officials and professional diplomats. According to their defenders, they acted in privacy and with discretion for flexibility that would advance their national interest. According to their critics, they acted in secrecy to promote their own self-interests or hide decisions that might lead their countries into armed conflict. The tension between these two positions reached an explosion point during the First World War with popular cries for "democratic control" and a more open "new diplomacy." It continues with even greater force in our own day, especially with the expansion of information, well-organized pressure groups, and democratic governments. This certainly challenges those responsible for statecraft to be ever-mindful of opinion and explains why so much attention is now devoted to what is called "public diplomacy." Its

impact is felt in the use of armed force as well, for as General Wesley Clark writes in frustration about the Kosovo campaign in *Waging Modern War*:

> The weight of public opinion was doing to us what the Serb air defense system had failed to do: limit our strikes. The impact of this hasn't been lost on military or political leaders. . . . [F]or sustained operations, public support will be essential. This, in turn, can only be gained by accepting the restraints of public opinion and sensibilities on future operations.

Other challenges are presented by changes in the geographical extent and scope of international relations itself. The focus of attention throughout the classical system of diplomacy was upon the continent of Europe, and statesmen could enjoy the relatively simplicity of a small number of culturally homogeneous actors. But powerful historical forces transformed this Euro-centric system into something different, bringing the United States, Japan, and increasingly China into world affairs and into a complex and heterogeneous system of truly global scale. One of the challenges of our time, therefore, is the necessity of developing an understanding of the resulting diversity of cultures, political and social systems, and perspectives in the world today.

This process of expansion and extension has been accompanied by growing interaction and integration, or by what is described as "complex interdependence" and "globalization." The world is becoming increasingly interconnected, and what affects the people of one state affects those of another over many issues and at a variety of levels. Virtually no country can remain uninvolved or untouched and, in this age of the indivisibility of security, any search for the security of one's own country alone is a strategy that will fail. The results bring not only benefits, but also serious challenges—to the human security of individual people, the security of nation-states, and to the security of the international system as a whole. Indeed, this is precisely why the largest gathering of global leaders in history met together for the much-anticipated 2005 World Summit convened at United Nations headquarters. They understood that a diverse and broad array of threats confront us in our interdependent, contemporary world: international war between states, civil violence within states, the proliferation of weapons of mass destruction, terrorist networks, a single superpower pursuing unilateral policies, the threats posed by failed or collapsed states, human rights abuses, transnational organized crime, poverty and starvation, population growth and migration, HIV/AIDS and other deadly infectious diseases, resource depletion and climate change, and environmental degradation, among other dangers. "Depending upon wealth, geography, and power," observed Secretary-General Kofi Annan,

> we perceive different threats as the most pressing. But the truth is that we cannot afford to choose. Collective security today depends on accepting that the threats which each region of the world perceives as most urgent are in fact equally so for all. In our globalized world, the threats we face are interconnected. . . . [and] whatever threatens one threatens all.

In order to find collective ways to address these challenges with their potential for catastrophic consequences, it will be necessary first to understand their

nature. Of essential importance in this regard—and especially in a book with the title of *Force and Statecraft*—is to recognize that some of these threats clearly involve war and armed force, and others do not. Security and survival are increasingly defined in different ways. Moreover, power itself is composed of, and measured by, many different elements. These range from military might to economic wealth, from industrial capacity to the morale and education of citizens, from information to the level of technological sophistication, and from the "moral force" of religious beliefs and ethical values to the capacity of words, cultural and political ideas to influence behavior. Given this wide range, some of the ever-widening and global challenges ahead simply do not lend themselves to the utility of armed force as an instrument of policy at all. Stated more directly, not all of the diplomatic challenges of our time are military problems. Not all solutions, therefore, will be military solutions.

So many of the changes in the diplomatic revolution, of course, are the result of developments in modern technology. Highly sophisticated telecommunication satellites in orbit around the planet, computers and the World Wide Web, fiber optics, nanosensors, and wireless environments of the digital age have created an information revolution that dramatically affects diplomacy, the collection and analysis of intelligence, and the command, control, and communications of military operations as readily as they do other aspects of daily life in the twenty-first century. The same can be said of advances in the area of transportation that allow a person from one part of the world unprecedented mobility and speed (some traveling faster than the speed of sound) to reach almost any other location within hours. Technological inventions increasingly shorten time, decrease distances, and expand opportunities for communication and interaction. They also enable political leaders to completely bypass resident ambassadors and professional diplomats if they so desire.

While each of these technological developments presents both opportunities and challenges, the most serious for force and statecraft are nowhere more evident than in modern weapons. During the classical system of diplomacy, the capabilities of armed force were extremely limited. Statesmen viewed war as controllable and, therefore, usable. It was serious enough that leaders might try to prevent it, but mild enough to enable them to invoke the threat or resort to force when necessary. This is why they considered force to be a legitimate and useful instrument of foreign policy, or, in the words of Clausewitz, "policy by other means."

But it is no longer as simple as this. At Waterloo in 1815 an infantry soldier could fire two or three times a minute at an enemy standing only a few yards away. At the Somme in 1916 the machine gun fired 600 rounds a minute. The "Battle of the Drawing Boards" during the Second World War accelerated this process even further. The capabilities of today's weapons from the revolution in military affairs on the ground, at sea, in the air, and from space against adversaries continents away are almost unbelievable.

In some ways, technological advances actually are making armed force more useable. Precision-guided munitions, stealth aircraft whose profiles and materials render them virtually invisible to radar, and the Global Positioning

System, for example, make it possible for weapons operating at extremely long distances and relying on gigabytes of information to hit very specific targets with unprecedented accuracy. One result of this development is the possibility of significant reduction in the amount of collateral damage and loss of life by combatants and by innocent civilians trapped in war zones. Despite the obvious and tremendous advantage in sparing lives, however, there is growing concern that such new precision weapons—and the ability to deliver them electronically with minimal risks and near immunity—may appear to lower the costs of war and lead to an exaggerated overconfidence in high-tech armed force. In this way, the military option may become more seductively easy for policy makers to select, blinding them to the need for caution and use only as a "last resort," the possibilities of diplomacy and persuasion, the vulnerability to debilitating cyberattacks, or the dangers of wars against ill-equipped but nevertheless determined insurgents fighting in unconventional ways.

Even more challenging is the fact that certain kinds of weapons technology fulfill the ultimate irony and tragedy of the "the fate of Nemesis," in which man was punished by fulfilling his wishes too completely. There is now such a thing as an excess of power. Weapons exist that cannot be controlled and that bear little or no proportion to rational objectives. This feature, by its very nature, alters important dimensions in the calculus of the relationship between ends and means in statecraft.

Armed force remains, as it has been throughout history, a necessary instrument of policy in particular situations against certain kinds of adversaries, especially when diplomatic efforts prove to be inadequate or unsuccessful. It can be threatened and used by individual nation-states, by coalitions and alliances, or by the international community acting within the United Nations for a variety of purposes. It can increase credibility in defensive deterrence and coercive diplomacy designed to protect peace and security or enhance negotiation and crisis management. It can be used to defend vital interests, to protect allies and others under attack from aggressors, to provide collective security in such a way as to maintain the international system, to support normative values and enforce international law, to shield innocents from genocide and other egregious human rights abuses, to police cease-fire agreements in peacekeeping missions, and to furnish particular means for practical peacemaking and for preventive diplomacy.

But armed force, as extensive historical experience demonstrates, is best used to check certain kinds of threats rather than solve fundamental problems, and entails many serious challenges. It is a blunt and dangerous instrument of statecraft containing an inherent tension between the logic of war as a political act for limited objectives and the "logic of the instrument" of war itself, which stresses the use of ample force to destroy or render impotent an enemy's forces. The very existence of military force threatens others, creates vast uncertainties, and increases the risks of escalation in any crisis. It can be treacherously seductive for those leaders who mistakenly believe that military might alone will enable them to act as they wish and get what they want in the world and, therefore, that they can substitute force for diplomacy. Armed

force cannot always be controlled, can endanger delicate negotiations or crisis management, and can threaten the existence of the international system when used offensively to coerce and intimidate opponents, to inflict pain, to launch wars of aggression, to conquer or exterminate, to overthrow legitimate governments, or to engage in terrorist acts against innocent civilians.

Policy makers can expect to be confronted with these challenges and the difficult choices that they entail in the future as they have in the past, but with the full knowledge that the dangers become even more acute when they involve weapons of mass destruction. Technology and scientific discovery have vastly increased the capacity to quickly and easily kill such large numbers of people, and thus raise profound questions about the proportionality of ends and means and whether any conceivable political objective can possibly justify their use. To make matters worse, even weak and economically collapsed states and nonstate actors like terrorists can acquire chemical and biological weapons. More resources are required to procure nuclear capabilities, yet they are within reach of even impoverished and starving countries like North Korea. Moreover, none of these weapons require sophisticated missiles for delivery. They may be easily concealed and taken to targets with deadly accuracy by airplanes, cars, boats, or backpacks, thereby penetrating the defenses of even the strongest of states. The dangers posed by these weapons of mass destruction, including their accidental or unauthorized use, of course, are not limited to their use by terrorists or rogue states—but by all who possess them. As commentator Jonathan Schell writes in his thought-provoking book, *The Fate of the Earth*:

> As scientists and technicians we live in the nuclear world, in which whether we choose to acknowledge the fact or not, we possess the instruments of violence that make it possible for us to extinguish ourselves as a species. But as citizens and statesmen we go on living in a pre-nuclear world, as though extinction were not possible and sovereign nations could still employ the instruments of violence as instruments of policy. . . . In effect, we try to make do with a Newtonian politics in an Einsteinian world. The combination is the source of our immediate peril.

This statement is not just an observation about existing weapons capabilities and the potential for cataclysmic war; it is vital reminder of the critical importance of attitudes and values.

There is much to consider here. As technology increasingly minimizes or even eliminates many of the physical barriers or limitations of the past, it makes those restraints that we are willing to place on ourselves all the more essential. As a consequence, we need to give the issue of self-imposed restraints particularly careful consideration.

The relative simplicity and manageability of the classical system of diplomacy at times seem far removed from the complexities of our own day. Some of its elements, of course, are gone forever: five European powers alone making decisions for everyone else, sovereign nation-states as the only actors in foreign affairs, a minimal influence of domestic opinion or economic interests, and limited technological capabilities for communication, transportation, and

armed force. But it is worthwhile to remember that one of the most critical features that enabled the classical system to be successful did not reside in things, but in ideas and values. That is, statesmen realized that no nation, however powerful, possibly could protect itself on its own and therefore know that their own long-term self-interests would be best served when defined in terms of collective security and the common interests of the system as a whole. They came to recognize in this regard the critical importance of working together to develop shared normative values and to accept certain self-imposed restraints.

Statesmen of the classical system realized that they had to find some way to avoid anarchy by regulating the level of their rivalry before it destroyed them. Competition, they came to understand, could not be allowed to become fatal to the competitors. A series of completely unregulated conflicts, the catastrophic revolutionary and Napoleonic wars, and the possibility of still others thus convinced them of the absolute necessity of reaching agreement on shared values. They came to understand through painful experience that no international system can possibly survive unless there is a consensus by all the major participants upon fundamental goals and objectives and upon basic rules of accommodation and ethical norms of conduct with limits on what is acceptable and unacceptable behavior. For this reason, they agreed to accept certain self-imposed restraints upon themselves. They recognized the legitimacy of the system, their mutual co-existence in a balance of power, the use of limited means in the pursuit of limited ends, and the validity of existing treaties and they believed that they possessed a shared responsibility to cooperate in the collective defense of these norms and to work as diplomatic partners rather than only rivals to maintain the system itself.

The acceptance of such norms and self-imposed restraints is a matter of political will among the participants in the international system. This will can change through time, depending again on context. One thinks, for example, of the evolving support for the norm of self-determination in the process of decolonization following the Second World War, or the willingness of states to impose restraints or rules upon themselves (and thereby surrender some of their sovereignty) in order to protect the value of human rights and hold those who abuse them responsible for their actions. It is the presence—or absence—of these shared norm values that tells us much about the successes —or failures—of the classical system, the interwar years, the efforts of the United Nations, the Cold War, and the evolving international system of today.

The significance of shared values and self-imposed restraints in statecraft is nowhere more evident than in the threat and use of force. Leaders at the time of the classical system of diplomacy realized that armed force could be regarded as a legitimate instrument of policy as long as limited means were utilized for limited political ends. The technology of the time, of course, restrained the capabilities of the means, but values restrained the objectives and determined *jus ad bellum*, or the justice of war, and *jus in bello*, or the justice in war. This is an essential point to bear in mind, especially in today's world where seeking to establish *jus post bellum*, or justice in the aftermath

of war (in such places as Kosovo, Afghanistan, and Iraq) is so important for peace and security and where weapons of mass destruction possessed by either terrorists or nation-states demonstrably unwilling to abide by established international norms or to accept self-imposed restraints are so frightfully dangerous.

It is precisely for these reasons that the organizers of the recent World Summit —the largest gathering of global leaders in history—devoted so much attention to the challenge of trying to build what they called "a new consensus" on norms that could provide the basis of restraints for the future. Indeed, the very first agenda item for the conference as a whole was entitled "Values and Principles." Time and time again, the participants stressed that the degree to which they could achieve peace and security would be a function of their ability to find "common ground," to recognize that what binds them together is much more important than what separates them, to reach agreement on "shared values" concerning "moral imperatives" as well as "objective interests," and to accept mutual restraints. They declared that these requirements applied to all aspects of statecraft, but particularly and most poignantly to armed force.

Here, they immediately found themselves struggling with the challenge of the wide disparity in attitudes toward normative restraints involving nuclear weapons. Under the terms of the Non-Proliferation Treaty, a remarkable 183 nations have agreed to impose upon themselves a total renunciation of these weapons of mass destruction, even as a means of deterrence. Of these, four once possessed such weapons but voluntarily decided to give them up. Together, these nations strongly encourage others to accept similar restraints. Nevertheless, under the same treaty, five nuclear powers (the United States, Britain, France, Russia, and China) promised to "pursue negotiations in good faith" leading to a treaty on "general and complete disarmament," but none of them has been willing to do so. Israel, India, Pakistan, and North Korea refuse to be bound by the treaty at all, and Iran currently gives every indication of developing a nuclear industry capable of producing weapons. These problems are compounded by the fact that more than forty countries currently possess the means to make fuel for peaceful nuclear power, but this easily can be modified to make material for nuclear weapons. It is not technology, but political will based upon interests and values that keeps them from doing so. Moreover, and in sharp contrast, recently-discovered attempts to smuggle highly enriched uranium across international borders indicate that terrorists actively are seeking to acquire precisely these kinds of weapons.

The leaders assembled at the World Summit also faced one of the most difficult of all challenges: namely, the urgency of developing normative guidelines for when, under whose authority, and how armed force could be legitimately used in the world today. This centuries-old and persistent problem was raised anew after the end of the Cold War in the context of using force for humanitarian intervention in Somalia, Bosnia, and Kosovo. It virtually exploded, however, over the American-led war against Iraq. The United States insisted that in an age of terrorism and weapons of mass destruction,

the United Nations Charter's old rules governing the use of force and some of the criteria of traditional just war theory no longer applied, that it did not need authorization or a "permission slip" from an overly timid Security Council to take military action and, thus, was free to launch a preventive war against perceived threats when and where it chose. Most others, in sharp contrast, argued that whenever any state or nonstate actor refuses to accept established restraints and the rule of law, claiming that it unilaterally can define if and when force should be used irrespective of the norms or interests of the system as a whole, others will feel free to make the same claim for themselves and a recipe thereby will be created for international anarchy rather than international order.

When these kinds of difficult issues and sharp differences of opinion arise, it is particularly interesting to note how frequently reference is made, in one way or another, to history and to theory. It was not at all uncommon, for example, to hear speakers at the World Summit refer both to the "lessons of history" as well as the "new historical realities." They made frequent reference to history and to the past serving as a guide to the future. They also observed that we live in the context of the dynamics of the diplomatic revolution that has produced a number of dramatic transformations in the world, some of which present serious challenges of a new order of magnitude. At the same time, conference participants also recognized that many of the challenges are not completely new, that continuities exist as well as changes, and that in some respects many of the diplomatic challenges of our time are enduring and similar to the diplomatic challenges of previous times. In the effort to make discriminating judgments about which is which in these vital matters, it was not unusual to hear the more thoughtful participants and analysts draw upon the impact of people, process, possibilities, perspective, and sense of proportion in the past or to watch them seek guidance from the principles of negotiation, deterrence, coercive diplomacy, crisis management, and ethical restraints. In attempting to find workable solutions to the many challenges for peace and security ahead, therefore, there may be much to be gained from the lessons of history and insights of theory as found in the study of force and statecraft.

SUGGESTIONS FOR FURTHER EXPLORATION

The challenges ahead can be monitored more closely today than at any other time in history. Daily news can be followed on those Web sites with international capabilities such as the British Broadcasting Corporation at http://news.bbc.co.uk; CNN at www.cnn.com; *Le Monde* at www.lemonde.fr; *New York Times* at www.nytimes.com; *Die Zeit* at www.zeit.de; al-Jazeera at www.aljazeera.com; and the UN Wire Service at www.unwire.org. Thoughtful discussions, analyses, opinion, as well as notification and reviews of newly published books appear in leading journals such as *Ethics and International Affairs, Foreign Affairs, Foreign Policy, International Affairs, International Conciliation, International Organization, International Security, International Studies Quarterly, Internationale Politik, Journal of International Affairs, Orbis, Review of International Studies, World Affairs,* and *World Politics,* among others.

In addition, all major nation-states and regional and international organizations now use technology and the Internet to maintain active Web sites as a means of presenting their positions on contemporary challenges of force and statecraft. Among these, see the African Union at www.africa-union.org; the British Foreign Office at www.fco.gov.uk; the Chinese Foreign Ministry at www.fmprc.gov.cn; the European Union at http://europa.eu.int; and French Foreign Ministry at www.france.diplomatie.fr; the German Foreign Ministry at www.auswaertigesamt.de; the Japanese Foreign Ministry at www.mofago.jp; NATO at www.nato.int; the Organization of American States at www.oas.org; the Organization for Security and Cooperation in Europe at www.osce.org; the Russian Foreign Ministry at www.mid.ru; the United Nations at www.un.org in several different languages; and those of the United States government, including the Central Intelligence Agency at www.cia.gov, Department of Defense at www.defenselink.mil, Department of Homeland Security at www.dhs.gov, Department of State at www.state.gov, and Office of the Director of National Intelligence at www.odni.gov.

The most recent collective efforts of the international community to prepare for the challenges ahead can be found in the documentation surrounding the 2005 World Summit found at www.un.org; Secretary-General Kofi Annan's report, entitled *In Larger Freedom: Towards Development, Security, and Human Rights for All* (New York, 2005); the report from the High-Level Panel on Threats, Challenges, and Change under the title of *A More Secure World: Our Shared Responsibility* (New York, 2004); and the *United Nations Millennium Declaration* (New York, 2000). Other discussions that offer speculations about the future include Dan Caldwell and Robert Williams, Jr., *Seeking Security in an Insecure World* (Lanham, MD, 2006); Joseph Nye, Jr., *Soft Power* (Boulder, CO, 2005); Donald Snow, *National Security for a New Era: Globalization and Geopolitics* (New York, 2004); Ivo Daalder and James Steinberg, "New Rules on When to Go to War," *Financial Times*, August 2, 2004; Peter Hough, *Understanding Global Security* (New York, 2004); U.S. National Security Intelligence Council, *Mapping the Global Future* (Washington, DC, 2004); Paul Gordon Lauren, "Toward the Future," in *The Evolution of International Human Rights: Visions Seen* (Philadelphia, 2003); Philip Bobbitt, *The Shield of Achilles* (New York, 2002); Thomas Ricks, "A New Way of War," *Washington Post National Weekly Edition*, December 10–16, 2001; Wesley Clark, *Waging Modern War* (New York, 2001); Martin van Creveld, *Nuclear Proliferation and the Future of Conflict* (New York, 1993); and the still thought-provoking Jonathan Schell, *The Fate of the Earth* (New York, 1982).

INDEX

FORCE
AND
STATECRAFT